The Best of Intentions

THE

Best

OF

Intentions

The Triumphs and Failures of the Great Society Under Kennedy, Johnson, and Nixon

IRWIN UNGER

DOUBLEDAY

New York London Toronto Sydney Auckland

PUBLISHED BY DOUBLEDAY
a division of Bantam Doubleday Dell Publishing Group, Inc.
1540 Broadway, New York, New York 10036

DOUBLEDAY and the portrayal of an anchor
with a dolphin are trademarks of Doubleday,
a division of Bantam Doubleday Dell
Publishing Group, Inc.

Library of Congress Cataloging-in-Publication Data

Unger, Irwin.
The best of intentions: the triumphs and failures of the Great
Society under Kennedy, Johnson, and Nixon/Irwin Unger.
p.   cm.
Includes index.
1. United States—Social policy. 2. Economic assistance,
Domestic—United States. 3. United States—Politics and
government—1961–1963. 4. United States—Politics and
government—1963–1969. 5. United States—Politics and
government—1969–1974.   I. Title.
HN59.2.U52   1996
361.6'1'0973—dc20   95-38406
CIP

ISBN 0-385-46833-4
Copyright © 1996 by Irwin Unger
All Rights Reserved
Printed in the United States of America
April 1996
First Edition

1   3   5   7   9   10   8   6   4   2

In Memory of Dear Friends Robert Greenberg
and Allan Naimark

Contents

CONTENTS

Foreword

THE GREAT SOCIETY of the 1960s has left its mark on the land. Anyone who has crossed the country by car can see, and hear, its traces. My wife and I experienced this as we drove—appropriately—to Austin, Texas, some time ago from our East Coast home. Junkyards and commercial road signs had been largely banished from highway shoulders. There were clean, well-equipped public rest stops every hundred miles or so to make our daily mileage stint more comfortable. Cruising down the interstates, far from metropolitan centers, we tuned into National Public Radio for classical music, in-depth news programs, sophisticated discussions, and intelligent interviews. On our return route we stopped at Assateague Island, in Virginia, a national seashore preserve established in 1965 by Lyndon Johnson, to see the wild ponies and walk the nature trails. And our car itself bore the marks of the Great Society. The seat belts we (usually) wore, the collapsible steering columns, and other safety features were mandated by safety measures of the 1960s. The Great Society had made our trip pleasanter and safer.

Conventional histories usually ignore these by-products of the Great Society. It is the social programs aimed at the restless poor, the enfeebled aged, the ill-schooled ghetto kids that get the attention. But in fact there was another Great Society aimed at the educated middle class, or intended for its advantage. Though little noted, this "quality of life" movement may in fact be the one that succeeded best.

The Best of Intentions is not primarily about the Great Society's middle-class agenda, however. It gives more space to Medicare, federal aid to education, and the War on Poverty than to highway beautification, automobile safety, truth in lending, clean water, and nature preservation. The first three were the big, expensive programs that called forth the greatest White House effort and got the limelight. They deserve special attention. Yet I have thought it proper to give more than usual heed to the programs that expressed a new 1960s perception of America's problems and opportunities in an age of seemingly assured affluence. They have meant much to millions of Americans but they have been largely ignored by the very people—the journalists, the scholars, the social scientists—who have benefited the most from their creation.

On the other hand I bypass the civil rights movement. This choice may seem arbitrary. Very little of the 1960s escaped the powerful influence of the decade's drive for racial equality. Yet I believe it a reasonable course to take. Essentially, my plea is the traditional *ars longa, vita brevis.* Let scholars who have spent their lives mastering the vast literature of the subject and are prepared to enlarge the work of Taylor Branch, Clayborne Carson, David Garrow, August Meier, and the other accomplished historians of the Second Reconstruction attempt a reconsideration of civil rights in the sixties. I have no such qualifications or ambitions. No doubt much remains to be learned and said about the post–World War II civil rights revolution, but readers interested in a new view of it would be better served by looking elsewhere.

The reader of *The Best of Intentions* will encounter the civil rights movement, as well as Vietnam, prosperity, and other facets of the decade, as aspects of the background in which the Great Society began and evolved. But they are beyond the scope of this work.

Scholarship is a cooperative venture. This work is no exception; I have been helped by many people. First, let me thank two colleagues—Ari Hoogenboom of Brooklyn College and David Burner of SUNY, Stony Brook—who read early drafts of the book and gave me wise and skilled advice on its style and content. Professor Dick Netzer of New York University shared with me his knowledge of the National Endowment for the Arts. I owe a large debt to my agent, Alex Hoyt, who had faith in my proposal from the outset and was able to communicate his enthusiasm to a major publisher. Roger Scholl, my editor at Doubleday, provided the sort of skilled reading and imaginative editing rare in publishing today. He immeasurably improved the final draft. I also wish to praise Karen Richardson, my copy editor, who performed her essential tasks with unusual precision.

Librarians, as is their wont, were wonderfully helpful. I would like to thank the professionals at the New York Public Library, at the Elmer Bobst Library of New York University, and at the Monmouth College Library in Long Branch, New Jersey. The staff of the John Fitzgerald Library in Boston were most helpful with interlibrary-loan materials.

For sheer efficiency and generosity, however, no library and no group of library experts equaled those at the Lyndon Baines Johnson Library at Austin, Texas. All were cheerful, cooperative, and kind, but I would especially like to single out Linda Hanson, Mary Knill, and John Wilson.

But my greatest debt is to Debi, my wife, my collaborator, and my friend, who shared the ups and downs, the fun and the pain of the research and composition of *The Best of Intentions*.

The Best of Intentions

Prologue

LYNDON BAINES JOHNSON, president for only six months, arrived in Detroit on *Air Force One* on the morning of May 22, 1964. He was greeted at the airport by Governor Romney, Mayor Cavanagh, Henry Ford II, and thirty thousand enthusiastic voters. Half an hour later he was on the speakers' platform in the immense oval of the University of Michigan stadium at Ann Arbor to receive an honorary degree and address the eighty thousand parents, faculty, friends, and graduates seated before him.

His theme in that spring commencement address was the Great Society, a phrase he had begun to use a few weeks earlier. Teddy Roosevelt, early in the century, was first to name his reform agenda (TR called his program the Fair Deal), but it was his Democratic successors who had standardized the practice, and every Democrat since Franklin Roosevelt had his own version: New Deal, Fair Deal, New Frontier. "Great Society" would begin to catch on as Johnson's program following the Ann Arbor commencement address.

As Johnson described it that sunny spring day, his Great Society blended the old and the new. It aimed first at rounding out the New Deal's promise of security against the uncertainties of life. That was not surprising. Johnson had had many mentors in his long political career, but none had left such an indelible mark as the smooth Squire of Hyde Park. LBJ both worshiped FDR and envied him at the same time. He never ceased as president to test his own performance against the greatest American leader of the century.

But the Great Society was to be more than just the New Deal perfected. The United States in 1964 was not the country of thirty years before. Roosevelt had come to office during world capitalism's greatest crisis. Twelve million Americans, a never-equaled quarter of the work force, were jobless in March 1933 and millions despaired of the future. Now, the United States was rich. The 4,900 University of Michigan graduates seated before the president were about to be launched into a world of dazzling possibilities. Recently a few pundits and academics had uncovered pockets of the disadvantaged, of the excluded, but the public mood was of wonder at the sheer quantitative performance of the economy and a bounding confidence in the future.

The Great Society envisioned at Ann Arbor was infused by the sense of affluence achieved. During the century past, the president boasted, the nation had created "an order of plenty for all of our people." But that was not enough. The challenge ahead was to "use that wealth to enrich and elevate our national life and to advance the quality of our American civilization." The Great Society rested "on abundance and liberty for all." But that was "just the beginning."

The Great Society would be a place where every child could enrich his mind and enlarge his talents. It was a place where leisure would be an opportunity "to build and reflect, not a feared cause of boredom." It would be a place where "the city of man serves not only the needs of the body and the demands of commerce but the desire for beauty and the hunger for community." In the Great Society people could "renew contact with nature" and would be "more concerned with the quality of their goals than the quantity of their goods."

To achieve the Great Society the nation must build in three environments. First was the decaying cities, where housing and transportation were inadequate, where open land was vanishing and old landmarks were being destroyed. Then there was the physical environment. "The water we drink, the food we eat, the very air that we breathe" were threatened with pollution. The nation's parks were overcrowded, its seashores overburdened. Green fields and primal forests were disappearing. Americans must work to "prevent an ugly America," for "once man can no longer walk with beauty and wonder at nature his spirit will wither and his sustenance be wasted." Finally there was education. "Our society will not be great until every young mind is set free to scan the farthest reaches of thought and imagination." As things stood millions had not finished high school; thousands could not afford college; teachers were poorly trained and underpaid; classrooms were overcrowded. All of this would have to change.

The speech could not have been extrapolated from Johnson's own heritage of Southwestern populism and New Deal liberalism. Many of his points and phrases expressed a new, distinctive sensibility. The Great Society perspective was created by intellectuals, who as the 1950s wound down began to conceive a new liberalism that would wrestle with quality of life, now that quantity of life had been largely attended to. The speech had been written by Richard Goodwin, a brilliant young Harvard Law School graduate whom Johnson had inherited from the Kennedy White House. The thirty-two-year-old Goodwin was very much a man of his times. Law clerk for Supreme Court Justice Felix Frankfurter, he had reached political consciousness after World War II, when a rich and triumphant United States appeared a colossus among nations. But if all was right materially with America, it was not right esthetically and spiritually, in the view of Goodwin and his peers. Measured by standards of physical beauty, cultural achievement, and personal fulfillment, the nation remained impoverished. Beneficiaries themselves of the new affluence, it made them uneasy. Wealth had not produced a new Athens, a new Florence. Instead, it had encouraged suburban conformity, kitsch, and shopping malls.

The focus on quality rather than quantity went back to the mid-fifties, when the historian Arthur Schlesinger, Jr., in an article for the *Reporter,* first brought it to public attention. The times, "The Challenge of Abundance" said, called for a " 'qualitative liberalism' dedicated to the bettering of people's lives and opportunities."[1] At the end of the decade Schlesinger would become an influential voice in the circle of thinkers forming around Senator John Kennedy of Massachusetts. But he was not alone in formulating the new vision. The idea of "quality" was clearly in the air among the intelligentsia by the early sixties. During the 1960 presidential campaign, academics at the Maxwell Graduate School of

Public Affairs at Syracuse University urged Kennedy to emphasize the "politics of affluence" rather than "concentrating so much on full employment, economic growth, and economic security."[2] At an early 1964 conference called by White House intellectual adviser and Princeton historian Eric Goldman, Norman Podhoretz, editor of *Commentary*, called for "a spiritual revolution in the American character in order to cope with affluence and automation." Richard Rovere of *The New Yorker* warned that there was "very little gain in economic growth" when it was "achieved by stimulating the production, distribution, and consumption of trashy things, the creation of trashy houses and landscapes, the dissemination of trashy education and ideas."[3]

A qualitative emphasis even seeped from the Port Huron Statement, the June 1962 manifesto for change that marked the birth of Students for a Democratic Society and the New Left. The student insurgents who foregathered at the United Automobile Workers' FDR Camp near Lake Huron insisted that the problems of America were largely the problems of meaning and connection, not of simple abundance. "Loneliness, estrangement, isolation, describe the vast distance between man and man today," the statement announced. "These dominant tendencies" could not be "overcome by better personnel management, nor by improved gadgets, but only when a love of man overcomes the idolatrous worship of things. . . ."[4]

Johnson was never comfortable with the intellectuals. A graduate of Southwest Texas State Teachers College, he played the role of passive-aggressive in their presence. He sneered at "the Harvards" who populated the Kennedy White House and at times went out of his way to humiliate and even degrade them. Academics on the White House staff tell tales of being forced to confer with their chief while he was seated on the executive bathroom "throne." But he also admired and envied them and flattered them by emulation.

Now, on this bright spring day at Ann Arbor, LBJ was pronouncing as his own their new message to the American people. He did not have precise blueprints for change at this point, he told the graduates and honored guests, but he would "assemble the best thought and the broadest knowledge from all over the world to find . . . answers for America." There would be White House conferences and meetings on the cities, on natural beauty, and the quality of education. Whatever solutions emerged, he promised, would not flow from "a massive program in Washington" but would require a "creative federalism between the National Capital and the leaders of local communities."[5]

All told the speech was no more than two thousand words long and took only twenty minutes to deliver. But it touched a resonant chord in the educated audience and they applauded frequently. On the return trip to Washington on *Air Force One,* Johnson was "absolutely euphoric." With a scotch highball in hand, he came back to the press pool at the rear of the plane. "Well, what did you think of it?" he asked Charles Roberts of *Newsweek.* Roberts told him he had gotten "a hell of a reception." He had counted applause bursts twenty-seven times. No, said the beaming president, it was twenty-nine. Jack Valenti, his special assistant, had counted and it *was* twenty-nine.[6]

The ideas Johnson conveyed on that sunny May day infused the Great Society. He would repeat them many times in the months ahead and labor to turn concept into reality. At Ann Arbor he had invoked a special moment in time when many things seemed possible. It was a moment that could not last, and would never be repeated.

ONE

Moving Again

JOHNSON YEARNED, then, to carve out a reform agenda appropriate to the expansive new day. The Great Society, as LBJ described it at Ann Arbor, posited a large middle-class constituency and it sought specifically to please that constituency. Clean air and water, new and improved national parks, highway beautification, consumer protection laws, federal subsidies for the arts and humanities, public broadcasting, loans to college students—all these would touch the lives of solvent, well-educated, and politically literate men and women, the people who read books and weekly newsmagazines, bought classical records, toured America by car, and traveled abroad. Eric Goldman, who came to the Johnson White House as the intellectual-in-residence to replace Kennedy's Arthur Schlesinger, Jr., called them the "Metro-Americans," a term that never caught on.

But in the end the reform wave we call the Great Society was more than the itinerary announced at Ann Arbor. The programs of the sixties were a hybrid. Johnson added his own, distinctive "New Agenda," but most of the big, expensive Great Society programs rounded out those Roosevelt, Truman, and Kennedy had proposed but failed to complete. This "Old Agenda" aimed at achieving "security" against life's mishaps through federal intervention. Begun at the century's birth in response to the hazards of a new urban-industrial society, it expressed modern liberalism's faith in rational, benevolent, centralized planning in a world of graft, inefficiency, consumer vulnerability, predatory economic power, and social inequality. Lyndon Johnson hoped to move beyond his predecessors' policies, but in the end the Old Agenda is the part of the Great Society that has registered most vividly on our historical memories.

Though the Great Society Old Agenda programs go back at least to the New Deal of the 1930s, their immediate inspiration was John F. Kennedy. Larry O'Brien, the Massachusetts politocrat who served both Kennedy and Johnson as chief point man for congressional relations, believed that the two presidents had "the same goals, objectives, whether it was called the New Frontier or the Great Society."[1] He exaggerated. Kennedy, for one thing, had little of LBJ's interest in a post-scarcity agenda. In the mid-fifties, when Arthur Schlesinger, Jr., sent the Massachusetts senator a memo imploring him to move beyond the New Deal to a program of "qualitative" social reform, Kennedy advised caution. It was impossible, he said, to get a "very advanced program of social legislation" through Congress; the Democratic leadership would stymie it.[2] Nor was he a special friend of black Americans. Their plight, like that of the poor, was hearsay to him and, especially at the beginning, he risked his limited political capital on their behalf only reluctantly. And even where Johnson sought to fulfill his predecessor's policies, he gave them his own twist.

But there were also differences in commitment between the two men. John F. Kennedy was not an ardent reformer. His family's Democratic allegiance derived more from historic ethnic loyalties than from principled liberalism, and his father, Joe Kennedy, though a prominent New Deal official, never liked Roosevelt and what he stood for. Second son Jack entered politics more to appease his imperious parent and win fame and power than to realize a social vision. As representative and senator he was not the favorite of the party's liberals and never joined Americans for Democratic Action or the Democratic Advisory Council, the avatars of the party's reformist wing.

And yet, once in power, circumstances propelled him into a reform program. During the 1960 presidential campaign Kennedy had promised to make the country "move again." After eight years under Eisenhower, the bland old uncle in the White House, the country wanted something different. Besides, youth must act, not conserve. And the party's traditions could not be ignored. Ever since FDR had replaced "Dr. New Deal" with "Dr. Win-the-War" in 1943, the Democrats' social welfare state remained unfinished. The foundations were in place, some walls were standing upright. But the structure as a whole existed only in blueprint. For a Democratic president to extract the old plans from the drawer was inevitable. Still, Kennedy was more interested in challenges abroad than problems at home, and his commitment to reform was never passionate or tenacious.

The Kennedy domestic agenda, the New Frontier, was spliced together in the weeks between the election and the inauguration by a circle of academics, congressional staffers, business leaders, and members of the Kennedy entourage organized into twenty-nine task forces. Recruited by the president-elect's brother-in-law, Sargent Shriver, the supercharged head of the Chicago Merchandise Mart, these thinkers and planners, meeting during the ten-week transition period in airport motels and empty New York and Washington offices, concocted a legislative program for the incoming administration. The task-force approach suited Kennedy. He had been a member of Congress since 1947 but he neither knew nor liked the senior executive department bureaucrats who had generally initiated new legislation in the past. The new system seemed to give him greater control over the legislative development process. As given final form at a late-December pre-inauguration meeting with Democratic leaders in Palm Beach, the task force recommendations were mostly warmed-over Truman-era Fair Deal proposals: a higher minimum wage, low-cost-housing legislation, hospital insurance for retirees, and federal assistance for public schools. Only two items on the "must" list were new: aid to "depressed areas" and a program to retrain the unemployed.

The chances of getting this program through Congress did not look good. The Democrats had lost twenty House seats in the 1960 election, all in the North and mostly liberal. The new president had slightly better congressional numbers than Truman. In Kennedy's first Congress the Democratic majority would be 65 to 35 in the Senate and 262 to 174 in the House. Truman's numbers for his 1949–50 Congress were 54 Democrats to 46 Republicans and a 263-to-173 Democratic majority in the House. But while both men had nominal Democratic majorities, neither had liberal majorities. Ever since Roosevelt's second administration a coalition of Republicans and Southern Democrats had controlled the legislative process on Capitol Hill through committee seniority and the filibuster, and had foiled the liberals' every attempt to round out their domestic programs. The congressional liberals had not let up during the uncongenial Eisenhower years, but even the legislative wizardry of Lyndon Johnson, the Democratic Senate majority leader, had been unable to break the logjam. Whatever the voters wanted, the conservatives in Congress determined the lawmaking process.

As the New Frontiersmen trickled into Washington in early 1961 to locate apartments and find schools for their kids, they could not have been too hopeful. Kennedy had experienced the power of the Southern barons and their GOP allies in Congress firsthand and was under no illusions about the New Frontier's chances on the Hill. Nor could he count on his personal influence. During his fourteen years in Congress he had never been close to the inner circle of either house. They did not know him. As O'Brien said of his chief's three House terms, "He was just another guy that came by once in a while."[3] Nor could he use the stick of grassroots presidential popularity to beat a mulish legislature into obedience. He had won the election with a plurality of just over 100,000 votes out of a total of almost 69 million. It was a "razor-thin margin of victory and no mandate of any kind," O'Brien later recalled. Kennedy's "coattails didn't mean a thing to anybody who was in Congress; that hadn't helped them get there."[4]

But the Kennedys were always tenacious competitors and the president, however tepid his reformist zeal, did not intend to surrender without a fight. As inauguration and the opening of the Eighty-seventh Congress approached, the party's top congressional leaders—Mike Mansfield, the Senate majority leader-designate; Speaker Sam Rayburn; and Vice President Lyndon Johnson, Mansfield's powerful predecessor—came to Palm Beach for a two-day strategy session. On the flagstoned patio of the Kennedy mansion the Democratic chieftains considered how to restrain Senate debate and deprive the House Rules Committee chairman—the notorious mossback Howard Smith of Virginia—of the power to control the flow of legislation.

Congress opened in January with an unprecedented donnybrook over rules and procedures. The Senate liberals tried to weaken the filibuster roadblock by making it easier to invoke cloture—the motion to cut off debate. They failed, though the bruising battle, Congress-watchers said, did shake the conservative Senate diehards.

In the House the administration was more successful. The speaker was Democrat Sam Rayburn of Bonham, Texas, a somber, compact man who dressed in the dark suits of "a capable undertaker."[5] Rayburn was humane and generous, and his life revolved around service to his party and his country. A bachelor, the House was his life. He was not a classic liberal, but "Mr. Sam" wanted the young Democratic president to succeed, and despite failing health he now summoned up all his remaining energies to expand the House Rules Committee by two Democrats and one Republican to override Chairman Smith. Conservatives resisted ferociously. Minority leader Charles Halleck made the rules-change fight a party issue and browbeat fellow Republicans into voting no. Outside Congress, the Southern press, the segregationist White Citizens' Councils, the American Medical Association, and the powerful national business associations mounted a campaign to retain the conservative grip on legislation by defeating the Rules Committee packing scheme. Rayburn deployed all his persuasive powers. Reluctant Democratic members were summoned to the speaker's office and presented with an uncompromising alternative by Mr. Sam: "Are you with me or old man Smith?" Cabinet members with friends on the Hill trekked to the Capitol to badger and cajole. When Rayburn at one point was about to give up, the White House liaison office propped him up. The final vote to pack the committee was wafer thin: 217 to 212. When the victory was announced, cheers went up on the Democratic side of the House and liberal members gave Rayburn a standing ovation.

The procedural successes did not clear the way for the New Frontier, however. The times were not yet ripe. In early 1961 the polls showed that the American public liked the president but were indifferent to the proposals he was sending to Congress. That body in turn was in no mood to enact major programs with big price tags. At odds with the White House during the Eisenhower administration, the congressional Democrats, knowing their chances for success were limited, had often acted like bold innovators. During the previous eight years, they had submitted a flood of bills that got nowhere on Capitol Hill. Now, with their own man at 1600 Pennsylvania Avenue, actual change seemed frightening. Rayburn's victory in the end did not make a major difference; Congress would still block the liberal agenda.

To make matters worse, on August 31, after twenty-five consecutive terms in the House, Rayburn resigned and went home to Bonham. There, in November, just as the first session of the Eighty-seventh Congress was drawing to a close, he died of pancreatic cancer. His successor, John McCormack of Massachusetts, never developed quite the skill, or enjoyed quite the respect, or wielded quite the power of Rayburn. At seventy, McCormack was a wavery old man and both Kennedy and Johnson would feel the loss.

Estimates of the Kennedy legislative record are a classic illustration of conflicting perception. Larry O'Brien, a fierce Kennedy loyalist, has described in rich detail the unprecedented and innovative Kennedy White House congressional liaison office. He and his assistants kept precise head counts of volatile congressional opinion and were able to pinpoint where pressure had to be applied. They beefed up the liaison offices of the major executive departments and mobilized them for legislative battles over pending bills in each department's area. The White House, O'Brien notes, sent fifty-three major bills to the Eighty-seventh Congress and, though it "was a struggle every inch of the way," got thirty-three passed.[6] The president himself was proud of this record and he and his aides were "astounded" at the media's conclusion that he had "failed."[7]

That is one view, an insider's view. Others were not convinced. One year into the new administration, Joseph Rauh, a leader of Americans for Democratic Action, would observe that "compared to Ike or Nixon, Kennedy is OK," but "compared to the 'high hopes' we had, he's a bitter disappointment."[8] Harry McPherson, a Johnson aide, looking back soon after the 1968 election, would declare: "Kennedy was unable to get anything done."[9]

The truth lies somewhere between. Compared with the somnolent Eisenhower years the Kennedy era was fruitful in legislation; compared with the supercharged Lyndon Johnson years it was barren. The political realities of the time must be factored in to fairly compare New Frontier with Great Society: Kennedy simply did not have the votes that his successor enjoyed. Still, it was not

entirely bad numbers that defeated JFK. He did not invest personally in his domestic programs as much as Johnson did. To move
legislation, Kennedy presided over thirty-two "leadership breakfasts" and invited more than five hundred members of Congress
to White House coffee hours. But he almost never directly asked
legislators for their votes and seldom made personal phone calls.
He had little taste for the sweaty glad-handing, easy camaraderie,
and not-so-gentle blackmail that Johnson used to get what he
wanted. He was too fastidious. By the time the "lace curtain"
grandson of Boston pols Patrick J. Kennedy and John Francis
("Honey Fitz") Fitzgerald came along, the drive and sure political touch of his forebears had become attenuated.

During his first Congress Kennedy gave top priority to two measures that his liberal predecessors never considered: a depressed-
areas relief bill and a program to retrain the chronically unemployed. In different ways these were attempts to deal with stubborn "structural" unemployment, an affliction newly discovered
and said to explain why it was so hard to squeeze the unemployment rate down from almost 7 percent. It was not, the argument
went, that the economy as a whole was operating at less than full
throttle—though that was true; it was that no matter how fast the
GNP engine raced, certain regions and certain classes remained
unaffected.

Structural unemployment afflicted entire regions. In the Ap-
palachians, the coal mines were shutting down as Americans
turned to natural gas and petroleum to heat their homes and fuel
their trains and factories. The surviving coal industry had mi-
grated to the cost-efficient strip mines of the Midwest and mountain states. With little left but steep, worn-out fields to farm, the
mountain folk were fleeing to Detroit, Chicago, and Cincinnati,
leaving behind a sad residue of families without jobs or livelihoods, living in shacks, eating beans and cheap carbohydrates,
and going barefoot. Harry M. Caudill's angry 1962 exposé of
Appalachian social conditions, *Night Comes to the Cumberlands,* only
dramatized and publicized a long-festering problem much pon-
dered by the economists and regional sociologists.

Structural unemployment also afflicted individuals. There was a
mismatch between the skills the economy needed and the skills
workers had, and the disparity, it was said, was growing worse. As

two Bureau of Labor Statistics officials noted in 1962, the decade ahead would offer "fewer and fewer job opportunities for the unskilled," and many workers would have to be "retrained for different jobs."[10]

In the mid-1950s a new element—"automation"—became a critical component of the structural unemployment issue. We had achieved bounding abundance through technology but it was beginning to seem a Faustian bargain: Human beings would be permanently replaced by machines. In the past the addition of new machines and new processes had been incremental and society could take the changes in stride. But the new breakthroughs promised to overwhelm the capacity of the economy to absorb them.

This was the latest version of the "technological unemployment" panic, which went back at least as far as the English Luddites, the handworkers and craftsmen of the early 1800s who had physically attacked the new power-run textile machines that threatened their livelihoods. The enormous surge of pent-up consumer demand after 1945 had absorbed into the labor force almost everyone able and willing to work, new technology notwithstanding. But fear of displacement by machines had returned during the late 1950s with the introduction of the computer, electronic feedback mechanisms, and continuous-flow operations. These innovations promised to supersede the smoky, congested old factories with miraculous shiny and silent new plants where a dozen engineers and technicians would supervise an army of robotic machines. Automation quickly became a specter haunting America. By 1960 a body of scare literature had emerged that foresaw disaster ahead for those without the esoteric new skills to survive in the "cybernetic" age. In that year a Gallup poll showed more Americans feared automation than the Soviet Union. At a press conference in February 1962 President Kennedy declared that "the major domestic challenge of the Sixties" was to "maintain full employment at a time when automation is replacing men."[11]

Obviously, one way to rescue people from poverty was through upgrading workforce skills: Teach the poor how to deal with the new technological age; show them how to use the new machines. Faith in technical education would undergird many Great Society programs. But unfortunately, the problem was not that simple. The "culture of poverty" would also have to be overcome.

As described in anthropologist Oscar Lewis's widely read 1961 study of a Mexican-American family, *Children of Sanchez,* the poor not only had poor skills; they also had poor habits and poor attitudes. They lived for today and had little capacity for deferred gratification. They had no faith in existing institutions and were often in trouble with the law. Their sexual relations were irregular; their families were unstable. They were apathetic and seldom shared interests and causes with others. Their "culture," moreover, was enduring. It was passed down from parents to children and consigned each successive generation to the same dismal poverty trap.

Besides *Children of Sanchez,* Lewis wrote the even more popular *La Vida,* about a poor Puerto Rican family, which appeared in 1965. Lewis's books were not dry dissertations. They read like novels and became national best-sellers. Widely discussed by the people Eric Goldman described as "Metro-Americans," they planted in the minds of policymakers and "policy publics" the notion that the behavior and values of the poor themselves were at least in part responsible for their fate. In later years liberals and radicals would attack the culture-of-poverty formula as conservative. It was "blaming the victim" rather than society. It was also, some charged, a racist devaluation of black ghetto mores and an example of bourgeois condescension toward the "lifeways of the poor. . . ."[12] But at first the formula seemed a valuable pointer to the direction that poverty amelioration must take. Just ending discrimination or even providing skills would not suffice. It would also be necessary to restore the hope, morale, and confidence of the poor if they were to be rescued.

The culture-of-poverty idea colored the thinking of the New Frontier-Great Society social engineers. Like the skills deficiencies of the poor, they believed, the poor's cultural inadequacies could be handled by education rather than redistribution. It would not be necessary to massively transfer to them income others had earned. The way to rescue the poor was to purge them of their bad habits and values. This approach not only avoided the pain of robbing prosperous Peter to pay impoverished Paul; it also appealed to the endless faith of Americans in the possibilities of schooling and teaching as a way to transcend one's personal origins.

Structural unemployment was not abruptly discovered in late January 1961. All through the Eisenhower era mayors, governors, social activists, and economists had agitated for federal measures to deal with the stagnant pockets of idleness and despair. Congressional committees had held hearings and bills had started their slow legislative trek, only to be blocked by the conservative coalition or cut down by Ike's vetoes.

Kennedy's election loosened the barriers. During the 1960 nomination campaign he had been genuinely appalled by the wretchedness of life in the squalid West Virginia "hollows." When Democratic West Virginians chose him over rival Hubert Humphrey in the presidential primary, he vowed to help them if he was elected. Within minutes of the first day of the first session of the new Congress, in both the House and Senate, Democrats introduced a bill to ease the agony of the nation's laggard regions. The measure benefited Appalachia and the South disproportionately while skirting the loaded race issue. It sailed through Congress. On May 1, as his first legislative victory, Kennedy signed the Area Redevelopment Act authorizing loans to businesses willing to relocate in "depressed" areas and providing grants to improve roads and bridges in these regions, the whole to be administered by an area redevelopment agency.

Retraining workers to fit the needs of modern industry proved more controversial than regional revival. In 1961 the Senate had passed a generous five-year, $655 million bill to retrofit workers with "obsolete or insufficient skills." But the House had balked, and not until March 1962 did Congress present the president with a bill that responded to the automation panic. The Manpower Development and Training Act provided $262 million for retraining 410,000 workers displaced by new technology. Preference would be given to workers from families with incomes of less than $1,200 a year. Youths in the program would receive $20 a week while learning new skills; older workers who were heads of households would receive allowances equal to their home states' jobless compensation benefits.[13] Other Kennedy measures in the Eighty-seventh Congress to close the gap between the deserving poor and the prosperous middle class included raising the minimum wage from $1 to $1.25 an hour and increasing Social Security payments to retirees.

Structural unemployment was not the only kind of joblessness that worried the experts as the new Democratic president got his bearings. Idleness and poverty clearly were also the result of slow economic growth. The country had basked in prosperity since World War II. But there had been recessions and economic slow-downs. During the 1960 presidential campaign the economy had performed poorly. Growth for the year had been a feeble 2 percent, and on Election Day the unemployment rate touched 5.5 percent, then considered unacceptable. Political analysts believed that it was this listless performance, more than anything else, that had given Kennedy his slim margin of victory over Richard Nixon.

But more than purely cyclical unemployment was at stake. Slow growth guaranteed persistent poverty. Get the economy moving at a fast clip, and the number of chronically poor would inevitably decline. More than one prominent economist believed that economic expansion was likely to reduce poverty faster and more permanently than all the efforts to alter the "personal characteristics" of the poor.[14] Kennedy, a famous Sunday sailor and navy man, is reputed to have described this process as "a rising tide [that] lifts all boats."

And how was the economy to be revved up? By fiscal policy, by manipulating taxes and government spending—by applying the gospel according to Saint John Maynard Keynes, the dapper Cambridge don whose mid-Depression *General Theory of Employment, Interest and Money* had revolutionized academic economic theory. Posited on the belief that treasury spending beyond treasury revenues could restore full employment of capital and labor in a period of sluggish private demand and investment, the book had offended the orthodox laissez-faireists and "marginalists," and its ideas had been applied only feebly during the dismal Great Depression itself. World War II, however, had mandated colossal federal deficits for national self-preservation, and the ensuing surge of growth had vindicated counter-cyclical finance. After 1945, Keynesian economics had swept the university economics departments and become the standard fare of the undergraduate textbooks at all but the most benighted freshwater colleges. Within the business community Adam Smith and Alfred Marshall still reigned and were stubbornly defended. But by the waning years of the Eisenhower administration, the most influential American economists—John Galbraith of Harvard, Paul Samuelson of MIT, Leon Keyserling of Truman's Council of Economic Advisers—were ardent Keynesian practitioners and publicists. Each of them, while remaining at the sidelines, fed Kennedy a steady diet of suggestions, proposals, and stratagems for rebuilding the American economy and ending stagnation.

Kennedy's own Council of Economic Advisers was a hotbed of Keynesian ardor. Its chairman, Walter Heller, a slender, bespectacled professor from the University of Minnesota, was known to favor Keynesian "tax tools" rather than "credit tools" as mechanisms to manage the economy.[15] His goal, almost to the point of obsession, was growth. Other CEA Keynesian proselytizers were James Tobin of Yale and Kermit Gordon of Williams College, soon to become director of the budget.

The fiscal policy tool could be used in several ways. The most liberal wing of the Democratic party endorsed Galbraith's approach. In his best-selling 1958 book, *The Affluent Society,* the towering, droll Canadian had celebrated the postwar American economic miracle. But he had underscored the persistence of "public squalor." While private opulence abounded, the nation's parks, roads, shorelines, schools, public buildings, and other facilities that formed the common wealth of the American people were shabby and unsightly. It was natural, then, that "left" or "progressive" Keynesians like Galbraith should favor stimulating the economy by increasing public spending on what today we call infrastructure. Let the deficits to spur growth benefit the public sector. Create jobs and at the same time improve public amenities and augment the future productive capacity of the nation. It was consistent with big-government liberalism of the sort that dominated intellectual and academic circles.

Progressive Keynesianism was endorsed by Americans for Democratic Action (ADA), the central committee of left-of-center Democrats. The Kennedy administration, liberal economists Leon Keyserling and Robert Nathan told ADA at their 1962 convention, put "undue emphasis on the principle of a balanced budget . . . at the expense of achieving full employment."[16] Among Kennedy's close economic advisers, Paul Samuelson was the chief progressive. In a twenty-four-page report prepared before the inauguration, he proposed a $3 billion to $5 billion spending program. Some of this would be assigned to expanded jobless pay for the unemployed, but the rest would go for urban renewal and highway and school construction.

There were also conservative Keynesians who emphasized cutting taxes to spark the economy through an upsurge in private demand. To the progressives this meant more tail-fin cars, private boats, expensive vacations, and home swimming pools—the conspicuous private consumption that Galbraith deplored. In fact, most conservative Keynesians probably agreed privately with Galbraith that deficits from public, rather than private, spending was wiser. But they were realists. Cutting taxes, even if it meant going into the red, might appeal to Congress, but running deficits by enlarging the federal budget and the federal government's scope seemed impossible. Too many congressmen—virtually all the Republicans and most Southern Democrats—would see such a course as dangerous heresy. Cutting taxes seemed to be the quickest and most expedient way to economic growth.

And Kennedy himself was an old-fashioned fiscal conservative who shuddered at deficits, however derived. He had learned more of his economics from his father, the Wall Street operator, than from his Harvard professors, and neither version of deficit spending struck him as wise. At a March 1961 White House meeting, Walter Heller proposed a $9.5 billion cut to revive the economy. The president turned it down. "I was universally complimented on the cogency and clarity of the memo," Heller reported, but the proposal was rejected "on the basis of political unacceptability."[17]

Though refusing to adopt an overt fiscal stimulus package, Kennedy backed into one by pushing extra spending on national defense in the wake of worsening Cold War relations with the Soviets. By the end of the 1961–62 fiscal year the federal budget was $6.3 billion in the red. And however unintentional, it gave the economy a needed kick. Unemployment declined a percentage point by mid-1962.

Then came the stock market plunge of late May and early June 1962, when the Dow-Jones fell a dramatic 25 percent below its 1961 high. The "Kennedy crash" jolted the president's confidence in traditional economic wisdom and pushed him over the line. In August he told a national TV audience that the time had

come for a tax cut. High taxes were a brake on the economy, he
told the viewers. They dampened private investment and weakened consumption. He intended to ask Congress for a substantial
cut in taxes when it convened in January.

The bill Kennedy sent the legislators asked for $10 billion to
$12 billion in tax cuts and more equity in the tax code. It quickly
bogged down in committee, entangled in conflicting interests,
philosophies, and egos. By the fall of 1963, however, the business
community had begun to anticipate the delights of lower corporate and personal income taxes and the promised fiscal stimulus.
In September the House finally approved the measure by a substantial majority.

Still, the tax cut bill had not passed when Kennedy went to
Dallas in November to meet his tragic fate, and it became one of
the first items on the new president's agenda.

Heller, for one, considered Kennedy-Johnson-era fiscal policy a
vital component of the Great Society. But Kennedy himself did
not perceive affluence as an opportunity for new directions, and
the New Frontier contained little of a post-scarcity new agenda.
The president's legislative program aimed at filling in the blanks
of the social welfare state inaugurated by Roosevelt. It imitated
Harry Truman's Fair Deal and, like the Fair Deal, it bogged down
in a conservative-dominated Congress.

Especially vulnerable was Kennedy's proposal for federal health
care. The chief New Frontier-Great Society health care measure
was the culmination of almost a half century of debate over gov-
ernment-sponsored health insurance. Before World War I a handful of reformers had pushed unsuccessfully for health insurance
to be paid for by the states. During the retrograde, conservative
1920s the issue languished, but revived with the New Deal. Franklin Roosevelt seriously considered adding a federal health insurance scheme to his breakthrough Social Security program in
1935. But FDR collided head-on with the organized medical profession.

By the mid-1930s doctors had come to cherish the one-on-one
doctor-patient, fee-for-service system for medical practice. It established an invaluable doctor-patient relationship, they insisted,
that benefited the public. The doctors had a point. The arrangement made for good medicine, as we are coming to understand

today, when bureaucratic medicine is eclipsing the older system. But it had also made physicians prosperous, powerful, and privileged. The hint, in 1935, that health insurance might be included in the proposed federal Social Security program produced a firestorm of protest from the American Medical Association. Rather than jeopardize unemployment insurance or other important features of the Social Security bill, Roosevelt dropped the health care scheme from the package.

The brilliant and heroic work of doctors in World War II and the miraculous medical breakthroughs of sulfa drugs, penicillin, and the polio vaccine brought medicine enormous new prestige after 1945. The public's faith in medicine made it eager for better health services. Simultaneously, unions and large employers alike found health insurance a "fringe" both pleasant and relatively painless, and more and more labor contracts included insurance schemes to pay hospitals and doctors. Meanwhile, hospitals, concerned with the heavy burden of charity patients and deadbeats, scrambled to insure reimbursement for their expensive services. By 1949 even the AMA had bowed to the public's desire for security against disastrous health costs by accepting voluntary, private health insurance as a vehicle for patient medical payment. By 1960 more than 100 million Americans were covered by private health insurance schemes. Ominously for cost containment, many of these policies had no deductible; they paid from the first dollar of medical cost.

Despite the boom in private health insurance, many Americans remained with no other means than their paychecks or savings to meet medical costs. Nonunion workers, the jobless, and the retired, especially, were without coverage. Millions simply did without medical attention entirely. A shocking proportion of the population did not see a doctor or a dentist in an entire year, some for years on end. Others settled for the meager and begrudging services of free clinics or charity wards. The elderly were especially vulnerable. Few worked, or worked at jobs that included health insurance benefits, yet as a group, frail and isolated, they were beset by more than the usual health problems.

No political leader was more alert to the failings of the nation's health delivery system than that old Midwestern populist Harry Truman. In 1949 Truman submitted to Congress the Murray-Wagner-Dingell bill providing federal money to pay home nursing charges, sixty days of hospital costs a year, and doctors' and dentists' fees. Almost everyone would be covered, and the plan, like Social Security's old-age pensions, would be paid for by a payroll deduction, with the nonworking poor subsidized by federal grants. Administered by the states, this generous plan would disburse payment to the health providers either directly or through health insurance companies, and doctors could either receive fees for service or accept a fixed annual payment for each patient.

The administration tried to convert the doctors but failed. The AMA mounted a ferocious, all-out attack on the bill. It assessed every member $25, and with a $3.5 million war chest hired the firm of Whitaker and Baxter to make its case. The Chicago-based PR concern was soon spewing out a stream of printed material denouncing "socialized medicine" as expensive, bureaucratic, and destructive of the sacred doctor-patient relationship. One of its most effective propaganda efforts was a poster, prominently displayed in many doctors' waiting rooms, showing a kindly, worried physician at the bedside of a sick little girl while her distraught parents hover nearby. At the bottom of this saccharine nineteenth-century print was the slogan: KEEP POLITICS OUT OF THIS PICTURE!

The administration's measure never got out of the House Ways and Means Committee. Truman introduced the bill again in the next session with no better results. During the 1950 congressional elections the AMA targeted pro–health insurance candidates for defeat. When a number lost, it declared a decisive victory over "socialized medicine."

The fifties were lean years for every sort of social legislation. A self-congratulatory decade, when most Americans marveled that they had survived the Depression and World War II and cherished their good fortune, it was also an era of ideological timidity, when every political innovation could be quelled by painting it communist red. Yet the champions of federal health insurance did not lose hope. Operating from within the walls of the Federal Security Agency, the administrative body of Social Security, a cluster of bureaucrats, led by Wilbur Cohen and I. S. Falk, worked to save federal health insurance by scaling it down to fit a conservative era.

A graduate of the University of Wisconsin when it still basked in the glow of pre–World War I La Follette progressivism, Cohen had come to Washington in 1934 as a very young man to help launch the Social Security system. He had stayed with the Social Security Administration and, over the years, as a high-level bureaucrat, had gotten to know most of the movers and shakers on Capitol Hill. Cohen was a dedicated proponent of health insurance as the capstone of the Social Security system, but he was a gradualist or, as he admitted, a "salami slicer," who recognized the innate resistance of the American political system to rapid change.[18] During the lean fifties he and Falk designed a new health care bill that shaved off another thin slice of the health care sausage. The Murray-Wagner-Dingell bill had sought to benefit all age groups; the Cohen-Falk health insurance plan was aimed solely at retired people receiving Social Security benefits and focused exclusively on hospital costs.

Given the American milieu, this limited approach had many advantages. Everywhere else in the Western world government health insurance had come first to low-income wage workers and was subsidized through general tax revenues. But in the United States, with its tradition of self-help and individualism, this smacked too much of socialism—taking from the rich to give to the poor. Social Security, on the other hand, seemed an "earned" benefit rather than a handout and so had a special legitimacy. The public, moreover, by the fifties was familiar with and liked the old-age pension system to which the health plan would be attached. And its beneficiaries seemed especially deserving and worthy of compassion. Unlike people still working, who were likely to have private health insurance through their employers, retirees were generally unprotected. Why should old folks, who had worked all their lives and now faced unusual, perhaps catastrophic medical costs, be denied protection from financial ruin when they became sick? The scheme also sought to finesse the antipathy of the organized medical profession. Doctors' fees were not included. Called Medicare by the popularizers, the Cohen-Falk plan, in several variants, became the center of the federal health care debate for the next decade.

In 1958 Medicare came before Congress as a plan sponsored by Rhode Island Democrat Aimé Forand of the key House Ways and Means Committee. Unfortunately, the hope of appeasing the MD's came to naught. This time the AMA raised a quarter of a million dollars to head off the danger. Allied with the doctors were the National Association of Manufacturers, the American Farm Bureau Federation, and the National Chamber of Commerce, regulars in the never-ending battle to oppose "socialistic" national legislation and expanded federal powers. In March 1960, after weeks of hearings and a major investigative report by the Department of Health, Education, and Welfare, the House Ways and Means Committee, headed by Arkansas Democrat Wilbur Mills, rejected the Forand bill by 17 to 8.

But by this time all but the most hidebound Americans agreed that something must be done to help the old and the poor pay their medical bills. Unable to resist the tide, the organized medical profession gave its begrudging support to a bill that promised to meet their objections. Sponsored by Mills and the powerful Senate baron Robert Kerr of Oklahoma, the Kerr-Mills bill was the conservative answer to Medicare but in some ways was actually broader than the Forand measure. Kerr-Mills paid for up to six months of hospitalization; provided funds to pay doctors, dentists, and surgeons; and covered the costs of X rays, drugs, and private nursing. But—crucially important—unlike Medicare, it was means-tested: Only the "medically indigent," who could prove their inability to pay, were eligible; most Social Security pensioners would not be covered. It also required that beneficiaries absorb large deductibles. And the program would be state administered. This avoided the bogeyman of centralized federal control and allowed the states to set standards of benefits and need. It would satisfy the 1990s conservative faith in localism. But like all state-administered federal programs, it inevitably ensured gross inequalities across the nation. The weakest part of the bill was that the states must contribute up to 50 percent of the costs, an arrangement that many states could not, or would not, afford.

Despite skepticism at both ends of the political spectrum, the bill passed and became law in 1960. Touted by its supporters as a plan that would "enable every state to improve and extend medical services to aged persons,"[19] by 1963 only thirty-two of the fifty states had Kerr-Mills programs operating, and the programs in most of these states were grossly underfunded. Since federal money was allotted on a matching basis, five of the most prosperous states received 90 percent of all the federal funds disbursed.

Dissatisfaction with Kerr-Mills's limitations kept the federal health care issue bubbling during the 1960 presidential campaign. Kennedy denounced the law as inadequate and tore into the Republicans for defeating the Forand bill. His administration, he promised, would enact a Medicare law to cover all Social Security pensioners. During the campaign even Nixon acknowledged that more should be done to defray the costs of medical care, but insisted that the "American people . . . must not have a compulsory health insurance plan forced down their throats. . . ."[20] John Kennedy's election placed health insurance once more on the congressional agenda.

The Kennedy Medicare measure, called the King-Anderson bill, drafted by a task force on health and Social Security headed by Wilbur Cohen, was a retread of the Forand bill but without the surgical benefits clause. All Social Security recipients would be covered for hospital and nursing home costs. The expense would be defrayed by a one quarter of 1 percent increase in Social Security taxes. Beneficiaries, however, would be required to pay ten dollars a day for the first nine days of hospitalization. The modesty of the bill was designed to disarm anticipated opponents; the administration sought to allay everyone's fears. "The program," Kennedy declared, "is not socialized medicine. . . . It is a program of prepayment for health costs with absolute freedom of choice guaranteed. Every person will choose his own doctor and hospital."[21]

Liberals denounced the measure as timid and criticized the president as too eager to placate the enemy. Yet it gratified union leaders and older Americans' groups. Forand himself, now a private citizen, helped organize the National Council of Senior Citizens to fight for the bill. By the end of the year the National Council had more than half a million members.

The council proved to be a vigorous body. It organized mass rallies in Miami and Detroit for King-Anderson and sent out thousands of flyers and letters urging its passage. It allied itself with organized labor in a joint Medicare campaign. Walter Reuther, the forceful president of the United Automobile Workers, addressed the gray-polled delegates at the 1962 National Council meeting and pledged that "the American labor movement will work with you, stand with you, and fight shoulder-to-shoulder with you. . . ."[22] During the weeks that followed Big Labor prodded its members to write their congressmen to get the Medicare legislation moving.

Neither Kennedy's caution nor the old folks' enthusiasm defused the opposition. The AMA responded like one of Pavlov's dogs to the ringing bell. Early in 1961 it sent its members packets of anti-King-Anderson leaflets for distribution to patients and a poster for their offices entitled "Socialized Medicine and You." The material called the pending bill a denial of freedom—"Your freedom to choose the doctor *you believe is best for you*. And your doctor's freedom—his freedom to treat you in an individual way. . . ."[23] In April the AMA launched an anti-King-Anderson letter-writing campaign and buttonholed individual congressmen, paying special attention to members of the Ways and Means Committee. The bill was an expensive tax bill, not a health bill, it insisted. Determined to present a health-professions united front, the AMA pressured individual nurses to break ranks with the pro–health insurance American Nurses Association. In the fall the AMA established a political action committee to rally voters against pro–health insurance candidates in the 1962 congressional election.

Planted squarely athwart the Medicare entrance was the smooth-haired, bespectacled Wilbur Mills of Kensett, Arkansas, chairman of Ways and Means. Diligent, stubborn, in total command of detail, a political animal with no visible life beyond Congress—spectator sports and crossword puzzles excepted—Mills guarded the portals to expanded health care and indeed to the entire Great Society. Mills was proud of his offspring, Kerr-Mills, and refused to see its imperfections. He also resented every effort to pressure him to move when he believed the votes were not there. In part Mills's power was based on his astounding record of success in passing legislation his committee approved, but that reputation in turn depended on knowing when he had the votes needed to carry it in the House. Now he was dubious; the votes weren't there.

As King-Anderson approached a critical point, the administration decided to go over the heads of Congress and make a direct appeal to the public. Larry O'Brien and Cohen, now assistant secretary at HEW, preferred to work with Chairman Mills than to confront him; Mills would just dig in. But they had been overruled, and in late May the White House authorized a weeklong blitz of public opinion that took Interior Secretary Stewart Udall to Kansas City, Commerce Secretary Luther Hodges to Boston,

Labor Secretary Arthur Goldberg to Miami, and Cohen to San Diego. The president himself addressed 17,500 cheering senior citizens at Madison Square Garden while an estimated 10 million viewers watched him on TV.

Kennedy positioned Medicare as the fulfillment of the New Deal, still a blessed political era to millions of seniors. He also appealed to the self-interest of active young adults, who, he said, should not be "heavily burdened" by the medical costs of their aged parents. He denied the bill's opponents' charge that it would drain private initiative and responsibility. "I can't imagine anything worse . . . to sap someone's self-reliance," Kennedy said, "than to be sick, alone, broke. . . ."[24]

The PR campaign was not a success. Kennedy had not prepared well and his Madison Square Garden speech was an ad-libbed harangue that drew cheers from the partisans in the hall but came across as strident to the TV audience. In Washington the UAW staffers who watched the performance on TV concluded "the President . . . wasn't really behind the bill at all. Otherwise, how could he have given such a terrible speech?"[25] As loyal Democrats they made excuses for Kennedy, but the speech in fact may have betrayed the president's limited commitment to domestic change.

The AMA did better. To answer the president, it asked for equal free time from the networks. When they refused, the doctors bought broadcast time to reply the next night. The organized medical profession won the propaganda exchange hands down. Miami surgeon Edward Annis, head of the AMA's speakers bureau, moved viewers with an eloquent plea for Americans to trust their doctors' judgment. He called the administration's bill a "cruel hoax and a delusion" that would benefit millions who could afford to pay while ignoring many not covered by Social Security. He lauded the ineffective Kerr-Mills Act and disparaged King-Anderson as certain to put an impersonal, bureaucratic wall between patients and their doctors.[26]

Kennedy had failed to mobilize massive public support to overcome the forces of entrenched conservatism, and the campaign, intended for twenty cities, was soon called off. If anything, backing for the president's bill visibly softened; its enemies gained confidence. The shift in public mood was not lost on the politicians, and the Ways and Means Committee continued to sit on the bill despite efforts by HEW secretary Abraham Ribicoff to liberate it by compromise. In August, as Congress prepared to go home for the mid-term elections, the Senate decisively defeated the Medicare bill, confirming the impression that the second session of the Eighty-seventh Congress had been marked by administration incompetence and a stubborn refusal of Congress to see that times had changed. Kennedy attempted at least twice more to get a Medicare bill enacted but failed. At his death in late 1963, Medicare remained stalled, checked by organized opposition too powerful for a weak, preoccupied, and inept administration to overcome.

Another leftover from the New Deal-Fair Deal era was federal aid to education. The urgency of the issue reflected the American credo that education could conquer all—poverty, superstition, social inequality, crime, racism, and even ill-health. Give individuals the tools of literacy and numeracy, it held, and they could achieve the American dream for themselves. The door of the little red schoolhouse was the portal to a free, equal, healthy, rewarding, democratic, and prosperous society.

Yet for all their faith in education, Americans found it vexing to pay for it. The nation's primary and secondary schools were administered by more than twenty thousand local school districts and financed by a combination of state and local taxes. Richer states and richer districts could support their schools generously. New Trier near Chicago, Beverly Hills in Southern California, Scarsdale in New York's Westchester County, Newton outside of Boston, and their like could construct high school buildings with laboratories, libraries, gymnasiums, auditoriums; could hire teachers with M.A.'s and even Ph.D.'s; could provide a feast of courses as opulent as those of a small liberal arts college. Poor southern and farm-belt states could not equal New York, Connecticut, New Jersey, Illinois, California, and Massachusetts in their education outlays, while hundreds of local school districts, even some in richer states, did not have the tax base to supplement state contributions.

During the immediate post–World War II period, public school districts came under unusual pressure. The fertility explosion of the "togetherness" era made the need for new classrooms and more teachers a painful financial burden everywhere. During the baby-boom period, aid-to-education partisans made federal funding for teachers' salaries and new classrooms their prime goals. Then, as the bulge began to pass out of the school pipeline, data that revealed a shocking illiteracy rate among military draftees, especially those from the South, created new alarm. Many experts today are skeptical of higher outlays per student as the key to quality education, but these doubts in part were planted by the experiences of the sixties programs enacted under Lyndon Johnson. As the Great Society got underway, few educators disputed that inequality and insufficiency in funding were serious problems of American education and that solving them would contribute to social amelioration generally.

Like Medicare, federal aid to education had been part of the liberal agenda for decades. Its rationale changed over the years, but it remained a fixed feature of the liberal landscape. Also like Medicare, it had a history of defeat at the hands of fiscal and states-rights conservatives. Yet it differed from Medicare in at least two ways. From the mid-fifties on it had been caught in the crossfire of civil rights partisans and Dixiecrat segregationists determined either to use federal aid as a wedge to end Jim Crow schooling or keep it from being so used. More than once in the late fifties and early sixties Harlem's high-profile black congressman, Adam Clayton Powell, had given federal aid bills the kiss of death by tacking on amendments requiring that federal funds be denied segregated schools.

More daunting was the issue of local control. The "religion of localism" is deeply entrenched in the American consciousness, especially in the matter of education. Many Americans feared that federal financing would end local autonomy and impose a lockstep uniformity on neighborhood schools, perceived, for all their actual flaws, as friendly, human-scale places. And certainly local and state education officials saw the federal government as a potential despot ready to take over the school systems and impose curricula, standards, and goals from Washington. Money, yes! But not if it threatened one iota of local independence. For their part, education reformers often saw the local and state educators as time-servers, careerist bureaucrats who cared little for education, fought every effort to make themselves accountable, and thirsted only for higher salaries and bigger budgets. During much of the decade the reformers' prime villain was Edgar Fuller, head of the Council of Chief State School Officers, who seemed to epitomize the self-protective and self-serving qualities of the state education bureaucracies.

Most perplexing of all, however, was the issue of separation of church and state, a principle cherished by secular liberals and pious Protestants alike and deemed a foundation stone of American civil liberties.

If the nation had remained overwhelmingly Protestant, the "separation" question might not have arisen. But of course it had not. During the nineteenth and early twentieth centuries millions of Catholics had arrived on America's shores. Like other immigrants they anticipated a better life and they generally found it. But the United States was also an alien land in religious terms, where the Catholic faith was not respected. The public schools seemed hostile preserves that taught either a godless secularism or a disguised version of Protestantism. Conscious of their exposed minority position, the First Provincial Council of Catholic Bishops, meeting in Baltimore in 1829, authorized a system of church-sponsored parochial schools to help defend the ancient faith against its Protestant detractors and preserve it from the erosions of a materialistic, secular society. The system grew slowly at first and then, with the leap in Irish and German immigration in the 1850s, exploded. It surged again at the end of the century as new waves of "wretched masses," primarily from Catholic eastern and southern Europe, crashed on America's shores. By 1965 there were 3.5 million students enrolled in more than fourteen thousand Catholic elementary and high schools.

The cost of this vast parochial school system ran to some $3 billion annually. All of it was borne by Catholic parents and the Church. But why should they have to do so, Catholics asked? Every child educated in a Catholic school was one less imposed on the local taxpayer. And Catholic parents not only shelled out for their own children; they also paid the local taxes that supported other people's offspring. Why must Catholic parents be kept from sharing in the public school fund from whatever source derived, local or federal?

The arguments against federal funding of Catholic schools appealed to both sacred rights and garden-variety self-interest. Any attempt to divert public revenues to religious schools, said civil libertarians, violated the hard-won protection against oppressive "established" churches incorporated into the First Amendment of the Constitution. Separation of church and state was as precious a principle as free speech. Catholics, moreover, had the option of sending their children to the public schools. If they preferred private schools, they should pay.

But more than principle was at stake. The 1.5 million public school teachers of the nation plus the state public school administrators formed a powerful lobby against federal aid to parochial education. Give the Catholic schools money and there would simply be less for the rest. Though their constitutional scruples were undoubtedly sincere, the National Education Association and the American Federation of Teachers, the country's premier teachers' lobbying groups, clearly also feared that sharing the tax pie with Catholic schools would leave their members with a smaller slice. Organizations like the American Association of School Administrators and the Council of Chief State School Officers added to this a concern over sharing power and influence with another agency.

None of the arguments for local autonomy had excluded the federal government from the education business entirely. In 1917, under the Smith-Hughes Act, federal funds had supported vocational education through matching grants to the states. Beginning in World War II and continuing through the 1950s, Washington gave money to local school districts "impacted" by military bases or war industries, although these grants often benefited prosperous communities. Higher education had aroused less controversy. Ever since the 1860s the federal government had funded the "land-grant colleges" through gifts of land from the vast public domain. The 1944 GI Bill and its extensions paid the tuition at college and trade schools of millions of World War II and Korean War veterans. And even the conservative Eisenhower administration supported the National Defense Education Act of 1958, the spawn of post-*Sputnik* hysteria. NDEA provided federal loans for college students in fields deemed vital to America's strategic interests, with generous payback terms for those who became teachers, and grants to state schools to encourage programs in science and modern languages, all designed to help America catch up to the Soviet Union. But each of these federal outlays was a "categorical" grant for a specific, designated purpose; none was a "general," across-the-board stipend for day-to-day school operations themselves.

Until the Great Society, virtually every effort to secure general federal aid to elementary and secondary education had foundered on the rock of the church-state separation issue. Civil libertarians and the teachers' lobbies denounced every aid measure that included private and parochial schools as a betrayal of a holy American principle. The Catholic hierarchy, through its social mouthpiece, the National Catholic Welfare Conference, assailed every aid measure that did not include parochial schools as bigoted discrimination against Catholic citizens. A flurry of bills during the forties and fifties to funnel federal taxes into public school construction and public school teachers' salaries met the united opposition of segregationists, fiscal and cultural conservatives, states-righters, and the Catholic hierarchy, and all crashed in flames.

The Kennedy administration was to meet its own aid-to-education Waterloo. Kennedy was not as devoted to public education as his successor would prove to be. A beneficiary of elite private education, he lacked special devotion to the venerated "common schools." Yet, like other Northern Democrats, JFK was committed to some sort of federal program to help finance and improve public schools and universities, and soon after the election had established a small task force on education headed by Frederick L. Hovde, president of Purdue University, to concoct a new federal-aid-to-education package.

The distinguished panel proposed an ambitious $9.4 billion program, spread over four and a half years, for elementary- and secondary-school grants, loans to the states, and for college dorms and other higher-education construction. But the proposal was a budget buster. Dean Francis Keppel of the Harvard School of Education, one of the task force members, later admitted: "We came up with a report that if Mr. Kennedy had adopted would probably have broken the federal government bank in no time at all."[27] More damaging, however, was the response of the Catholic hierarchy. Kennedy could not yield on the religious issue. As a Catholic himself he had, during the election campaign, pledged strict adherence to separation of church and state. But the task force proposal offended Catholic leaders. Soon after its issuance Cardinal Spellman of New York, a powerful voice of conservative Catholicism, told an audience that it was "unthinkable that any American child be denied the Federal funds allotted to other children which are necessary for his mental development because his parents chose for him a God-centered education."[28] Views like the cardinal's easily translated into votes. Like the president himself, many of the Northern liberal congressmen who would otherwise have favored the bill were Catholic with Catholic constituencies. They did not intend to defy the Church. Their defection promised to be crippling.

The administration did not adopt all the task force proposals. Early in the first session of the Eighty-seventh Congress, it submitted two major education bills, one for elementary and secondary education, the other for higher education. The lower-education bill proposed a three-year, $3.3 billion program of federal grants for construction and teachers' salaries for the public schools exclusively. It also included a provision to continue the impacted-areas subsidies that liberals charged primarily rewarded rich school districts, but to reduce their amounts.

As opposition to the administration's bill mounted, Kennedy, feeling he must be less Catholic than the pope, told reporters that direct loans and grants to parochial schools were unconstitutional. The statement was not very helpful. Pulled one way by party loyalty and the other by Church pressure, leading Northern Democrats on the Rules Committee—James Delaney of New York, Tip O'Neill of Massachusetts, and Ray Madden of Indiana—defected from the administration and, joining with Republicans and Southern Democrats, blocked action by the House Rules Committee. Hoping to rescue some federal aid to education, the White House tried to push through an extension of the National Defense Education Act. To appease the Church the bill authorized federal construction loans to private and parochial schools. The loophole failed to work. This time, a coalition of segregationists, fiscal conservatives, and church-state separationists in the Senate defeated the administration's bill.

Kennedy made several further attempts to pass a federal aid to education law during his "thousand days." Several additional bills went into the legislative hopper during the next two years, but none of them was as generous or as broadly gauged as the first. And all failed.

JFK also failed to get his higher education bill through Congress. Kennedy subscribed to the hypothesis, just gaining acceptance, that economic growth depended as much on human capital—what people had in their heads—as on machines, factories, and chemical processes. His proposals to Congress in 1961 and 1962 promised several billions in federal grants as well as loans to colleges, both secular and religious, to improve programs, especially in math, science, engineering, and modern languages; to build libraries, classrooms, and laboratories; and to provide both federal scholarships and loans for deserving and needy students.

The measures encountered the usual coalition of skeptics, bigots, strict constructionists, cheese-parers, and naysayers. Some opponents raised the religious issue: Should Catholic colleges get the same help as other private institutions? Federal loans to sectarian institutions had precedents; outright grants had none. The National Education Association came out against it, and William Carr, head of the NEA, shot off telegrams to every member of the House warning that providing federal construction grants for sectarian colleges "imperils America's traditional concept of separation of church and state."[29] The scholarship program was especially attractive to upwardly striving, lower-middle-class families, who saw the road to their children's future success paved with diplomas. But it ran into the resistance of conservatives to straight-out federal scholarships as opposed to loans. Willing to accept a subsidized college loan program, men like Frank Lausche of Ohio recoiled at outright federal handouts as extravagant and a dangerous extension of federal commitments. In February 1962, a $2.67 billion college aid bill allocating $924 million for 200,000 four-year scholarships that would average about $700 a year went to a joint conference committee. But the measure, when reported back, went down to defeat in the House in late September by a narrow 214 to 186 vote.

Higher education rose from the mat before the ten-count, however, in Kennedy's last year. The administration's higher education bill of 1963 dropped the scholarship provisions, and to mollify enemies of aid to religious institutions, it provided grants to colleges and universities only in the form of construction loans and earmarked grants for libraries and programs in science and engineering, mathematics, and foreign languages. This bill, after conference committee reconciliation, passed the House in early November. Senate approval was a foregone conclusion when Kennedy was shot in Dallas at the end of the month. It passed the

upper house on December 10, to be signed into law by Lyndon
Johnson a week later.

There was, then, something to show for three years of effort to
revise and upgrade the nation's educational system. But the
Higher Education Facilities Act of 1963 was a modest measure,
the most that a legislatively weak and marginally concerned administration could accomplish.

At least one Kennedy initiative—the War on Poverty—fed on the
new post-scarcity sensibility. Scholars clash over the ultimate origins of the War on Poverty. One circle insists the push came from
below, the other that it came from above. Bottom-up, says one
side; top-down, says the other. The disagreement is not merely an
academic squabble. It is an issue that separates two models of
America's social essence.

In the reform-from-below version, the Kennedy administration
was goaded reluctantly into a poverty program by fear of black
unrest and the need to court a volatile proletarian constituency
essential for reelection in 1964. By August 1963, when Martin
Luther King moved the nation with his "I Have a Dream" speech
at the Washington march "for jobs and freedom," the civil rights
movement had already shifted from voters' rights and integration
to poverty issues. The reform-from-belowers describe a buildup of
ghetto anger and a resulting sense of foreboding among federal
officials two years into the Kennedy administration.

The reform-from-below partisans are found predominantly on
the hard political left. Skeptical of individualism, suspicious of
capitalism, emotionally allied with the nation's poor and minorities, they scorn liberal reform as essentially a defense of the status
quo. Progressivism, the New Deal, the Fair Deal, the Great Society
are to them successive manifestations of "corporate liberalism"
designed to save capitalism by smoke and mirrors. The War on
Poverty is a perfect example of liberal sleight-of-hand, they say.
Moreover, to see the poor as passive objects of change denies
them the respect they deserve. In reality, these partisans believe,
the poor did not wait for the rulers to confer benefits on them.
They forced the rulers' hand. There is a paradox here. On the
one hand, says the hard left, the Great Society was a shallow effort
of underfunded programs. On the other, the proletariat deserved
the credit for creating it.

On the whole I believe the top-down view more persuasive. The sixties antipoverty programs were not, initially, a response to black militancy. The timing is wrong. Until 1964 or 1965, racism still seemed the key to black poverty. Even civil rights leaders believed that. Eliminate bigotry, render society color-blind, and economic inequality would decline. The way to reduce black poverty was through civil rights legislation, not special antipoverty measures. Opponents of the early federal antipoverty programs would occasionally play the race card. But its defenders, a louder chorus, proclaimed that poverty was not confined to one group and denied that concern for race governed the antipoverty program. Adam Yarmolinsky, one of the War on Poverty's creators, said in a freewheeling 1973 Brandeis University–sponsored discussion of sixties Great Society urban policy, "The poverty program was in no sense a help-the-blacks program, and not only were we saying this, but we didn't think it was."[30] Other participants seconded Yarmolinsky. Economist William Capron, another War on Poverty founding father, insisted at this meeting that the civil rights leadership had nothing to do with the poverty program. "There was no attempt to consult. There was no input of any kind that was directly targeted on the development of this program that came from [them]."[31]

Capron and Yarmolinsky were right as far as they went. They were drawing on their experience with the Kennedy-Johnson poverty task force in 1963–64. But in fact, by the following year the ground would begin to shift as a new militancy suffused the civil rights movement and the nation began to tremble under the first blasts of ghetto rebellion.

The top-down perspective identifies the antipoverty initiatives as the work of liberal technocrats in the Kennedy-Johnson White House and a top layer of bureaucrats and administrators in the executive departments. There—among the White House staff, the Council of Economic Advisers, the Social Security Administration, the Budget Bureau, the Departments of Labor and of Health, Education, and Welfare, and even in Defense and Agriculture—economists, lawyers, sociologists, and assorted social scientists, inspired by the insights of behaviorism and the precedents of Europe and Australia, yearned to fulfill the promise of the social welfare state. Daniel Moynihan—himself a participant in the Kennedy administration's early antipoverty planning—calls it the "professionalization of reform." The War on Poverty was "preeminently the conception of the liberal, policy oriented intellectuals, especially those who gathered in Washington, and, in a significant sense, came to power in the early 1960s under the Presidency of John F. Kennedy."[32] Much later Robert Lampman, another founder of the War on Poverty, in a symposium on federal antipoverty programs, stated bluntly: "The initiatives for a poverty program came from inside government . . . ; they certainly did not come from well-organized pressure groups. . . . It was an elite group inside the Kennedy administration that started talking about this," he added, "and I think they saw it as an attempt to follow in some logical way in the spirit of the Social Security Act and the Employment Act [that is, the Full Employment Act] of 1946."[33] And their conclusions are confirmed by studies of welfare states around the world. Recently, Theda Skocpol, a Harvard sociologist, has called attention to the autonomous role of political leaders and bureaucrats in the political process. Politicians and administrators, she says, are "not merely agents of other social interests. They are actors in their own right. . . ."[34]

Some members of this "new priesthood of action intellectuals"[35] were holdovers from the FDR-Truman years. Wilbur Cohen of HEW is their perfect representative. Many were novices attracted by the new Democratic administration. Adam Yarmolinsky, Charles Haar, Richard Goodwin, Walter Heller, Kermit Gordon, Alice Rivlin, and Moynihan himself are examples. Frustrated by the dominant conservative stasis, they finally found their voices in a new era of liberal presidents. Many of their programs had only shallow, grassroots constituencies. The propulsive force was a combination of altruism, professional pride, and the urge—powerful among the politocrats—to deploy the new social science insights and techniques of their fields. In a time of swaggering national confidence and a profound sense that with enough will and money any goal was within reach, these people prepared to take on the age-old scourge of poverty.

This emphasis on the bureaucrats' role is itself a battlefield within the larger war over the War on Poverty's origins and agents. It is the position of old New Deal liberals, moderates, neoconservatives, and assorted nonliberals. Leading the charge against it were Richard Cloward and Frances Fox Piven, two radical professors of social work. Cloward especially was a pivotal player in the preliminaries of the poverty war. Both would later mobilize the poor to confront and challenge the whole liberal welfare state. At the 1973 Brandeis conference Cloward objected to the claim that the "main actors were some intellectuals and some bureaucrats." That conclusion left out the "broader context" of Martin Luther King's Birmingham campaign, the March on Washington, and other civil rights events immediately preceding the decision to attack poverty. When Fred Hayes, a former Kennedy housing official, claimed that the highly publicized New Haven urban renewal programs had been geared primarily to the specifications of architects and urban planners, Piven objected: "And it didn't have anything to do with protests . . . in the ghettos?" "No, no," Hayes responded, "there was no protest in the ghettos in New Haven at that time."[36]

Even if the top-down, Moynihan-Lampman perspective on the origins of the War on Poverty is closer to the facts, it is not the whole truth. A small circle of instigators did not impose their will on a reluctant public. At the outset a substantial part of the educated middle class embraced the poverty war with zeal as a fitting response of a rich nation to those left out.

Undoubtedly many of these people were moved by Christian charity. Americans have always been generous donors to good causes and to the afflicted. But the claim of top-down derivation of Great Society antipoverty programs does not require exaggerated faith in class altruism. It assumes, rather, that many prosperous Americans accepted the "post-scarcity" attitude that no dark shadow fell across the future and that the age-old curse of poverty could finally be lifted. Lyndon Johnson himself, in his March 1964 message to Congress accompanying the Economic Opportunity Act, the War on Poverty law, would express the mood concisely when he announced that "today, for the first time in our history it is possible to conquer poverty."[37]

But middle-class Americans also craved emotional comfort. All things considered, Americans enjoy their prosperity more if its benefits are not confined to the rich. As the decade began, however, this did not seem to be the case. In a time of roaring prosperity "Metro-Americans" were troubled that too many fellow citizens had been left behind. Affluent Americans could not bask in their own good fortune, could not be at ease in paradise if millions of impoverished fellow citizens did not share the boon to

some degree. Poverty was a blot on American life, like ugly highway billboards or polluted streams. And there was another consideration: The existence of poverty weakened the United States in
the global struggle with communism. How could we claim our
system was superior if millions continued to live at the edge of
survival? The power of the East-West international rivalry to influence domestic policy is vividly illustrated in the case of *Sputnik* and
the resulting race to the moon. Before it was over billions would
be spent to vindicate the American democratic, capitalist system
through technology. The same urge would have its muted equivalent in the War on Poverty and other Great Society programs.

This does not mean that every doctor, lawyer, accountant,
teacher, storekeeper, middle manager, engineer, and business executive perceived poverty as a major national problem or a cur-
able one. In fact a Gallup poll in early 1964 showed that 83 percent of Americans did not believe that poverty would ever be
entirely done away with. It only requires that influential and politically sophisticated Americans, more than previously, acknowledged the existence of intractable poverty and were willing to
invest in its reduction.

One more quality of the early sixties middle-class *Zeitgeist* was
essential, however, to launching the Great Society: the relative
suspension of class blame. There is a long history in America, and
elsewhere in the Western world, of distinguishing the "deserving" from the "undeserving" poor. The first, the worthy, are
widows and children, the chronically sick and disabled, the men-
tally deficient, the insane; the second, the unworthy, are the lazy,
the improvident, the addicted, the dishonest, the criminal. The
two sorts of poverty have not been considered morally equivalent.
Widows and orphans, victims of acts of God, deserve compassion
and succor without stigma. The slothful and the "vicious," far
gone in drink and other depravity—victims, we would say today, of
self-destructive behavior—do not. Such people cannot be allowed
to starve or to die of medical neglect, perhaps, but they should be
given minimum aid and be made to pay a price for every dollar.
For a time in the early sixties, however, fewer Americans than in
the past made these distinctions. The poor as a whole seemed,
somehow, deserving. In the months to come, middle-class impatience and even anger at the poor would overwhelm guilt, and the
prosperous could ease their discomfort by resurrecting the ano-

dyne of the undeserving poor, who had no one to blame but themselves. But that would be later.

But the *Zeitgeist* was only the background noise to the War on Poverty. In the foreground, improbably enough, was the federal effort to deal with juvenile delinquency.

Each decade of the twentieth century has had its emblematic crime that aroused public fear and ire beyond its actual due. In the Progressive Era it was the "white slave trade"; in the twenties it was bootlegging. Bank robbery was the 1930s larceny of preference. The 1950s crime-of-the-decade was juvenile delinquency.

During that sober-side postwar era, the behavior of adolescents alarmed good, respectable folk to the point of hysteria. Free of the material restraints of their Depression-era parents, the young acted out with fast cars, provocative hair, and lustful music. Worst of all, at the fringe, young males gathered in gangs that murderously "rumbled" with other gangs, took drugs, and mugged upstanding citizens. During the decade juvenile delinquency, violating all predictions of affluence's likely fruits, became a towering cultural anxiety that inspired novels, TV broadcasts, Broadway musicals, legislative investigations, and an avalanche of analytical books and articles. In 1955 the movie *Rebel Without a Cause*, starring James Dean, broke all box office records. In January 1955 even the Eisenhower administration was vexed enough to propose a $5 million program of grants to the states to combat juvenile crime.

Efforts to establish the causes and cures of juvenile delinquency engaged all the usual suspects—politicians, social workers, judges, police officials, and the eleemosynary institutions. In the thick of it all was the Ford Foundation, the $3.7 billion powerhouse of good intentions in Manhattan.

In its earliest years of full operation the foundation had come under withering attack from anti-communist warriors as a sponsor of left wing, socialistic projects. Under its third president, Henry Heald, a former head of New York University, it drew in its horns. A narrow conservative who epitomized the cautious rigidity of the McCarthy era, Heald closed down the foundation's controversial behavioral sciences and mental health programs and poured most of its revenues into irreproachable aid to higher education programs. But even Heald was not able to squelch the natural ten-

dency of big foundations to sponsor change, and during his tenure Paul Ylvisaker, who came to Ford in 1955, established a
beachhead for social activism in its public affairs program.

Son of a Lutheran minister, Ylvisaker was inspired by the social
gospel philosophy of the liberal Protestant denominations associated with the World Council of Churches. He had arrived at Ford
in the midst of the urban renewal craze of the fifties, which saw
massive slum clearance and downtown "redevelopment" as the
way to rejuvenate the older cities. By this time the most famous of
the redevelopers and urban planners was Edward Logue, development administrator of New Haven. Logue had become a celebrity
among Metro-Americans for his bold transformation of the old
college town inhabited by Yale by razing squalid slums, constructing shiny new office buildings, opening up park areas, and building new, middle-class housing. But Logue himself had begun to
worry about the poor people that "renewal" displaced. They were
more often the victims than the beneficiaries of the planners'
changes.

Renewal did not solve the social pathologies of the older cities.
Around the centers of these remained a transitional area between
the commercial heart and the suburbs—a "gray area"—where
newcomers collected in squalid housing, enduring decrepit public facilities, poor schools, and little opportunity for social advance. These were what used to be called the "slums," but unlike
the slums of the past, they were not way stations for their inhabitants in the climb up the American social ladder.

Inspired by Logue's insight, Ylvisaker searched for an urban
program that looked beyond bricks and mortar to the human
problems of the gray areas. If slum clearance could not end poverty, what could? Here Ylvisaker borrowed the insights of a group
of sociologists and social workers who had learned their lessons,
first- or second-hand, from the University of Chicago School of
Sociology, which emphasized the "competent community." Such
a community, able to exert pressure on the politicians and impose
discipline on its members, was far better equipped to check slum
crime and delinquency than case workers and psychologists.

In the late fifties the chief prophet of community competence
was Leonard Cottrell, director of the Russell Sage Foundation. As
Cottrell had written in 1929, when he was a thirty-year-old graduate student at Chicago, the spread of business and industry into

residential areas and "the influx of foreign national and racial groups" caused "a disintegration of the community as a unit of social control." In this state "community resistance is low. Delinquent and criminal patterns arise and are transmitted socially just as any other cultural and social pattern is transmitted. In time these delinquent patterns may become dominant and shape the attitudes and behavior of persons living in the area."[38]

One of Cottrell's students was Lloyd Ohlin, professor of social work at Columbia. Like Cottrell, Ohlin had taken his graduate training at the University of Chicago, but he also had learned from Saul Alinsky, the maverick social activist who, in the late 1930s, had fathered the Back-of-the-Yards project in Chicago as the instrument to rally the poor against their afflictions and oppressors. Alinsky's community self-help movement would challenge political elites and disturb the complacent. He would become persona non grata to local officials and moderates and would later rail against the federal War on Poverty program as hierarchical and bureaucratic. Poverty warriors would try to distance themselves from Alinsky, but he shared the University of Chicago milieu with Cottrell, Ohlin, and other War on Poverty founders such as Richard Boone of the Ford Foundation, who originally was a Cook County (Chicago) official, and William Cannon of the Budget Bureau. It is difficult to deny a common intellectual heritage.

Within the larger issues of slums and their pathologies, Ohlin's special interest was delinquency, its causes and its cures. In the late fifties he linked up with a younger colleague at Columbia, Richard Cloward, to develop a theory of delinquency that would help provide a philosophical rationale for the poverty programs of the Kennedy-Johnson administrations.

The approach became known as "opportunity theory." As spelled out in *Delinquency and Opportunity,* published in 1960, it ascribed gang affiliation and adolescent crime to frustration. Delinquents were not made by failed socialization. They understood the difference between right and wrong. As the prospectus for Mobilization for Youth, the early showcase for opportunity theory, expressed it: "They [delinquents] may enjoy flouting the rules of the game. . . . But to say this is not the same as to say that they do not understand the rules."[39] The problem was that slum youths internalized the material goals of the affluent society but then could not attain them. Crime and delinquency represented a rational response to blocked opportunity. If you could not attain money and status in the larger community, you could in the gang through criminal activity. ". . . [P]ressures toward the formation of delinquent subcultures," Ohlin and Cloward wrote, "originate in marked disparities between culturally induced aspirations among lower class youth and the possibility of achieving them by legitimate means."[40]

At the very conclusion of their influential book Cloward and Ohlin criticized the popular slum-clearance programs that were displacing the poor and destroying whatever social cohesion slum communities had. Ways should be found to reconstruct the mechanisms that provided "social control and the avenues of social ascent."[41]

But the implications of *Delinquency and Opportunity* went far beyond this modest proposal. The way to solve the delinquency problem was not through counseling of slum youth by earnest teachers or idealistic social workers. It was not by merely doling out cash. It also was not, by implication, through strengthening the family. Delinquency would be abated by providing opportunity to the inner-city young. Give them jobs; give them focused training. Make it possible for them to succeed within the legitimate world and they would abandon the underworld. If the goal was to transform the slums, "gobs of giving would be wrong," Ylvisaker said. "It is not dependency we want to encourage, but independence and choice."[42]

Community competence and opportunity theory had different ideological textures. The opportunity model was philosophically more radical. It blamed existing society. The criminal youth's choice of crime was a rational one given the injustices of the social order. The system had to change to end delinquency. The community competence model was a version of the culture of poverty. It assumed that any healthy community must accept conventional middle-class values and transmit them to the young. It blamed the slum community itself, though it did not absolve the larger society from culpability for community demoralization. It also called for "social control." At the same time both models rejected the elitist, top-down approach that relied on missionaries from the middle class—social workers, classroom teachers, and "mental hygienists"—to save the slum communities and rescue delinquents from sin. And in the end the community competence model, with community empowerment at its core, would prove far more effective in roiling the system than most people expected.

Without attempting to keep the two views distinct, the Ford Foundation applied the theorists' models in a number of Ford Foundation Gray Areas programs. In 1959 Ohlin and Cloward became advisers to Ylvisaker.

That same year, the Chicago superintendent of schools asked the foundation to fund a series of meetings to discuss education for the "culturally handicapped."[43] The foundation proposed a more ambitious scheme. In March 1960 it made an initial grant of $1.25 million to create new schools in urban renewal neighborhoods that would not only teach local children but also serve as community centers, like old-fashioned settlement houses. It soon sponsored a cluster of other antipoverty, juvenile delinquency programs emphasizing education, jobs, housing, health, welfare, and other services. The foundation selected seven cities as Gray Areas demonstration projects and poured $2 million to $7 million into each.

Meanwhile the foundation was drawn into a New York City program that would serve as a preview of coming attractions of the Great Society War on Poverty.

Mobilization for Youth (MFY) was conceived in 1957 by the directors of New York's venerable Henry Street Settlement to deal with the juvenile delinquency problem of the Lower East Side. Early in the century the area had sheltered the city's Jewish immigrants. Many had moved out—to Brooklyn, the Bronx, and the suburbs—as they assimilated and raised their economic status. Some remained, along with many ethnic Irish and Italians. But none of these older groups contributed appreciably to the local delinquency problem. As an MFY document noted, "Only one Jewish boy was reported as currently in a gang."[44] The problem came from the large influx of Puerto Ricans and blacks, many of whose young men drifted into criminal and violent gangs that threatened the stability of the neighborhood. The area had always been poor, but this time there were few signs that residents were ever going to escape poverty and social pathology.

The settlement workers' proposal to address the problem recommended more social workers and sports programs as well as

"Big Brother" relationships with the gangs. Neither city officials nor local philanthropies found this conventional approach interesting, and the Henry Street officials turned to the National Institute of Mental Health in Washington. NIMH itself had begun to lose faith in the value of mental health clinics to cure "disturbed youths" and was beginning to shift to Cottrell's "community competence" approach. The Cottrellites at NIMH now saw an opportunity to use the Henry Street proposal as a springboard to test new strategies, and in 1958 they went to Ohlin and Cloward at the Columbia School of Social Work and asked them to revise the original scheme. Cloward contacted David Hunter of the Ford Foundation and the two cobbled together a grant proposal that emphasized the project's attraction as a social experiment. The NIMH took the Ohlin-Cloward-Hunter scheme, further revised it to meet its guidelines, and made a $450,000 planning grant to the project, to be run jointly by the Henry Street Settlement and the Columbia group. Cloward would become one of its directors and the Ford Foundation would provide the project with a $2 million additional grant.

A completed blueprint for what was now called Mobilization for Youth (MFY) appeared in December 1961 as a 617-page tome. It called MFY a "demonstration project" to test "the prevention and control of delinquency by expanding opportunities."[45] But in fact it went beyond opportunity theory. It also proposed "community competence" as part of the solution. Neighborhood people themselves would be consulted and recruited for programs to improve the opportunities and amenities of the community. Nor did the proposal neglect more traditional remedies for youth crime. In fact, the plan ruled out no promising answer to juvenile delinquency.

Mobilization for Youth would send strong ripples through the Kennedy-Johnson Great Society. In 1961 the MFY experiment seemed part of an exciting new departure for dealing with the urgent issue of youth gone wrong, and it attracted favorable attention from the eager, fresh-faced New Frontiersmen. As Daniel Moynihan, the Kennedy administration's young assistant secretary of labor, would later note, "expanding *opportunities* had suffused the Washington atmosphere, just as it had that of New York."[46]

One who caught the fever was David Hackett, a close friend of

Attorney General Robert Kennedy from Milton Academy days. Hackett had been only a day student at Milton, but he had also been a golden boy, the best athlete in school, whose friendship with Robert had made the runty Catholic misfit acceptable to the WASP preppies who dominated the school. The Kennedy brothers' own youth helped to focus their attention on the juvenile delinquency problem. Within a week of the 1960 presidential election, John Kennedy chose Hackett to mobilize the administration's future antidelinquency program.

Hackett had no experience in the field and inevitably turned to the experts. Soon after the inauguration he summoned David Hunter, the man in charge of MFY concerns at Ford, to pick his brain. He then called a conference on delinquency, as much to learn himself as to facilitate interchange. The discordant messages at the conference only confused him. One voice stood out, however—Lloyd Ohlin's—and thereafter Hackett became an unquestioning disciple of opportunity theory. Together he and Ohlin decided that the executive branch needed a coordinating body to deal with delinquency.

In mid-May 1961, at Hackett's urging, JFK established by executive order the President's Committee on Juvenile Delinquency consisting of Attorney General Robert Kennedy and two other cabinet officers, with Hackett as executive director and Lloyd Ohlin and Sanford Kravitz, an expert on youth crime, as special assistants. Richard Boone of the Ford Foundation public affairs department soon joined the group. The committee was charged with coordinating all federal JD programs, developing new ones, and encouraging federal, state, and private agencies to cooperate and make recommendations to the federal government "on measures to make more effective the prevention, treatment, and control of juvenile delinquency and youth crime."[47] The very day he issued the order Kennedy submitted to Congress the Juvenile Delinquency and Youth Offenses Control Act. Passed that September, the bill established the Office of Juvenile Delinquency, with a three-year budget of $30 million. Formally under the Department of Health, Education and Welfare, the JD programs now were actually under the control of David Hackett in the White House and, through him, Richard Cloward, who came to the capital as director of OJD. Leonard Cottrell, too, was drawn into OJD as chairman of its demonstration review panel.

Still untested and unchallenged, Mobilization for Youth, itself the beneficiary of a $2.1 million federal grant in May 1962, became, not surprisingly, the prototype of the federal juvenile delinquency projects. Hackett and Ohlin used their sparse money for planning grants for projects in sixteen cities to be modeled after MFY. This meant augmenting opportunity through total community involvement. However vague, the idea had the ring of bold innovation and made the reformers' juices flow. Once the plans were in place, they hoped the cities would find other sources of funds, public or private, to implement them and thereby ultimately demonstrate to a perplexed nation how to end the "rumbling," "bopping," and mugging that seemed to have become the chief occupation of many teenagers in America's inner cities.

True to the messy American way with reform, the Ford Foundation and OJD projects overlapped. Four Gray Areas city projects also received federal OJD funds. Mobilization for Youth got money from both Ford and the federal government and from other sponsors as well. OJD and Ford also duplicated each other in approaches. Both emphasized changing the environment rather than changing individuals, and both fixed on education and skills-creation as key ways to improve the slums.

During the remaining years of the Kennedy administration, the community action-opportunity theory circle around Hackett, Ohlin, Kravitz, and Cottrell, closely allied with Robert Kennedy, sought to expand its reach and impact. "Hackett's guerrillas" scrounged for loose money in federal department budgets to encourage more community planning groups. They worried that after the planning stage there would be no money for actual plan implementation, and bombarded the president with memos reminding him that the bills would soon come due and Congress would soon have to cough up real money.

Meanwhile, in the one project already underway, New York's Mobilization for Youth, problems were emerging that would become endemic in many of the Great Society War on Poverty community action programs. From the start MFY was a divided body. On one side were the older Lower East Side settlement-house staffers committed to the old ways of dispensing social services— the "welfare colonialism" that social activists would denounce. They did not oppose local input. In fact they were happy to encourage neighborhood councils. But they assumed these would serve primarily as conduits for information and advice from the experts and abet the social workers and the authorities. The Ohlin-Cloward group of Columbia intellectuals, of course, rejected all this as a denial of opportunity theory and community competence principles. But how were these to be implemented within the bounds of a small New York City neighborhood? One way was to create as many neighborhood jobs as possible, but clearly a few million dollars of federal funds was not going to break the logjam for most of the local poor. But opportunity theory implied more than a program to create jobs. It was a challenge to existing American society. By creating a program that confronted the local establishments—educational, political, and economic—MFY could become a revolutionary model for the nation. The Columbia people had little use for the sort of genteel-consensus views of traditional social service liberals. They saw the people of the Lower East Side as victims of a callous and even oppressive system who deeply resented their status. These feelings, the activists believed, should be encouraged so that the poor might awaken the inert power centers of the neighborhoods and the city and through disruption seize autonomy for themselves.

In 1963 Frances Piven, Cloward's associate, wrote a training program proposal for MFY that laid out this policy explicitly. The poor, she said, had "no regular resources for influencing public policy." Their only recourse, therefore, was "disruption." This meant violating "the implicit 'social contract' of major institutions and . . . the explicit social contract of the law as well." But, "If our analysis is correct . . . disruptive and irregular tactics are the only resources, short of violence, available to low-income groups seeking to influence public policy."[48]

At first the cracks between the two factions were papered over by dividing the available funds between the Columbia group and the settlement people. Each would pursue its own policy. The Columbians would take charge of community development programs; the settlement professionals would work with educational, employment, and family services. The community development programs received the smaller share of MFY money, but were dominant in the investment of manpower and energy. One MFY official told Jack Newfield of the *New York Post* that the organization's three hundred-person staff spent more than 80 percent of its time and effort "organizing the unaffiliated—the lower fifth of the economic ladder . . . who will overturn the status quo [and solve the problems of] delinquents, alcohol, and drug addiction."[49] Community development would also attract by far the most attention and notoriety.

Inherent in the policies of the MFY activists was a fundamental paradox that bedevils all proponents of deep social change: The revolution is made for the masses but inevitably is conceived and conducted by an elite. History suggests that insurgency from below, beyond brief spasms of blind rage, is not self-starting. So what are activists to do? Should they seek to incite social upheaval? Sensitive to charges of elitism and manipulation, they usually insist the masses are ready for fundamental change and need only a small spark to ignite. But too often the "people" are not as inflammable as the theory asserts and require a major accelerator. And before long the incendiaries have taken over. It then becomes their revolution, not the people's.

Mobilization for Youth embodied this paradox. Its initial board of directors was composed predominantly of professionals and notables who lived "uptown." Its three-man staff directorship included Cloward and George Brager, both of whom believed that results flowed from confrontation rather than cooperation. Community Development Program Director Brager's appointees to MFY's large staff included men and women with roots in the left political culture of New York—Trotskyites, former Stalinists, people with old socialist backgrounds, Castroites, incipient New Leftists. Many represented a new breed of social workers who rejected the services-delivery approach of their predecessors, and even the non-Marxists among them were excited by bold, anti-establishment initiatives. Inevitably they treated the community programs as opportunities for confrontation with what would later be called the power structure, with the goal of "empowering" the local people.

But the first phase of the community development program, running through mid-1963, was intended to be catalytic, not directive. Operating out of their grungy East Second Street headquarters, MFY community development staffers brought together bodega owners, Pentecostal ministers, tenant groups, and Puerto Rican war veterans, who, they hoped, would spontaneously initiate action programs of some useful kind. They soon learned how naive they were. People who came to the meetings did not have the same goals as the staffers. As one MFY leader confessed, "Most of them were more interested in Mobilization's resources of money and staff than in programs of community change."[50]

By the summer of 1963, the frustrated staff began to take a more aggressive role in raising community consciousness. They would now be more directive. They would aggressively rally the Lower East Side poor around issues—bad housing, unresponsive schools, poor city social services—and organize mass protests and strikes that would get the attention of the powerful. In the process, the activists hoped, the poor would slough off their despair and skepticism and discover a new sense of autonomy. Regardless of merit, the new approach was a sure formula for trouble.

The first challenge to the powers-that-be was a "conflict confrontation" between Puerto Rican mothers, organized as MOM, and Irving Rosenbloom, principal of P.S. 140. At a parents meeting in October 1963, the principal had insulted them, the mothers charged. They responded by picketing the school and shouting slogans, some of which smacked of anti-Semitism. MOM in fact was "a phantom organization led by MFY staff members" and not above committing outright fraud. Its two-hundred-signature petition to the New York school's superintendent contained only twenty valid names.[51]

MFY also encouraged the Negro Action Group (NAG), a band of black militants affiliated with Jesse Gray, a Harlem activist who specialized in rent strikes against white landlords charged with neglecting maintenance and exacting excessive rents. In early 1964 Mobilization brought together NAG, the East Side Tenants' Council, CORE, and other groups to form the Lower East Side Rent Strike Organization. MFY did not provide direct rent-strike leadership, but it did contribute leaflets, office supplies, staff, and small amounts of cash.

MFY would soon stir up a storm, but fortunately in 1963 the ruckus was still confined to New York, and the national media did not take note. There was still room for bold experiments by the technocrats in Washington.

The juvenile delinquency program would be one source of the War on Poverty. It would contribute ideas and personnel directly to the antipoverty planners and shape their early outlines and approaches. But the juvenile delinquency community, in turn, was being reshaped by a new intellectual and cultural climate. By 1960–61 the ice cap of McCarthyism that had chilled social innovation and speculation for a decade was retreating, and novel ideas and initiatives were beginning to poke through the thawing soil all over the nation.

The change within the juvenile delinquency community was marked by an uncommon literary event. In 1852 the best-seller, *Uncle Tom's Cabin,* confirmed and legitimized antislavery feelings among literate Northerners and fanned the flames of North-South angers. Eleven decades later Michael Harrington's *The Other America* touched the conscience of educated Americans and awakened a sense that something must be done for the poor.

A Midwesterner educated at Jesuit Holy Cross, Harrington had come to New York in the early 1950s to join Dorothy Day's Catholic Worker Movement and soon became an editor of its publication. He also joined the Young People's Socialist League, the youth section of the Socialist Party of America, and the League for Industrial Democracy, the parent of the later Students for a Democratic Society. Harrington was never a Stalinist. His brand of "Third Camp" socialism was always more humane and democratic than the rigid line of those who looked to Moscow. Yet he never ceased to believe that the state must intrude to reduce the inequalities of wealth and power inherent in the existing capitalist system.

Harrington became interested in the issue of poverty amid plenty just as the Eisenhower era was winding down and a sense of new political possibility was stirring. The project that culminated in *The Other America* began as a long article for *Commentary* magazine, then entering a brief left-liberal phase. The book itself appeared in 1962 as part of a miniwave of poverty books. That same year Gabriel Kolko, another democratic socialist, and Robert Lampman, a University of Wisconsin economist who had made wealth and income distribution his special field, also published books on the continued existence of poverty and gross economic inequality in America.

Harrington's foil was Galbraith's *Affluent Society* of 1958, a work that gave high marks to postwar American capitalism at least as an engine of private wealth creation. "Case" poverty—of the sick, the aged, and the physically handicapped—and "insular" poverty —of depressed areas and special industries—still existed, Galbraith admitted. But the great unfinished task of the American economy was not how to wipe up the remaining spills of private want but to make the starved and squalid public sector equal to the private opulence of the booming postwar economy.

Harrington believed that Galbraith had been too dismissive of private poverty in America. There were as many as 50 million poor people in America, more than a third of the total population. They were migrant laborers, transplanted hillbillies, alcoholics, sharecroppers, unemployed Appalachian miners, the chronically sick, and the old. Significantly, they were largely white. "Poor" had not yet become a euphemism for "Negro." But the crude message that entered the consciousness of literate Americans by way of *The Other America* was that poverty was a major unsolved problem of their avowedly rich society.

Harrington's impact was given resonance by Dwight Macdonald, a brilliant, peripatetic radical who had flirted with every sort of non-Stalinist socialism to be found. By the early sixties Macdonald had become a popular commentator on mass culture and a writer for *The New Yorker,* the journalistic boutique that purveyed the wares of dissident intellectuals to the liberal professional classes. In January 1963 Macdonald's article reviewing *The Other America,* as well as the book by Kolko and one by the University of Michigan Survey Research Center, appeared in the magazine under the title "Our Invisible Poor." It helped catapult Harrington's book to the best-seller list and scatter his ideas widely around the country.

The Other America was like a flash of light to policy makers grappling in the dark with related issues. As Henry Cohen, a staffer in the Office of Juvenile Delinquency, later noted, he and his colleagues began to say: "Gee, but that's really what we're after. . . . This gives us a broader framework." In a sense, Cohen noted, "We'd gotten caught in a youth framework because that had been the battle of the fifties."[52] Jack Conway, a union leader working for the Kennedy administration, recalled that after reading the Harrington book "things kind of came together and had a different meaning. . . ." It was "a real blockbuster."[53]

Opportunity theory was implicitly an attack on poverty. Poverty, after all, rather than personal maladjustment, was the force behind delinquency. But the advent of the Harrington-Macdonald pieces made the implicit overt. In 1962 David Hackett and his associates had begun to refer surreptitiously to the OJD programs as poverty programs rather than delinquency programs. By early 1963 Hackett's guerrillas and a group of earnest and idealistic midlevel bureaucrats from several federal agencies were meeting in the Justice Department and talking of how to attack national poverty. Meanwhile Mobilization for Youth had gone public with the new approach. In a statement of goals adopted in June 1963 the directors of MFY declared that its first priority was to "reduce poverty" so that "new opportunities are created."[54]

More important than Harrington's impact on mid-level bureaucrats was his effect on JFK himself. Myth has it that John Kennedy, a literate man, read Harrington and was impressed. In fact, it was more likely that he read the Macdonald review; it was shorter and a president's time is limited. According to Kermit Gordon, his budget director, JFK had also been reading articles on the poverty of eastern Kentucky by Homer Bigart of *The New York Times*. But whatever the source, the poverty issue caught his attention. So steeped in affluence himself that he scarcely knew that cash existed and seldom carried any with him when he left home, he was touched by *The Other America* and in December 1962, in a year-end review of economic conditions, he exclaimed to Walter Heller: "Now look! I want to go beyond the things that have already been accomplished. Give me the facts and figures on the things we still have to do. For example, what about the poverty problem in the United States?"[55]

Heller seized the ball and ran. In fact Gardner Ackley, Heller's successor as head of the Council of Economic Advisers, believed that "the whole idea of the War on Poverty really did originate with Walter Heller." Heller, in his view, was more eager and committed than the president himself.[56] During the summer of 1963 he brought Robert Lampman to Washington to vet the poverty issue in the United States. Lampman was soon running off memos faulting New Frontier programs for limited results in reducing the nation's poor. A staff paper prepared under Lampman's direction in early spring 1963 confirmed that poverty was an intractable problem. Setting $3,000 a year per family as the bottom line for the nonpoor, it concluded that since 1956 overall economic growth had reduced poverty only two percentage points, from a high of 23 percent.

This figure of $3,000 lacked a good rationale. It was superseded in 1965 by the calculations of Mollie Orshansky of the Social Security Administration. Orshansky adopted a Department of Agriculture estimate of seventy-five cents a day for food per person and then multiplied it by three to include all the other assumed essential expenditures for a nonfarm family. In any case, the Orshansky figure of $3,335 for a family of four—suitably adjusted for price changes—became the official "poverty line" in 1965 and remained so for many years.

Heller sent this memo to the president. Soon after he asked Lampman and other CEA staffers to prepare "a practical Kennedy anti-poverty program." This would be incorporated into the president's 1964 economic report.[57]

During the summer of 1963 Lampman, William Capron of the Council of Economic Advisers, HEW's Wilbur Cohen, and various Labor Department officials met several Saturday mornings for brainstorming sessions to hammer out a set of proposals. The bureaucrats toyed with many approaches, including a redistributionist "negative income tax," but nothing very useful or convincing came out of these sessions. In effect, no one really knew what to do about poverty besides more of the same: providing "relief" and services under the Aid to Families with Dependent Children (AFDC) provision of the 1935 Social Security Act.

The lack of focus was not surprising. The federal functionaries were still far ahead of the voters. The poverty problem as yet disturbed only some intellectuals and a top layer of the public; most Americans were still unaware that it existed. In the early summer of 1963 Heller tried out the poverty issue in a speech to the Communications Workers of America. The country needed a tax cut, he declared, but it also needed "to open more exits from poverty."[58] When CWA president Joseph Beirne thanked Heller at the end, he endorsed the tax cut but ignored the antipoverty suggestion. Later in the summer, on a lecture circuit, Heller talked up the poverty issue with reporters but they were uninterested. The topic was simply not exciting to newspaper readers.

Nevertheless, in September Ted Sorensen, White House counsel and JFK's alter ego, ordered the CEA and the Budget Bureau to form a special poverty task force and come up with specific proposals. The results were once again unimpressive. Budget Bureau staffer William Cannon later called them "awful."[59] But

Kennedy, unaware of the bureaucrats' disarray, remained hopeful. By October, Heller remembered, "President Kennedy had given us a green light to pull together a set of proposals for a 1964 attack on poverty."[60]

In some desperation Heller sent out a memorandum on November 5 to various executive departments and agencies asking for suggestions for "widening participation in prosperity." He wanted, he said, "imaginative new programs."[61] Attached to the memo were fifty-eight proposals he had received from the task force. During the remainder of the month, as the department inputs straggled in, the president made frequent references to his antipoverty initiatives for 1964, and on the nineteenth he again told Heller to go full speed ahead on the poverty proposals.

On November 20 the president flew to Texas with the first lady to help Vice President Johnson cool the passions among squabbling state Democrats and improve his chances for reelection in 1964. On November 22, while the Budget Bureau and the White House staff were reviewing the executive department poverty proposals, news arrived that he had been assassinated.

As a formal entity the New Frontier ended on that frightful day in Dallas. It will be remembered as a failed effort by a president who seemed more interested in world affairs and private affairs than in broad domestic issues. But JFK's initiatives began the spring thaw, after eight frozen years, that his successor would bring to full summer bloom.

TWO

Let Us Continue

A CROWD of three thousand waited silently as the presidential plane, just arrived from Dallas, braked to a stop on the Andrews Air Force Base runway. They had come to glimpse the remains of the martyred president and pay their respects to Jackie, his beautiful widow. A few perhaps hoped to see the new president and size him up.

Not many who stood vigil on that bone-chilling late-November evening knew a great deal about Lyndon Johnson, and those who did were probably not reassured. A world-champion manipulator and maneuverer, he had been able to make people do his bidding from childhood on. The hunger for influence, power, and domination often seemed his primal emotion. His political tactics, critics said, could not bear close moral scrutiny. During the 1948 race for the Democratic nomination that sent him to the U.S. Senate, he had defeated his challenger by eighty-seven votes out of 980,000. His opponents, masters of hanky-panky themselves, claimed that the Johnson forces had practiced fraud shocking by even lax Texas standards to defeat their man, Coke Stevenson. For years thereafter Johnson found himself dogged by the ironic tag "Landslide Lyndon."

Johnson was not a standard liberal. He had no argument with private wealth. He had won the patronage and support of the powerful Texas business classes by securing for them bountiful favors and contracts. As senator, he never failed to defend the oil depletion allowance that allowed the petroleum companies to reduce their federal taxes by billions. And he had made himself rich by using his political influence to win lucrative radio and TV franchises in Austin.

But he was also not a conventional conservative. LBJ, in fact, was a composite of apparently incompatible political parts. The self-serving, power-hungry wheeler-dealer was not the only Lyndon Johnson. If he heeded the conservative rich, he had also been a loyal follower of Franklin Roosevelt when frightened Americans turned to the New Deal for salvation. He had worked for the Roosevelt administration as head of the Texas branch of the National Youth Administration and never forgot that federal programs had enabled young men and women to stay in school and had brought to the Hill Country of his parents the blessings of modern appliances through the rural electrification program.

He hobnobbed with liberals as well as tycoons. In his years in the House of Representatives, during the 1930s and 1940s, he was a regular partygoer at the Georgetown home of Arthur "Tex" Goldschmidt and Elizabeth Wickenden Goldschmidt, two liberal Texans. Other guests included Abe Fortas, a brilliant young Yale Law School graduate from Memphis who worked with Goldschmidt in the Interior Department; Clifford and Elizabeth Durr, liberal Southerners related to Supreme Court Justice Hugo Black; and William O. Douglas, a Securities and Exchange commissioner whom Roosevelt would appoint to the Court in 1939. Johnson did not always agree with the liberals he met on the Georgetown party circuit, but he never lost touch with them or his New Deal roots. He would later say that "FDR was like a daddy to me."[1]

Mid-American populism also contributed to his political makeup. His father, Sam Ealy Johnson, fought for the common folk in his two terms in the Texas legislature and Lyndon, as he often said, had learned his politics at his father's knee.

Ideology aside, Johnson was a soft-hearted man. He truly felt the pain of the deprived and despised. Larry O'Brien recalled that "It was his nature to become almost emotionally involved in this subject [poverty]." His war on poverty "underscored his often-mentioned concern about the poor, his often-repeated stories about his childhood and his youth."[2] Harry McPherson, the literate and outspoken Texas lawyer who Johnson brought to the White House as special counsel, admitted soon after LBJ left office that Johnson was "as self-centered a man as ever was." But he also had a rare capacity "to empathize." When "an old woman falls down in the street his shins ache a little."[3] He also cherished the role of benefactor. Since his days as a young teacher in Cotulla, Texas, when he fought to get hot lunches and sports equipment for his poor Mexican-American students, he had played Big Daddy to others in need. Paternalism suited the style of a Southwestern leader and he deployed it with verve.

And there was a final element in the mix. As president, he was now on the biggest stage of history. His constituents included the 180 million of the fifty states, not the 9.5 million of Texas. There could be no higher office, no more exalted official honor. The only goal remaining was the judgment of history. When a *Newsweek* editor in mid-1965 asked LBJ why as president he seemed more liberal than as senator, he replied: "I'm more aware of the problems of more people than before. . . . I'm a little less selfish, a little more selfless. . . . In this place, you can't go any higher and the only thing you want to do is what's right."[4]

But LBJ never shared the class resentments and anti-business biases of the populists and New Dealers. To defend "the people" did not mean seeking enemies and villains. In private Johnson was capable of condemning the selfishness of the rich but he seldom rabble-roused. He deplored divisiveness and craved "consensus," the cliché tag often applied to his governing style. This was more than a political tack; it suited his personality. LBJ wanted to be loved. He had a mean streak that he could not always restrain and he drove his subordinates cruelly, often without regard for their personal lives. But at the same time he was capable of startling acts of generosity toward people who worked for him. In the political realm he was loathe to make enemies if they could be avoided. Ideally, opponents should be converted, not defeated.

In the hours and days following November 22, Johnson made all the right moves to reassure the public and inspire confidence in his leadership. He spoke to the press, to labor leaders, to business magnates, and to the politicians, asking them all for their guidance and help. He reassured members of the diplomatic corps and the heads of state who attended the funeral for JFK that American policies would be firm and steady. He addressed the men and women of the military services around the world and told them that America continued to seek an "honorable peace" and "a world free of the causes of hatred." He displayed his compassionate side in touching letters about their father to Caroline and John-John, Kennedy's small children. *Newsweek* said his first week in office had "inspired admiration in nearly everyone who saw him or heard him. . . ."[5]

But the president's tact stopped at the borders of politics. The new administration exploited to the hilt the public's guilts and griefs to push through the stalled New Frontier program. At times, admitted Larry O'Brien, it seemed "crass,"[6] but in fact no president could have resisted the stratagem.

"Let us continue" were among Lyndon Johnson's first words to the Eighty-eighth Congress. Speaking to a special session of both houses on November 27, less than a week after the assassination, he endorsed the pending civil rights legislation, the stalled tax bill, the delayed federal education bill, and a measure to encourage youth employment. He also intended, he announced, to promote the Kennedy-conceived campaign against poverty.

Without question LBJ embraced the New Frontier out of conviction. But there was also the politically expedient dimension. Nineteen sixty-four was a presidential election year and Johnson wanted a record of achievement to run on. To look good, he must get as much of the deadlocked Kennedy agenda through as possible. But even if he failed, he would gain—by blaming the Republicans for obstructionism.

In fact the logjam of the Eighty-eighth Congress did not abruptly break up. The die-hards, in and out of Congress, had no intention of reopening the closed books of the New Frontier. Not that LBJ did not try. In his January "State of the Union" address he announced that a Medicare bill would be one of his first priorities. In early February he sent a special health message to Capitol Hill. "We are going to fight for medical care for the aged as long as we have breath in our bodies," he announced.[7] His proposal tripped the alarm bells at the AMA and set in motion Operation Home Town, an aggressive counterattack built around telephone calls, radio and TV programs, and propaganda "kits" with more than fifty proposals on how to generate letters, place ads, and contact influential people to stymie the administration. Doctors were advised to use these themselves and hand them out to patients who sympathized with the AMA's cause.[8]

Prodded by the president, the Senate Finance Committee held hearings on Medicare in August 1964 but refused to report out its own bill. Johnson, however, did get the Senate to approve a Medicare amendment to a House bill increasing Social Security payments. This was the first time in the long battle over federal health insurance that at least one house of Congress had approved the principle, and optimists took heart. But Medicare got no further in the Eighty-eighth Congress. The House-Senate conference committee refused to accept the Social Security bill as amended by the Senate, and when the administration's supporters declined to yield, the conference committee deadlocked. The entire bill, including the Medicare clause, died when the Eighty-eighth Congress adjourned.

Yet Congress was not totally unyielding. On July 6 it passed the Urban Mass Transit Act appropriating $375 million to aid commuter facilities. In early August, as part of a big farm bill, it approved a food stamp plan to provide subsidized food to the poor. Food stamps had been part of a JFK pilot program in forty communities in twenty-two states to test the costs and benefits of subsidized food for welfare families. Now it was to be expanded to the entire nation and extended for two years, though it remained a modest, local option program. In September Congress gave Johnson the Wilderness Preservation Act, closing 9 million acres of federal land to development to keep it pristine for all time. The administration also put into the hopper a flock of key social policy bills to await passage when the new Congress assembled in January.

It was Johnson who finally signed the tax cut bill that Kennedy had proposed. Though a fiscal conservative who ran from deficits, he retained Walter Heller as head of the Council of Economic Advisers and embraced JFK's tax cut package. The bill LBJ approved on February 26, 1964, cut taxes by $10 billion spread over 1964 and 1965.

In many ways the tax cut proved to be the most important legislation of Johnson's first year. The results were spectacular, far more potent than those following the Reagan tax cuts of two decades later. By 1965 unemployment was down to the 4 percent the experts considered purely "frictional," that is, the result of normal job turnover. The United States had reached "full employment." The GNP soared. Between 1961 and 1965 it advanced at a rate of almost 6 percent a year. And all this without serious inflation: Price increases during this period averaged only a little more than 1.5 percent a year! As early as May 1965 *U.S. News & World Report,* no friend at first to the new economic policies, noted: "Tax relief, in massive doses, appears to have achieved something like magic."[9]

The Great Society would swim on a sea of prosperity. Federal revenues leaped from $94 billion in 1961 to $150 billion in 1967. What to do with all the extra money would become a puzzle to the Treasury and Congress. A further tax cut, of course, was a possible way out of the happy dilemma, but it was difficult not to be tempted at this point by a little "progressive" Keynesian response. In any case, innovative social programs need not require sacrifice. Helping the poor, renewing the cities, improving education and health care, cleaning up the environment, making America more beautiful, and encouraging the arts and scholarship could all be accomplished painlessly. No one would have to give up anything he already enjoyed. Never could a generous public impulse be so cheaply indulged. Johnson's programs would be blessed by a sustained economic boom almost unique in our history. In 1968 Walter Heller would summarize it in his professorial way: "An expanding economy enables the nation to declare social dividends out of growing output and income instead of having to wrench resources away from one group to give to another, and thus enables presidents to press ahead with a minimum of social tension and political dissent."[10]

But without question, the centerpiece of the second, post-assassination congressional session was the War on Poverty.

The vice president had not shared in the White House discussions of poverty in 1963. But Johnson learned about them the day following the tragic events in Dallas, when a regiment of aides and dignitaries descended on his office in the Executive Office Building to touch base with the new president and discuss what now had to be done. One of the visitors was Walter Heller, who had come to brief Johnson on his predecessor's economic plans. Heller told LBJ about Kennedy's antipoverty initiatives and asked if he wanted the work to go forward. "I'm interested," Johnson told Heller. "I'm sympathetic. Go ahead. Give it the highest priority.

Push ahead full tilt."[11] In that brief exhortation, Lyndon Johnson had signed aboard the War on Poverty.

For a birthright populist like Johnson, the issue of poverty amid plenty, raised by Kennedy in the last weeks of his Thousand Days, seemed God-sent. Here both dimensions of LBJ came into play. His liberal, compassionate, paternalistic side made the campaign against poverty naturally congenial. Big Daddy would make all Americans happy. This easily merged with his yearning to be included in the liberal pantheon alongside his hero FDR. Lyndon Johnson would be a great president in the only way he knew: by wielding the power of the federal government to change the lives of Americans for the better. This was before the Vietnam War, before Watergate, before the soaring crime rate in the cities undermined the public's confidence in national institutions. Everything still seemed possible for government; problems would inevitably yield to intelligent central planning. In 1961 Kennedy had promised to land "a man on the moon and return him safely to earth" during the decade. By 1964 the space program, enthusiastically supported by LBJ, was well on its way to realization. If the United States could put a human being on the moon, surely it could solve more mundane problems by an equal outlay of brains and energy? The Great Society and the moon race displayed the same overweening confidence in human ability to shape reality.

Johnson himself assigned the War on Poverty to the Old Agenda of the liberals from 1933 on. And it *was*, literally speaking. His first important legislative initiative in the jittery days following the tragedy in Dallas, it was borrowed from his martyred predecessor. But Johnson's War on Poverty reflected the new spirit and met the standards of the Ann Arbor manifesto better than its patron knew.

Unfortunately, at Kennedy's death the antipoverty campaign was an idea without a plan. All the jawboning of the fall had produced little in the way of concrete proposals. Then, on December 1, Hackett submitted a thirty-nine-page memo to Heller that finally started the wheels rolling.

Hackett's proposal was not a bold initiative; it called for little more than a pilot program. Using the Kennedy approach, the White House would create a clutch of task forces focused on various target groups: slum dwellers, marginal farmers, Indians, Mexican-Americans, and others. Their deliberations and studies would lead to specific "federally-supported . . . demonstration projects," which in turn, after soliciting local input, would try out various antipoverty approaches.[12] These pocket social experiments could be paid for by shifting funds from existing programs; in fact, the plan suggested, they might include the ongoing Ford-OJD projects. Later, after several years of trial and error, with solid knowledge in hand of the causes and cures for persistent low incomes, the government would be ready to launch a large, well-funded, broad-fronted drive against poverty and social despair. This scheme sounded more like an academic experiment than a major federal program.

On December 20 Heller submitted a Council of Economic Advisers proposal to Ted Sorensen that retained the experimental emphasis but expanded on Hackett's original proposal. It called on the president to submit to Congress a plan for a ten-year campaign against poverty with a major emphasis on youth, "to *prevent* entry into poverty." Money should not be scattered, but rather focused on "a number of major demonstration projects," each of which would emphasize a "significant poverty situation." Heller suggested that the administration concentrate on no more than ten demonstration areas—one rural and one urban area in each of the five major regions of the United States. After consulting with Ylvisaker and several Ford Foundation Gray Areas officials, Heller made community action a key component of his program. But Heller's community action agencies would not be totally autonomous. "[U]nder the aegis of local governments," they would provide "well-organized local initiative, action, and self-help" of federally approved and funded plans. At the top would be the Council on Poverty, consisting of the appropriate cabinet and agency heads and chaired by a presidential appointee.[13]

Every year the Johnsons left Washington to spend the Christmas-New Year's holidays at their ranch in the Texas Hill Country. Nineteen sixty-three, despite the calamity in Dallas, was no different. But LBJ never spent his days on the banks of the Pedernales solely in relaxation. A work addict, he carried the business of governing with him wherever he went. During those last days of December a constant stream of bureaucrats and politicians flew to the Ranch to brainstorm with the president. When discussions flagged visitors could expect to be dragooned into touring the grounds at breakneck speed with LBJ at the wheel of his white Lincoln.

Heller arrived with Budget Director Kermit Gordon on the twenty-seventh to sell the president on the new CEA poverty proposal. Initially Johnson balked. He wanted "to continue" his predecessor's policies but he also wanted to make his own mark before the election, less than a year away. This puny plan was not his kind of program; it had no drama, no punch. And it would not get through Congress easily. He wanted a program that would be "big and bold and hit the nation with real impact."[14] He was not interested in a demonstration program. Why bother with the preliminaries? Start with the main event itself. And why only a handful of projects? Put a poverty program in every community that wanted one. On the twenty-eighth the president told the reporters who had gathered at the Ranch that he intended to mount a fight against poverty in the coming congressional session. But his exuberant confabs with Heller and Gordon notwithstanding, he was careful to reassure fiscal conservatives. The poverty program would not be a budget-buster; he would run a tight fiscal ship. It was an early version of the Johnson hype combined with the Johnson parsimony. If he could, he would please liberals and conservatives simultaneously.

At this point LBJ saw no problem with the community action feature of the proposal. But what in fact was community action? Hackett and the JD people equated it with community competence. The Council of Economic Advisers considered it primarily a convenient way to deliver services. Budget Director Gordon, a former member of the CEA, believed community action agencies would "act in effect as the coordinating body for all those categorical federal programs."[15] The president, apparently, had no idea what "community action" meant. But it reminded him of his time at Cotulla when he had recruited the parents of his Mexican-American students to help with their children's education. It had worked then; students had learned better when their parents became involved. To Johnson, this was pretty much the same. Johnson would later claim that he, as well as Gordon and Heller, recognized the political dangers of community action, but in fact he—and they—almost certainly did not. Gordon himself later noted that he and the other authors of the War on Poverty thought that the community action agencies would be "domi-

nated by local government."[16] In truth, no one, except a few
activists on Mobilization for Youth in darkest New York, who observed the school protests and the rent strikes, actually understood how divisive and disruptive community action could be.

Back from the Ranch soon after the new year, Heller and
Gordon proposed additional refinements. The new plan abandoned the pilot project aspect, gave much greater emphasis to
community action local initiative, and proposed "a single outstanding public figure . . . to exercise the basic control of the
Community Action Program." Reflecting the importance of education in the poverty program, the two economists also recommended including in any poverty bill $200 million for special
school improvement projects.

Johnson launched the antipoverty program with a flourish in
his first "State of the Union" address on January 8. His speech to
the joint session of late November had only hinted at things to
come, and the public awaited the "State of the Union" expec-
tantly, anxious to know what the new president had in store for
the nation. LBJ spoke softly, but his language was "brisk." Over
120 people had contributed to the final product; the speech had
gone through more than ten drafts. Johnson focused on domestic
programs and within these made the assault on poverty the core.
"This administration today, here and now, declares unconditional war on poverty in America," he proclaimed. The struggle
would not be easy, but "we shall not rest until that war is won." It
would be waged "in city slums and small towns, in sharecropper
shacks and in migrant labor camps, on Indian reservations,
among whites as well as Negroes, among the young as well as the
aged, in the boom towns and in the depressed areas." Its weapons
would be "better schools, better health, and better homes, and
better training, and better job opportunities to help more Americans, especially young Americans, escape from squalor and misery
and unemployment. . . ."[17]

Hackett and the CEA people always deplored the president's
military metaphor; they considered it hype and feared it created
expectations of unconditional victory that were sure to be disappointed. But it was now LBJ's program and they had to go along.
Toward the end of the month the president assigned close to a
billion dollars for the poverty program, including about $500 mil-
lion for the community action groups, in his annual budget mes-

sage. A week later he appointed Sargent Shriver, the Kennedy
kinsman and admired head of the popular and successful Peace
Corps, to take over poverty program planning.

Meanwhile the annual economic report of the CEA set the
stage for the legislative drive. Twenty percent of all American
families were poor, it stated, with the proportion of poor among
the old, black Americans, rural dwellers, Southerners, and families headed by women well above the national average. The nation
needed a "strategy against poverty" that employed tax cuts, area
redevelopment, adult education, health insurance for the aged,
and civil rights legislation. All of these, however, should be
molded into a "coordinated and comprehensive attack" through
the new community action programs.[18]

But for all the airy suggestions and fine phrases, the administration did not yet have a bill to send to Congress, and Shriver
scurried to convert the CEA proposal into a viable piece of legislation. To help him, the Peace Corps director borrowed personnel
from executive agencies and recruited private volunteers. With
$30,000 wangled from the president's contingency fund, he and
his reconstituted task force set up shop, first in three rooms tem-
porarily vacated by the peripatetic Peace Corps staff and then in
the magnificent old Court of Claims building until blasting from
an adjacent construction site brought down chunks of the ceiling.
At this point the task force was split up, with one part retreating to
a former District of Columbia hospital, and the other to an abandoned Washington hotel.

The men who assembled the administration's legislative proposal were primarily midlevel bureaucrats, mostly young, idealistic, and full of confidence. They called themselves the Poor Corps
and they worked with passion. As one participant put it, it was a
time "of chaos and exhaustion when energies were fueled by
excitement and exhilaration—itself . . . the product of . . .
'the beautiful hysteria of it all'. . . ."[19]

Heading the group as Shriver's deputy was Adam Yarmolinsky,
a young lawyer with Ivy League training whose mother was the
distinguished poet Babette Deutsch. Yarmolinsky had worked for
the Ford Foundation's Fund for the Republic and there got to
know Ylvisaker. Most recently he had been one of Defense Secretary Robert McNamara's "whiz kids" at the Pentagon, where
he had absorbed his boss's "system's analysis" administration

method that emphasized policy choices based on the ratio of costs to benefits. The costs-benefits approach came originally from the RAND Corporation, a Pentagon-funded think tank that analyzed new military technology, defense issues, and administrative policies, primarily for Cold War purposes. Like other cutting-edge groups of the early sixties the system's analysts made a fetish of the amazing new computers and the information manipulation they could achieve. It reinforced their exuberant confidence in social engineering and their certitude that any problem could be solved. At times, critics would say, their love of technique would eclipse content. Other important members of the task force were Hyman Bookbinder, a Department of Commerce consultant; Harold Horowitz, a lawyer at Health, Education, and Welfare; James Sundquist, deputy undersecretary of agriculture; and Daniel Patrick Moynihan, assistant secretary of labor. Moynihan's distinguished career in politics would remain intertwined with the poverty issue for the next thirty years.

Besides the "sub-cabinet" bureaucrats, Shriver consulted academics, businessmen, foundation executives, labor leaders, and an assortment of certified pundits. Yarmolinsky invited to Poor Corps sessions various outside social observers and poverty "experts," including Ylvisaker; Frank Mankiewicz of the Peace Corps; Michael Harrington, author of *The Other America;* and Paul Jacobs, a left-wing author and journalist who would soon be a celebrator of the emerging student left. Yarmolinsky would later belittle the contribution of the two radicals, Harrington and Jacobs. Their suggestions, he claimed, stressed the need for basic structural change in American society, but seemed completely unrealistic. "They'd tell us over and over again what the problems were, but we said 'what do you do about them? What kinds of legislation?' And it wasn't their bag."[20] Also present at the sessions were Hackett and Richard Boone, who were there to see that the community action concept remained a central feature of the program.

The task force system, as JFK had already demonstrated, was a inventive way to generate ideas. LBJ would create fifteen task forces in 1964 and another twenty-seven from 1965 to 1968 to brainstorm issues, concoct programs for the Great Society, and deal with various administration concerns. But each was enveloped in secrecy. Meetings were held in private and members were ordered to avoid the media. One task force member who dropped his guard a little told a nosy reporter: "I could get my head handed to me for even talking to you about this thing."[21] For all his virtues, LBJ was a devious man who had little respect for openness as such. And besides, he believed that he could get more honest opinions if staffs and experts could deliberate away from the glare of publicity. (Hillary Rodham Clinton's 1993 task force on health care reform resembled the Johnson approach in its cloak of silence during its deliberations. She was sharply criticized for excluding the public, and some observers believe that the approach helped defeat her husband's federal health insurance plan.) In the end, however, the covert nature of the task force deliberations only reinforced the elitist, top-down process by which the Great Society was created.

Down the road, community action would become the most embattled and clamorous feature of the War on Poverty. But it vexed Shriver and Yarmolinsky from the outset. For one thing, no one was clear what it meant. To people at the Budget Office, it was primarily a device to deliver services to poverty clients, something like a local welfare office. But to Hackett and Boone it meant grassroots democracy, and they pushed relentlessly to make it the keystone of the new program. At an important meeting of the task force in early February, Boone repeated the mantra "maximum feasible participation" so often that Yarmolinsky chided him: "You have used that phrase four or five times now." "Yes," Boone replied. "How many times do I have to use it before it becomes part of the program?" "Oh, a couple of times more," Yarmolinsky quipped.[22] In the end the Ford Foundation-Office of Juvenile Delinquency crew got the phrase "maximum feasible participation of residents" in the development, conduct, and administration of programs written into the poverty bill. But Shriver managed to demote the Community Action Program (CAP) section of S. 2642 to the second of the five "titles" that would make up the final bill.

Besides the few utopians and the CAP partisans, the poverty task force received suggestions from Willard Wirtz and the Department of Labor people. Why not establish a substantial public works program, they said, to create jobs, financed by a five-cent tax on cigarettes? But the proposal smacked too much of the make-work programs the New Deal had adopted to fight mass unemployment and imposed a painful sacrifice on the general public, still relatively guiltless about cigarettes. When Shriver proposed it at a Cabinet meeting the president gave him an "absolute blank stare." As far as LBJ was concerned, Yarmolinsky later reported, "We weren't even going to discuss that one."[23] Wirtz also suggested raising the legal age for leaving school from sixteen to eighteen to improve the education of poor youths. This seemed likely to swell the school dropout rate and was also rejected. Yarmolinsky would later describe the special concern of task force members with school dropouts, not because they were potential social tinder—that would be a later concern—but because "having clearly identified themselves as needing help, hopefully, they could be saved before they continued the poverty cycle through yet another generation."[24] In the end the task force turned to a job corps, modeled roughly on the respected New Deal Civilian Conservation Corps (CCC), to prepare young people at special training camps for work in the economy. This program became Title I of the bill as finally submitted.

Putting the Job Corps first in the bill was a calculated decision. The program emphasized youth, the group among the poor who seemed most salvageable and most promising. It chose, as Yarmolinsky later wrote, to prepare people for jobs rather than prepare jobs for people. Job creation would be taken care of by the tax cuts, which would lift economic growth rates. In addition the task forces crammed into their proposal work-training programs for local youths between sixteen and twenty-two (Neighborhood Youth Corps); a work-study program for poor kids attending college; $1,500 annual grants to low-income rural families; provisions, later dropped, of land reform; loans to the chronically unemployed to help them start businesses, and to businessmen to encourage them to employ the jobless; and payments to finance experimental schemes to get parents off welfare. Hidden away in each of the titles were vague authorizations that would evolve into full-blown programs themselves, several of which would eclipse the initial specified programs.

To administer, coordinate, and guide the ungainly whole would be the Office of Economic Opportunity (OEO), headed by a single director. That arrangement would highlight the program, give it the flexibility needed to be effective, and spare it the bureaucratic sclerosis of the traditional cabinet departments. Included in the section creating the "poverty czar's" office was a provision for Volunteers for America, a sort of domestic Peace Corps (later renamed Volunteers in Service to America, or VISTA) that substituted for a proposed national service corps proposal long stalled in Congress.

The bill that Shriver gave the president and that he in turn handed Congress was in fact a modest proposal clothed in bold rhetoric. It did not attempt a massive transfer of income from the prosperous to the indigent. The first-year cost of the poverty program would be less than a billion dollars—less than 1 percent of the federal budget and only one six-hundredth of the GNP. And much of its funding would represent transfers from other programs rather than new money. It did not seek to alter the basic structure of American society, to create different winners and losers. Instead, it sought to change the poor. It incorporated, implicitly, the "culture of poverty" concept that poor people were handicapped in the race of life by their values, habits, and knowledge. The proposed bill provided modest amounts of seed money to enable the poor to acquire the skills, motivation, and attitudes they needed to better cope with the existing economic rules of the game. The president and his aides expected future congresses to increase funding, but no one expected the program to strain the nation's financial resources.

Describing the Economic Opportunity Act in this way may appear to belittle the War on Poverty. But there really were no serious alternatives at the time. Neither income redistribution nor planned social reconstruction was politically feasible in the early 1960s—or at any other time in America, for that matter. To believe otherwise is to allow ideology to obscure reality. However generous—or guilty—the middle class felt, however self-confident and eager the technocrats to make changes, neither wanted an economic and social revolution nor believed one possible. That postwar America had done extraordinarily well was a given of the times. That we as a country could do still better was assumed, but a twinge of social guilt doth not a revolution make. We should not be dismissive of the early poverty warriors' efforts. The War on Poverty was a distinct break with the past. It stated, for the first time, that it was the policy of the United States to end the age-old scourge of want. The New Deal had also attacked poverty, but that was at a time when an enormous proportion of the American people had fallen victim to economic catastrophe, and their condition was viewed as temporary. The few New Deal programs, like the Resettlement Administration and the Farm Security Administration, designed specifically to deal with chronic poverty were brief, grossly underfinanced, and limited to rural regions. Another possible exception was the Tennessee Valley Authority, one goal of which was to ameliorate chronic poverty in a specific region of the mid-South. But TVA was at least as much a conservation and resource-development program as an antipoverty program.

Johnson's War on Poverty might not seem bold by the standards of social theorists and revolutionaries, but it broke new ground for liberal capitalism in the United States.

LBJ sent his War on Poverty bill to Congress with the usual covering recommendation on March 16. The president's message was a composite. It was, first, a liberal manifesto that pledged a "national war on poverty" with "total victory" as its objective. "[F]or the first time in our history," he declared, "we have the power to strike away the barriers to full participation in our society. Having the power, we have the duty." Johnson called the program a commitment by the president, by Congress, and by the nation "to pursue victory over the most ancient of mankind's enemies."

But the message also took into account conservative fears and mainstream prejudices. The government had no intention of creating dependency, LBJ said. Instead, it hoped "to give people a chance . . . to develop and use their capacities. . . ." The tax cuts just enacted would "create millions of new jobs—new exits from poverty," but for the tax cuts to work there would have to be new policies to "strike down all the barriers which keep many from using those exits."[25] As poverty warriors would often express it, Johnson wanted to give people a "hand-up," not a "hand-out." There was good reason for calling the bill the Economic *Opportunity* Act: It would give people the tools to help themselves. The bill, moreover, would benefit all. For much of his political life Johnson had cherished social peace. He yearned for consensus; he wanted to be loved by all Americans. Lest the middle class feel left out, he promised that the War on Poverty would be an investment in people that would provide dividends for everyone. "Giving new opportunity to those who have little will enrich the lives of all the rest." And the whole thing would be a bargain. The new program was within the nation's means. In January he had, by a feat of fiscal legerdemain, managed to submit to Congress a budget of only $98 billion, $2 billion under the arbitrary round sum that then signified extravagance. This amount included the cost of the administration's social programs. The War on Poverty, he noted, would cost only $970 million, 1 percent of the federal budget.[26]

In Congress the Economic Opportunity Act went before both chambers simultaneously on March 16. In the House the measure was steered to the Education and Labor Committee, presided over by Adam Clayton Powell, and dominated by Northern liberals. Powell was an ordained minister and spiritual leader of Harlem's flourishing Abyssinian Baptist Church, but he was also a flamboyant high-liver who flaunted his taste for worldly opulence and did not let his clerical robes hobble him as he rushed after beautiful women. As the House hearing opened he was in the news in a libel case. But Powell was also a "race" man who identified with Negro issues and fought for legislation in Congress that benefited the poor. He simply would not permit the opposition much leeway in delaying the bill.

The House hearings opened on March 17 as Sargent Shriver, with Moynihan at his side, reinforced the president's claim that the bill was not a budget buster. Its costs were all contained within the administration's recently announced barebones budget; it would not require a nickel more. The Economic Opportunity Act was sound, Shriver told the legislators; the country would get a dollar's value for a dollar spent. The programs represented "the best thinking in the nation on this subject." Businessmen, farmers, and scholars had all vetted it, he declared. It was Shriver's job, of course, to laud the administration's proposal. But he was not telling the whole truth. It had taken Shriver and his Poor Corps only six weeks to do their work and at times, as critics would claim, the War on Poverty would reveal the haste involved. The bill was a grab bag of untested programs. By contrast, the food stamp program, soon to make its way through Congress as an auxiliary to the Economic Opportunity Act, had been tried out in forty different cities before being submitted as a permanent program. But of course Johnson had rejected the pilot-program approach to poverty in favor of a broad-fronted legislative campaign. The antipoverty programs were as experimental as the skeptics feared; not even "the best thinking in the nation" really could tell if they would have a serious impact on poverty.[27]

The testimony of Walter Heller, head of the Council of Economic Advisers, was less political and more genuinely informative. Growth since the war had reduced but not ended poverty. Broken homes, ill-health, poor skills, illiteracy, and racial discrimination still consigned millions to destitution. Heller repeated the culture of poverty mantra: Not only were many born into poverty; it was passed along from generation to generation. The solution was the hand-up approach. The "essence of the President's attack on poverty," Heller noted, was "the creation of new economic opportunities, a chance for the poor . . . to earn their way out of poverty." Heller allowed the tip of a hand-out, redistributionist approach to peek through, however. It would cost $11 billion a year, about 2 percent of the GNP, to raise the incomes of all families above the $3,000 a year poverty line by just giving it to them in cash. But then he drew back. Such a gift "would be an unacceptable 'solution' because it would leave the roots of poverty untouched and deal only with its symptoms." And besides, he told Congress, the American people would not buy it. In the last analysis, "the key to an enduring victory over poverty" lay "in helping the poor help themselves: by creating jobs for them and by giving them access to those opportunities through the essential skills, knowledge, health, and environment which our society has all too often denied them."[28]

Another strong advocate for the bill was Attorney General Robert Kennedy, who came to the hearing room with the aura of family tragedy draped around him like some magical cloak. A scrappy in-fighter for his programs, Bobby used his moral power openly. "President Kennedy was totally committed to confronting and dealing with these problems," he assured the subcommittee, and then went on to describe the impressive work of JFK's President's Committee on Juvenile Delinquency and Youth Crime in getting summer jobs in Washington for unemployed youths. The War on Poverty bill would help even more, he said.[29]

Over the next five weeks a steady parade of well-wishers and ill-wishers, individuals and organizations, came through the doors of the hearing room to testify on the Economic Opportunity Act. Once proposed, EOA became a rallying point for several important constituencies. Walter Reuther, the liberal president of the

United Automobile Workers, then at its postwar zenith, told the subcommittee that "the labor movement has made it clear to the President that we enlist with him in the war against poverty for the duration of the war."[30] At its recent convention in Atlantic City the UAW had adopted a document entitled "Full Mobilization for a Total War on Poverty" that paralleled the president's plan. The convention had also called for an alliance between the civil rights movement and the drive to end poverty.

The civil rights movement itself was represented, though rather pro forma, by Whitney Young of the moderate National Urban League, who noted that the Negro would not be satisfied to "end up with a mouthful of civil rights and an empty stomach." Stronger support came from a covey of big-city Democratic mayors. Robert Wagner of New York, Richard Daley of Chicago, Jerome Cavanagh of Detroit, Raymond Tucker of St. Louis, and others took their seats before the microphones and proclaimed their enthusiasm for the bill. Bedeviled by the backbreaking costs of social services, the mayors saw the measure as a federal subsidy that would check the soaring costs of welfare. Wagner noted that back in 1927 New York City had spent $12,000 on public welfare and poverty. In 1964 poverty and its effects were costing the city more than a billion dollars a year, one third of its total budget. That could not go on; the cities had to be rescued. Daley, who later became an outspoken critic of OEO and Shriver, looked forward not only to federal cash but to federal coordination of diverse poverty programs. Like several other outside witnesses, Daley had obviously not read the bill. When Republican Peter Frelinghuysen of New Jersey asked whether the cities should accept the community action programs in Title II, Daley first acted surprised but then recovered to say that local officials should control the CA groups and programs. At the very beginning, then, without knowing it, Daley had stepped on a land mine, part of a major explosive field that would eventually cripple the War on Poverty.

Outside of Congress, meanwhile, public opinion began to rally to the administration's program. Early in the year the liberal public was only mildly interested in the issue of poverty. But the president's declaration of war touched a nerve of idealism and generosity that no one had anticipated. Labor leaders, liberal journalists, and organizations with liberal agendas all rushed to endorse the campaign. The general secretary of the National Council of Churches wired the president that it "heartily endorsed" his announced "concentrated attack on poverty."[31] Eighty-five-year-old Upton Sinclair, the old socialist muckraker and California gubernatorial candidate during the 1930s, chimed in with "My goodness—it's the beginning of what I've been begging for."[32] The AFL-CIO executive council, at their meeting in Bal Harbour, Florida, praised the president for "forthrightness and courage" in forcing "affluent Americans to face up to the fact that one-fifth of the families in the richest and most productive nation of the world still live in poverty."[33] With more than a little exaggeration, staff reporter Marjorie Hunter wrote in *The New York Times* "News of the Week in Review" section of March 29 that "the elite of many communities have turned from symphony and art center drives and horse show benefits to working up plans to combat poverty."[34] On April 1 she reported that there had been "an outpouring of American thought" about poverty from all classes. Tens of thousands of letters had descended on the White House "scribbled in pencil and neatly typed on business stationery," almost all supporting the president. "The picture is of an affluent but vaguely disturbed American who asks: 'What can I do to help?' "[35] Time would show how thin this support was, but clearly the War on Poverty at the outset touched a resonant chord of public sympathy.

Passage of the Economic Opportunity Act was probably never in serious doubt. Yet that did not restrain opponents. Its enemies focused on a number of predictable points. At the hearings, Republican Congressman David Martin of Nebraska raised the inevitable question of cost. During his testimony Bobby Kennedy had predicted that the War on Poverty might last twenty years. If he was right, noted Martin, the tab could reach $50 billion or even $100 billion before the job was done. That cost would bankrupt the country, making *every* American eligible for the poverty program. Robert Taft, Jr. of Ohio, son and namesake of the eminent conservative senator, professed to be puzzled at why, suddenly, at this point, it was necessary to mount a war on poverty. The nation had had a poverty problem from the very beginning and had been fighting it all along by various means. Could it be, he asked archly, that the War on Poverty was connected with the upcoming presidential and congressional elections? Meanwhile, conservative congressmen were also transmitting their doubts to their constituents. In a letter to voters back home, Texas congressman O. C. Fisher called the antipoverty bill "the biggest boondoggle in modern history." It was New Deal make-work, "leaf-raking" all over again, he wrote, and to top it all, it mandated integration. Norman Thomas, the "veteran socialist," Fisher claimed, "says the bill is the biggest step we've ever taken to convert this country into a socialist welfare state."[36]

Predictably, representatives of the National Association of Manufacturers and the U.S. Chamber of Commerce attacked EOA at the hearings. It would cost too much, do little good, and open the door to more big government. And besides, poverty was being reduced every day by the success of American business in creating wealth. The conservative Farm Bureau Federation also denounced the measure. And not even all Democrats were happy with the proposed new law. Roman Pucinski of Chicago's 11th District, who *had* read the bill, expressed reservations about Title II. Pucinski was well aware that, in his home city, the local community advisory board of the Office of Juvenile Delinquency project had recently clashed with the mayor over who was in charge. The battle between city hall and the board had been heated. Might this not happen again, he asked the attorney general? There seemed to be "a tendency on the part of the government in Washington to deal directly with organizations in local communities, bypassing the local governments," he noted. The private organizations that would receive funding under Title II had become "somewhat notorious as empire builders. . . ." Pucinski, as a good Democrat, did not intend to oppose the president, but he hoped that Title II would not repeat the problems of the juvenile delinquency programs.[37]

Democrat Edith Green of Portland raised another uncomfortable point. The "Gentlelady from Oregon," as some called her, was "gentle" only by the conventions of old-fashioned congressional courtesy. A smart, sharp-tongued former schoolteacher and an independent feminist, she asked Shriver pointedly why the proposed Job Corps was restricted to males. Women were a third of the labor force and should be decently represented among the beneficiaries of the new training program. Shriver demurred. The Job Corps, like the juvenile delinquency programs and the old Civilian Conservation Corps, had targeted men. Clearly still enchained to old-fashioned views that women were frail and vulnerable, he found it difficult to swallow the idea that they might be sent off to paramilitary camps for training. It would require rethinking the programs, he noted. Green persisted through the hearings and managed to get the administration to promise that Title I of the Economic Opportunity Act would be revised to include women.

Leading the Republican attack through the early congressional hearings was Peter Frelinghuysen. Bearer of a venerable name in American politics, the New Jersey congressman charged, within the hearing room and without, that the head of the new agency would be an all-powerful poverty czar who would make "door mats" of the established cabinet department secretaries. To counteract "Petulant Peter" the administration sent to the Hill a parade of cabinet officers—Luther Hodges of Commerce, Robert McNamara of Defense, Willard Wirtz of Labor, and Anthony Celebrezze of HEW—to deny that they felt in any way threatened by the powers to be conferred on the OEO administrator.

Meanwhile, both in the committee room and in the House corridors, the Republicans tried to play the race card: The bill was primarily intended for blacks, they whispered to Southern Democrats. The administration fought back. In his testimony Robert Kennedy had specifically denied that the bill was geared to blacks. But it was Phillip Landrum of Georgia who most effectively squelched the charge. Landrum, a Democratic loyalist despite his home region, had been chosen by the White House to lead the floor fight rather than the abrasive liberal Powell, to head off just such claims. Not only was Landrum a white Southerner, he was also a certified conservative best known for the 1959 union-regulating Landrum-Griffin Act. Organized labor hated him, and when O'Brien told George Meany, head of the AFL-CIO, of the White House strategy, Meany was flabbergasted and "disbelieving."[38] But Landrum came through. The program "is and should be color blind," he told the press in early April. The Republican charges were "not going to lessen my enthusiasm for this bill."[39]

One demurrer to the administration's poverty program made only the back pages of the press on March 22. This was the report of the "Ad Hoc Committee on the Triple Revolution," whose signers included: Gunnar Myrdal, the Swedish economist and author of the seminal work on American race relations, *American*

Dilemma; W. H. Ferry, of the Ford Foundation–funded Center for the Study of Democratic Institutions of the Fund for the Republic; the liberal economist Robert Heilbroner; the left literary critic Maxwell Geismar; Michael Harrington of *The Other America* fame; Todd Gitlin and Tom Hayden, founders of Students for a Democratic Society; Irving Howe of *Dissent* magazine; A. J. Muste of the radical pacifist Fellowship of Reconciliation; peace advocate H. Stuart Hughes, of Harvard's history faculty; Stewart Meacham of the American Friends Service Committee; and the brilliant Stanford University biologist Linus Pauling, a polymorphous defender of "progressive" causes. Devoted to the future of the American economy, this private group of old leftists, budding New Leftists, and assorted left-liberals would man the ramparts of sixties insurgency in the years ahead.

The committee called into question the administration's basic antipoverty strategy. The imminent cybernation revolution would require more heroic medicine than the Johnson administration was offering. Upgrading traditional skills would be of little help when electronic circuits had made many of them obsolete. There would simply not be enough jobs out there when machines had taken over. The visionaries embraced the "incomes policy" that Heller had touched on but rejected. The nation must make an "unqualified commitment" to provide "every family with an adequate income as a matter of right" without regard to jobs. That was "the only policy by which the quarter of the nation now dispossessed and soon-to-be dispossessed by lack of employment can be brought within the abundant society."[40]

The Triple Revolution circle was breaking new ground. Their voices and their proposals would be heard again. But this was 1964, not 1970, and the redistributive, guaranteed-income proposal that Richard Nixon would make a national issue made scarcely a ripple on Capitol Hill.

The House hearings concluded on April 28, and for the next two weeks the Democrats barricaded themselves in the committee room refining the bill. The tireless Shriver was present much of that time to help. Seeing himself as the indispensable salesman, the Peace Corps director arrived on the Hill at nine in the morning and many days did not leave for home until seven or eight at night. The Republicans were miffed at being excluded from the Democrats' discussion and held their own caucus. In mid-May the two groups finally got together and revised the administration's bill, especially the community action section. In this altered form the bill was reported out in late May to the entire House by a straight-party vote.

But now, Rules Committee czar Howard Smith, confirming his reputation as conservative ogre, held it up for the whole month of June, forcing administration leaders to mobilize the Senate to prod the lower house off dead center. The problem in part was time. The Fourth of July holiday was coming up, to be followed by a week's congressional recess for the Republican National Convention. If the Democrats wanted a poverty bill to show at their own Atlantic City convention in August, Senate consideration would have to hustle.

Hearings before the Senate Select Committee on Poverty did not begin until mid-June. Though drastically foreshortened, they were more illuminating than those of the House. Attorney General Kennedy made another appearance, once more to deny that the poverty program was primarily aimed at blacks. The War on Poverty was not to be confused with the civil rights movement. "After all, Negroes comprise only twenty percent of the poor in this country," he noted. The administration was equally concerned with people from Appalachia, Mexican-Americans, Puerto Ricans, Indians, Alaskans—all Americans without opportunity.[41]

This time the Republicans were better prepared. By 1964 the GOP was a deeply divided party. One wing represented seasoned old wealth and the home-owning middle class anchored predominantly in the Northeast, upper Midwest, and West Coast. Its leaders and supporters accepted much of the emerging social welfare state constructed since the New Deal, though they worried about costs and deplored excesses. Their stars were named Rockefeller, Lodge, Scranton, and Kuchel. The second wing, lodged predominantly in the South and Southwest and financed by the new wealth derived from oil, cattle, and real estate, considered most of the political and social changes since Herbert Hoover crimes against America's founding principles of individualism and localism. In the country as a whole the hard right was still in a minority, but in the spring of 1964, it was about to capture the heights and impose its candidate, Barry Goldwater, and his agenda on the national GOP.

The Republican senators mirrored this right-wing surge. The

diminutive John Tower of Texas noted sarcastically that each Job Corps enrollee would cost the government more than sending a student through an Ivy League college. A more potent voice was Barry Goldwater's. The handsome, silver-haired Republican senator from Arizona, the front-running challenger and defier of his party's moderate Eastern wing, pointed to a horrendous dropout rate for a California program similar to the Job Corps. The federal program was certain to have the same problems, he said. Senator Winston Prouty of Vermont proposed as an alternative to the administration's measure a tax incentive to businessmen to provide job training to the poor.[42]

The most methodical counterattack, however, came from Frelinghuysen, a moderate Republican, who had come over from the House as a witness to bolster the Senate opposition. The New Jersey congressman had been pushing his own antipoverty plan, one that emphasized state control, omitted a central federal poverty agency, incorporated some of the EOA programs into separate bills, and provided less money. He denounced the administration's bill as "a grab bag . . . , something for everyone." Its costs were certain to balloon, he claimed. The initial outlay of a billion dollars would only whet people's appetites. Americans were "creating a monster that we will regret," he warned. Frelinghuysen had no doubt that the bill was politically motivated: The Democrats were playing to the voters in this presidential election year. He acknowledged that it packed considerable political punch. If Congress wanted to establish a job corps, for example, he plaintively remarked, let it do so, "but do it on its own merits, not by wrapping it up in the magic words of poverty and daring everyone to vote against it because if they do it will rebound to hurt them at the polls in November."[43]

The Senate Select Committee concluded its hearings on June 25, and on July 7, just before recessing for the Republican presidential convention, reported the bill out, slightly altered, by a vote of 13 to 2. Goldwater and John Tower cast the two "nay" votes and issued a minority report calling the Economic Opportunity Act a "hodgepodge of programs treating only the results, not the causes of poverty."[44]

The Republican convention opened in San Francisco's Cow Palace on July 13, with its outcome never in doubt. Goldwater and his allies had won more delegates in the grueling months of caucuses and primaries than their Eastern opponents and completely dominated the proceedings. They heckled Nelson Rockefeller, New York's liberal governor, when he challenged the majority platform written by the new Republicans of the South and West, and jammed through their own. The official platform announced that poverty had fallen faster and further under Eisenhower than under Kennedy, claimed the administration's antipoverty proposals overlapped forty-two existing programs, and predicted that poverty would be ended by free enterprise, not big government. But in fact, few of the delegates at San Francisco cared deeply about the War on Poverty at this point, and the media paid little attention to the issue in their coverage of the convention. The reporters, interviewers, and anchors preferred to report the acrimonious struggle between the far-right-wingers and their enemies and had a field day with Goldwater's praise of extremism and blunt defiance of the GOP compromisers and "weak-willed" moderates in his acceptance speech.

Debate on the poverty bill began in the Senate when Congress reconvened the third week in July. Chairman of the Select Committee, Pat McNamara of Michigan, was in charge. Democratic whip Hubert Humphrey worked the floor rounding up votes. A principled Midwestern liberal, from Minnesota's farmer-labor tradition, Humphrey had won the respect of even the conservatives by his good nature and sincerity. Johnson appreciated Humphrey's loyalty and hard work and would soon reward him. At the sidelines, but very much in ultimate charge, was the president himself.

Johnson campaigned personally for EOA. As far back as April he had warned the Doubting Thomases of the U.S. Chamber of Commerce that a class of permanent poor was destabilizing for the economy and they, the rich and powerful men seated before him, had a major stake in transforming people into productive members of society. Now, during the Senate debate over the War on Poverty bill, the president cajoled, flattered, and arm-twisted the senators. He needed the measure to win in November, he told Democrats, and he would put a star next to the names of each senator who voted for the bill and who got others to vote for it. He did not specify what the star meant, but few members of the upper house could doubt that it represented a line of credit in the powerful Lyndon Johnson political bank.

The Republican counterattack was robust, with Senator Tower, pumped up by the triumph of his man in San Francisco, leading the charge. The combative conservative bantam from Texas targeted the Job Corps in particular. The program was just a renamed "old Civilian Conservation Corps of the 1930s," he asserted. If there had been need for conservation then, there was not now. But more than this, school administrators would undoubtedly use the proposed Job Corps as a dumping ground for students who were flunking out and were hard to handle. And to top it all, the bill implied that the public schools could not do the job and only "the Federal Government in its infinite wisdom, knowledge, ability, and omniscience can accomplish anything in the world."[45]

Senate conservatives knew they could not sink EOA. Poverty, like crime, was an unquestionable public evil and no one could afford risking the voters' wrath by refusing to oppose it. Unable to block the bill entirely, they attacked its more controversial and vulnerable provisions. Southern senators, still largely Democrats, did not intend to let the liberals in Washington use the poverty bill to erode further the social order in Dixie. The Job Corps seemed especially menacing since many of the enrollees would assuredly be black adolescents. Job Corps centers in the South would be integrated under the bill, and liberal administrators in Washington would use them to further school "race mixing." If he wanted his bill passed, Southern Democrats told Sargent Shriver, the governors would have to be given veto power over locating Job Corps centers in their states.

Shriver balked. Such a proviso would effectively eliminate such centers in the South. A huddle between Shriver and key senators in chambers off the Senate floor produced a compromise. The governors would have thirty days to accept or reject a Job Corps facility in their state. If they did not act, the project would go ahead. If they rejected the project, the head of the Office of Economic Opportunity, after review, could order it to proceed nevertheless. The amendment passed by voice vote.

And then there was the question of the governors and the community action programs. Should the highest elected state officials be excluded from the process of approving grants to the locally derived antipoverty programs? This issue was less about race than about local power versus federal power and about who got to feed at the patronage trough. It was a critical matter, for the very essence of the community action idea was to empower the neighborhoods. And besides, neither Shriver nor his lieutenants had much faith in the probity or efficiency of the men in the state houses; if they were in charge the red tape would become strangling and the money would be squandered. The Peace Corps director was adamant on this point: State officials must not be allowed to control the flow of money to the local communities under Title II.

But here the administration came close to defeat. As jittery poverty task force staffers in the Senate gallery bit their fingernails, an amendment by Senator Prouty to give the state governors power over the community action programs almost squeaked through. On several quick roll calls the administration forces managed to defeat the amendment by consistent 46 to 45 votes. Inexplicably, the Republican presidential nominee, Barry Goldwater, failed to cast his vote.

Despite the narrow escape the Economic Opportunity Act passed the Senate on July 23, by a vote of 62 to 33. Clearly, compassion toward the poor still ruled. Almost a third of the Republicans had voted "yea."

Back in the House final passage proved more difficult. Here, too, the administration had to make concessions. To break the logjam on the Rules Committee it agreed to replace the $1,500 rural "grant" in Title III by the less generous and less expensive "loan," a change demanded by the fiscal conservatives. On July 28, the committee, by an 8 to 7 vote, finally sent OEA to the full House for debate. Washington reporters predicted the results on the floor would be close.

Johnson once more pulled strings—in fact he grabbed at every loose end he could. The president buttonholed his business allies and, prodded by the relentless LBJ, prominent executives picked up the phones to call undecided congressmen. The Pennsylvania congressional delegation shook their heads in disbelief when Stuart Saunders, president of the Pennsylvania Railroad, phoned to ask their support for the poverty bill.

At this point in mid-summer it became clear that the choice of Phil Landrum to floor-manage the bill had been inspired. On July

18 New York's Harlem exploded in an orgy of window smashing, rock throwing, looting, and sniping following the shooting of a teenage black youth by a white New York City policeman. The mayhem soon spread to Brooklyn's even poorer Bedford-Stuyvesant neighborhood. A week later the Rochester ghetto detonated, forcing New York governor Rockefeller to call out the National Guard. Riots erupted in Jersey City and other towns as well soon after. It was the first of the "long, hot summers" that would shake the nation's confidence that racial problems could be solved within the limits of liberal consensus politics.

But for now compassion still outweighed resentment in the public mood and Landrum was able to use the riots for constructive purposes. If the Poor Corps functionaries were moved primarily by liberal compassion or professional pride, the Georgia congressman was frank in depicting the War on Poverty as a measure of social control. The poor, he observed, were piling up in urban slums, where they represented "social dynamite." The EOA bill accordingly was "the most conservative social program" he had "ever seen presented to anybody." It was a bulwark against "anarchy."[46] In a year or two Landrum's argument would be condemned as "rewarding" rioters, but for now it seemed wise and prudent. In August 1964 the congressman from Jasper, Georgia, scored points where they counted.

The administration proved aggressive in other ways too. Administration officials, indifferent to politesse and appearances, swarmed over the House to wheedle and twist arms. Liberal Republican Representative Charles Goodell of New York would complain that "unprecedented pressure" had been brought on him and other congressmen to pass the bill. The administration was agile as well as assertive. For some time two groups had been fighting over the primary focus of the Job Corps. One, composed of old-line conservationists, had been pushing Congress for a Youth Conservation Corps (YCC) on the model of the New Deal Civilian Conservation Corps (CCC) to preserve and improve the nation's natural endowment. In their minds, the Job Corps was the substitute for the YCC, and they believed it should emphasize work experience in the national forests and parks. The poverty task force staff, however, were more interested in making the enrollees literate and capable of handling office equipment and factory machinery. Kids, they said, were more important than trees. During the intense two days of debate and maneuvering in the House, the task force people yielded and agreed to assign at least 40 percent of all Job Corps enrollees to conservation work. The administration also yielded on an amendment to require a loyalty oath from Job Corps members.

One other concession proved necessary—the dumping of Yarmolinsky, the young, hotshot Defense Department official whom everybody assumed would be Shriver's first deputy when the Office of Economic Opportunity got rolling. Bright, articulate, arrogant, and, at times, socially awkward, Yarmolinsky had offended many Southerners by his aggressive implementation of armed forces racial integration while at the Pentagon under Robert McNamara. The Republican far right also accused him of left-wing associations and dubious loyalty; there was, besides, an undercurrent of anti-Semitism in the attack. As debate raged on the House floor, a group of North Carolina representatives gathered at Speaker McCormack's office and told Shriver and other administration leaders that Yarmolinsky would have to go or they would not vote for the bill. Trying to protect his protégé, Shriver denied that any OEO administrators had been designated, but the Tar Heels would not be put off. The president would have to promise that Yarmolinsky would be barred from any part in the new agency. At this point a quorum call interrupted the meeting and during the break Shriver and McCormack called Johnson. When the North Carolinians returned, Shriver told the rebels that "the President has no objection to my saying that if I were appointed I would not recommend Yarmolinsky."[47] With this statement, eight Southern votes swung to the "yea" side.

Observers expected a close call when the House voted on Friday, August 7. And so it proved to be. A vote for recommittal of the bill in the Committee of the Whole passed 170 to 135. This would have returned the bill to an earlier stage of the legislative process. It was now in serious trouble. Fortunately, voting as a body, the House reversed the count and on the final roll call the Economic Opportunity Act passed 228 to 190. The eight North Carolina votes had not been needed after all.

That evening the poverty task force staff and other friends of the bill, a hundred strong, celebrated their hard-fought victory with a bibulous party in Georgetown that did not adjourn until the early hours of Saturday. But some hearts were heavy for Yarmolinsky, who had been a needless sacrifice.

On August 20 LBJ signed the Economic Opportunity Act into law on the broad steps overlooking the White House Rose Garden. It was a perfect summer morning and the president was smiling broadly. Squinting into the bright sun he promised "a new day of opportunity" for the nation's poor. The "days of the dole" (Johnson certainly meant Aid to Families with Dependent Children [AFDC], the program that provided most of the "welfare" funds to poor families.) were "numbered." Those who participated in the War on Poverty programs, he announced, "would vindicate" the thinking of the measure's creators.[48] His guests, apart from the media, were all Democrats. The Republican leaders had been invited but none had chosen to come. Johnson used seventy-two pens in signing the legislation and, as had become the practice, handed them as souvenirs to those who had shepherded the bill through to passage. The first went to Adam Clayton Powell, who also accepted a second pen for the absent Phil Landrum. The third went to Senator McNamara. Sargent Shriver, Hubert Humphrey, and Mayor Wagner got keepsakes too. Even Yarmolinsky received a pen as a consolation prize. He accepted it with a rueful smile.

The Great Society was not the core issue of the 1964 presidential campaign. The public cared about the fate of "older people" and, where polled, expressed overall support for the War on Poverty. But the poverty issue, as it turned out, did not loom large during the contest.

The Democrats meeting at Atlantic City in late August, soon after the poverty bill passed, gave more attention than their opponents to social programs. They boasted of their stand on Medicare and pledged to expand the War on Poverty into a total war against human want. But again the media, seeing this as standard liberal rhetoric, seemed indifferent to the issue.

This is not to say that on some level the public was not conscious of party differences over social issues. The two candidates were personally as far apart on government activism, self-help, and fiscal restraint as any could be within the framework of American two-party politics. Goldwater had voted against the war on poverty and against Medicare in the recent Congress and had denounced virtually all the social welfare legislation since Herbert Hoover. Obviously a Goldwater victory would sink the Johnson programs.

But the campaign turned less on issues than on fears. The Arizona senator seemed to the great electoral center to be outside the mainstream of American party government. Convinced that the tragedy at Dallas was an expression of political excess, the public blanched at his acceptance speech statement that "extremism in the defense of liberty is no vice! And . . . moderation in the pursuit of justice is no virtue!" They also recoiled when he suggested privatizing the Tennessee Valley Authority and the social security system, and proposed allowing local military commanders to use nuclear weapons without prior approval from Washington if attacked. When he did mention the poverty issue during the campaign, he managed to offend rather than convert. On September 18, speaking before an audience in the depressed setting of Appalachia, he called the War on Poverty "phony," "cynical," and "irresponsible," a "hodge-podge of handouts" being used by Johnson "to further selfish political ambitions." And, he insisted, there was really very little poverty in the United States. The administration's poverty line, supposedly marking off the rich from the poor, represented "material well-being beyond the dreams of a vast majority of the people of the world."[49] William Miller, the scowling arch-conservative from upstate New York whom Goldwater had chosen as his running mate, attacked Medicare. It would "destroy and bankrupt the social security system."[50] Like the acrimonious convention, the GOP candidates' remarks seemed another display of a death wish.

Johnson spent forty-two days on the stump, covered more than sixty thousand miles, and made almost two hundred speeches. As his motorcade wound through towns, he would stop the car and urge people to "come down to the speakin'." When the crowd collected he told them about his colorful family and his boyhood in Texas, all in corn-pone language. James Reston wrote that Johnson conducted the "most peripatetic campaign in the history of the Republic."[51] Most of the time the president ignored legislative specifics. With Goldwater as his opponent he could afford to. The overriding issue was whether the voters trusted the trigger-happy kooks who had seized control of the GOP. When the president touched on ideology or policies it was to take a balanced, philosophical, and statesmanlike middle course. Only occasionally did he play the Great Society card. In October at Pittsburgh he promised that in the future, under his policies every slum "would be gone from every city in America. Every child would have a first rate education. Poverty would end; life would have meaning, purpose, and pleasure. The place is here and the time is now."[52]

It is unlikely that the War on Poverty, or the promised Great Society generally, changed many votes on November 3. The Democratic strategy was on the money. Americans were more against than for anything in 1964. The public deplored Goldwater's saber rattling and his threats to Social Security. In the White House the president and his advisers were discussing how to rescue South Vietnam from the communist danger, but in the fall of 1964 Johnson seemed less bellicose than his opponents. And he clearly did not intend to dismantle the social welfare state that his Democratic predecessors had constructed.

On November 3 LBJ took forty-four states and 61.1 percent of the popular vote, an all-time record. The new Eighty-ninth Congress would have 295 Democratic representatives, thirty-seven more than its predecessor; the new Senate would have sixty-eight Democrats, a gain of two. Both houses of the new Congress would have Democratic majorities of more than two to one. And almost all the new members were liberals. To get legislation through the Eighty-eighth Congress, Johnson had been forced to play the "martyred president" card. And even this had not been enough to break the hold of the old guard on the law-making process. Now it would be different; LBJ had congressional majorities that few other liberal presidents had ever enjoyed.

The election was not a public mandate for another New Deal. It was as much a repudiation of the hard right as an endorsement of liberalism. Still, the outcome would have momentous consequences for the Great Society. Regardless of the reality, Johnson would claim a mandate, and in the face of the political tsunami of 1964, his opponents would be hard-pressed to deny that the American public supported his policies. It is difficult to argue with 61 percent of the popular vote. In the months ahead, Johnson intended to put both mandate and majority to good use.

Under the guiding hand of the president's young Texas protégé, Bill Moyers, the task forces had been busy preparing a legislative program for the Eighty-ninth Congress ever since the summer. Of the fourteen (after the Civil Rights Act passed on July 2, the civil rights task force was dropped), the "big three," pinpointed in the Ann Arbor speech, were targeted on education, natural beauty, and cities, headed respectively by John Gardner of the Carnegie Corporation, Charles Haar of Harvard Law School, and Robert Wood of MIT. The marching orders for all was to have proposals for new Great Society laws ready by November 10, just a week after the election.

THREE

The Fabulous
Eighty-ninth

LYNDON JOHNSON'S inaugural festivities cost a half million dollars more than his predecessor's. There were five inaugural balls, the largest at the National Guard Armory, where the resplendent guests danced to the tunes of the Air Force band and laughed at sallies by Johnny Carson, Carol Channing, and Alfred Hitchcock. Johnson enjoyed himself immensely; he was among the few presidents who actually danced at the traditional balls. Lyndon and Lady Bird managed to get to all five galas, but they saved the festivities at the Sheraton Park Hotel, where many of the guests were fellow Texans, for last. As LBJ left the ballroom he told the remaining revellers: "Don't stay up late. There's work to be done. We're on our way to the Great Society."[1] The president was back at the White House and in bed by 12:20 A.M.

In fact, the first session of the Eighty-ninth Congress would create the core of the Great Society. Between January 4 and October 23, 1965, Congress put together one of the most impressive legislative records in history. The administration submitted eighty-seven bills to Congress and Johnson signed eighty-four, for a batting average of .960. Two of these measures—national health insurance for retirees and the poor and the first-ever general federal-aid-to education law—were historic landmarks of the social welfare state. But several others—the higher education bill, the revision of the immigration laws, highway beautification, the

National Foundation for the Arts and Humanities, the Clean Air and Clean Water acts, a new department of housing and urban development—were major pieces of legislation in their own right. Larry O'Brien, stage manager for the legislative program, called the session "just miraculous," "unbelievable." "Nothing like that had ever occurred in terms of depth and impact."[2] O'Brien was a partisan, of course, but by any measure of legislative output, the Eighty-ninth Congress, and especially its first half, deserved the labels "fabulous," "great," and "amazing," bestowed on it by admirers.

The election returns were still blaring from the TV sets on November 3, when Democratic leaders took the first steps to translate landslide into legislation. As he watched the mounting numbers, House Speaker John McCormack picked up the phone to call members of the Democratic Study Group, the liberal congressional caucus. McCormack was not as vigorous a leader as his predecessor, Mr. Sam, but he could see that this time a liberal mandate must not be frustrated by the rigged seniority structure of the lower house of Congress.

The DSG had been organized in 1959 by a group of Democrats fed up with the conservative roadblock to liberal change. In the Eighty-seventh Congress DSG members had backed Rayburn's move to enact the New Frontier by expanding the House Rules Committee. The change had not been enough, however; the liberals had continued to butt their heads futilely against the conservative barrier.

Now, following the presidential election, the congressional liberals were ready to try again. At a meeting in early December, the DSG proposed further reform of House practices. One change expedited use by a committee chairman of the twenty-one-day rule to free legislation from the grips of a balky Rules Committee and allow it to be brought to the House floor for action. A second ended the practice by which an objection by any House member could delay a reconciliation conference with the Senate when a bill had passed the upper chamber in a different form. A third prevented obstructionists from delaying final action on a measure by requesting an engrossed copy of a bill. More important than these rules changes, however, was a shift in all committee party memberships to reflect the new Democratic 7 to 3 majority in the lower house. A month later, on January 2, backed by the White House, the suggested reforms sailed through the Democratic caucus and became the legislative rules of the Eighty-ninth Congress. There were also key committee changes, with at least two conservative Democrats who had supported Goldwater denied chairmanships.

The new House rules undoubtedly made a difference. But the sheer Democratic preponderance was more important than all the procedural changes. The Eighty-ninth Congress had the largest Democratic majorities since 1937. And the shift in ideology went beyond the raw party numbers. The forty-six Republicans defeated in 1964 had averaged a healthy ten years in office. Their departure stripped away more than four hundred years of accumulated conservative seniority and the power and influence that seniority conferred. At the same time, on the other side, many of the freshmen Democrats owed their success to LBJ's coattails. Both inexperienced and grateful, they were sure to take the advice and guidance of the White House and administration leaders in the new Congress. As the president contemplated the congressional prospect before the session opened he remarked: "It could be better, but not this side of paradise."[3]

On election eve, as the vote figures poured in, Johnson had called his chief congressional liaison aide, Larry O'Brien, and told him: "We can wrap up the New Frontier Program now, Larry. We can pass it now."[4] O'Brien had planned to leave Washington after the election, but Johnson refused to let him go. He would be needed in the new Congress. But LBJ was too much the realist— or too much the fatalist—to rejoice in the numbers for long. Just before Congress convened in January he reflected: "I was just elected President by the biggest popular margin in the history of the country—sixteen million votes. . . . I've already lost about three of those sixteen. After a fight with Congress or something else, I'll lose another couple of million. I could be down to eight million in a couple of months."[5] Clearly, the administration's marching orders must be "Forward!" Move fast or the chance would be lost. The first session of the Eighty-ninth Congress would be, O'Brien later said, a "full court press."[6]

O'Brien and his staff would perform their magic on the Hill. But it was the president who provided the added push for success. LBJ was far more effective than his predecessor. Though a Kennedy loyalist reluctant to diminish the luster of his first boss, O'Brien conceded that JFK was never as adept with Congress as Johnson. When Kennedy met with congressional leaders "he would not force the issue." He could argue with them vigorously, but "he would stop short of putting his finger on the fellow's chest and saying 'Are you with me? You've got to be with me . . .' "[7] By contrast Johnson was "fully committed to the nitty-gritty of legislative progress."[8] LBJ poked congressmen in the chest all the time. He also grabbed them by the lapels and leaned into them while coaxing, cajoling, and threatening. The "treatment" almost always worked. Few victims could deny this force of nature.

Johnson demanded as much of his subordinates as of Congress. A work addict himself, he made it clear that no one on the White House staff could expect to lead a nine-to-five life under his administration. Staff and aides had to be at the president's beck and call at all times. Joe Califano recounts how, shortly after he joined the White House staff, the president phoned him at his office. Califano's secretary told Johnson that her boss was in the bathroom and could not answer immediately. "Isn't there a phone in there?" the astonished president asked. "No, Mr. President," she answered. "Then have a phone put there right away." Califano vetoed the order, but the next day when the same thing happened the president took the decision out of his hands. Within minutes two Army Signal Corps technicians arrived at Califano's office and installed a telephone, including the special direct line to the Oval Office, in his john.[9]

The marching orders went all the way to the top. Shortly after the election the president told his cabinet officers and chief agency heads that he counted on them to strain every muscle to both formulate "imaginative new ideas and programs" and carry out "hard-hitting, tough-minded *reforms* in existing programs." The Great Society would be expensive, so they must ruthlessly cut the failed programs and the completed programs to free up money for the new programs. They must get "to know personally the new members of Congress, Republicans as well as Democrats." There would be a congressional reception at the White House from six to eight P.M. on December 9, LBJ told his chief advisers—"I want each of you to attend."[10]

Through the first session of the Eighty-ninth Congress the president deployed all his awesome persuasive and manipulative powers to enact the Great Society. Johnson adopted and refined several strategies and devices used by Kennedy. Like JFK, he cemented relations with key representatives and senators by inviting them on evening Potomac cruises on the presidential yacht, the *Sequoia*. On these relaxed, informal trips down the river to Mt. Vernon, the congressmen and their wives would consume a buffet dinner and join in sing-alongs accompanied by an accordion. The conversation was never "heavy," but the legislators would discuss specific bills and consider how to expedite committee deliberations. Like JFK, LBJ also invited Democratic leaders to weekly leadership breakfasts at the White House, where he and his staff could review with them the progress of the administration's programs. Johnson introduced the use of flowcharts at these breakfasts to make his points. At one end of the dining table was a large display board on an easel, divided on the left into two columns, one labeled "House," the other "Senate." The right side of the board had boxes corresponding to the legislative stages of specific bills, from submission to final passage. As the leaders returned each week to the White House to consume scrambled eggs and deer sausages from the Ranch and listen to LBJ's pep talks and advice, they could see the cards representing each important bill advance gradually toward deposit in a bowl that marked final passage.

LBJ and his staff immersed themselves in every wiggle of the legislative process. At critical points, as the year before, the president manned the phones and buttonholed important legislative players. Meanwhile his loyal lieutenants—Bill Moyers, Douglass Cater, Wilbur Cohen, Harry McPherson, Joe Califano, Larry O'Brien—were in a perpetual trot to Capitol Hill to consult, advise, wheedle, and demand. Chief White House lobbyist O'Brien constantly briefed the cabinet on legislative progress and often hectored the department heads when HEW or Labor or Interior or Commerce seemed not to "be moving that bill."[11] Wilbur Cohen, then assistant secretary of Health, Education, and Welfare, would remember that he never worked so hard in his life as he did between February and June 1965.

□   □   □   □

The Johnson landslide reset the clock on Medicare, the federal health insurance program. Even the skeptical Wilbur Mills of Ways and Means could read the returns.

Mills is an enigmatic figure. Most Americans today remember him as a buffoon who disgraced himself in 1974 by drunkenly cavorting with his mistress, the stripper Fanne Foxe, in the Tidal Basin near the Jefferson Memorial. In fact, he was an astute Harvard Law School graduate who hid behind a deep-South drawl and owlish glasses to survive politically in conservative Arkansas. Mills was a political chameleon. Unlike many of the Southern congressional barons, he was a pragmatist, sensitive to shifts in the political winds. And November 1964 had marked such a climatic change. In a speech to the Kiwanis Club of Little Rock just after the election, Mills announced that he had "always thought . . . that wage earners during their working lifetime should make payments into a fund to guard against the risk of financial disaster due to heavy medical costs. . . ."[12] Mills was expressing the view of many moderates: Medicare was primarily a way to avoid personal bankruptcy, not the first step in a comprehensive national health plan. But for the moment, that would do to get Medicare moving. It now seemed that the last legislative barrier to a minimal federal health care measure was gone.

Introduced in the Eighty-ninth Congress as H.R 1 in the House and S. 1 in the Senate, the first bills in the hopper, King-Anderson (after Representative Cecil King of California and Senator Clinton Anderson of New Mexico), was still a modest proposal. As a HEW staff guide that accompanied the bill pointed out, the proposed law's coverage "left a substantial place for private health insurance . . . [particularly] for physicians' services" at the hospitals. Under the measure, private insurance companies would administer and audit payments and the hospitals could choose the companies. The measure was "hospital insurance for the aged through social security," and no more.[13] It did not cover ordinary doctors' bills; it did not cover drugs. The paid hospital-stay period was a meager thirty days.

But even its modesty did not protect the bill from attack. In fact, its limitations gave the enemies of federal health insurance a weapon for belaboring it. This time the political conservatives and the AMA realized it was not enough merely to oppose. Instead, they came up with their own plan that promised to limit the damage from federal intrusion into medical practice by narrow-ing the program. Called Eldercare, it proposed federal and state subsidies of private health insurance for only the "means-tested" elderly poor, but covered physicians' and surgeons' fees, drug costs, and lab and nursing home charges, as well as hospital care. The plan would be administered by the states. This proposal be-came the center of the conservative campaign to defeat Medicare, led, as usual, outside of Congress, by the AMA. During the first quarter of 1965 the AMA spent almost a million dollars to influ-ence the course of medical insurance legislation in the Eighty-ninth Congress.

The transformed political climate notwithstanding, the spon-sors of Medicare were forced to engage in some fancy legislative footwork to keep their proposal alive. The House Ways and Means Committee began its hearings on January 27 in closed session. There had been enough opportunity for posturing and propa-ganda on health insurance in the previous session, declared Chairman Mills; this time the witnesses would discuss the techni-cal details of financing and administration, not play to the public. Meanwhile, the ranking Republican on Ways and Means, John W. Byrnes of Wisconsin, introduced a version of Eldercare that dropped the means test and assigned the health care costs as one third to the beneficiary and two thirds to the federal treasury. The plan, however, was entirely voluntary, so that many of the poorest and most infirm seniors would be left out. Still, the Byrnes bill distanced the Republicans from the AMA. Gerald Ford of Michi-gan, the new House GOP leader, reflecting the party's determina-tion to transcend Goldwater obstructionism, endorsed it.

The Republican alternative made Ways and Means liberals un-comfortable. By including drugs, nursing home costs, and physi-cians' and surgeons' fees, the Republicans had outbid them with senior citizens; Mills, they insisted, must produce a more gener-ous response than the pending Democratic bill. Mills later claimed that he always wanted "a total package," that he pre-ferred "to do a complete job."[14] In fact, as we saw, he also kept close track of the shifting political winds. But whatever his mo-tives, he now moved quickly to steal the Republicans' thunder. There would be a Part B to the new law to cover doctors' bills. Enrollment in Part B would not be automatic, however. Pensioners would have to elect it and agree to pay a small monthly fee, though most of the cost would be defrayed by the treasury.

But Mills did even more. He had been thinking for some time about upgrading the imperfect 1960 Kerr-Mills law that subsidized general health care for the indigent elderly. However flawed, it was a measure in which he still felt pride of authorship. According to Wilbur Cohen, Mills also wanted to head off any scheme for universal national health insurance—to include everyone, not just retirees—the goal of many committed liberals. Mills asked him during the Medicare debate, Cohen later recalled, how to refute the claim that the administration's proposal was an "entering wedge" for broader, nationwide "compulsory insurance for everyone." Cohen told Mills that he could fend off the critics "if he included some plan to cover the key groups of poor people. . . ." "Medicaid evolved from this problem and discussion," Cohen later claimed.[15]

Cohen often sounds like Zelig—the Woody Allen movie character who turns up at every important historic event of the century. But this account has the ring of truth. Cohen may well have been the immediate inspiration for Mills's change of heart. In any event, Mills now proposed a separate title for the Medicare bill to pay the medical costs of welfare recipients and the medically indigent, regardless of age, the costs to be defrayed by joint state and federal outlays from general revenues. It came to be called Medicaid. Convinced that the liberal tide could not be stopped and determined to leave his brand on the historic breakthrough legislation, Mills pulled off a coup. Using the opening given him by the AMA and the Republicans, he managed to enlarge the administration's spare measure into something far broader than anyone believed possible. It was "the most brilliant legislative move I'd seen in thirty years," Cohen remarked.[16] When Byrnes heard of Mills's stroke he "just sat there open-mouthed."[17]

Though the add-ons promised to cost the federal government an additional $500 million a year, Johnson approved. The president wanted expanded access to medical care above all; cost considerations were secondary. Anything to get the bill enacted. On March 24 he endorsed the enlarged version of Medicare as "a tremendous step forward for all of our senior citizens." Chairman Mills, he noted, deserved great praise for what he had accomplished.[18]

But the game was not yet won. Johnson could see trouble ahead in the Senate and moved to head it off. The problem was the crusty, conservative Harry Byrd of Virginia, head of the critical Senate Finance Committee. A First Family of Virginia blueblood whose American roots went back to the seventeenth century, Byrd gloried in the past and saw little reason to change anything. He had not signed on for Medicare, and Johnson laid a plot to trap the senator into supporting the health bill against his wishes.

On March 26 Moyers notified Byrd that there would be an important meeting that afternoon at the White House and dispatched a car to the senator's farm in the Virginia countryside to pick him up. Byrd thought the summons had something to do with foreign affairs and came expecting a confidential White House briefing. He walked straight into a nationally televised meeting in the cabinet room with the president and nine influential congressional Democrats. On camera Johnson mounted a grade-A performance of the "treatment" suitably adapted for TV. After a glowing account of the Medicare bill's provisions, the president called on the congressmen one by one to express their support. All complied. When he got to Byrd, the president remarked pointedly: "I know that you will take an interest in the orderly scheduling of this matter and giving it a thorough hearing." Nonplussed, Byrd said nothing. Johnson prodded: "Would you care to make an observation?" The senator tried to duck. The House bill had not yet come to the Senate and so he was not familiar with it, he said. Johnson would not be deflected. The senator knew nothing, therefore, that would delay hearings on the bill in the Finance Committee? Byrd was trapped and reluctantly agreed that he knew nothing that would. LBJ swooped in for the kill. "So when . . . [the House bill] is referred to the Senate Finance Committee, you will arrange for prompt hearings . . . ?" Byrd managed to squeeze out a faint yes. With a broad smile Johnson looked full-faced into the TV camera and banged his fist on the desk in front of him. "Good!" he exclaimed.[19] After the session, the bemused senator said to O'Brien: "If I had known what you had in mind I would have dressed more formally."[20]

In the House passage was swift once the bill cleared committee. On April 8, after a single day of debate, the lower chamber endorsed the health care bill by a vote of 313 to 115, with forty Southern Democrats included among the "nay"s.

The Senate began consideration of the House bill at the end of April with a round of open hearings. HEW secretary Anthony Celebrezze, the first witness, predictably praised the measure but then raised a significant cost control issue. Celebrezze recommended that the charges of anesthesiologists, radiologists, pathologists, and physical therapists be folded into general hospital costs under the compulsory hospitalization section of Medicare rather than, as the Mills bill provided, placing them under Part B, the voluntary physicians' fees section. The Mills separation pleased the doctors. They had long opposed the hospitals on how these specialists' fees were paid. They considered the prevailing practice an example of the despised "corporate practice of medicine," equivalent to treating physicians as salaried employees.[21]

The Mills formula was a concession to a powerful group that still had to be appeased. It did not thrill the hospitals, however. Besides reducing their influence as "the central institution in our health service," as the American Hospital Association put it, the scheme would raise patients' costs.[22] The AMA denied that separate fees for the prescribed groups would be more expensive, but in fact the claim proved to be valid.

No amount of truckling to the AMA ensured the bills' approval, however. When Democratic majority whip Russell Long proposed a "catastrophic illness" amendment, the doctors seized on it as a chance to check the Medicare juggernaut by sowing confusion. Long's amendment actually addressed a major problem of health care: financial disaster caused by costly chronic illness. It would pay for any length of hospital stay, no matter how prolonged, but would tie benefits to income and make the middle class pay a large part of their coverage. In the view of Wilbur Cohen it would add exorbitantly to the cost of the health care program, while making the plan "attractive only for very low-income people."[23] The Louisiana senator, more conservative than his famous father, Huey Long, was probably not serious about his scheme. Mike Manatos, O'Brien's contact man with the Senate, reported that Long had introduced his amendment primarily "for the purpose of convincing the doctors and his constituents back home that he made a good try, and when the Committee rejects it he will then be able to say he had to support whatever bill the Committee reports. . . ."[24]

Though it was divisive and distracting, the Long amendment picked up some support from liberals as well as from AMA lobbyists, but administration managers were able to convert it into an innocuous extension of the length of hospital care if the patient paid part of the extra cost. The administration also got the Senate to accept its more frugal formula for reimbursing the anesthesiologists, pathologists, and other in-hospital physicians.

As the Finance Committee completed its work on the bill, the AMA rallied for the last time. On June 8 it announced it would insert ads in a hundred major papers proclaiming the administration's program "the beginning of socialized medicine."[25] Later that month, at the association's annual convention in New York, eight state medical societies submitted resolutions pledging their members to boycott the federal health care program if enacted. It looked like the old game once more and liberals feared the worse. But in fact the political and ideological climate had altered with the Johnson landslide, and many doctors saw they were now in danger of looking like monsters of self-serving greed. Dr. James Z. Appel, the incoming AMA president, warned members against employing "unethical tactics" to defy Congress, and the AMA governing body, the House of Delegates, refused to adopt any of the boycott resolutions. Still, in a final, truculent fling, the delegates declared that physicians should not work under conditions that "tend to interfere with or impair the complete and free exercise of [their] medical judgment and skill or tend to cause a deterioration of the quality of medical care."[26]

Johnson had played a significant role in weakening the doctors' opposition. The president believed in consultation, and in June he had summoned the AMA leaders to the White House. There he simultaneously flattered and cajoled them. He recalled his fondness for his old family doctor, who had tended his father and mother, and told them that he respected doctors and the medical profession deeply, and that the American public cherished them as well. Physicians enjoyed a "favored position," so they could not "do anything but work for the public interest." They simply had to do it. "It's expected of you and you are equal to it, and I expect it of you."[27]

On June 24 the Finance Committee reported out the amended

House bill, and floor debate in the Senate began on July 6. The discussion was brief and the bill passed on the ninth by a vote of 68 to 21, with almost all the Northern Democrats approving and Southern Democrats and Republicans about evenly split.

The joint conference committee accepted the Senate's modest extension of hospitalization time, but Mills continued to insist on the inclusion of charges for radiologists, physical therapists, anesthesiologists, and pathologists in the physicians'-fees rather than the hospital-costs section. Johnson understood the cost-inflation effect and urged Mills and Hale Boggs to drop the provision. But when they refused to budge the administration conceded the Mills formula. It would become a mechanism for pumping up hospital charges for the next generation. As one of the Senate conferees later claimed, "Mills had promised the doctors that he would never put any of them under any compulsory system and he kept his word." "Unfortunately," he added, it was "going to cost the American people hundreds of millions of dollars. . . ."[28]

And it was not the only expensive concession to appease the doctors. Mills also insisted in the conference that there be no prescribed rate structure; doctors could charge "reasonable" and "customary" fees, those "prevailing" in their communities. This formula opened the door to a vast ballooning of medical costs. Johnson understood the cost-inflation danger, but it seemed another unavoidable concession for enacting a Medicare bill. As Wilbur Cohen confessed, he had to "promise before the final vote in the executive session of the . . . Ways and Means Committee that the [Social Security Administration] would exercise no cost control."[29] According to O'Brien: "There was nobody in that conference who was going to buck Wilbur Mills on the House side. . . ."[30]

And yet the administration did not give up entirely on medical cost containment. The president and his advisers worried not only about sweeteners to doctors; they also feared that when Medicare came on line in 1966, demand for medical services would soar, imposing additional pressure on health care costs. The politically expedient way to keep doctors' fees reasonable, the White House concluded, was to multiply the number of doctors, dentists, and health facilities and so increase competition for patients. To implement this market-force approach, in the fall session's closing

days, Congress passed the Health Professions Education Assistance Act, authorizing almost $800 million over four years for
hospital construction and medical-dental education with the goal
of doubling medical school enrollment from eight thousand to
sixteen thousand. Still not satisfied, in May 1966 Johnson would
appoint the National Advisory Commission on Health Manpower
to investigate rising health care costs and make further recommendations.

As we know today, the supply-side route to containing medical
costs failed; medical cost inflation would defy all efforts to contain
it. (Competition in medicine, in fact, had paradoxical effects. See
Epilogue.) But the evil effects would become visible only much
later. In the meantime the liberal community savored the victory
of Medicare. Writing from New York, Elizabeth Wickenden, Arthur Goldschmidt's wife, his old friend from New Deal days, con-
gratulated the president for putting the "capstone on all our long
hopes and aspiration for better health care for the aged."
"Wicky," as her friends called her, recalled an event years before
when Arthur, along with Abe Fortas, William Douglas, and other
liberal guests at her Georgetown home, were prodding the tall
young Texas congressman on "some current cause of the day." In
exasperation Johnson had turned on his tormentors. "But where
would you be with all your liberal ideals if people like me couldn't
get elected to Congress to fight your battles for you?" "And you
were right," Wickenden now confessed.[31]

The president wanted to sign the bill at the Truman Library to
honor the man who had first placed federal health insurance on
the national agenda. Harry and Bess Truman would be issued the
first two Medicare cards. Horace Busby, a conservative Johnson
aide and speechwriter, warned the president to abandon the plan.
Truman's health proposals, to cover everybody, had been seen as
"socialized medicine," and the president must not associate
Medicare with it. The public might believe that Johnson intended
to go beyond the bill Congress had just passed.[32]

LBJ ignored Busby's advice and on July 30 flew to Independence, Missouri, with his entourage. More than two hundred dignitaries and celebrities attended the signing ceremonies in the
Truman Library auditorium. On the stage, next to the lectern, a
leather-bound "enrolled" copy of the bill lay on the mahogany
desk on which Truman had signed the momentous 1947 mea-

sures defining the Cold War containment policy. The ex-president, frail but clear-eyed at eighty-one, thanked Johnson for bringing the gift of federal health insurance to the American people. It was a measure "which puts the nation right, where it needs to be right." It made him glad "to have lived this long." Johnson praised his predecessor's pioneer role and then—fulsomely—explained the significance of the legislation. "No longer" would "older Americans be denied the healing miracle of modern medicine." "No longer [would] illness crush and destroy the savings that have been so carefully put away. . . . No longer [would] young families see their own incomes, and their own hopes, eaten away simply because they are carrying out their deep moral obligations to their parents. . . ." The ceremony concluded with the usual tiny strokes of many pens. Perhaps with some covert irony, one of the souvenirs went to Russell Long for his "able and effective work" in getting the bill enacted.[33]

Federal aid to elementary and secondary education was the other breakthrough law of the Eighty-ninth Congress. By the time Lyndon Johnson became president, federal aid to education had become a key component of the liberal arch, sanctified by a generation of reformers. LBJ considered it his mandate to complete that arch.

But the president also felt an intense personal commitment to improving and expanding American education. No American had greater confidence in the power of schools to cure and transform than Lyndon Johnson. His experience as a teacher and administrator in Cotulla, and then as an instructor of speech at Sam Houston High in Houston, gave him the hands-on experience in education that few presidents in this century have had. And his own life seemed to confirm the power of education to uplift. In the presence of the "Harvards" who surrounded Kennedy, Johnson was always apologetic about his Southwest Texas State Teachers College education. But he also recognized that the freshwater school in San Marcos had given him an essential leg-up in his climb to the heights. George Reedy, his White House press secretary, would later say that LBJ had "an abnormal, superstitious respect for education. I believe he even thought it would cure chilblain."[34] It was Lyndon Johnson, rather than George Bush, who first expressed the wish to go down in history as the "education president."[35]

As in health insurance, Johnson could build on the Kennedy experience. In the three previous years the supporters of federal aid to education had hit all the potholes and soft shoulders on the road and now knew where they were located. The president could also take advantage of his non-Catholicism. In 1947 the Supreme Court, in *Everson* v. *Ewing Township,* had upheld a New Jersey law authorizing state funds for transporting parochial school children on the grounds that the money went to the students, not their schools. In the court's eyes, then, church-state separation was not violated. Kennedy's advisors had urged him to invoke the *Everson* child-benefit principle for his own aid-to-education proposal, but he refused. *Everson* was a stretch, he said, and a Catholic president had to be above reproach on the church-state issue. The Protestant Johnson was not so burdened. He could afford whatever expedient handle he could grasp.

Another significant change was the refocus on poverty. Still dimly perceived in 1961, the plight of the poor amid plenty had become a major national concern by 1965, in part thanks to Johnson himself, and escape from poverty seemed closely linked with education. Previously alarmed by schoolroom shortages and slumping teachers' salaries, the aid-to-education lobbyists could now point to Appalachia and the inner-city ghettos as broad public concerns. The poor whites of the former and the poor blacks of the latter would be the chief beneficiaries of federal aid.

The redirection of the argument no doubt reflected the change in the *Zeitgeist*. But it was also expedient. The aid-to-education zealots knew it would be more difficult for groups like the Catholic Welfare Conference and the National Education Association to oppose a bill intended primarily to benefit the nation's disadvantaged children. And the poverty focus promised to reduce state rivalries. The rich states had always objected to paying collectively for the education of children in the poor states. But if the payout went to school *districts* with a given proportion of poor children, the objection blurred. Every state had plenty of such districts, so all would gain to some extent. According to John Gardner, head of the Johnson task force on education and later secretary of Health, Education, and Welfare, this formula, conceived by Commissioner of Education Francis Keppel, "dissolved the whole sense of the state feeling that its money was going somewhere else; it dissolved this whole geographic paralysis."[36]

The Johnson bill, eventually labeled the Elementary and Secondary Education Act (ESEA), was the product of much behind-the-scenes churning and maneuvering. During the summer and fall of 1964 Commissioner Keppel, the most forceful member of the Gardner task force, met frequently with the two groups, the National Catholic Welfare Council and the NEA, whose support was essential for success. Former dean of education at Harvard, Keppel was an effective conciliator. He not only talked to the traditional antagonists; he also got them to talk to one another. A high Episcopalian, he particularly enjoyed working with "the monsignors." One participant later noted, "This marked the first time that the Council began to communicate with the NEA."[37]

The task force was divided on one issue: the role of state departments of education. None of the task force members had much faith in the efficiency or commitment of state school officials. They seemed, Keppel said, "the feeblest bunch of second-rate, or fifth-rate, educators who combined educational incompetence with bureaucratic immovability."[38] But Keppel wanted to reform them by better financing, while William Cannon, the Bureau of the Budget staffer who served as the task force's executive secretary, wanted to bypass them. Cannon, as a contributor to the War on Poverty, had already expressed his distrust of entrenched local bureaucracies and once again plumped for new structures and local input. In his view the federal government should finance supplementary education centers and educational research labs, along with a network of local educational experimental centers to challenge both the sclerotic federal Office of Education and the local establishments.

The Gardner task force recommendations reached Johnson just after the election and he took the time to read them through. After Thanksgiving he discussed them at the Ranch with Celebrezze, Wirtz, Moyers, Cohen, Keppel, and Cannon. Press ahead, he told them. After Congress assembled, he would propose specifics in a series of communications culminating in a special education message on January 12.

The January 12 message covered education from kindergarten through graduate school. Johnson asked Congress for $1.5 billion for the first year, two thirds of which would go to elementary and secondary school districts with a large proportion of poor children. A further quarter of a billion would go for a range of higher education programs, including the first federal college scholarships, guaranteed student loans, and money to upgrade small colleges and improve the holdings of college libraries. The federal government would also provide money for the states to buy textbooks and purchase books for schools and libraries. It was a cornucopia combining every education wish-list ever concocted and conferring benefits on every constituency in the education forum.

As a practical legislative matter, elementary and secondary education was soon split from higher education and submitted as a separate bill. In the House, ESEA went to Carl Perkins of the education subcommittee of the House Education and Labor Committee, and in the Senate to Wayne Morse, chairman of the education subcommittee of the Labor and Public Welfare Committee.

The bill contained five titles, each designed to beguile a separate constituency while not provoking an equally powerful opposition. The crucial title was the first. It accounted for five sixths of the total amount of federal funds to be spent and was the heart of the bill. Its announced target was educational inequality. To pacify states'-rights advocates and the local school establishments and to avoid charges of federal domination, Washington would supply funds (about $1 billion the first year) to the states, on a formula that took into account the states own education contribution per child, with more generous states receiving more money. In turn, these dollars were to be allotted by the states to individual school districts in accordance with the number of children from low-income families, defined as those earning less than $2,000 a year and those who received more than $2,000 a year in federal "relief." Any school district with as little as 3 percent eligible children would get something. The districts would not receive the money automatically. It would be given for programs that were specifically designed to help poor children, under guidelines developed by the U.S. commissioner of education. Nothing was said about parochial schools as such, but in assessing the needs of poor children the school districts would be required to count the number in private schools (read: "parochial schools") as well as those in public schools and provide these non-public-school children with services, such as educational radio and TV, mobile laboratories, and assorted instructional materials. In the end only a tiny 4 percent of private school pupils, compared with 19 percent of public school pupils, actually participated in Title I programs.[39]

Title II, which allotted another $100 million of funds, promised further benefits for Catholic parents by making available library resources and textbooks to all poor students, provided these materials were nonsectarian and approved for all students alike. Title III, following Cannon's approach, sought to establish a system of "supplementary education centers and services" to provide remedial instruction, physical-education and recreational facilities, adult education, and educational counseling, and to encourage creation of experimental programs by local educational groups, an approach paralleling the community action programs of the Economic Opportunity Act. Title IV funded research by universities and other agencies into the problems of elementary and secondary education in America but not those connected with sectarian issues. Title V, inspired by Keppel, provided money for the upgrading and improvement of the state boards of education, which administered the nation's elementary and secondary schools.

Unlike all the other general federal-aid-to-education measures of the past, this bill seemed likely from the first to have clear sailing. The 1964 Civil Rights Act, passed the previous July, had removed the school integration issue, a stumbling block for the Kennedy measures. Title VI of that landmark bill for racial justice explicitly prohibited federal contributions to any activity or agency that discriminated on the grounds of race, color, or national origin. The education bill also promised to provide especially generous funds to both urban and rural constituencies, both overrepresented in Congress, while spreading a little federal money even to prosperous suburbia. Best of all, the church-state issue had been largely finessed. Keppel's honest brokering and the concessions to Catholics were critical. But the Church had also changed in the past five years, becoming more ecumenical and liberal under the transforming rays of Pope John XXIII's revolutionary opening to modernity. On the day the president delivered his education message, Monsignor Frederick Hockwalt, spokesman for the National Catholic Welfare Conference, declared the administration's bill fair to children of all religions and praised it for emphasizing cooperation of public and private schools. Meanwhile, a shift had taken place on the other side as well. National Education Association leaders, like other Americans, read the November election returns and concluded that a federal aid bill with benefits to Catholic schools was inevitable this time around. They were also moved by professional politics. NEA's more liberal rival, the American Federation of Teachers, an AFL-CIO-affiliated trade union, had recently endorsed federal financing of private education. The NEA could not be left behind. The same day Hockwalt praised the administration bill, the NEA called it "politically feasible" and pledged to support it.[40]

In fact not all the roadblocks had crumbled. Conservatives suspicious of all government, and some liberals who considered ESEA's outlays too meager, still hoped to stop the juggernaut. Suburban representatives also remained skeptical. The bill short-changed their constituents, who had taxed themselves to the limit to support their local schools and were now being asked to pay for someone else's children. Finally, the religious objections had not been completely surmounted; not all the misgivings of the church-state-separation breed had been fully addressed.

The administration strategy was to hurry the bill through Congress before the agreements worked out became undone. In the House, Carl Perkins, an administration stalwart from the coal mining region of Kentucky, opened hearings on H.R. 2362 on January 22. He concluded them expeditiously twelve days later.

The hearings displayed the full range of opinion on federal aid to education, but had little overall effect on the bill's progress. Keppel and Celebrezze predictably lauded the bill's approach to education as new, imaginative, and promising. They were followed by a stream of school superintendents, school principals, and assorted professional "educators" so uncritically pro-ESEA, now that their fears of federal controls had evaporated, that upstate New York Republican Charles Goodell expressed doubts that they had anything in mind beyond hauling in more money. Despite the change in intellectual climate and the administration's preliminary ground clearing, several witnesses raised all the old doubts and objections as if nothing had changed since 1963. Howard Squadron of the American Jewish Committee, for one, charged that the nation's glorious "universal free public school system" would "be gravely threatened" by the bill's provisions.[41]

A few friendly witnesses and at least one liberal subcommittee member raised the question of effectiveness: Would the bill actually improve the quality of education for the poor? In fact, breaking with most previous reform legislation, the bill required periodic self-evaluation of several programs. Keppel claimed that these provisions would measure how well the bill achieved its goals. But would this be enough, asked John Brademas of Indiana, a House Democratic whip, but also a former Rhodes scholar. How much did anyone really know about overcoming the disabilities and pathologies of poverty? Other witnesses raised doubts of the innovative capacity of local school bureaucrats. Could people so hidebound, so accustomed to the old ways, be expected to use the money they got effectively? As one Rutgers professor noted, if Congress did not closely monitor the law, the school systems would use the money "any old way they care to."[42]

Perkins had little patience even with the most constructive criticism and rushed the legislation through committee. Republicans protested that they had not had a chance to call most of their witnesses. Given the Democrats' haste, they complained, the bill should be called "the Railroad Act of 1965."[43] In full committee, the prickly Edith Green of Oregon, a former schoolteacher and defender of the state education establishment, unnerved the bill's sponsors by a barrage of amendments. First she wanted local school districts to have the right to challenge in the federal courts decisions regarding money allocations to private schools. The Catholic members saw this as an effort to exclude them from benefits. If passed, it might well have scuttled the bill. Next, she objected to the funding formula on the grounds that it gave too much money to the richer states and not enough to the poorer. The administration was convinced that the Oregon "gentlelady" was allied with Republicans Goodell and Albert Quie of Minnesota to defeat the measure. She was not; in the end she voted for the bill, though her objections were voted down. On March 8 the full Education and Labor Committee approved the bill.

The Goldwater disaster had stigmatized GOP negativism, and the House Republican leaders tried to evade the charge of mere obstructionism. Rather than opposing federal aid to education in toto, they presented their own alternative. Called, soberly, the Education Incentive Act by its supporters and, wryly, the "Constructive Republican Alternative Proposals" (CRAP) by the unimpressed Democrats, this scheme promised tax credits for parents who paid school taxes but sent their children to private schools. The Republican House leaders asked the Rules Committee to delay reporting the administration bill to the House as a whole until their proposal had gotten a full airing.

No one expected the committee to comply. Indeed, given the newly revised formula for selecting committee personnel, no one expected it to alter or delay the administration bill in any significant way. And it did not. On March 22 the Rules Committee sent H.R. 2362 to the House floor for final debate and vote.

This was the last chance for the bill's enemies to block or alter it, and they failed. To the administration, the bill was the touchstone of success or failure during the session. It was, declared Larry O'Brien, "the cornerstone to the entire Administration legislative program for the Eighty-ninth Congress." If the president could "hold the troops together on this one, it will surely make things that much easier during the remainder of the session."[44] The administration forces ran out all their big guns to contain their opponents. But on March 24, for a few hours, the adept attacks of Quie, Goodell, and Robert Griffin of Michigan, primarily on the funding formula, went unanswered and several key Democrats began to waver. Meanwhile, in the House gallery, White House aide Douglass Cater and Samuel Halperin of the Office of Education watched the proceedings, "scared as hell" that the bill was in trouble.[45]

The Republican assault was contained that day by artful counterattacks by Brademas and Frank Thompson of New Jersey. But the threat of defeat was not over. That evening Vice President Humphrey phoned ten key Democrats pleading with them to keep the faith. The next morning the Democratic whips and assistant whips foregathered to plot floor strategy for overcoming obstructionist amendments and delaying tactics. For the next two days the Democratic leaders fought off their opponents. On the twenty-sixth the opposition, armed with Edith Green's judicial review and revised funding formulas, was stopped in its tracks. At ten-thirty that evening the speaker put the bill to the final vote and it passed 263 to 153, with almost every Northern Democrat in favor, as well as 40 percent of the Southerners. When McCormack announced the tally a cheer went up from the floor. Weary of debate and maneuver, and conscious they had enacted a landmark measure, even opponents, it was said, felt relieved.

In the Senate, hearings on ESEA began on January 26 and drew the usual parade of witnesses pro and con. Commissioner Keppel and Secretary Celebrezze appeared to praise the proposed measure and answer critics. Lobbyists flocked to the Hill to rehearse their objections or announce their support. The remarks of only two participants, both named Kennedy, are of interest, however.

Robert, the newly elected junior senator from New York, once again expressed concern about the possible misuse of Title I money by the hidebound local education bureaucrats. Bobby's suspicions had deep roots. Not only had the Ohlin-Cloward opportunity theory of juvenile delinquency left him skeptical of local establishments, but his newly acquired constituency of militant civil rights leaders was beginning an attack on the New York City Board of Education as remote from the public and racist that would erupt three years later as the rancorous and divisive Ocean Hill-Brownsville school war. In this imbroglio black activists, led by Ocean Hill-Brownsville administrator Rhody McCoy, and their supporters clashed with white schoolteachers, the teachers' union, and their partisans, triggering a wave of teachers' strikes that badly divided New York along racial, class, and religious lines.

Kennedy asked Keppel whether the money spent under Title I would not be swallowed up by the bureaucracy and fail to benefit the students. Might Congress not be "just . . . investing money where it really is going to accomplish very little if any good"? One "of the really great problems we have in this country . . . is the school boards in some of these communities, in some of these States," he noted. They "are just not going to take the necessary steps to deal with the problem."[46] In fact the White House already knew Kennedy's concerns; he had communicated them to the Office of Education before the bill went to the House. Now, at the Senate hearings, Keppel assured the New York senator that the administration would guarantee that the bill retained an evaluation clause. As we shall see, that decision would have consequences.

Edward Kennedy, "Ted," the youthfully handsome junior senator from Massachusetts, for his part joined with Gaylord Nelson of Wisconsin in urging that the bill include a teachers corps, modeled on the Peace Corps. The new agency would dispatch volunteers to the nation's impoverished school districts to improve the quality of education for the poor. Committee leaders assured them that their proposal would be given careful consideration before final enactment, but that now was not the time to take it up. Eventually a teachers corps proviso would be made part of the higher education bill passed later in the session.

The Kennedy-Nelson proposal fell victim to LBJ's fear of delay. Johnson knew that support for a federal-aid-to-education bill was more solid in the Senate than in the House. But he dreaded the crapshoot of a House-Senate conference committee at the end, where opponents would get a second chance to do damage to the bill. To spare ESEA the ordeal of double jeopardy, administration strategists induced Wayne Morse to delay the Senate's own action until House passage and then accept the House measure intact. After much arm twisting, on April 6 the education subcommittee of Labor and Welfare submitted H.R. 2362 to the Senate as its own bill.

Cantankerous in the public spotlight, in the privacy of the Senate Morse was a fair and reasonable man respected by his fellow legislators. His adroit maneuvering hurried the bill through floor debate in a mere three days. Morse, Majority Leader Mike Mansfield, and the other Democratic leaders effectively rallied the troops to defeat damaging amendments by Republicans and Southerners and brought the bill to a final vote on April 9. The results were stunning: 73 "aye"s and only 18 "nay"s, with the "nay"s composed of the usual Western and Midwestern Republicans and a sprinkling of Southern Democrats.

Johnson, like the entire liberal community, was jubilant. In fact the measure was not really a *general* federal-aid-to-education bill as everyone claimed. Rather, it was an elaborate and detailed categorical bill; every bit of money was targeted at a specific program or beneficiary. Virtually none was handed over to the local school administrators to do with as they wanted, though in fact it would prove difficult to get the local school administrators to obey the law. Still, it was a major breakthrough and Johnson was proud of the administration's accomplishment. At a White House victory reception, he told congressmen that he had "worked harder and longer on this measure than any measure . . . since [he] came to Washington in 1931. . . ."[47]

On April 11 the president flew to Texas and, a mile from the Ranch, on the lawn next to the simple building where he had gone to school, he signed the Elementary and Secondary Education Act. The ceremony was steeped in Johnsonian sentimental nostalgia. The guest of honor was Kathryn Deadrich Loney, "Miss Kate," who had taught Lyndon at the one-room Junction School, where he learned to read. Seven middle-aged Mexican-Americans, former students of the president at the Cotulla school in La Salle County back in 1928, and four of the Sam Houston High debaters he had coached in 1930, were other guests. This time Johnson used only one pen to sign his name and presented it to Miss Kate. The old lady did not understand the gesture, and true to her old-fashioned ethic of mine-and-thine left it on the bench as she walked off at the ceremony's end.

Medicare and ESEA were the two blockbuster bills of the first session of the Eighty-ninth Congress. Both were items of the old liberal agenda; both represented old promises finally fulfilled. Each had also been part of the Kennedy program left unfinished on November 22, 1963.

But they were not the only wrap-up measures of this session. On March 9 Johnson signed an Appalachia bill, an expansion and upgrading of the Kennedy Area Redevelopment Act, which had already expended several hundred million dollars with few visible results. The new law appropriated $1.1 billion for redeveloping the depleted highlands region of eleven Eastern states, earmarking much of the money for improved roads and infrastructure. On April 27 the president approved the Manpower Development and Training Act of 1965, a liberalized version of a Kennedy measure that increased proportionately federal funding for upgrading job skills and provided for longer-term programs. The Older Americans Act created the Administration on Aging within HEW and appropriated $17.5 million to the states for programs to teach the aged new job skills. In the fall, after sometimes rancorous debate over the Teachers Corps provision, Congress enacted the Higher Education Act, which finally established federal college scholarships for poor students and provided federal underwriting of private tuition loans for the middle class (the federal government would absorb part of the interest rate charged by private loan agencies), and authorized funds for improving academic quality at small colleges and for upgrading college and university libraries. Title V created the national Teachers Corps, first suggested by senators Kennedy and Nelson. Congress, however, refused to appropriate the funds for the Teachers Corps in the $4.8 billion appropriations bill at the end of the session. These did not become available until the following session. (For the controversy over the Teachers Corps, see Chapter 5.) LBJ signed the bill at his alma mater, Southwest Texas State, on November 8.

The Eighty-ninth Congress righted a long-rankling ethnic affront with passage of the 1965 Immigration Act. In the racist, tribal 1920s, Congress had enacted an immigration restriction law rigged against the "inferior" breeds of southern and eastern Europe and favoring Nordics. The new measure replaced the geographical quota system with a selection process based on first-come, first-served, regardless of race or ethnicity, though preference was given to those with family relations in America and with useful occupational skills. The United States would now accept all "the huddled masses," not just Britons, Celts, and Germans, though if they were doctors or engineers it would be a little easier to stay. On October 3, the president stood in the shadow of the Statue of Liberty in New York Harbor; a half mile behind him floated Ellis Island, where millions of immigrants had first set foot on American soil. While a chorus sang "America the Beautiful," LBJ signed the new Immigration Act into law. For good or ill, it would have an immense impact on the nation's demographic profile.

In early 1965 the ghetto and its pathologies had not yet become shorthand for urban problems; that awaited the angry inner-city uprisings of the months and years ahead. But social scientists and planners already worried about blight, decay, white flight, and other city problems. LBJ went to some trouble to address urban concerns this session. In a special message to Congress of March 2 he called for a cabinet-level department of housing and urban development and 500,000 new housing units for citizens too rich for public "projects" and too poor to pay for decent private living quarters. The bill offered a federal subsidy to owners of housing who made available cheap rental accommodations to any family that met certain modest income standards, if they were elderly, physically handicapped, or lived in existing substandard housing. The families targeted were those whose incomes were above the maximum level for public housing eligibility but too meager to buy decent private housing.

Folded into two separate bills, the president's proposals quickly ran into trouble. Federal housing programs of any kind had become suspect in recent years. Initiated by the New Deal during the thirties, urban housing built at federal expense had provided living space for many thousands of "deserving" poor families at a time when a third of the nation or more seemed unable to pay its rent. As a matter of fact, as a young congressman from Texas, Lyndon Johnson had gotten one of the first New Deal housing projects for his home district in Austin. Postwar prosperity and the generous subsidies to suburban homeowners through tax breaks and mortgage loan guarantees, however, had drawn off many solid, working-class families from the cities, and many low-income "projects" had deteriorated into slums as the unstable, the sick, and the defeated took their place. By the mid-sixties public housing was in bad repute and few politicians were anxious to support further expansion of what they considered a sick system. The proposal for a new cabinet-level housing and urban affairs department, moreover, was tainted by the disdain for the central cities felt by many middle-class whites. Rural and suburban congressmen, representing voters who had fled the cities in disgust, had little reason to support such a bill.

But it was the rent subsidy provision that proved the hardest sell. Conservatives considered the rent subsidy likely to open a Pandora's box. Senator John Tower of Texas attacked it as a dangerous precedent. "Next we would have subsidies for groceries, then for clothing, then maybe for guaranteed incomes."[48] Opponents in Congress called it socialistic. Unspoken, but very much alive under the surface, was the race issue. The subsidies were likely to go to black families primarily, and by now many Southerners believed blacks already had gotten too much special treatment. Many on the Hill, O'Brien remembered, considered it as "implementing civil rights legislation."[49]

Faced by such opposition, the president was forced to compromise. To win House passage of the Housing and Urban Development Act he agreed to restrict subsidies to families poor enough to be eligible for public housing, cutting off many lower-middle-class people from its benefits. In this form it passed the lower house in late June by a vote of 208 to 202, a far tighter squeeze than most Great Society legislation of this session. In the Senate the rent subsidy, deserted by moderate Democrats, barely squeaked through. Johnson signed the housing bill on August 8 with the rent subsidy intact, though without funding. Just before adjournment in late October, the joint House-Senate conference committee on the $4.8 billion appropriations bill deleted the $30 million rent subsidy allotment, and the president had to induce the second session of the Eighty-ninth to make it good. (See Chapter 5.)

During this miraculous first session of the Eighty-ninth Congress, Johnson built on and extended the natural-resource and environmental policies of the Kennedy administration.

The environmental awareness of the nation had been evolving and expanding since the 1950s, when naturalist Rachel Carson published *Silent Spring,* a graphic and moving exposé of the blighting effects of DDT on birds and animal life as the pesticide seeped into the food chain. The book had set off a great debate that raised the nation's environmental consciousness. By the beginning of the sixties a new "ecological" perspective had appeared that would swell into a mass movement during the following decade.

Kennedy had responded to the emerging environmental concerns by endorsing federal funding for sewage treatment plants, for air pollution controls, for wilderness preservation, for national park expansion, and for improved recreation facilities on federal lands. His support in Congress, however, except for wilderness preservation, was at most half-hearted, and conservatives either killed off or seriously watered down the proposed legislation. Still, for the first time since FDR, the federal government had taken the initiative in environmental policy.

Prospects for environmental legislation improved after November 1963 and especially after November 1964. At the outset of his political career Johnson, like his mentor FDR, had been a conservationist. He never lost his appreciation of nature and always preferred the country to the city. As a senator he changed his constituency and his positions. Between 1949 and 1960, any sensitivity to environmental concerns was hard to detect. Texans, by and large, belonged to the other tradition of resource management: Get it while you can! Senator Johnson had been friendly to the oil, natural gas, and cattle interests of the Lone Star State and had endorsed the 1953 tidelands oil bill that shifted control of the nation's rich coastal oil resources from the relatively independent federal government to the lobbyist-dominated states. But LBJ had a different constituency in the White House and soon reverted to his conservationist, progressive roots.

Another force behind the administration's position on environmental concerns was the influence of Secretary of the Interior Stewart Udall. A former Arizona congressman, Udall had absorbed the new environmentalism that was in the air in the early 1960s. The old "conservation" emphasized prudent and "scientific" use of resources to extend their life and maximize national wealth. The new approach emphasized the need to protect and improve the quality of life. As Udall had explained in his 1963 book, *The Quiet Crisis,* although the country stood "on a pinnacle of wealth and power," Americans lived in a land of "vanishing beauty, of increasing ugliness, of shrinking open space, and of an overall environment that is diminished daily by pollution and noise and blight."[50] The fact that these words echo concerns addressed in LBJ's May 1964 "Great Society" speech is not accidental. Richard Goodwin, the author of the Ann Arbor address, had borrowed many ideas from James Reston, Jr., an assistant to Udall at Interior, and a disciple of the new environmentalism.

Though it was Goodwin who made life quality the theme of the Ann Arbor speech, surprisingly he himself was not certain what the "beauty" issue really meant or what its limits were. Assigned the job of assembling task forces on the environment, Goodwin was nonplussed. "This thing they were trying to put together. They weren't quite sure what it was," he later remarked. "It was the environment, it was the quality of life, it was beauty, and it was a very amorphous and difficult subject."[51] Harvard Law School professor Charles Haar, a friend of Goodwin's who ended up chairing the natural beauty task force, was equally puzzled. The task force was groping, he later said. "It was the beginning of the movement that somehow the standard of living, the gross national product, was not enough. That as the most powerful, most technologically advanced country in the world, we also ought to have some kind of environment, some kind of physical setting which was worthy of this kind of production power and some of the more emotive ideals."[52]

In fact there were two distinct issues at stake. One was fairly traditional: the safety and health of the public. It was the other—natural beauty and the enjoyment of rivers, lakes, forests, and mountains—that seemed novel as a subject deserving federal attention. But in truth few issues better epitomized the Great Society's quality-of-life focus.

In November 1964 the task forces on environmental pollution and on preservation of natural beauty, which Johnson had created in July, reported on their work. The experts and environmentalists proposed a shift in conservation emphasis from the wide-open spaces of the West, with its minerals, grazing lands, and forests, to the metropolitan East and Midwest, with their visual blight, air and water pollution, congestion, and sparse recreational areas. We would emphasize beauty, Haar recalled, in the "damned standard metropolitan statistical areas." The president's version of conservation would focus on the "working class areas where the people were. . . ."[53] It did not take into account, he later noted, the special concerns of black Americans. "We were not in the black period at this time," he later told historian Joe Frantz. "I don't think there was a full awareness. . . ."[54] The reports did not have a strong legislative focus; still, their underlying philosophies became the basis for a raft of separate proposals over time.

Johnson's "State of the Union" address on January 4, 1965, called on Congress to protect "the beauty of America" and preserve a "green legacy" for the nation's children. It was the first time any president had made esthetic concerns a significant item of national policy. He endorsed more attractive landscaping for highways, streets, and open spaces; proposed enhanced powers for the government to check air and water pollution "before it happens"; asked for a wild rivers bill to preserve the pristine quality of streams; and recommended measures to make the Potomac "a model of beauty." At the conclusion of the environmental section he announced that he intended to call a White House conference on natural beauty.[55]

On February 8, in a message on the environment infused with the quality-of-life theme, Johnson proclaimed a "new conservation" that would lift the human spirit and establish that "beauty must not be just a holiday treat, but part of our daily life."[56]

Johnson and his advisers were mixing two issues. At no time, even during these confident, early months of the Great Society, was there a strong public groundswell for federal policy on "beauty." Conservatives, who looked balefully at any expansion of federal power, could not be expected to cheer when Washington announced that it was assuming responsibility for the nation's esthetic values. As for what was still being called "the common man," judging by the country's physical and cultural landscapes, he was perfectly content with modest standards of excellence in landscaping, the arts, and in matters of taste generally. No doubt Americans were richer, better educated, and better traveled than "before the war," but they were still "middlebrows" at best, to the dismay of the country's aesthetes, sophisticates, arts practitioners and consumers, and intellectuals. For most men beauty remained the province of "the ladies," the place where all social frills properly resided. But if unconcerned about beauty, few Americans wanted to be choked, poisoned, or nauseated by bad air and bad water. Pollution—chemicals in the lakes and rivers, smog in the air—made you sick and *that* was a problem deserving of Washington's attention.

Johnson's February 8 message to Congress on the environment called for a bill to check pollution "at its source" through enhanced water quality standards and better enforcement rather than by waiting to "cure pollution after it occurs." In the post-scarcity mode, it also called for a "new conservation" that would not only "protect the countryside" but "salvage the beauty and charm of our cities." The nation must not be concerned "with nature alone," Johnson noted, "but with the total relation between man and the world around him." The object of the new conservation was "not just man's welfare, but the dignity of man's spirit."[57]

Rather than send its own recommendations to Congress, however, the administration chose to second the bill of Senator Edmund Muskie of Maine, introduced in 1963 in the eighty-eighth Congress and blocked by the National Association of Manufacturers and other industry groups and only feebly supported by the Kennedy White House. Now, in the new Congress, once more the measure ran into trouble, with Muskie's demand for strict federal standards the sticking point for conservatives. This time, however, administration pressure bulled the bill through with the Muskie demands intact though it took most of the session to accomplish it. On October 2 Johnson signed the Water Quality Act of 1965 with the grandiose announcement: "Today, we proclaim our refusal to be strangled by the wastes of civilization. Today we begin to be masters of our environment. . . ."[58]

LBJ seemed more concerned about clean water than clean air. Larry O'Brien believes that Johnson was personally offended by the pollution of the Potomac. He remembered outings on the *Sequoia* when the smell was so bad the president had to hold his nose. But more likely Johnson preferred clean water because it seemed harder politically to clamp down on the manufacturers of cars, the major source of air pollution, than on the despoilers of the nation's water. Besides, LBJ had a close political relationship with Henry Ford; was it smart to alienate him? The upshot was that the White House declined to take the initiative on clean air. Once more Senator Muskie led the way, introducing a bill early in the first session to establish car exhaust emissions standards and regulate fetid garbage dumps.

The White House was slow to support the Muskie bill. Appearing before the Maine senator's subcommittee, James Quigley of HEW asked for a delay until smog devices being tested in California proved their worth and the president had had a chance to meet with auto leaders to gain voluntary compliance. The liberal jeers that greeted the administration's solicitude for Detroit was a jolt. In a second appearance before the subcommittee, Quigley, newly briefed by the White House, endorsed the Muskie bill, though he asked for presidential leeway in determining exhaust standards. Suitably modified, the bill passed. Though a Johnny-come-lately, the president signed the Clean Air Act on October 20 with the ringing declaration that beginning that very day the nation was reversing humanity's age-old suicidal destruction of the environment.

Johnson's commitment to natural beauty was grounded in fundamental commitments. Besides the quality-of-life emphasis of his Great Society theme, he himself cherished the countryside. Raised in the scenic Hill Country of south-central Texas, he had created a Texas-style arcadia at his ranch on the Pedernales that brought him joy and solace. He invariably told visitors: "I'm going to show you the greatest treasure that no money can buy—sunset on the Pedernales."[59] He took a special interest in the roads people traveled as they traversed the countryside. As director of the Texas National Youth Administration in the 1930s he had helped create 250 roadside parks with picnic tables and rest room facilities where drivers could stop to refresh themselves.

The most potent force in the beautification movement, however, was Lady Bird Johnson. The First Lady had made it her signature "cause," but it was rooted in a long-standing interest in natural beauty. While the Johnsons resided in the White House she devoted her amazing energies to the outdoor landscaping of Washington and ending blight along the nation's highways. The historian Lewis Gould has concluded that "her commitment to the beautification of the environment was of lasting importance."[60]

The White House Conference on Natural Beauty held in May gave the administration's beautification program a needed kick. The conclave of architects, planners, and aesthetes recruited by the civic-minded Laurance Rockefeller proposed little to preserve and enhance the beauty of the nation that had not been heard in academic circles for a decade: urban planning, landmark inventories, landscaping of federal highways. But the meeting served as a showcase for these ideas and schemes and was, says Gould, a "catalytic event" that gave the Johnson beautification policies a "national impetus."[61] As Ada Louise Huxtable, architectural critic for *The New York Times,* noted at the conference's end, "Natural beauty now becomes a matter of public opinion and public action."[62]

The president appeared at the closing session of the conference and praised its work. To the applause of the thousand participants, he announced that he would shortly introduce four bills to check the despoiling of the American landscape. The first would require the states to prohibit billboards within one thousand feet of interstate and other federally subsidized ("primary") highways outside of commercial or industrial zones or lose some portion of federal aid for highway construction. Although the nation already had a billboard control law for the interstate system, passed in 1958, that paid states a small bonus if they limited outdoor signs, fewer than half had complied. The second would prohibit new junkyards within one thousand feet of federal highways and require that existing ones either be removed or screened by July 1, 1970. A third encouraged the states to use part of their federal highway aid to construct scenic secondary roads and access roads to beauty spots. A fourth required the states to earmark 3 percent of their federal highway subsidy to roadside landscaping.

The legislation that eventually emerged from Congress and was signed into law was a flawed act. If its purpose was to eliminate all visual blight along America's highways, it failed, as anyone traveling on the interstate system even today can see. At every interstate exit, commercial signs set on high pylons tell motorists of local gas stations, motels, restaurants, and assorted "attractions." And many of the lesser U.S.-subsidized "primary" roads of the country resemble strip malls or elongated shopping districts.

The bill as initially submitted was acceptable to the Outdoor Advertising Association of America, the lobbying group for billboard advertisers in the cities and towns. Formerly opposed to all restrictions on location of billboards, the association was now willing to accept confinement to designated business areas. But the bill ran into the adamant opposition of roadside motel, restaurant, gas station, and convenience store proprietors. Without billboards announcing their services, their livelihoods would be destroyed, they insisted. Allied with them were the Roadside Business Association, representing rural billboard owners, and a portion of organized labor that feared the loss of jobs among sign-painters and restaurant and motel workers. Since all highway beautification proposals targeted roadside junkyards for removal, junkyard owners naturally were determined members of the pro-billboard coalition.

Small business always caught the legislators' ears. But the congressmen also worried, noted Henry Hall Wilson, O'Brien's lobbyist in the House, "whether their people [constituents] will be irritated at not being able to learn twenty-five miles in advance what kind of restaurant or service station is down the road."[63] And the politicians themselves used roadside billboards extensively for their campaigns for office. But LBJ was resolved to fight aggressively. The president considered the bill a debt he owed Lady Bird and decreed that everyone on the White House staff must work to get it passed. The investment of so much political capital in the measure disturbed some White House advisers and a few referred facetiously to Lady Bird as "our 'beauty queen.'"[64] Lady Bird Johnson herself coaxed and lobbied to the point where some Republican congressmen felt annoyed at what they called "petticoat government."

The congressional hearings and debate on highway beautification pitted the extremes against both the administration and the Outdoor Advertising Association. The state "roadside councils," women's garden clubs, and the small cluster of other beautification groups preferred a federal law that would remove roadside blight completely and not reward the blight-makers with a penny of the taxpayers' money. The pro-billboard lobby, if it could not stop the bill entirely, wanted to maximize state control—the states were more pliable than Washington—and guarantee generous compensation for any billboards or junkyards removed. They also wanted the extended network of noninterstate, primary roads withdrawn from consideration. Congress was soon wrangling over who would pay for the programs and how: Would the money come from general treasury revenues? from an excise tax on automobiles? from the federal Highway Trust Fund? And what agency should designate commercial or industrial zones where the billboard exclusion might be suspended? Should existing signs and junkyards be removed under the government's police power or should owners of such eyesores be given "just compensation"? How far from the highways would signs be permitted? Should the scenic roads provision be retained or junked? The administration proved less adept on the beautification bill than on others. "I must inform you," O'Brien wrote the president in mid-September "that our performance on the Highway Beauty bill has fallen far below the standards of our usual work." Administration managers had, inadvertently, he wrote, created "confusion" and angered friendly senators and representatives.[65]

In the end Congress allowed the states to designate "commercially zoned" business areas where signs would be unaffected. The federal government would retain some say in determining these zones and could designate standards of size, lighting, and spacing of signs, but the new law exempted "on-premises" signs for restaurants and motels and authorized compensation to owners of billboards to be removed from places not authorized. Junkyards too could remain in areas of commercial and industrial use, and elsewhere their owners would be compensated for removing, landscaping, or screening them. The administration had proposed withholding all federal highway funds if the states did not comply with the guidelines on removal of blight, but Congress reduced this incentive to only 10 percent of the federal grant. Congress accepted in modified form the president's proposal for creating roadside rest stops and recreation areas, for landscaping, and for scenic property purchases, but it rejected his scheme to designate scenic roads for special protection.

With these and other modifications, the bill passed. At the East Room signing ceremony in late October Johnson, just back in harness after his gallbladder operation, announced that the law would "bring the wonders of nature back into our daily lives," after years when, "in our eagerness to expand and improve, we have relegated nature to a weekend role. . . ." He conceded that the bill did not "represent everything we wanted." But it was a "first step" and he believed the grandchildren of those in the room with him would some day "point with pride" to those who helped pass the bill.[66] He gave Lady Bird the first pen and a big kiss on the cheek.

Nothing embodied the soul of the Great Society more faithfully than the arts and humanities endowments. American painters, sculptors, writers, and musicians had tried to finagle public support of their vocations for generations. In Europe a tradition of royal patronage had survived the democratic revolutions of the nineteenth century, and orchestras, theatrical troupes, opera companies, as well as individual artists and performers, could count on public patronage. The United States had not been a total desert for cultural subsidies. Local governments had provided support for the arts through museums and libraries, and the states, through their public universities, had inevitably underwritten humanist scholars. And even the federal government had at times helped. Besides permitting individuals and corporations tax deductions for contributions to the arts and humanities, Washington had occasionally directly funded the finer things. No other activity of the New Deal had endeared it so much to historians, writers, and artists as the federal arts, federal writers', federal music, and federal theater projects under Harry Hopkins's Works Progress Administration, which kept scholars and creative men and women from starving during the Great Depression and allowed them to continue to practice their vocations.

But the WPA experience was short-lived. In 1943, in the middle of World War II, Roosevelt canceled all WPA programs. Thereafter, the direct federal contribution to high culture and humanistic studies in America was begrudging and remained so through the Truman-Eisenhower years. Once again, it was the New Frontier that would breathe new life into a previous era's liberal impulses.

The National Endowments for the Arts and the Humanities were not end products of a grassroots movement. Federal subsidies for the arts and scholarship had the backing of the learned societies, the universities, the performing arts professional troupes and organizations, and prominent painters, scholars, writers, choreographers, and musicians. Americans were better educated and better traveled than before 1945, no doubt, but the audiences for high culture were still relatively small. All told, they did not form a political mass large enough to impress the politicians. Not that the creative thinkers and performers were totally without political clout. In late 1963 Arthur Schlesinger, Jr., Kennedy's emissary to the intellectuals and academics, advised his new chief, Lyndon Johnson, to pursue JFK's recent cultural leads for political reasons. It could "strengthen the connections between the administration and the intellectual and artistic community," he wrote, and that was "something not to be dismissed when victory or defeat next fall will probably depend on who carries New York, Pennsylvania, California, Illinois, and Michigan," states presumably where the highly educated and culturally sophisticated could make some difference.[67]

Schlesinger's views notwithstanding, there is little reason to see the New Frontier-Great Society cultural thrust as a response primarily to constituent demands. In fact, closer to the grassroots was the reaction of one Paducah, Kentucky, woman to a proposal by Labor Secretary Arthur Goldberg in late 1961 that the federal government accept a modest responsibility for the arts. (The occasion was Goldberg's arbitration of a musicians' strike against the Metropolitan Opera in New York. The secretary's proposal for a subsidy for the arts was written by the ever-present Daniel Moynihan.)

"Is this Russia?" asked Mae Gough. "Why should Americans who detest Opera and Symphonie [sic] be forced to pay taxes to support them . . . ? If you and the Kennedy bunch like Opera, you support it. You can afford it. . . ."[68] Ms. Gough's populistic philistinism would be echoed in Congress each time the lawmakers considered the issue of subventing the arts.

In fact, once again, the impetus for new programs came from the top. Outside of Washington rich patrons of the arts like John D. Rockefeller III and bluebloods like August Heckscher were in the thick of the battle for federal arts subsidies. In government circles the dearest friends of performers and creators were people with patrician names—Livingston Biddle, Jr., Claiborne Pell, John Vliet Lindsay, and Ogden Reid. Linking arms with the bluebloods were culturally sophisticated Jews. Behind Johnson's cultural urges was his good friend Abe Fortas, a talented amateur violinist who was now a rich and influential Washington lawyer and one of the president's close advisers. Goldberg, Richard Goodwin, and Abe Ribicoff in the Kennedy administration were other agitators for federal support for the arts. In Congress, besides Pell, Reid, and Lindsay, there were senators Jacob Javits and Herbert Lehman, and congressmen Emanuel Celler and Adolph Sabath. Others, neither aristocrats nor Jews, supported the arts and humanities legislation, of course, but it clearly did not originate in a log cabin. Fortas frankly expressed the elitist view in a letter to Heckscher in January 1964. The arts as a field were of the "greatest importance," he noted. He doubted "its political importance," but he "couldn't care less." "It is nationally important and I am sure that is enough for you and me."[69]

Yet this position can be pushed too hard. Whatever class-derived values fueled their founders and however disproportionately the educated middle class benefited from their programs, in later years the endowments would often be defended on the grounds of their broad social utility. Each time federal subsidies for the arts and humanities came under attack, their champions would laud them for preventing crime and anomie, encouraging home craftsmanship, and keeping adolescents off the streets. In a democracy the *demos* must be served.

The long battle for federal arts funding finally yielded results in the Kennedy years. John Kennedy was not a culture enthusiast. His favorite reading matter besides history was James Bond thrillers and he was not much interested in either music or art. Jackie was a genuinely cultivated woman whose tastes impressed her husband. But beyond the influence of his wife and her friends, JFK recognized the decorative value of the arts to his administration.

The first signs of the new attitude came with the inauguration itself, when Kennedy invited 155 artists and scientists to Washington to witness the historic event. The poet Robert Frost graced the swearing-in ceremony at the Capitol. Thereafter, the president got good PR mileage from White House soirees featuring the cellist Pablo Casals and the violinist Isaac Stern. Kennedy, like others, also viewed culture as a weapon of Cold War rivalry. In the war for men's minds, the Soviet Union must not be allowed to portray the capitalist United States as a grossly materialist society indifferent to the finer things and incapable of encouraging beauty.

Still, Kennedy's cultural leadership was tentative and meager. In December 1961 he asked August Heckscher, a former newspaper editor and director of the Ford Foundation's Twentieth Century Fund, to join the administration as a part-time special consultant in the arts. In May 1963 Heckscher issued a report, *The Arts and the National Government,* which justified at least a marginal federal presence in the arts field on grounds of quality of life, international rivalry, and the economic importance of the arts. One of his recommendations was an advisory council on the arts in the White House. Bills for this purpose had come before Congress, sponsored by Representative Frank Thompson of New Jersey, but had been voted down like other Kennedy legislation. So, too, had bills sponsored by Javits and Senator Joseph Clark of Pennsylvania to provide actual subsidies, though modest ones, for the arts. In June 1963, having abandoned hope of congressional action, Kennedy established a White House arts advisory office by executive order.

Meanwhile the historians, anthropologists, linguists, musicologists, geographers, philosophers, and literary critics had begun to catch the subsidy fever. Their sparkplug was Barnaby Keeney, the enterprising president of Brown University in Providence, Rhode Island. A scholar of the Middle Ages, Keeney believed that Congress should support the humanities as it had the natural sciences since 1951, through the National Science Foundation. Prompted by Keeney, in early 1963 a group of scholarly organizations established the National Commission on the Humanities, which, in April 1964, issued its report calling for a grant-giving national humanities foundation modeled after its science predecessor.

By the time the report appeared, LBJ was ensconced in the Oval

Office and it was to him that the growing number of supplicants for federal largesse turned. Johnson had few interests beyond public affairs, a lack, White House counsel Harry McPherson later remarked, that had been "a major limitation of his."[70] His favorite piece of music, it was said, was the insipid pop tune "Raindrops Keep Falling on My Head." Even Lady Bird admitted that her husband had "no natural cultural bent."[71] But Johnson was surrounded by friends and aides who enjoyed and respected performers and scholars. Abe Fortas, his trusted legal adviser, was an especially important influence. LBJ also hoped to win the nation's culture leaders to his side. Schlesinger, the president could see, had a legitimate point: The writers, artists, and intellectuals spoke in a louder voice than their small numbers warranted. He was also moved, as in so much else, by the need to emulate, and even exceed, his predecessor. And then there was the logic of the Great Society vision. When Americans were finally freed of necessity by the power of modern technology, what would they do but embrace the grace notes of life?

Once in the Oval Office LBJ wasted little time making his cultural intentions known. In February 1964 he appointed Roger Stevens, a prominent New York businessman, Broadway impresario, and good friend of Fortas, to an arts commission advisory post established by Kennedy's executive order. During the summer, he endorsed the long-delayed legislation to establish the National Council on the Arts, to serve as an advice-giver to the government on artistic matters, and signed the bill on September 3. Later that month, while campaigning in Providence against Goldwater, he told a Brown University audience that he would propose a national humanities foundation to fund worthy humanities projects.

LBJ's efforts on behalf of culture continued after he swamped Goldwater in November. Using the gold-plated spade Franklin Roosevelt had wielded to break ground for the Jefferson Memorial, in December he inaugurated the long-delayed Kennedy Center for the Performing Arts. The law establishing the National Cultural Center was passed under Kennedy, but construction had not begun at his death. Congress renamed it the Kennedy Center in January 1964. Also in January, in his "State of the Union" address, LBJ endorsed a national foundation for the arts. "We must also recognize and encourage those who can be pathfinders for the Nation's imagination and understanding," he told the opening session of the Eighty-ninth Congress.[72] In fact, Johnson's inaugural outdid Kennedy's in its tribute to art and culture. Amid the more conventional hoopla there was a reception for the nation's prominent artists and writers hosted by Roger Stevens, a ballet performance by Margot Fonteyn and Rudolf Nureyev at the inaugural gala, and a concert by Isaac Stern and Van Cliburn with the National Symphony.

A raft of arts and humanities bills dropped into the legislative maw soon after the Eighty-ninth Congress began its work. Senator Ernest Gruening of Alaska and Congressman William Moorhead of Pennsylvania introduced bills to create a humanities foundation into which the arts could be tucked. Jacob Javits introduced a straight arts foundation bill. Pell, meanwhile, though his primary loyalty was to the arts, prepared two bills to give both endeavors equal status. His approach was seconded by Frank Thompson in the House. By late February joint House-Senate hearings were under way on the proposed cultural legislation, with Pell and Thompson sharing the chair.

The witnesses at these hearings were the predictable roster of impresarios, performers, academics, and leaders in the professional performers' unions. Barnaby Keeney talked loftily of "the lives and aspirations of men" and "our hopes, our imaginings, our beliefs."[73] Howard Mumford Jones of the Modern Language Association waved the ever-useful Cold War banner: If the United States was to "lead the world" it "must understand the world it wants to lead."[74] Andrew Biemiller, the chief Capitol Hill AFL-CIO lobbyist, weighed in for the bill because, he explained, he was concerned with the earnings and working conditions of people in the theater. Even conservative actor Charlton Heston endorsed the bill. He was a Jeffersonian, he said, and believed in limited government. But the proposal was a good one, especially if government support did not mandate government control.

On March 10 the administration cut through the confusion of voices by submitting its own bill, possibly authored by Fortas, to establish an independent agency to parallel the National Science Foundation. The bill's preamble rang the changes on the Great Society qualitative theme. During America's early history it "was largely engaged in mastering its physical environment. . . . [M]ore recently, advancing technology, defense, and space needs have put a claim on energies that might have gone into humane and artistic endeavors with the result that our social, moral, and aesthetic development has lagged behind our material advance." It was the "national interest that the social, cultural, and educational imbalance be redressed."[75]

The new agency would be called the National Foundation on the Arts and the Humanities. Under this umbrella title would be two separate "endowments," administered by national councils or boards of trustees and coordinated by a federal council on the arts and the humanities. The National Council of the Arts, established in 1964, would become the arts endowment's advisory body. The humanities equivalent would be a new body. The endowments would distribute federal grants to deserving individuals and organizations, including sums on a matching basis with private money. But after promising much, the preamble made clear the scheme was little more than a pilot. The total amount of funding proposed for the first year was puny: $20 million for both endowments.

In June, as the bill struggled in Congress, one sector of the artistic community perversely turned on the president. The occasion was the White House Festival of the Arts, conceived by Eric Goldman, Schlesinger's successor as intellectual-in-residence, to add luster to the administration by bringing prominent artists and writers to the White House for a day of readings and performance. Most of the artists and literati accepted the invitation and behaved politely, but several rebuffed the president churlishly. Poet Robert Lowell, in protest against the administration's Vietnam policy, publicly reneged on a promise to read his poetry. Dwight Macdonald, the *New Yorker* critic who had publicized Harrington's *The Other America* back in 1963, came to the festival but rudely circulated a petition among the guests praising Lowell's stand; twenty other cultural luminaries sent a telegram seconding Lowell.

Though angered and bruised by the snubs, the president continued to press for the arts and humanities bill. The cosmopolitan Senate proved accommodating, but the more parochial House balked. In September, as the session was winding down, the bill finally made it to the House floor after Johnson labeled it "must" legislation. There, Representative H. R. Gross of Iowa, hoping to laugh the bill to death, proposed to append basketball, golf, pinochle, and poker to the arts subsidy list. To clarify the bill's definition of "dance" he suggested adding the words: "including but not limited to the irregular and/or rhythmic contractions and coordinated relaxation of the serrati, obliques, and abdomnis recti group of muscles—accompanied by rotary undulations, tilts and turns timed with and attuned to the titillating and blended tones of synchronous woodwinds."[76] In effect, belly dancing. Frank Thompson retorted that the "gentleman from a farm state does not know the difference between a belly dancer and a bale of hay."[77]

The bill finally passed the House and Senate on September 16. Javits later claimed that it was the humanities constituency, with the higher-education lobby behind it, "that put the bill through. Otherwise, it could never have passed. . . ."[78] Each endowment got $5 million for fiscal 1967, and half of this diminished sum in turn was reserved to meet matching private grants. At most it was a beginning. Yet when Johnson signed it into law two weeks later in the standard Rose Garden ceremony, he announced that it would have "an unprecedented effect on the arts and humanities of our great nation."[79]

Without question, the first session of the Eighty-ninth Congress was the high water mark of the Great Society. As bill after bill slid through the legislative mill, the country marvelled. On August 10 *Times* columnist Tom Wicker noted, "They are rolling the bills out of Congress these days the way Detroit turns supersleek, souped-up autos off the assembly line. . . . The list of achievements is so long that it reads better than the legislative achievements of most two-term presidents."[80] The politicians echoed the journalists. Carl Albert, House majority leader, called it a legislative performance "far greater than Roosevelt's."[81] To Speaker John McCormack, it was the "Congress of fulfillment . . . of accomplished hopes . . . of realized dreams."[82] The president himself could not restrain his joy. The first session of the Eighty-ninth Congress, he said, had been "fabulous, the greatest in history. . . ."[83] As historian Paul Conkin has noted, LBJ had the same body-count view of legislative gains as his generals did of progress against the enemy in Vietnam. But the performance was truly extraordinary.

Yet Johnson was beginning to feel uneasy. On August 11 rioting broke out in Watts, a black neighborhood of Los Angeles, and at the end of five tumultuous days thirty-four people were dead, more than a thousand injured, and 977 buildings had been damaged or destroyed. The ghetto disturbances in New York and other Eastern cities the previous summer had not set off national alarms, but Watts touched a sensitive collective nerve. Johnson worried, and with reason, that such violence would undermine public support for social programs. Whatever the initial motivation behind them, several of the most visible Great Society programs, and certainly the War on Poverty, were beginning to seem disproportionately tailored to black Americans. Would the reservoir of goodwill among whites soon run dry?

And then there was Vietnam. Americans paid little attention to the ominously unfolding events in Southeast Asia until 1965. They seemed too remote and too confused for serious concern. In August 1964 Congress had given Johnson a blank check to use force against the Vietnam communists in the form of the Tonkin Gulf Resolution, but only two senators voted against it and none of the rest considered it a mandate to escalate American intervention. During the fall presidential contest, LBJ had carefully skirted the Vietnam problem lest he trump one of his high cards against Goldwater—that his opponent was a hothead and he a man of peace. But then in early 1965 the American stake in the bitter, dangerous fight in Vietnam finally registered on the public consciousness.

At the very time the administration was ticking off one legislative victory after another in the Eighty-ninth Congress, it was beginning to entangle itself and the nation fatally in Southeast Asia. In February 1965 Johnson launched Operation Rolling Thunder, a massive bombing campaign to check the North Vietnamese conquest of South Vietnam. In early March the first U.S. combat troops stepped ashore on the beach at Nam O. During the summer Johnson took the fatal step of ordering American soldiers to attack the communist enemy.

Resistance at home to American Vietnam policy began almost at once. On March 24 students and faculty held the first anti-Vietnam teach-in at Ann Arbor, the campus where the Great Society had been first proclaimed. Teach-ins soon erupted on campuses across the country, driving a wedge between the administration and the nation's intellectuals. It was this growing alienation that Johnson had first experienced at the White House Festival of the Arts. That May pacifists and the emerging New Left student movement held the first march on Washington to denounce U.S. involvement in Southeast Asia.

Johnson knew, very early in the game, that the war seriously threatened his Great Society. Charles Haar, the Harvard law professor who had headed the task force on beautification, remembered coming to Washington in June 1965 for a White House stag dinner arranged by Moyers and Goodwin for the chairmen of the first round of Johnson task forces. June 1965 was perhaps the Great Society's apex and the mood was exultant. Over steak and lobster tails, the chairmen took turns describing the wonderful legislative accomplishments of the task forces. In the midst of the bibulous self-congratulation, the president himself walked in. Johnson had not had dinner and accepted some of the food, including a large helping of vanilla ice cream. He praised the group for their good work and then launched into a monologue on Vietnam. He had consulted all the foreign policy experts, including Dwight Eisenhower, and they had told him that the United States must not abandon its commitments in Southeast Asia. But he feared the effects on the Great Society. World War I had eclipsed Woodrow Wilson's New Freedom. World War II had aborted the New Deal. "I don't want that to happen to the Great Society," Haar remembered the president saying. "I don't want to get involved in a war. I don't want to get involved in entanglements abroad. We've got here the makings of the greatest people, the greatest country. We have your programs. We'll develop more programs, and I don't want that to happen."[84]

As we know Johnson's fears were prescient. But in June 1965 most knowledgeable Americans would surely have considered them misplaced. The president and his policies were wildly popular. Polls in the fall of 1965, as the senators and representatives left for home at session's end, showed that no president in three decades enjoyed such consistently strong support from all major segments of the population.

Meanwhile, field reports on the War on Poverty were arriving at OEO Washington headquarters and appearing in readers' morning newspapers. The Great Society was about to stall.

FOUR

The Culture of Poverty

LYNDON JOHNSON had every reason to rejoice as Congress adjourned. The first session of the Eighty-ninth had given him a spectacular record of achievement, even by the measure of his revered predecessor, Franklin Roosevelt. But the president, a natural pessimist, was not satisfied. By the end of the summer, he later wrote, he began "to sense a shift in the winds." Congressional leaders were telling him that the country "needed time to catch its breath . . . to consolidate and digest the laws we had already passed." In his memoirs Johnson would point to the defeat in September of his bill to provide home rule to Washington, D.C., as a turning point.[1] He clearly was exaggerating. The bill was not an indispensable component of the Great Society. Yet its defeat did hint at trouble ahead for the larger program. Designed to give some political autonomy to the residents of the District of Columbia, until now ruled entirely by Congress almost as a colony, the bill ran into a wall of racial fears. Washington was already a predominantly black city and many members of Congress, including prominent Southern Democrats, distrusted its capacity for self-government.

The defeat of home rule for the District of Columbia reflected a growing public distrust of local autonomy generally, and as expressed in heavily black communities specifically. Even as the Great Society bills rolled off the assembly line, the problems of the War on Poverty and particularly its community action pro-

grams began to trouble mainstream white Americans and drain
the pool of goodwill that had sustained the president's programs.
By the time Congress recessed for the year-end holidays, a part of
the middle-class public had turned sour on the poor and lost faith
in the campaign to rescue them.

The bill creating the Office of Economic Opportunity had passed
in late August 1964 but the first grants to poverty programs were
delayed until after the presidential election. Not until the votes
were all counted did OEO begin to function out of headquarters,
in a decrepit, soon-to-be-demolished hotel near downtown Washington. (OEO soon moved to new offices at 19th and M Street,
also in downtown Washington.)

Those first months pulsed with enthusiasm and hope. The new
agency attracted some of the country's brightest young lawyers,
economists, journalists, and social workers. Most believed they
could make society juster and more compassionate. Shriver himself was one of the enthusiasts. Born into an old Maryland family,
he was a Catholic liberal whose moral guide was *Quadresimo Anno,*
Pius XI's encyclical condemning economic inequality and praising social reform. His wife, Eunice, was herself a social activist with
a particular interest in juvenile delinquency and mental retarda-
tion. The two together had created the Special Olympics for physically handicapped athletes. Shriver was also a dapper charmer
and a skilled player of the Washington political game. Though a
Kennedy only by marriage, he shared with the clan an ironic sense
of humor and a respect for toughness. His Peace Corps office
door carried signs saying NICE GUYS FINISH LAST and GOOD GUYS DON'T
WIN BALL GAMES. He had new signs for his office at OEO: BRING ME
ONLY BAD NEWS; GOOD NEWS ONLY WEAKENS ME.[2] He would need to be
strong in the months ahead.

Shriver was a work addict. When an associate suggested a morning meeting at "about ten," he responded: "By ten o'clock the
day is half over."[3] The directorship of the Peace Corps, a post he
would not surrender until January 1966, further burdened his
strenuous days. The Economic Opportunity Act had conferred
unusually broad powers on a federal agency. Shriver was in fact a
"czar," to use the media phrase, who could shuffle money and
resources from program to program almost without accountability. As he would later admit: "There are very few occasions in

government history where any administrator of a program had the kind of freedom and power I had at OEO."[4] That power was not always well deployed. Wilbur Cohen called Shriver a poor administrator. Cohen undoubtedly reflected Health, Education, and Welfare's chagrin at being excluded from a major role in the War on Poverty, but events would confirm his estimate.

From the outset budget constraints quickened the poverty warriors' sense of urgency. The bill creating the Office of Economic Opportunity had appropriated $1.5 billion. Congress, however, had authorized only $800 million to spend for fiscal 1965. Community action programs were to get $250 million, all of it to be spent by June 30, 1965. With so much to do it should have been easy to find ways to spend the money, but formulating and administering poverty programs were daunting problems. For a decade or more, educators, social workers, economists, and sociologists had been churning out ideas about poverty and the poor. But no one knew what really worked. How to choose winning programs and avoid losers would engage the attention of OEO administrators for the next five years.

The question of community action was particularly baffling. Congress had mandated "maximum feasible participation" by the community in the planning, coordination, and administration of local antipoverty programs, whether funded by cities, states, or the federal government. But what did this mean? Some antipoverty warriors considered the community action agencies (CAA's) simply tools for distributing largesse to clients. William Capron, one of the War on Poverty planners, has said that he and his colleagues saw community action primarily as "a device for focusing federal dollars and getting the right mix. . . ."[5] The plans themselves, in this view, would originate with the OEO officials in Washington, the experts and skilled administrators. This was the traditional paternalism of old-fashioned "social work" (it has been called the "social service model") and it was deeply embedded in the professional culture.[6] Conveying the full flavor of this response, one New York City poverty administrator remarked: "You can't go to a street corner with a pad and a pencil and tell the poor to write you an anti-poverty program. They wouldn't know how."[7]

But initially this was not the dominant view within OEO itself. Most agency officials sincerely believed that community action groups should both plan and implement programs. Within the agency, moreover, there was a circle of poverty warriors with a broader objective. Richard Boone, Shriver's choice to head community action planning and policy, was the former Kennedy juvenile delinquency aide and community action activist who had transfused his vision into the War on Poverty task force. The OEO inspector general was William Haddad, a former Peace Corps executive, journalist, and leader of the Tammany-challenging New York Reform Democrats. Both men saw CAP as the vehicle of empowerment, as a device to challenge local, entrenched "establishments" even if they were controlled by liberal Democrats. Beyond this they envisioned a transformed society with fewer disparities of wealth and poverty. Robert Levine, a historian of the War on Poverty, discreetly calls them and their circle "theoreticians and ideologues" whose "primary solution was political and quasi-political organization of the poor . . . through vigorous use of the participation language in order to change various political balances."[8]

Above them, initially, in the chain of command, as OEO's CAP division head, was Jack Conway of the AFL-CIO Industrial Union Department, an associate of Walter Reuther. Conway became acting head of the Community Action Program in October. Six months later, in May 1965, although reluctant to take the job he considered rightly Yarmolinsky's, he was made deputy director of OEO, Shriver's second in command. Conway's replacement at CAP was Theodore Berry, a soft-spoken black Kentuckian and a former vice mayor of Cincinnati, who shared the views of Boone, Haddad, Edgar May, Edgar Cahn, Sanford Kravitz, and the other "theoreticians." Some of the other early administrators included Otis Singletary, an academic historian and college official, who was appointed head of the Job Corps, and Glenn Ferguson, an original member of the poverty task force, who became head of VISTA.

But in the selection of programs and the allocation of money and energies, the bureaucrats would not be completely free agents. The public was watching closely, with high expectations, and would pounce on mistakes. And there were the politicians. The poverty war was almost a billion dollars of found money. Could the pols resist treating it as a giant pork barrel? And the poor themselves? In the black community, consciousness and militancy were rising by the week. Many black activists had come to see standard government benefit programs as "welfare colonialism" —top-down largesse conferred by whites on "natives" in the slums.[9] How would they respond to the new programs? Would the militants sit by and let others have a free hand?

The idealistic Boone-Haddad-Kravitz circle quickly learned that the poor were not self-starters. Community action groups were often confused, ill-informed, and slow to act. OEO mailed out hundreds of brochures advertising the new federal programs and urging local communities to establish city-wide community action boards to prepare proposals and forward them to Washington. The responses dribbled in so slowly that OEO had to devise its own "demonstration" programs and assign these to local governments and community action agencies without prior approval. Later, OEO would also establish "national emphasis programs" that it offered to community action agencies like prepackaged meat cuts at the supermarket. However effective in getting things moving, these schemes were top-down arrangements that subverted the empowerment goal the theoreticians valued. But if national emphasis programs undercut "power to the people" in principle, they retained the potential for social militancy and attacks on the social order.

The first community action city-wide boards were thrown together by local officials and inevitably represented the old order. In October 1964, with OEO scarcely past the start-up phase, Philadelphia mayor James Tate submitted an antipoverty plan written entirely by city officials. The plan designated as the city's community action board an existing Ford Foundation anti-delinquency panel that critics considered bureaucratically musclebound and remote from its clients. In January he appointed a new Philadelphia antipoverty action committee consisting of handpicked supporters plus a selection of businessmen, civil leaders, and social workers. Cleveland, New York, Los Angeles, and San Francisco soon repeated the Philadelphia performance—mayor-appointed boards composed of all the usual worthies: clergymen, social workers, civic-minded ladies, academics, and local politicos— while folk claiming to be closer to the grassroots remained outside, looking in.

A related problem emerged in the South. In Dixie whites were reluctant to allow blacks proportionate representation on community action bodies. In Sumter County, Alabama, for example, where blacks outnumbered whites more than three to one, the Area 14 Community Action Committee was composed of four whites and two blacks. The whites were all supporters of segregationist governor George Wallace, while the blacks did not even live in the district. This arrangement, claimed the Reverend R. H. Upton, head of the Sumter County Movement for Human Rights, "controverts the philosophy of the Economic Opportunity Act and the war against poverty."[10] In Memphis, the mayor and city commission refused to admit any blacks to the CAP committee despite the intervention of OEO's Southeastern regional director.

Mobilization for Youth in lower Manhattan mounted the first local community challenge to political establishments and middle-class sensibilities. As we saw, MFY was the very inspiration for Shriver's community action programs, but it was also a foretaste of community action's administrative and political troubles around the nation.

Just as Congress was putting the finishing touches on the War on Poverty bill, MFY became a public relations disaster. On August 16, the front-page headline of the Sunday New York *Daily News* blared: YOUTH AGENCY EYED FOR REDS. The lead story below the headline charged that MFY was under investigation by federal and city agencies as "a suspected Red honeycomb for leftists." Communists and assorted radicals "by the score" had "infiltrated" Mobilization and had "diverted its funds . . . to disruptive agitation."[11] The article, and four others that followed during the week, charged that MFY was guilty of serious financial irregularities, that it was affiliated with rent-strike radical Jesse Gray, and that it had helped foment that bitter Harlem anti-police riot in July 1964. These claims were soon seconded by the New York City Council president, Paul Screvane, an ambitious politician eager to run for mayor.

The *News* spoke with the voice of blue-collar New York at its mean-spirited worst. Defiantly anti-intellectual, anti-elitist, and antiliberal, it was the Archie Bunker of New York journalism before that TV character had been created. An investigation by the Department of Justice of Communist Party infiltration found the charges exaggerated. And several of the *News*'s specific claims—

that rent-strike leader Jesse Gray had a direct telephone line to MFY headquarters, for example, and that MFY mimeograph machines had printed up inflammatory handbills during the 1964 Harlem riot—were flatly untrue. This did not mean, however, that many MFY staffers were not radical, politically and ideologically, with views of drastic social change that went beyond the liberal consensus. Joseph Helfgot, a trained social scientist, believes that MFY attracted a "select" leftist segment of the social worker population, including "ex-communists" and socialists.[12] However garbled the message, the *News* did get right the politicization and radicalization of MFY programs and conveyed the message effectively to the blue-collar voter public.

Antipoverty officials defended Mobilization. David Hackett, the father of community action, told the New York *World-Telegram and Sun* that "all the information we have indicates that Mobilization for Youth . . . is doing an exceptional job."[13] But the bad publicity undoubtedly undermined Washington's support of MFY. Hackett himself would not stay around for long to fight for the project. His patron, Robert Kennedy, was preparing to quit the Justice Department to run for the Senate from New York, and Hackett intended to accompany him. And the departing attorney general himself felt no compelling desire to entangle himself in the sticky MFY spiderweb just as he was about to face the voters of the Empire State. During the fall 1964 election campaign Bobby managed to avoid the MFY issue entirely. Johnson had even less incentive to support the controversial New York program. In December, after passage of EOA, the president announced that another agency, the city's Antipoverty Operation's Board, would be receiving a $5 million grant under the War on Poverty program. In late 1965, after a period of "reappraisal and search for new directions,"[14] MFY regained federal support but only by ejecting most of the radicals and changing its strategy. On the occasion of a HEW grant of $600,000 in October 1965, Marilyn Bibb, MFY's new community development chief, described the process coyly as "moving to the second level," but admitted that it meant abandoning "the big dramatic things that can rally people."[15]

The poverty warriors in Washington were lucky that MFY attracted little attention outside New York; its doings would have given conservatives a potent weapon against the Economic Opportunity Act as the bill worked its way through Congress. But in fact, the New York experience would be reprised more than once under OEO's own auspices during 1965, and the results would drain off much of the poverty program's support and goodwill.

One of the most damaging blows to public support of the War on Poverty was the disastrous Syracuse community action experiment launched in February 1965. Ironically, the Syracuse program was headed by a mayor—Republican William Walsh—who had testified in favor of EOA during the congressional hearings preceding passage of the act. Walsh, a former social worker, was not your ordinary local Republican functionary. The mayor was an early enthusiast for the juvenile delinquency project of the Kennedy administration and, at the time of the hearings, had just submitted a grant proposal to the President's Committee on Juvenile Delinquency for his Mayor's Commission on Youth. In his testimony, he told the House committee that he endorsed "the philosophy that the people who are served by programs must be involved in their planning and development."[16] Yet within a year the city's poverty program would transmogrify into a campaign by militants to take power from the city's elected authorities.

The Syracuse antipoverty program began as an OEO demonstration project launched by Sanford Kravitz. The $314,000 grant went to Syracuse University for funding the Syracuse Community Development Association project to teach community members techniques for organizing the poor.

Two separate streams of sixties insurgency came together in the Syracuse project. Most of the nineteen "organizers" the association recruited were black militants who brought to the city the lessons they had learned in Birmingham and Selma. Their governing axiom was that the elected officials of a community were immovable defenders of the status quo and enemies of the poor. What affected the program even more was the philosophy of Saul Alinsky, the people-power prophet, hired as a consultant to the Syracuse Community Development Center.

Alinsky combined an Old Testament prophetic streak with a radical egalitarianism and faith in community competence absorbed at the University of Chicago. He had started out as a criminologist for the state of Illinois but left that depressing field in the 1930s to rally working-class urbanites against the political and social status quo. In 1960 he moved his staff and his principles into Chicago's black Woodlawn slum, where TWO (The Woodlawn Organization) became the prototype of militant grassroots organizing. He often condensed his formula for social change into the slogan "To rub raw the sores of discontent."[17] He was soon advertising his approach as the model for social change and proffering his services as a professional agitator. Alinsky and his staff, when invited and suitably funded, would sweep into a community ripe for rebellion and teach it how to challenge city hall and the business establishment to reduce the disparities of wealth and power.

Alinsky was hired by Warren Haggstrom, a Syracuse social work professor who represented the new egalitarianism blowing through the profession. As Haggstrom explained it, the poor needed more than services. They needed to be pulled "into the mainstream of the community" and that required "a certain level of power."[18] The university paid Alinsky $10,000 for forty-eight visits to Syracuse to teach his techniques of community challenge and insurgency.

The project's unfolding was utterly predictable. Association-trained organizers mounted sit-ins, set up picket lines, and launched mass rallies to protest everything from poor garbage collection and greedy landlords to unfair welfare procedures. They conducted a voter registration drive in the ghetto to ensure that the city's poor became a political force to reckon with. Their goals were broader than the immediate aims of these campaigns, however. By this point in the decade an emerging New Left had appeared to challenge a society it saw as formally democratic but in reality hierarchical and unequal. The weapon to be wielded was "participatory democracy," grassroots involvement of ordinary men and women in the issues that affected their lives. As one Syracuse organizer, William Douglas Smith, a young civil rights worker from Minneapolis, asserted: "This is where the promise of democracy will be fulfilled. We must help the poor realize that they have power and they can use it."[19]

The reaction was also predictable. Local officials and elites concluded that the federal government, through the War on Poverty, was making gratuitous trouble for the worthy people whom Syracusans had legally chosen to lead them. Up for reelection that fall, Walsh saw the local CAP's voter registration drive as aimed at defeating him personally. (In fact, Walsh's reelection in November 1965 was quite possibly *because* of the attacks of antipoverty groups on him—an instance of emerging "white backlash.") But he also resented OEO's disregard of the city's official community action board, the Crusade for Opportunity. "I'm not going to take this lying down," he told a representative of OEO.[20] Beyond this, he and other Syracuse officials felt, with justification, that a federally funded training program was being used as an instrument of radical indoctrination. "We are experiencing a class struggle in the traditional Karl Marx style in Syracuse," declared the Syracuse Housing Authority director, "and I do not like it."[21]

Newark would present an especially direct case of the New Left's infiltration of OEO community action. Students for a Democratic Society (SDS), the flagship of the student New Left, had established the Newark Community Union Project (NCUP) in the summer of 1964 as part of the Economic Research and Action Project (ERAP). ERAP expressed the quest by the first generation of student radicals for a field of adult activism once college was past, and was a version of the "back-to-the-people" urge that had inspired privileged middle-class youths in the past. Under ERAP, young, post-college radicals would live in the poor urban neighborhoods and help fan the grievances against the oppressive establishments that denied the poor justice and a fair share of worldly goods. In all, SDS established a dozen ERAP projects during 1964–65 in working-class neighborhoods in towns and cities predominantly in the East and Midwest.

The founders of the Newark Community Union Project were Carl Whitman, a Swarthmore graduate, and Tom Hayden, formerly editor of the undergraduate *Michigan Daily* and chief author of SDS's founding document, the Port Huron Statement. In June 1964 twelve full-time ERAP workers set up shop in a converted store at 247 Peshine Avenue and prepared to change the lives of the local residents. In collaboration with the Clinton Hill Neighborhood Association, they were soon promoting rent strikes, demanding improved city welfare services, and organizing neighborhood clean-up campaigns. Joined by a core of fifty local people, the students distributed handbills and picketed landlords, welfare agencies, a department store, and police headquarters to demand racial justice and improved conditions for the poor. Meanwhile, the more scholarly ERAPers wrote a study dissecting the Newark "power structure" to reveal the inadequacies of the city's liberal leaders. The only significant "response by this Northern liberal city to the problems of Negro poverty," this paper concluded, was the neighborhood-wrecking process of "urban renewal."[22]

The New Left leaders never bought the War on Poverty as a serious effort to equalize power and wealth in the United States. Hayden, for one, would charge that it was all flash and no substance. But that did not prevent NCUP from agreeing to sponsor VISTA in Newark in 1965 and 1966 or keep Hayden from taking per diem expense money to come to Washington to explain the Newark project to the OEO headquarters staff.

SDS's involvement with VISTA in Newark created problems for OEO. Hugh Addonizio, the last of the city's white mayors, considered NCUP a nest of dangerous Marxists and the source of restlessness in the city's black ghetto. When the Newark project leaders agreed to serve as local sponsor of the storefront VISTA office, as required by OEO rules, the mayor protested loudly. OEO did not seem to take the mayor seriously, or at least did not cut SDS off from access to federal largesse. In 1966 and 1967 several ERAPers served as well-paid consultants to VISTA.

Through the spring and into the fall of 1965, troubles between the mayors and the militants involved in community action programs continued to bubble up. In San Francisco, Citizens United Against Poverty, formed at the Macedonia Missionary Baptist Church by young civil rights militants, fought with Mayor John Shelley, a loyal Democrat, over control of OEO funds. The Citizens United Against Poverty leaders rejected the mayor's appointed community action board, the Economic Opportunity Council, even though blacks were well represented on its executive committee, and insisted that full power over the community action programs be lodged with five local target-area advisory boards chosen by the people of the neighborhoods. Shelley soon lost control of the OEO programs to the target-area activists, whose focus was on "area development," the euphemism for organizing the poor to challenge local institutions.

In Chicago, a more forceful mayor, Richard Daley, the legendary Democratic boss who saved Illinois for JFK in 1960, squelched the grassroots revolt. When challenged by the Reverend Lynward Stevenson, the black Baptist minister who headed Alinsky's Woodlawn Organization, Daley and his chief antipoverty lieutenant, Deton Brooks, dug in. They denied Stevenson's request for $225,000 from OEO, and insisted that the Committee on Urban

Opportunity, their own community action agency, get the money instead. Appearing before the House Education and Labor Committee in mid-April, Stevenson charged that the membership of Brooks's community action agency "reads like the fund-raising list of the Democratic party." In Chicago, he announced, "There is no war against poverty. There is only more of the ancient, galling war against the poor."[23] Chicago's poor were being pushed out of the program by "men who drive Cadillacs, eat three-inch steaks, and sip champagne at luncheon meetings."[24] In the end, Daley won. Chicago became the most notable example of a mayor-controlled poverty program.

Viewed exclusively as a services delivery program, the Chicago community action program was a decided success. Chicago's community action board dispensed more than twice as much federal money to each poor family as New York's or Philadelphia's. Chicago also opened service centers for the poor more quickly than other cities and had a better record of honesty in handling funds. Yet the exclusion of local leaders from the decision-making process and the disregard of "participation" outraged the community empowerment forces. It was the Chicago experience that goaded Alinsky, still close to Woodlawn, to call the poverty program in general a massive relief program for the "welfare industry." It was a "macabre masquerade," he charged, and "a prize piece of political pornography."[25] Neither Shriver nor the mayors would ever forgive Alinsky for his harsh remark.

The struggles between the mayors and local city groups on the margins for money and patronage was no surprise. In the past, cities' services—police, fire, sanitation, schools—had provided jobs and income for Irish, Germans, Italians, Jews, Poles, and other nineteenth- and early twentieth-century immigrants. The immigrant newcomers often had to shake the urban machines hard to detach these plums from the tree. Efficiency, competence, and respectable accounting procedures often went by the board. For many of these people, city jobs were the surest route to middle-class respectability—and escape from the ghetto. Syndicated columnist Art Buchwald, writing in the early days of OEO, imagined asking a "local" what would be the first thing he would do if he got a paying job as a community action board member. The man replies: "Why, move out of the neighborhood, of course."[26]

After 1964, the local poverty agencies became patronage bonanzas for blacks, Latinos, and other groups new to the cities, with the process often following the same messy, morally dubious trajectory as the patronage scrambles of the past. For a circle of ambitious and assertive blacks and Latino ethnics, the community action boards and target area committees and directorships, as well as the poverty program as a whole, would be a cornucopia. Federal salaries, even under EOA, were far better than those most blacks earned, and for many strivers in the minority communities, getting on the War on Poverty payroll was the fastest way out of poverty. At the top, salaries often seemed extravagant by the standards of the day. Heads of local community action boards initially earned as much as $25,000 a year, more than many local mayors, a situation that aroused wide resentment. And these salaries soaked up a large part of all War on Poverty money. Of $8 million spent by Crusade for Opportunity in Syracuse, by mid-1967 $7 million had been expended for salaries. Worse, in several of the more militant community action agencies, flagrant rip-off artists used their power and influence to create political operations that made the old-time urban machines at times seem like the League of Women Voters. Wilfred Ussery in San Francisco, Boisfeuillet Jones in Atlanta, Livingston Wingate in New York, and their equivalents elsewhere treated the money coming from Washington as slush funds to be used for political advantage. That secure middle-class folk in the 1960s would bridle at this display was not surprising; their predecessors had scorned the patronage policies of the big-city white ethnic machines of the Gilded Age and the early twentieth century. And clearly, in both eras, xenophobia, bigotry, and class resentment would infuse their responses.

And below this top level were hustlers who used outright intimidation for personal gain. In the Bay Area, neighborhood con artists played like virtuosi on white guilt and middle-class dread to extort payoffs and de facto bribes from OEO officials. As one of them described the technique: "You made the white man quake. You brought *fear* into his face."[27] Unquestionably, some of these routines were purely larcenous. But they often expressed the urge for psychic revenge against "the man." Louis Zurcher reports that minority-member target-neighborhood committees in Topeka, until they gained confidence in the white officials of the city community action board, regularly razzed them.[28]

No antipoverty program, however, reached the intimidation level of Harlem's HARYOU-ACT during the summer of 1965. Painstakingly planned by the distinguished black psychologist Kenneth Clark, Harlem Youth Opportunities Unlimited, like Mobilization for Youth, both predated the War on Poverty and was funded initially by a federal juvenile delinquency grant. For a time HARYOU competed with ACT (Associated Community Teams), a program under the control of Harlem's erratic Adam Clayton Powell. But then, unable to resist the powerful New York congressman, Clark quit and HARYOU merged with ACT under Powell's protégé, Livingston Wingate, a vigorous but unsystematic man with more than a little of Powell's flamboyant attributes. (At least one author absolves Powell of the charge of outrageous takeover of HARYOU. Clark, he says, in effect surrendered HARYOU-ACT to powell.)[29] The combined organizations, HARYOU-ACT, soon became the Harlem agency administering money derived simultaneously from the juvenile delinquency, Neighborhood Youth Corps, and Manpower Development Act programs.

Several programs proposed in the HARYOU founding document *were* implemented. HARYOU established an afterschool study program for Harlem students and a narcotics institute to deal with the community's drug problem. It also set up the Cadet Corps, where Harlem youths who often got into trouble could strut their proud young male stuff without seriously damaging the social fabric.

Under Wingate, however, only a few of Kenneth Clark's original projects got going. Harlem Youth Enterprises, intended to create a number of youth businesses, collapsed along with Clark's schemes to improve Harlem schools and for a community action institute. Wingate, in fact, was as unwilling to share power with "the community" as Mayor Daley, and HARYOU shied away from community action.

Like many War on Poverty agencies, HARYOU-ACT was poorly administered. Clark described it as beset with "chaos and confusion" and called it a perversion of the agency he had planned.[30] To be fair, Clark was out of touch with Harlem. A celebrity since the Supreme Court had accepted his argument in the landmark *Brown* v. *Board of Education* decision that segregation was psychologically damaging to black children, he had moved from Harlem to the upper-middle-class community of Hastings-on-Hudson in

Westchester County. He was also a proud and touchy man who deeply resented the takeover of his creation by Powell and his associates. But many knowledgeable observers besides Clark had serious doubts about HARYOU-ACT. The organization, they said, was grossly top-heavy, with too many well-paid administrators who siphoned off funds that should have gone for the designated community beneficiaries. According to the black-run *Amsterdam News,* almost forty staffers were paid more than $10,000 a year, a generous salary for that time, and more than 80 percent of the money the organization received from the federal government went for salaries.

All this would have attracted only marginal public attention if not for Project Uplift during the summer of 1965. The events that took place during that steamy season in Harlem as part of Project Uplift seem to confirm the "bribe" formula for explaining the War on Poverty—that it was a payoff to smother rebellion in the ghettos. The truth, however, is more complicated. President Johnson, to be sure, wanted a cool summer in 1965 after the hot season of the year before and ordered Vice President Humphrey to channel federal funds into cities likely to explode during the sultry weeks ahead. But it was Wingate, the administrator from the Harlem community itself, rather than OEO officials in Washington, who initiated the actual payout, and it was as much a rakeoff to local poverty officials as a safety-valve for ghetto riot.

Livingston Wingate was a man of vivid imagination. According to his later account, Harlem was under siege by restless juveniles, ranging in age from thirteen to twenty-one, organized as the Five Percenters. Their name supposedly derived from Malcolm X and the Black Muslims, who identified 85 percent of American blacks as cattle and 10 percent more as "Uncle Toms." Only a remnant, 5 percent, were true black loyalists and only they knew how to deal properly with both whites and the black sellouts. In fact, though they professed to be inspired by black nationalist teachings, the Five Percenters seemed undistinguishable from plain hoodlums. According to one report, respectable Harlemites considered them delinquents inspired by a "hate philosophy" against both whites and middle-class blacks.[31]

These Five Percenters, according to Wingate, threatened to set off an armed summer uprising in Harlem that would have made Watts, the Los Angeles explosion, look like a garden party. The desperate youths "were prepared to die" if things did not improve in Harlem.[32] To head off trouble, by July 1 Wingate had put four thousand youngsters and a staff of five hundred on the HARYOU-ACT payroll. The jobs qualified as work-skill upgrading, but by Wingate's admission, they were just "blind-alley jobs."[33] If its purpose was to calm the community, the scheme was badly flawed. Marauding gangs, impatient with delays in getting their checks, threatened HARYOU-ACT itself, and Wingate had to hire armed guards to protect his offices at the cost of $15,000 a week.

Little of this came out until the fall, when Wingate's administrative competence came under attack and a number of investigations of graft and fraud were in progress. Wingate then told reporters that he had narrowly saved the city from destruction. The uproar was thunderous. Kenneth Clark claimed Wingate was using "black McCarthyism." His story of the Five Percenters was "fantastic, dangerous, irresponsible."[34] Other prominent Harlemites expressed doubt that the city had ever been on the verge of violent rebellion: Wingate had made most of it up to protect his reputation. In the end OEO suspended him without pay, only to reinstate him in the spring of 1966.

Militancy within community action programs was not confined to African-Americans. In San Francisco, the Mission Area Community Action Board, a target area group, became a battlefield between Mexican-Americans and blacks over hiring aides and professionals, with ethnicity a major qualification for employment. In California's Santa Clara County in early 1966, Mexican-Americans ousted Arthur Potts, the Anglo executive director of the county Economic Opportunity Commission, whom they resented as an outsider.

Some community action projects were dogged by charges of outright fraud. There is evidence that some HARYOU-ACT officials took large kickbacks from youths hired for the summer's Project Uplift. A neighborhood poverty leader in Trenton, New Jersey, confessed to Gregory Farrell, director of the local community action board, that he had demanded a payoff to authorize a neighborhood poverty center because he was "sure somebody was gettin' a nice rakeoff on rentin' that old department store," and he "figured [he] might as well get somethin' out of it too."[35]

If the militants had confined themselves to a little blackmail and a modest level of extortion, they might have escaped the wrath of the mainstream media and the middle-class white public. But by 1965 they were beginning to turn against the nonviolent, assimilationist credo of the civil rights movement—"black and white together"—replacing it with a separatist, black-power ideology that demonized white America and seemed to threaten savage social upheaval. One of the worst offenses of HARYOU-ACT against moderate sensibilities was funding of the Black Arts Repertory Theater School, forum of the militant playwright Imamu Baraka—at this point still known as LeRoi Jones. Founded in April 1965, the school received $40,000 of federal aid to put on antiwhite plays during the summer. One of these, *Jello,* depicted Rochester, the feckless black valet of Jack Benny's popular TV show, rebelling against his subservient role and killing all his white "oppressors," including Benny. That fall the group, still receiving money from HARYOU-ACT, heckled Abe Beame, the Democratic candidate for mayor, while he and Congressman Powell were on a walking tour through Harlem. When a reporter interviewed Jones, the slight, bearded playwright told it like it was: "There are a lot of people in black nations all over the world who want to kill white people," he opined. "Some of them are in Africa, and some of them are . . . here."[36]

It is important to see the community action program in its entirety. In the first four years of EOA, more than a thousand community action boards came into existence. Most of them were not committed to social apocalypse, racial catharsis, or revolutionary seizure of power. Instead, they were primarily distributors of government funds and services, as some had hoped and others had feared. And their harmonious relationship with local elected officials kept them out of the headlines even in their own locales.

An illustrative case both of goodwill and the difficulty of reconciling racial resentments is Topeka, a small city with a low poverty rate and a small minority population. If any city could be considered typically American, it was this community of 125,000 on the windy Kansas plains. The Topeka Welfare Planning Council categorically rejected the Alinsky confrontation model for community action when it developed its antipoverty plan under a grant by OEO. But it also avoided running the program from the mayor's office. The Economic Opportunity Board of Shawnee County, the city's overall antipoverty agency, adopted what its historian calls the "overlap" model of community action. As he notes, the Alinsky model assumed a zero-sum game: The poor could increase their power only at the expense of the privileged. The overlap model assumed "a community to be a relatively open power-system" and that authority did not "necessarily have to be taken from the Establishment to empower the poor."[37] According to the director of the city poverty board, the key words for the "Topeka Plan" would be "Compromise, Communication, Negotiation, Cooperation, Evolution, and Representative Democracy."[38] Members of the target neighborhoods would not confront and provoke the authorities and establishments. But they would be consulted by the public officials, the social workers, and the poverty experts in the planning and implementation of programs.

How did this eminently sensible scheme work out in practice? Not terribly well. Before long the program director, a Protestant minister with moderate views, was battling with the assistant director, a Mexican-American and former union official who admired Alinsky. The director favored keeping "within the fold" the target neighborhood committees, which represented the local poor. His assistant declared: "Let them go wherever they want!"[39] Cooperation across class lines proved difficult. The target area poor, their hopes newly awakened, were impatient with delays. The middle-class members of the antipoverty agency, concerned with administrative clarity and legal mandates, and knowledgeable about institutional limitations, sought to prevent what seemed ill-considered haste. Middle-class arrogance often contended with lower-class suspicion. Board meetings, accordingly, sometimes deteriorated into wrangles over details and symbols.

In November 1966, the director gave notice of his intention to leave the job early the following year. By the time he left, the Topeka program had spent slightly more than $1 million on preschool Head Start, adult education, Neighborhood Youth Corps, city and county beautification projects, and on a "neighborhood house" program for Topeka Indians. Several of these provided short-term employment for youths and adult laborers. Evaluators, however, considered changes in attitudes the most important result. Middle-class members of the poverty board acknowledged that they now understood the poor and their problems better than before. The poor of the target area committees in turn felt more optimistic about the chances for change. They seemed to have developed more self-esteem. A handful had acquired leadership experience. These were worthy changes but they did not dramatically transform the lives of poor Topekans. Even noncontroversial community action projects could point to little achievement during this first year.

But in any case, the blandness and moderation of most community action programs escaped the mainstream public. The press found the War on Poverty a mesmerizing subject and devoted more space to it than to any other domestic story except civil rights. Fifteen to twenty Washington reporters included OEO as their regular beat. And the meat of their reportage was horror stories detailing excesses and the doings of the community action kamikazes. It was yet another case of "Man Bites Dog" making a better story than "Dog Bites Man."

None of the press accounts, however, touched the public's raw nerve like the AP report in November of LeRoi Jones's summer escapades under the auspices of HARYOU-ACT. The piece, reprinted by papers all across the country, unleashed a wave of indignation that reached the president in a barrage of letters. "What justification" was there, wrote Mrs. I. Steinberg of Fairlawn, New Jersey, for giving money to a group aiming to "further hatred among the Negro people."[40] HARYOU-ACT was throwing away the tax payers' money by bowing "to loud, vocal, increasingly obstreperous groups. . . ." It was "blackmail, pure and simple," complained J. D. Magid of Bellrose, New York.[41] Mrs. William Clark of Caseyville, Illinois, called the Jones enterprise "a training school for radical strife" and observed it was "debateable" how long the country was "going to tolerate the complete lack of common sense in a program as this. . . ."[42] "What gives?" asked Jean Gettle of Tillamook, Oregon. She had never "heard of such a horrible example" of "foolish . . . expenditure" as described in the AP dispatch. It was "things as this that breed discontent."[43] "I cannot protest in strong enough terms how much I protest *my* tax money being spent to produce plays of hate," wrote Walter Hormell of Beverly Hills, California.[44] LeRoi Jones "advocates killing white people of whom I am one, and is living off my tax money," raged Richard Schalich of Marietta, Georgia. Negroes were using "the riots to . . . threaten the government into giving these funds."[45] These letters, apparently a very small sample of the total, were passed along to the president and referred to OEO for response.

By the end of the summer OEO officials felt embattled. Just before Labor Day, Bill Crook, an agency regional director, in a memo to his superior, noted OEO's "badly blurred and rapidly deteriorating" public image. OEO's lack of focus kept it from being effective. "At the end of the day," he said, "I have reacted to a dozen crises and leave my desk with the feeling that I have advanced not a foot. . . . The whole system is like a giant pinball machine. Problems, like steel balls, are periodically shot out—one by one all the desks light up—the ball bounces from station to station, and finally at the end of the day, drops out of sight."[46] Shriver himself remained cheerful and sought to reassure the president with a steady stream of positive news about the poverty war from his office, but at times his upbeat response must have seemed fatuous.

More damaging to OEO's reputation, undoubtedly, was the response of local political leaders. In May, as community action momentum built, mayors Shelley of San Francisco and Sam Yorty of Los Angeles introduced a resolution at the St. Louis meeting of the National Conference of Mayors condemning OEO for failure "to recognize the legal and moral responsibilities of local officials who are accountable to the taxpayers for expenditures of local funds."[47] In support of the resolution Shelley read a passage from Theodore Berry's OEO community-action agency workbook recommending "organizing low income residents for political effectiveness." Against whom? asked beleaguered Mayor Walsh of Syracuse.[48]

The resolution failed to pass. Most of the mayors, including Shelley and Yorty, were Democrats and did not want to embarrass the president. They concocted a facesaving formula: Vice President Humphrey, in St. Louis to address the convention, would listen to their grievances privately and transmit them to the White House. Humphrey reassured the mayors at the meeting that the "success of the program" depended on their leadership and that the president would not ignore their voices.

One historian has claimed that "the day the first letter of protest [against the War on Poverty] arrived in the White House from an aggrieved mayor was the day the administration began its retreat."[49] That is an exaggeration. The attacks by militants on elected officials offended LBJ. But the president at first discounted them and defended the antipoverty agency. In late April 1965 he acknowledged that in waging the War on Poverty "we will have difficulties." But he knew of no national domestic program that had "reached so many people so fast and so effectively."[50] A businessman's complaint about HARYOU-ACT brought a populist retort from the president. "You know the way to do something about Harlem?" he asked White House assistant Joe Califano. "Make those rich Wall Street bankers drive through Harlem to and from work everyday so they see poverty instead of riding in an air conditioned train drinking martinis and talking to each other about how much money they made."[51]

But at times OEO, and especially the community action programs, sorely tried Johnson's patience. Wilbur Cohen remembered that LBJ resisted efforts to appoint people associated with OEO to other federal posts. He had heard him say many times, Cohen reported: "Well, I don't want to appoint that fellow. He's from OEO. He's disloyal to me. He's a trouble-maker."[52] Community action, recalled James Gaither, a White House aide, probably subjected Johnson to more "political heat" than anything else except Vietnam.[53]

But Johnson understood that there was a constituency on the other side as well. Militants in the community had been skeptical of OEO all along. But originally this was not organized opposition. By late spring of 1965, however, the War on Poverty as conducted by Shriver and OEO came under fire from a newly defined, ideologically left-of-center organization in the form of the Citizens' Crusade Against Poverty (CCAP).

CCAP was the brainchild of Walter Reuther, the brisk, articulate union leader whose epic struggle to organize the autoworkers during the 1930s had made him a giant of labor history. He had been a socialist as a young man and never, even after becoming a powerful trade union boss, lost his sensitivity to social issues. All through the decade the United Automobile Workers was a major force behind the liberal commitment to racial equality and economic equity. The UAW even underwrote the Economic Research and Action Project's back-to-the-people program of the Students for a Democratic Society with a $5,000 check.

Early on Reuther identified himself to LBJ as "one of your loyal soldiers in the unconditional war against poverty. . . ."[54] In April

1964 he showed his support by organizing the Citizens' Crusade Against Poverty with a million-dollar subvention by the UAW. The CCAP sought to repeat the success of the UAW's civil rights lobby, the National Coalition of Conscience, and brought together at its preliminary conference in late June 1964 many of the same folk, plus labor leaders, businessmen, farm spokesmen, and social workers, to work for the new crusade.

During the debate in the Eighty-eighth Congress on the poverty bill the CCAP worked closely with the president and Shriver to help win passage. But by the spring of 1965 CCAP had become part of the left opposition. The ubiquitous Richard Boone, recently resigned from OEO, was its executive director and he brought with him the "maximum feasible participation" perspective double-distilled. Richard Cloward, too, was an important member of the new group's Commission on Community Action and Organization. Cloward and his close associate Francis Fox Piven were just months away from announcing their "action strategy" to "overload" the welfare system with enrollees and create so much turmoil that it would have to be replaced by a guaranteed income. Also participating were Michael Harrington, author of *Other America* fame, and Paul Potter, a founding father of Students for a Democratic Society. Providing moral support and lending respectability to CCAP was a contingent of prominent liberals, including former University of Chicago president Robert Hutchins; A. Philip Randolph, the revered black labor leader; famous baby doctor and author Benjamin Spock; the Harvard economist John K. Galbraith; and Richard Goodwin, the man who had composed the original Great Society speech. Martin Luther King agreed to head the organization's committee on public information and education.

In early 1965 CCAP advertised itself as a training and education agency. It intended to create a nationwide information exchange among individuals and groups fighting poverty. It proposed to establish several major centers where local antipoverty leaders could learn organizing and management techniques and where promising young "interns" from poor neighborhoods and from the Peace Corps and the civil rights movement would be taught how to organize the poor. It would teach local activists how to attract federal antipoverty grants and manage them once attained.

On the face of it there could be little objection to expediting OEO's community action programs in these ways. But a radical fringe at CCAP wanted to do more than give the poor a voice in local antipoverty projects. CCAP acknowledged, for example, that it was consulting Alinsky on training community activists. To the knowledgeable this promised confrontation and turmoil. Boone admitted that the organization expected to agitate and protest as well as train and educate. And it did. Though still loyal to maximum feasible participation, in April 1966 CCAP militants would boo, heckle, and physically threaten Shriver at the organization's first national conference and drive him from the stage when he told his audience that he was "not a bit ashamed of what has been done by the War on Poverty" and that instant satisfaction of the poor's demands was not possible. Commenting on this fiasco a few days later, Shriver ruefully noted that the disrupters seemed to be governed by a syllogism: "A real War on Poverty requires a social revolution. Government cannot subsidize a social revolution. Therefore the War on Poverty is a fraud."[55]

Even more hostile to the Shriver regime at OEO was the Organization for Black Power, formed in June 1965 by Jesse Gray, the Harlem rent-strike instigator. A precursor of the well-publicized black power groups of the following year, the group denounced the War on Poverty as a "fraud." The "so-called poverty program" was "little more than a bonanza . . . for the nation's middle-class social workers" and had "offered little or no help to those needing it most." The "dispossessed of the nation must be told to refuse to cooperate with the predominantly white social work lobby. . . ."[56]

In Congress, too, OEO and Shriver began to come under fire from the left for not heeding the needs and wishes of the poor. In mid-April 1965 the House opened hearings presided over by Adam Clayton Powell on the administration's request for increasing second-year War on Poverty funding to $1.5 billion, a sum far below the $3.5 billion for the second year everyone had anticipated when EOA was first enacted. A battle quickly erupted over the failure of OEO to conform to maximum feasible participation guidelines.

Powell blasted New York's mayor Robert Wagner for the undemocratic representation on the city's community action board and threatened to cut off the city's poverty funds if he did not change it. He also announced that the salaries of poverty program heads were "excessively high . . . wildly unrealistic."[57] No one doubted that the clash was as much over who got the money in Harlem as over the participation principle. Still, Powell used the hearings as an opportunity to charge that OEO had ignored the poor and that community action programs had degenerated into "giant fiestas of political patronage."[58] When OEO approved Los Angeles Mayor Yorty's scheme for a city-wide poverty agency that underrepresented poor neighborhoods, Powell called Shriver to his office to explain the agency's action. There the poverty czar confronted congressmen Augustus Hawkins, who represented the Watts district, and James Roosevelt, from the heavily Jewish Fairfax area, on OEO representation policies. Shriver reaffirmed the administration's commitment to community action and agreed to fund broader, city-wide grants in addition to programs encompassing small neighborhood projects. In the end Powell allowed the bill to move to the next steps of the legislative process.

The Senate hearings in late June on renewing OEO funding also squeezed the administration from the left. Black and Latino activists told the senators that entrenched power was shutting them out of the antipoverty planning process. Richard Cloward appeared to tell the senators some blunt truths. "Economic deprivation," he declared, was "fundamentally a political problem" and "power" would "be required to solve it." "[C]ontrol of vast poverty funds" was "at the heart of the current controversy over the involvement of the poor."[59]

In fact, Shriver and his aides sought to meet the charges that the community action programs were not democratically controlled. In June 1965 OEO set out informal guidelines for membership on community action city-wide and area boards that originated, planned, and administered community action programs. Representation could include public officials and social workers who dealt with the poor, as well as union, church, and civil rights representatives. But about a third of the members of each board should be residents of the target areas that received programs and funds. Nothing initially was said about how these people were to be selected. And besides the city-wide agencies, many target areas had their own neighborhood advisory councils. Where such existed, OEO headquarters directed, they should be composed of "locals." Though unpaid, these people would administer the programs and so have jobs and money to dispense.

The guidelines did not end the representation problem. Historians generally have favored the people over the politicians in the battles to control the community action agencies. The Mayor Tates look like narrow, unimaginative defenders of privilege against the legitimate aspirations of poor Americans, often black, seeking their rightful share of power and opportunity. Yet the reality is more ambiguous. Many who opposed the mayors were only marginally more representative of the poor than the elected city officials. They often were local landlords, ministers, shopkeepers, and teachers, exceptional men and women, often aggressive and articulate, who, in this era of crumbling social barriers, were on their way out of the ghettos and the slums in any case. Shriver, always the realist, was forced to concede early on that the one-third "community people" did not necessarily mean poor people, so long as they lived in the neighborhood. Representatives of the poor, he noted, did not have to wear "patches on their pockets."[60]

Hoping to make the community action boards more representative, OEO eventually required their selection by "democratic techniques." The formula did little to further democracy. When OEO established an election process for selecting city-wide advisory boards, turnouts were dismal. A campaign to get out the vote in Kansas City that cost $50,000 and employed four thousand volunteer canvassers induced only 8,287 voters to cast ballots, scarcely 5 percent of those eligible. In Los Angeles a similar effort produced a turnout of less than 1 percent. In Philadelphia only 4 percent of the 340,000 or so eligibles voted. In Cleveland, in early 1966, a major vote drive for the CA board featuring sound trucks, a poster campaign by the city's schoolchildren, and newspaper advertisements attracted only 4.2 percent of the eligible voters. In March 1966 Shriver admitted disappointment and OEO ceased to fund the elections.

The American Arbitration Association concluded that the reason for the dismal participation rate was that the poor saw no advantage to themselves in the CAA's, and most of the candidates running for the boards had little community credibility. Clearly another culprit, however, was the very culture of poverty the voters were enmeshed in. The apathy that consigned them to poverty in the first place kept them from the participation designed to empower them. Into this vacuum inevitably slipped the educated, the aggressive, the ambitious, and, all too often, the manipulative and larcenous.

But making community action palatable to the white middle-class public depended on decorum as much as fair representation. In the past federal programs had been administered either directly from Washington or, more recently, through local elective or appointive officials. Never before had the federal government sought to make informal grassroots organizations the primary agents for planning programs and dispensing substantial funds, thereby bypassing local political structures and challenging their authority and legitimacy. Still more unprecedented was the attempt to overcome the political apathy of the urban and rural poor and cut them in on a portion of the political and financial pie. Middle-class Americans, however aloof from the political process, took for granted that "the system" was fitted to their needs. Marginalized people were astonished when their views were consulted. Their lives were often desperate and chaotic and they lived hand-to-mouth, often by ruses and hustles. The community action programs seemed like another scam. Middle-class folk expected a reasonable level of propriety and financial probity in those wielding power and office. Given some power, the poor, not knowing much order in their own lives, had little interest in decorum and rules. And besides, they soon discovered, anger, insult, and invective were powerful weapons of intimidation against the authorities and their middle-class constituents.

Despite all the bad news, in September 1965 Congress renewed OEO funding for another year with a total budget of $1.78 billion, more than the administration had requested and almost double the initial, first-year appropriation, though less, as we noted, than had been anticipated for the second year of the War on Poverty back in early 1964. Congress did respond, moreover, to conservative pressure in reaction to a recent veto by Alabama governor George Wallace of an OEO grant to a biracial community action group in the Birmingham Congress. The revised EOA would permit the governors of each state to have veto rights over location of projects for the Neighborhood Youth Corps, community action, and basic adult education. The OEO director, however, could override the veto if he chose.

Meanwhile, the Job Corps, established under Title I of the Economic Opportunity Act, began to unravel even more messily than the community action programs.

EOA created two kinds of Job Corps centers, both removed from the presumably doleful influences of home, where poor youths, predominantly male, would live and receive training in those social and technical skills needed to lift them out of poverty. For those with virtually no education there would be places in the country—modeled on the New Deal–era CCC camps—where corpsmen could repair roads, build firebreaks, and help with conservation and resource management. These tasks would accustom them to the adult work experience. And they would also learn basic skills—reading and writing, primarily—that would prepare them for the world of work. For a second group, those at sixth-grade reading levels or better, there were to be "urban centers" just outside cities and towns that would emphasize the skilled crafts—carpentry, plumbing, electrical wiring, welding, and the like. A female division of the "urban centers," the brainchild of Edith Green, would actually be located within town and city limits.

In late 1964 Shriver launched a major advertising campaign to sign up Job Corps volunteers. OEO prepared thousands of kits with pamphlets, fact sheets, film strips, and applications and sent them to YMCA's, the Boys Clubs of America, religious groups, and to all fifty state employment agencies. The response was startling. By late January fifteen thousand applications and letters a week were flooding into OEO headquarters. Nor did the advertising cease with this first round. In the summer of 1965 Al Capp, whose "L'il Abner" was one of the most widely distributed comic strips of the day, prepared free of charge a thirty-two-page comic book featuring Danny Driftwood and Sloppy Belle, two high school dropouts who, induced to join the Job Corps, become successful and respectable citizens as a result. The booklet contained blue Job Corps "opportunity cards" prestamped.[61] The agency was soon buried under 300,000 little blue application cards.

The disproportion between demand and supply proved daunting. Shriver had hoped to have 100,000 Job Corpsmen living in camps by June 30. It soon became clear that such a goal was wildly unrealistic, and by March he had scaled back his plans to ten thousand. OEO met this modest target, but just barely, and only by contracting out the urban centers to private agencies that appeared equipped to do the job. Contractors included Litton Industries, IBM, Westinghouse, Federal Electric, and a number of universities.

The first actual Job Corps center opened in mid-January in a former Civilian Conservation Corps camp in the Catoctin Mountains close to the presidential hideaway at Camp David. During the next six months OEO opened fifty or so additional camps, including the first female center, established in a leased hotel in the heart of St. Petersburg, Florida. At its peak in mid-1967 the corps would have 123 centers with 42,000 enrollees. A majority of the centers were of the conservation type, though the total enrollment in the urban centers, male and female, was somewhat larger.

Troubles began almost immediately. Many of the recruits were black youths who had never before been away from home, and they found the new environments alien. Some brought with them social pathologies endemic to the inner-city ghettos. A startling half of the first contingent had criminal records; seven hundred of the original ten thousand had notations of "serious crimes" against persons and property in their personnel folders.[62] Another large contingent were Southern whites whose cultural baggage included a large ration of racism. The two groups together created an explosive mixture. Most recruits were school dropouts who could not get jobs in the most flourishing peacetime economy the nation had ever experienced. These, of course, were the very people targeted by Title I, but working with such human material would be frustrating to those—administrators, voters, and reformers alike—who expected quick results. And it promised to be costly besides.

And there was a final strike against the Job Corps: the reaction of local communities. Exposure to the kind of young men and women whom the corps recruited was certain to dismay middle-class citizens. This response resembled the town-gown tensions of college communities but it was made far worse by the class and race resentments just under the surface of American life.

During the first year news of the corps was almost uniformly bad. The first urban center was established outside Astoria on Oregon's wet, windswept coast. The small city provided few opportunities for recreation, and many of the recruits were disappointed with the limited range of skills and training available. A number quit in disgust. Then in mid-June, fifteen of the corpsmen were sent home for a brawl that had racial overtones. Governor Mark Hatfield complained to the president about the inadequate security at the camp and proposed that in the future the corps avoid the mixing of "northern Whites, southern Negroes, of unadjusted deviates, of those with past criminal records, and other problems" without adequate counseling and preparation.[63]

Worse was the riot in Kalamazoo, Michigan, touched off by the theft of a coat during a dance at the Lincoln Community School attended by sixty trainees. As the corpsmen, angry at accusations of dishonesty, waited for the buses to take them back to Fort Custer, they brawled with local youths and broke windows and damaged buildings in the downtown area.

The first women's center did not escape serious problems, either. Sixty percent of the young women housed in the old Huntington Hotel, in the heart of a retiree neighborhood in St. Petersburg, were black or American Indian. Their assignment was to learn typing, shorthand, cosmetology, and nursing—occupations that in 1965 no one felt ashamed to call female. But they were also young and from cultures not known for their puritanism. To the locals they seemed rowdy and promiscuous. The girls, residents complained, had converted the street in front of the hotel into a "courting lane" where they and their male partners engaged in shocking sexual acts.[64] The center's extravagant financing also offended the local media. Critics charged that the accommodations were plush and, with 122 officials and teachers to serve 237 students, wildly overstaffed.

And so the Job Corps story went through the rest of 1965. Residents of Edison, New Jersey, accused corpsmen at Camp Kilmer, reputedly Director Singletary's pride and joy, of drunkenness and narcotics use and claimed that they regularly stoned cars passing through the camp. At Camp Atterbury, Indiana, several corpsmen were arrested for sodomizing one of their fellow trainees. In San Antonio, recruits from the Gary Center near Austin wounded two air force enlisted men in the course of a holdup. The camp was soon causing "apprehension" among local people, and the authorities dispatched federal guards to keep the lid on.[65] One of the most loosely run centers was Camp Breckinridge, in western Kentucky, managed by Southern Illinois University. Breckinridge suffered from severe absenteeism, brutish hazing, and extortion by corpsmen, who were shaking down their fellows for $13.59 a month as "life insurance."[66] When racially charged fistfights broke out in the mess hall the administration called out the local fire department. Black corpsmen mobbed the firemen, and half of the corpsmen themselves, fearing for their safety, fled to town. In the end the state police had to be called in to quell the disturbance. The whole, squalid tale appeared at length in the Chicago newspapers, to the consternation and outrage of many middle-class readers. On August 4 *The Washington Post* carried an upbeat report on Breckinridge. Two weeks later, on August 21, the *Post* headed an article on recent events there NEGRO-WHITE FIST FIGHT STARTS RIOT AT JOB CAMP.[67] Together the two pieces suggest how the reality of American race relations could confound the best of intentions.

Nor was the Job Corps very impressive in its training role. In early 1966, one visitor to Kilmer observed that "half the kids were sleeping, the other half were indifferent and teachers were droning on and on with no involvement. They simply had not won the kids to either the subject matter or themselves."[68]

Undoubtedly, many critics of the corps had little faith in the Johnson poverty program overall. But there were also doubters from the left. In late 1965 an advisory committee of Rutgers professors attacked the Camp Kilmer operation as too regimented, too much like the army. The academics also criticized the way Federal Electric ran the project. "They make significant decisions regarding the programs, but decisions which give primary consideration to the profit motive." In an interview with *U.S. News & World Report,* Francis Purcell, head of the Rutgers advisory body, denounced the whole Job Corps idea of removing slum kids from their environments to make them more like middle-class white Americans. It reflected, he said, "a kind of demeaning attitude toward the poor that breaks through. . . ."[69]

The inexperience of OEO administrators and the pressure to spend the money fast before it disappeared were responsible for many of the unfortunate early errors. In 1966, though the program was considerably larger, discipline tightened and the centers ran more smoothly.

But even in its avowed goals of providing skills and improving job opportunities of the poor, the Job Corps was not an outstanding success. Analyses of whether it made young men and women from poverty backgrounds employable yielded at best ambiguous results. A longer stay in the Job Corps—more than six months—made a job more likely than a shorter stay. Whether this meant that Job Corps training helped, or whether the more persevering were inherently better able to get jobs, is unclear, however. Comparing Job Corps graduates with youths without Job Corps training produces similarly blurry answers. Carefully designed surveys showed that Job Corps applicants who never actually enrolled had *higher* employment rates than Job Corps graduates! Why this was so is not clear. As for wage differences between the two groups, Job Corps graduates, on average, earned a paltry nine cents more an hour than the no-shows, while Job Corps dropouts actually earned *less* than those never exposed to the Job Corps experience. There is another side of the picture. Since the Job Corps actually enrolled young people less able than the no-shows, it is not surprising that the latter started off earning more than the enrollees. But since the enrollees finally caught up, staying in the centers for six months or more obviously provided something that enabled students to make up the gap.[70]

What does all this show? The results are not unclouded, but taken together it is clear that the program had been oversold. Much of the taxpayers' money had been misspent on the Job Corps experiment.

The corps soon came under passionate attack. Conservatives charged that enrollees were being coddled. One senator noted that it cost $8,000 a year to house, feed, clothe, and educate a single corps member. It would be cheaper, he said, to send each one through the Ivy League. Shriver responded that the senator's figures were far too high and in fact each Job Corps recruit cost the government only $4,650 for nine months, about two thirds the expenses of a Harvard student. And given the gross imperfections of their previous training and education, "an objective critic" could "anticipate much higher costs for producing useful citizens out of Job Corps enrollees" than of Harvard-bound students.[71] By 1966, with thousands of draftees in Vietnam, the skeptics had a new line of attack. "Why should juvenile virtue be rewarded with military service in the Vietnamese nightmare," asked the truculently conservative Republican congressman from

New York, Paul Fino, "while a record of delinquency exempts punks from the army and puts them in line for Job Corps coddlings?"[72]

OEO defended the Job Corps but avoided claiming much educational success. Rather, as it would later say of Head Start, many of the benefits were medical. Corpsmen who spent the full nine months in the program gained more than ten pounds in weight. Thirty-five percent had been fitted with glasses and many had received medical and dental care for the first time. These were not trivial results, but all told there is no clear proof that the Job Corps helped very many of its clients to become self-supporting citizens. On the other hand, like most other Great Society programs, it clearly provided jobs for numerous bureaucrats, experts, and government functionaries.

The Community Action Program and the Job Corps were the two most troublesome and ambiguous titles of the Economic Opportunity Act. More successful—or at least less controversial—were the four "national emphasis" programs of OEO—Upward Bound, legal services, health centers, and Head Start—each included within the community action title but prepackaged at Washington headquarters and administered by local community action agencies.

Upward Bound was an attempt to extend to new, more problematic constituencies the merit principle in higher education. It reached down to social levels below those targeted by the scholarship provisions of the Higher Educational Act. But its commitment was to the old-fashioned American ethic of equality of opportunity.

During the late spring of 1965 OEO announced a "war on talent waste."[73] The program would seek out several thousand promising students among the poor in the third or fourth year of high school and send them to college campuses for six to eight weeks of instruction. The summer sessions, supplemented by a follow-up during the regular high school academic year, would broaden their cultural horizons, create or reinforce a thirst for knowledge, and prepare them generally for the long pull of higher education when they graduated. In 1965 OEO was able to make available only $2.5 million and enroll a little more than two thousand young people. But the program appealed to the idealism of the day. Widely praised, the following year it expanded a full ten times in both funding and number of participants.

The achievements of Upward Bound were limited. Some of its enrollees would not have gone to college without it, but it probably did not rescue very many. Moreover, most of its beneficiaries ended up in two-year institutions or in black colleges; few made it to prestigious schools. The college survival rate of Upward Bounders was as good as that of most students. But this may reflect the selective screening of those admitted to the program; the weaker candidates were simply weeded out. In the end it is unclear whether it was necessary to shell out the $1,000 a year per client the program cost to get such a select group into college. Almost all would have gone anyway through the auspices of existing private and public scholarship programs.

Legal services was a more consequential program. Poor people undoubtedly have greater need for legal advice and lawyers' services than middle-class folk. They are more often in trouble with the law and with their spouses; they are more often victimized by landlords, unscrupulous hucksters, finance companies, and assorted con artists; they more often need help to get their legal due under federal, state, and local welfare and public housing laws. For years the legal profession assuaged its collective class guilt through privately funded legal aid societies and by pro bono volunteer work. This system fell far short of filling the bill. Not enough lawyers were willing to give gratuitous legal services. Many legal aid offices, moreover, were located downtown, distant from their clients; they failed to alert the poor to their rights or advertise their services; they often refused to take cases such as divorces, which they considered unessential or morally ambiguous. It was understandable, then, that the liberal enthusiasts at OEO should consider legal services a natural choice for a community action national emphasis program.

OEO's own community action principles disposed it to more than the traditional dispensing of legal aid services. But this bias was reinforced by a widely circulated 1964 *Yale Law Journal* article by two young attorneys, Edgar and Jean Camper Cahn, both of whom would come to work for OEO. Both had experience in New Haven public service law and they urged the federal government to fund neighborhood legal firms to help the poor. These should not follow a "service oriented" model. Rather, the lawyers, a breed "particularly well equipped to deal with the intricacies of social organization," should serve a "representative function." They should establish clearly defined legal rights, seek to make the law simpler and more accessible, fight laws antithetical to slum communities, and help extend to new areas of claims the possibility of legal recourse. They should also seek, through legal challenge, to actually reform the law where it was antithetical to the poor. In effect, the neighborhood lawyers should function as advocates for the poor and as activists for change in the relations of the poor to the larger society.[74]

The Cahns' views borrowed from the new theory of entitlements as developed by Charles Reich, later to be a counterculture guru.[75] Just before the Cahns' article appeared, Reich had proposed in the same journal that a wide range of the "valuables dispensed by government" should be considered legal property that, no more than cars, stocks, or real estate, could be confiscated or denied by government fiat. "These interests," he affirmed, should be "vested" in the recipients.[76] Both essays together represented a new left-activist current in the legal profession that would eventuate in the interpretation of law, influential at Harvard and other law schools today, called critical studies.

Jean Cahn herself helped set up OEO's legal services program in late 1964, but it was never well funded. By July 1966 only some $25 million had been committed to legal services agencies in 125 communities. This was far more than the total budget of the private legal aid societies but well below the amount needed to take on "the system." In many cases, moreover, individual community action boards turned to the existing legal aid societies as their legal services agent.

And yet the program managed to offend part of the legal profession and threaten defenders of the existing social order. Law, as then constituted, was a profoundly conservative calling, and many established lawyers viewed the new legal services program as an open invitation to challenge authority and stir up social turmoil. They were especially suspicious of "law reform," the strategy implied, though not named, by the Cahns, aimed at changing policies or practices perceived as unjust to the poor through a barrage of litigation. Activist lawyers would challenge discriminatory measures through test cases in the appellate courts, would sue to force local agencies to change unfair practices, and seek to encourage community solidarity by keeping social injustice constantly in the public eye. Inspired ultimately by the NAACP's Legal Defense Fund challenge that had produced the 1954 landmark desegregation case, *Brown* v. *Board of Education,* law reform would help make the courts the final arbiter of issues regarding the environment, product liability, sex discrimination, housing, and much else in our litigious society.

In the spring of 1965 the Legal Aid Society protested OEO guidelines mandating law reform as a project goal. When OEO began to train a new class of "lay advocates," local neighborhood people primed on the rights of tenants, consumers, accused offenders, and others, the legal establishment bridled. In early 1966 the president of the Tennessee Bar Association attacked the Legal Services program as a plan "to tell the people how to carry out rent strikes and consumer strikes and demonstrations against lending institutions." His audience of fellow bar association presidents roundly applauded.[77]

In truth the lawyers objected to more than the program's ideology. The Trial Lawyers Association had no argument with government subsidies for legal services on the Medicare model of paying clients' professional bills. That would increase business for lawyers in general private practice with little downside. But many feared a system of full-time, government-employed attorneys, a scheme they labeled "socialization of the bar."[78] In June 1965 Shriver, in cooperation with the American Bar Association, organized a conference on law and poverty to build support among lawyers for "the war on poverty generally and the legal services programs to be funded by OEO in particular."[79] Addressing the conference, Shriver assured the lawyers that the government did not intend to disturb their relations with clients or turn legal aid into a political patronage trough.

In the end, OEO's propaganda was probably less persuasive than experience. OEO kept programs from cities where the local bar association opposed it. Most proved less divisive than expected and provided much needed work for young attorneys. In July 1966 the American Trial Lawyers Association, at its annual convention in Los Angeles, voted down a resolution to condemn the program.

During 1965, the first year, the Legal Services program made

relatively little impression on the public. Still ahead were its successful challenges to residency requirements for welfare recipients, to the "man in the house" rule disqualifying a poor family
for help under the Social Security Act's Aid to Families with Dependent Children provision, to rulings that denied the legal right
of tenants to withhold rent from landlords remiss in essential
house and apartment services and repairs, and to involuntary
commitment of emotionally disturbed people to public asylums.
After 1966, moreover, some law-reform-oriented attorneys would
ally themselves to the Cloward-Piven campaign to replace the
traditional welfare system with some version of a guaranteed income. In the process the OEO lawyers would help inflate the
welfare rolls and further enrage middle-class taxpayers against the
"undeserving poor" and their patrons.

The least-heralded OEO "national emphasis" program was
neighborhood health centers. First proposed by two professors of
medicine at Tufts, it came into being in mid-1965. The centers
were to provide one-stop care for the poor. Rather than scramble
from clinic to clinic, the ambulatory poor could find the medical
care they needed under one roof. Even the health centers were
infused with the participatory ethic. People in the neighborhoods
would help plan the centers' programs and see that they were
responsive to local needs. And wherever possible, local people
would be used as subprofessionals. The neighborhood health centers program evolved slowly. As late as mid-1968 there were only
thirty-two centers in actual operation.

Two other programs directly mandated by the Economic Opportunity Act, the Neighborhood Youth Corps and VISTA, received relatively little national attention. The NYC, administered
by the Labor Department, was a well-funded program to train
poor local youths in useful skills and put them to work in their
own neighborhoods, where they would help with traffic problems,
paint parking meters, pick up paper and cut bushes in city parks,
and the like. Though the promotion of job skills was its proclaimed mission, it resembled the WPA "leaf-raking" projects of
the 1930s, and like them, it made the pain of joblessness less
acute. The NYC proved particularly useful during the summers
when inner-city adolescents, inclined to mischief by their raging
hormones, were out of school. Local officials loved it because it
gave them money to dispense without having to cope with the

contentious boards of the community action programs. But the corps, too, was subject to abuse. In 1965, in some parts of the country, it provided cushy part-time summer work to the children of the prosperous. One beneficiary in Kansas City, it was reported, drove to his college classes in a new-model Thunderbird. In parts of the South and Midwest, critics charged, the program had also served as patronage, pure and simple. Jobs had been handed out to the politically influential, not the needy.

VISTA (Volunteers in Service to America) was the domestic version of the Peace Corps, first proposed by Kennedy in 1963 but defeated by conservatives and states'-righters. The idea was incorporated into the act establishing OEO when governors were given the right to veto any VISTA project in their states.

Meagerly funded, VISTA's first recruits began training in late 1964, their indoctrination emphasizing psychology, sociology, economics, and the culture of poverty. After six weeks VISTA volunteers, most of whom were young, middle class, and well educated, were assigned to one of six poverty areas called tracts, defined by geography, ethnicity, and economic problems. There, in the ghettos, slums, and rural wastelands, they taught classes in English and office skills, set up food cooperatives, advised local people about legal problems, helped with hostile landlords, brought ghetto schools in touch with ghetto parents, organized youth clubs, and built bus shelters for rural school children.

VISTA mined the same lode of idealism as the Peace Corps without the risks—or appeal—of foreign residence, and attracted a substantial number of recruits. During its first three years some 300,000 people contacted the VISTA office for more information; seventy thousand actually submitted applications. But the stingy $3 million initial congressional appropriation kept the program small. Planned for four thousand volunteers, by the end of the first year it had managed to recruit and train only about 1,100. Congress was never generous to the program. Of the seventy thousand applications received by mid-1968, VISTA could accept only about 20 percent, owing to funding limitations.

More than occasionally, the young idealists identified with their clients and, like their predecessors, the settlement house workers early in the century, became active in community efforts at betterment. VISTA volunteers in a number of communities led rent strikes and even helped organize labor actions against employers.

In Newark they were accused by the mayor of allying themselves with Marxists and assorted radicals with revolutionary agendas. Complaints by local political leaders led to several being fired from the corps. Yet all told, VISTA never became the same burr and irritant as community action and the Job Corps, perhaps as much for its lilliputian scale as for any other reason.

Head Start was undoubtedly the most acclaimed and popular of the national emphasis programs and remains one of the few War on Poverty programs still extant. In early 1993 the Clinton administration would extol Head Start and ask Congress to fund it with more than $9 billion over a five-year period.

Its popularity was predictable. It was an educational program, and like other educational components of the Great Society it supposedly challenged only the liberal society's imperfections, not its fundamentals. Its targets were young children, with their endearing innocence and winning ways. Few Americans, even the most conservative, can resist the appeal of little kids, whatever their race.

Shriver was fully aware of this partiality. Even in the harshest period of Jim Crow, white Southerners could allow themselves to be charmed by small black children. During the mid-sixties, the riot in Watts, the "long hot summers" that followed, and the cresting crime waves of the inner cities transformed the way many white Americans regarded their black fellow citizens, but young children remained largely exempt from the rancor and general mistrust. "There's always been a prejudice in favor of little black children," Shriver would tell an interviewer in 1977. "The old-time term 'pickanniny' was one of endearment. It wasn't until blacks grew up that white people began to feel animosity." He had hoped, he said, that Head Start "could overcome a lot of hostility . . . against the poor in general and specifically against black people who are poor, by aiming for the children."[80]

Shriver was also driven by practical politics. In early 1965 the turmoil surrounding the community action programs was still largely latent, but Shriver could see trouble ahead and wanted to give the mayors and local officials a program that was a popular winner. Moreover, there were millions of community action dollars still unused, with the new fiscal year only six months away.

Head Start was grounded on several virtually unchallenged liberal assumptions of the day. It bet on nurture against nature; it assumed that environment determined personal competence. Success in school and life was largely governed by experience, not heredity, and for most poor people the culture of poverty was the critical molding experience. Head Start shared these concepts with the War on Poverty generally, but also drew specifically on the experts who emphasized the importance of the earliest childhood years in stimulating mental capacity. Martin Deutsch and his associates at the Institute for Developmental Studies, Susan Gray at Peabody College in Nashville, and psychologists J. McVicker Hunt and Benjamin Bloom all proclaimed that IQ was the product of early childhood experience and could be substantially improved by enrichment during the preschool years. By 1964 their ideas had been tested in Chicago, Oakland, New Haven, New York, and other cities, several of the programs funded by the ubiquitous Ford Foundation. As Urie Bronfenbrenner, a Cornell University child development psychologist, would later note, Head Start was "an idea whose time had come," its principles impressed on the "minds of dozens of professionals . . . scattered over the land in universities, nursery schools, family agencies, and government offices."[81]

The program was set in motion in January 1965, when Shriver asked Dr. Robert Cooke, head of the department of pediatrics at Johns Hopkins, to form an advisory council of educators, doctors, economists, and psychologists to help plan an early childhood intervention project for OEO. Cooke was father himself to two retarded sons and had a deep personal interest in the welfare of disadvantaged children. The thirteen experts he assembled met eight times in New York and Washington and cobbled together a proposal. Late in the month the panel submitted its report to Shriver, and twenty-four hours later it was on the president's desk. Johnson had been alerted to the pending program, and in his January 12 education message had announced a preschool program under the War on Poverty. The president wanted to call the project "Kiddy Corps," but fortunately someone came up with "Head Start" instead.

Head Start was officially launched on February 19, 1965, at a White House ceremony presided over by the First Lady. Four hundred guests, many the wives of prominent Washington politicians, crowded into the East Room to listen to the advisory council and various experts describe the new program. Afterward, the guests adjourned to the Red Room for tea and cookies. The garden-party atmosphere was deliberate. Community action and the Job Corps had already incited public ire, and Shriver and the president wanted to make the occasion an event for the society columns rather than the hard-news reports. The ploy worked. Most papers carried the story on their society pages.

Like so many other early War on Poverty programs, Head Start was rushed into operation. Members of the advisory committee had proposed starting with a small pilot program before attempting anything ambitious, but Shriver needed both a big success to counter growing public unease and something to sop up leftover OEO funds before they were lost. The approaching summer vacation, moreover, assured the empty classrooms and idle teachers he needed for a large preschool program. He soon set as his target for the summer of 1965 an enrollment of 100,000 children.

Head Start established Washington headquarters in the decaying New Colonial Hotel on Fifteenth Street. There was no furniture at first, and at the early staff meetings almost everyone had to stand. Head Start director was Julius Richmond, a pediatrician and dean of the Upstate Medical School of the State University of New York, with Jule Sugarman, a former State Department staffer, as his deputy. The agency began with twenty employees and quickly expanded to three hundred, including some of the most skilled middle-management bureaucrats in Washington, many drawn to the project by its heartwarming goals. There was plenty of work for everyone. The advisory committee had already established criteria for funding community Head Start projects and laid plans for in-service teacher training programs. Head Start touched a resonant chord among Americans, and 200,000 people would eventually sign up as unpaid local Head Start aides that summer.

In a matter of weeks local groups from all over the country were applying for Head Start funding from OEO. To process the paperwork, the agency sent out a call for help, and hundreds of volunteers came to the shabby agency headquarters with its cardboard file cabinets to do their bit for poor children; many worked through the nights to meet the June deadline. Sugarman worried that the poorest communities would be left out and actively solicited applications from them. Under his direction Lindy Boggs,

wife of Louisiana congressman Hale Boggs; Sherri Henry, wife of
the federal trade commissioner; Dorothy Goldberg, wife of the
secretary of labor; and other "ladies bountiful" bombarded mayors, state legislators, Kiwanas and Lions clubs, the YMCA, and
other organizations with pleas to sponsor Head Start projects and
provide volunteers. The associate director also collected a hundred federal management interns and put them to work with
local groups to develop grant proposals. It all seemed to work. By
July Shriver, having initially anticipated an outlay of $18 million
for the program, had been forced to allot seven times as much.

Head Start's creators denied that the program was exclusively
for improving school performance and making culturally deprived children smarter. (On the planning committee itself, Edward Zigler, then a young associate professor of psychology at
Yale, had explicitly rejected the notion that the program would
raise the IQ's of participants.) It was also intended to benefit the
children's health, get parents involved in their children's education, encourage community self-governance, and create career
ladders in education for the poor. But most Americans assumed
that its main emphasis was intellectual and academic: poor kids,
caught before the ghettos and rural wastelands had time to undermine hope and prudence, would do well in school, better absorb
middle-class values, become self-supporting, and compete successfully in the race of life. Shriver, understanding the political value
of simplification, so presented the program. At one point during
the summer he told Sugarman that he would like to be able "to
say how many IQ points are gained for each dollar invested."[82]

Despite the early obstacles, Head Start roared off the ground in
May with ceremonies in the White House Rose Garden, where
Mrs. Johnson, Head Start's honorary chairperson, accepted the
program's symbolic flag from Sargent Shriver, and Danny Kaye,
the popular comedian and singer, entertained. The president,
with his usual modesty, announced to the assembled guests that
the summer effort would ensure that "thirty million man-years—
the combined lifespan of these youngsters—will be spent produc-
tively and rewardingly, rather than wasted in tax-supported institutions or in welfare-supported lethargy."[83]

All told, that summer more than half a million four- and five-
year-old preschool children in 2,500 communities, from rural Mississippi to the nation's largest metropolises, were enrolled in

eight-week Head Start programs. The cost was a resounding $82 million. Many were run by local school districts. Others were put together by local activists and volunteers through ad hoc organizations or local civic groups. Head Start projects were housed in every kind of facility: schools, churches, stores, apartments, civic centers, even abandoned sheds. Their teachers, each seconded by two volunteer aides, used an imaginative agenda of approaches to widen the horizons of their small clients. In Washington, D.C., one Head Start teacher took her charges to a suburban Grand Union supermarket to show them the great variety of fruits and vegetables available. Few of the preschoolers, she learned, had ever seen an eggplant, a cauliflower, or an avocado. Other teachers escorted their charges to fire stations, zoos, and working farms. For many children it was the attention that seemed to count. In one Mississippi project children for the first time were told their full names. In many projects the teachers' or aides' laps were the most effective learning platform for little kids who had never been cuddled.

The massive outpouring of hope, energy, and goodwill impressed even the hardest-hearted, most cynical observers. And the effort went where it promised to do the most good. A disproportionate number of Head Start's beneficiaries were black children of the urban ghettos and the Southern rural countryside. And among both races, the four- and five-year-olds who participated were those who scored lowest in achievement as measured by standard tests.

But some of the problems that jolted the community action programs overtook Head Start as well. Shriver recognized how easily OEO programs in general could succumb to slipshod financial accountability standards, and personally reviewed every grant made during the first eighteen months of the poverty program. As he told an interviewer, each one could have been "an entrance ticket to Leavenworth Penitentiary if the money was not spent correctly."[84] But his vigilance was sometimes not enough, and local Head Start officials would invite attack by their cavalier attitude toward record-keeping and receipts. Ideology too hobbled the project. In OEO's Washington office, the community action theorists pushed their agenda at the expense of Head Start's teaching mission. According to two later evaluators of the summer program, the CAP staff's indifference to the early childhood element of Head Start derived from "the conviction that Head Start should and would become part of an increasingly strong movement among the poor of our country to take control of the course of their lives, including the education of their children."[85]

One project in rural Mississippi incorporated both these unsettling elements. In May, bypassing the uncooperative state government, OEO made a $1.4 million grant to the Child Development Group of Mississippi (CDGM), organized by the Delta Ministry, a civil rights arm of the liberal National Council of Churches of Christ. The group was headquartered at the Mt. Beulah Center, not far from Jackson. The grant would be administered by Mary Holmes Junior College.

Most of the initial CDGM leaders were white civil rights activists who had participated the year before in the Mississippi Freedom Summer project that had riveted national attention when the Ku Klux Klan murdered three civil rights workers. They had registered black voters and taught freedom schools. They had helped create the Mississippi Freedom Democratic Party, the integrated political group that challenged the regulars of the Mississippi delegation at the Democratic Convention in August 1964 in Atlantic City. The novices had become politicized by their 1964 experience; the ideologues were confirmed in their adversarial politics.

During the winter of 1964–65, a group of Freedom Summer veterans and civil rights activists, led by Tom Levin, a radical New York psychoanalyst affiliated with the Medical Committee for Human Rights, began to talk about starting "freedom preschools" for Mississippi. When Polly Greenburg, OEO's Southwest regional analyst for Head Start, heard of their plans, she rushed to New York to persuade the group to make their endeavor an official Head Start project.

Mississippi Head Start under Levin's leadership was a militant organization from the outset. It did not see Head Start simply as a remedial program for young children. It regarded the OEO grant as "a mandate to go into every community in the state and organize the people politically. . . ."[86] The Student Non-Violent Coordinating Committee (SNCC), an offshoot of the student lunch-counter sit-ins of 1960, had been an important component of the Council of Federated Organizations, the umbrella organization for Freedom Summer in 1964, and it remained a presence in Mississippi when the Head Starters arrived. SNCC was initially skeptical of the Head Start project as an establishment enterprise. For activists to work for Head Start, said SNCC executive secretary James Forman, was like "people selling their souls and futures for a temporary loan."[87] But SNCC's Mississippi leader, Frank Smith, became director of the CDGM community staff, and of the forty CDGM summer central staff personnel, fifteen were SNCC activists. Other staffers were affiliated with the burgeoning student New Left. Jim Monsonis, Levin's chief administrative assistant, had been a founding member of SDS. Mary Varella, chief of Head Start's summer reading-readiness project, was also an early member of SDS. Another one hundred Northerners were recruited as "response teachers," as members of special projects, and as district coordinators. Many were college students from Berkeley, Bennington, Yale, and NYU, and their experiences in CDGM would further their politicization. There were also hundreds of local volunteers, almost all of them black, who conducted classes for black preschool children at eighty-six different locations— churches, renovated houses, outdoors.

For many of the central staff, the summer was an extraordinary personal adventure. The description of the project by the new-minted doctor who directed the medical program establishes its kinship with other transforming experiences of young activists during that idealistic, insurgent decade. The Northerners, he wrote,

> . . . were a motley crew: older professional people and semi-hippy students, liberals and radicals, New Yorkers and Californians, but the sense of uniting for a common cause in a hostile land quickly brought us together. We spent much of our free time at orientation singing folk and freedom songs. Orientation culminated in one wild morning session that began as a class in children's games and wound up in a foot-stomping, snake-dancing, freedom-singing hootenanny. Freedom was coming and we were to be part of it.[88]

During its seven weeks of actual summer operation, CDGM did a heroic job of bringing a more liberal and egalitarian culture into the sealed and meager lives of rural black Mississippians. At its eighty centers children were introduced to art, music, dance, and theater; intellectually spurred with puzzles and toys; and exposed to lively social interactions and verbal stimulation. The centers, as directed, also sought to improve the physical and psycho-

cal science and a friend of Marian Wright, a brilliant black Yale Law School graduate who headed the NAACP Legal Defense Fund in Jackson. One of the original planners of CDGM, she was also a pragmatist, and the change marked the beginning of a less political era.

In September CDGM's money ran out and for a time it looked as if it would die. But the organization was not friendless. White liberals and black civil rights leaders rallied to its side. In February Mississippi Freedom Democratic Party leader Lawrence Guyot telegraphed OEO in Washington to protest the withholding of CDGM funds. Hundreds of people in Mississippi would be forced on the state welfare rolls if they lost their Head Start jobs. In late 1966, over the protests of Martin Luther King, Jr., the National Council of Churches, and the militant, black-power SNCC and CORE, Shriver shifted OEO support to Mississippi Action for Progress (MAP), a body dominated by moderate establishment figures of both races, as an alternative Head Start agency in the state.

But CDGM would not die. Its many defenders in the liberal community bombarded the White House with demands that the group's funding be restored and took out advertisements accusing Shriver of bowing to conservative political pressure. Unable to ward off the group's influential friends, OEO eventually restored its funding and thereafter MAP and CDGM fought over where each should locate its programs within the state.

But CDGM was the only real static in an otherwise smooth Head Start transmission that summer. By the fall, Head Start stood out from almost all the other War on Poverty programs as an apparent success. The anecdotal information was all good. The kids seemed livelier, healthier, and better adjusted than before. When Lady Bird Johnson toured New Jersey Head Start centers with Shriver in August, she was captivated by what she saw. In Newark little William Purdie's mother told her "how much better he got along with other children at home since he started school. He had also learned for the first time how to dress himself."[91] In rural Lambertville, on the Delaware, Mrs. Johnson watched a home movie made by the Head Start teacher of the children's outing to a local farm. The First Lady noted how animated and happy the children were as they watched the film, far more so than their listless and dull parents.

On August 31, Johnson announced to an audience of several hundred doctors, psychologists, and educators at the White House that Head Start would become a full, one-year permanent program for 350,000 poor children, three years old and up. What had started as an experiment had "been battle-tested" and "proved worthy." Hope had "entered the lives of more than a half-million youngsters who needed it most."[92]

By the fall of 1965, OEO and its doings were at the hot center of an emerging war over class, race, and ideology that would strain American society in the years ahead. Much that had happened in the neighborhoods and the rural communities surprised and dismayed the liberal opinion makers and the well-disposed middle-class men and women who formed the nucleus of the Great Society's consensus. At the same time, it had politicized a stratum of intellectuals and students, generated a contingent of black activists, and raised in the ghettos exaggerated expectations, doomed almost inevitably to disappointment. Yet the administration still glowed with the achievements of the Eighty-ninth Congress. Americans generally still gave the president and his programs high grades.

Head Start gave the War on Poverty the bounce it needed, and as the Eighty-ninth wound down Shriver felt confident enough to propose a vast expansion and radical restructuring of the poverty war to pull everyone across the line to affluence with one great tug.

The idea of a federal cash subsidy to lift all families out of poverty had been in the air for several years. In 1963 the liberal economist Robert Theobald had written a book recommending a negative income tax as a device to set a floor under family incomes. In essence, the scheme proposed payments to families below the poverty line as a way to solve the dilemmas of welfare. As we saw, in early 1964, when Congress was considering the Economic Opportunity Act, the private Ad Hoc Committee on the Triple Revolution submitted to Johnson its proposal for a guaranteed family income. (For more on the negative income tax or the guaranteed income scheme, see Chapter 7.)

The embarrassments of the summer notwithstanding, in late October Shriver sent a memo to LBJ sketching out a grandiose plan to "end poverty in the United States, as we know it today, within a generation" that promoted a "universal negative income tax going to *all the poor* according to the single criterion of need."[93] The memo derived from a report by Joseph Kershaw, a former provost of Williams College, who had come to Washington to head the OEO office of Research, Plans, Programs and Evaluation, modeled after McNamara's touted systems analysis approach to efficiency at the Department of Defense. During the summer Kershaw and his staff assembled a five-year antipoverty plan that centered on a negative income tax and a mandated family allowance.

The guaranteed income proposal had little chance of enactment at this point. LBJ, for one, believed the scheme unrealistic. He also suspected that it was a political ploy by Robert Kennedy, Shriver's brother-in-law. The Kennedys, he felt, were bidding for the left-liberal vote, which Bobby would mobilize to challenge him for president in 1968.

During the fall of 1965, in fact, LBJ, though still committed to the Great Society and the War on Poverty, considered dismantling OEO as an entity. Optimistic in public, he recognized the drain of political capital as each week brought its new community action or Job Corps horror story. In mid-September, the new budget director, Charles Schultze, demanded that the OEO cease to encourage the politicizing of community action programs. *"We ought not to be in the business of organizing the poor politically,"* he wrote the president emphatically.[94] Later in the fall, the mayors again asked Hubert Humphrey to tell Johnson that something had to be done to check the community action kamikazes who were trying to destroy responsible city government. In November LBJ asked his assistant, Joe Califano, in "strictest confidence," to look into the possible dismemberment of the OEO and reassignment of its healthy parts to other agencies.[95] In the end, fearing negative political consequences, LBJ drew back, but he never felt as enthusiastic about the agency after mid-1965 as he had before.

The Johnsons always spent Christmas and New Year's at their Texas ranch. This time, the president flew down on December 21 and brought his new budget with him to work on. At the top of his agenda was figuring out how to pay for both the escalating war in Vietnam and his Great Society programs. Interspersed with the difficult decisions were the usual holiday festivities, made brighter now by the engagement announcement of the Johnsons' youngest daughter, Luci, to Air National Guardsman Patrick John Nugent. On Christmas Day the Johnsons attended services at the small stone Episcopal church in nearby Fredericksburg, and then exchanged presents back at the Ranch. The president gave his wife a new camera. There was good news about his health. He was healing well after the gallbladder operation in October, and the president's doctor pronounced him in "fine condition."

On January 2, relaxed and rested, Johnson returned to Washington. But the new session of Congress was about to begin and, given the news from the field, no one could be confident that the legislative momentum of the months just past could be sustained.

FIVE

Guns and Butter

JOSEPH CALIFANO, JR., arrived in Washington at the beginning of JFK's administration on the same wave that brought Richard Goodwin, Arthur Schlesinger, Jr., and Walt Rostow. Born in Brooklyn and a Harvard Law School graduate, Califano became one of McNamara's "whiz kids" at the Pentagon, where he learned the scientific management approach his boss had brought with him to government from the Ford Motor Company. When presidential special assistant Bill Moyers moved to the White House press office in July 1965, LBJ stole Califano from Defense to take Moyers's place as "a general-utility infielder on the domestic scene."[1]

Califano was an earnest liberal who shared the Great Society's social vision. During his first six months at the White House he spent much of his time fighting wage and price increases and bullying the feds into keeping interest rates low. But he was also LBJ's chief program planner for the second session of the Eighty-ninth Congress. During the summer and early fall, as the bounteous first session peaked, Califano was assembling task forces, consulting experts, and reading reports for a legislative agenda for 1966. At the Ranch, just before the New Year, he handed LBJ a document he had prepared entitled "The Great Society—A Second-year Legislative Program." For two hours the two men flipped through the loose-leaf folder, selecting the items to feed into the congressional mill in January. It was an extensive list.

There were initiatives to "reshape and reorganize" the executive branch, to shape new fair-housing legislation, to create a new department of transportation, and to reform campaign financing. The administration also proposed to expand the national park system, preserve historic sites, keep the rivers clean, construct hiking trails, improve the medical delivery system, build more schools, provide poor children with free school lunches, raise the minimum wage, and protect consumers through truth-in-packaging and truth-in-lending laws. In fact, most of this was minor stuff compared with the War on Poverty, Medicare, and federal aid to education. But there was one item in the thick book that seemed to break new ground. This was the "Demonstration Cities" program, an experiment in transforming the inner cities through an all-fronts attack on city pathologies—physical, social, medical, and administrative—more ambitious and imaginative than the "slum clearance" and "urban renewal" of the past.

In truth, few of the projects Johnson reviewed that winter's day at the Ranch were unfamiliar to him. The germ of Demonstration Cities could be found in the appendix of a 1964 task force report. It took on political weight when, the previous May, it came to the attention of Walter Reuther. And the scheme had been reworked and refined by a blue-ribbon task force ever since.

But Demonstration Cities was the only innovative program on the list. Reverting to his Ann Arbor vision of May 1964, Johnson would label the second session legislative array a "new agenda." The legislation of the first session had completed the New Deal, he later explained, but the new proposals tackled the problems that advanced technology had imposed on society. "Our growth in population, the massive decay of our cities, the steady separation of man from nature, the depersonalization of life in the post-industrial age . . . were the overwhelming problems of the future, demanding immediate action," he would declare in his memoirs.[2] This was more rhetoric than substance, however. Most of the proposals merely extended measures passed the session before. And the sad truth was that even this limited agenda would be difficult to enact. The second session would prove disappointing. With each passing month confusion, worry, fatigue, and anger would come to dominate public discourse and eat away at the broad middle-class consensus of the year before. And the sense of a changing climate of opinion would readily pass through

the Capitol's permeable walls to reach the impressionable minds
of the nation's legislators.

Few Washington insiders expected innovative, exciting programs
for the second session. Too much had taken place since the surging hopes of a year before. By December 1965 there were 185,000
combat troops in Vietnam, and 1,350 young Americans had been
brought home in body bags. During the forty-plus weeks the second session of the Eighty-ninth Congress lasted, the number of
American fighting men in Southeast Asia would soar to 375,000.
So would the carnage: There would be five thousand more American dead by New Year's Day 1966.

Vietnam had already begun to deflate the Great Society as the
new session opened. The Johnson coalition had been wide. At
one end was "enlightened" business, exemplified by Henry
Ford II, David Rockefeller, Thomas Watson of IBM, Ben Heineman of the Chicago and Northwestern, Edgar Kaiser of Kaiser
Industries, and Jack Straus of R. H. Macy—tycoons who had supported him against Goldwater. At the other end, briefly, stood
SDS, which, in the 1964 presidential campaign, had adopted as its
slogan "Half the Way with LBJ." Between was a broad band of
liberal academics and intellectuals, trade union leaders, African-
Americans, and the loyal blue-collar and ethnic constituencies of
the post–New Deal Democratic Party. This was the "consensus"
that Johnson had touted, and encouraged, after the 1964 landslide.

Vietnam rapidly disarticulated this loose confederation. Johnson was able to camouflage the country's growing role in Vietnam
during the 1964 campaign, but in February 1965 he had launched
a massive bombing campaign against North Vietnam to halt the
communist drive to overthrow the pro-Western regime in Saigon.
In March the first American combat troops came ashore on
Danang beach. Abruptly, what had been a "trouble spot" became
a war.

Vietnam first detached the anti–Cold War, non-communist left,
which had never been firmly anchored to LBJ. SDS, still an obscure campus group, held its first anti-Vietnam protest in April
1965, drawing eight thousand students and a modest crowd of
adult left-liberals, pacifists, and antiwar activists to Washington.
Academe had begun its long and bitter guerrilla war against Lyn-

don Johnson a month earlier when a circle of University of Michigan professors organized the first anti-Vietnam teach-in. The teach-in movement soon leaped from Ann Arbor to campuses in every corner of the nation. Its primary target was Johnson's foreign policy, but it undermined the administration's general credibility and destroyed its reputation with the liberal professoriat.

All through 1965 the antiwar movement grew in volume and strength, gathering in an ever-larger proportion of the nation's idealists, social activists, intellectuals, and opinion leaders. Before the year was out Vietnam had become an issue for the civil rights leadership. Martin Luther King began to denounce the war in February. SNCC leader Robert Moses addressed the SDS-inspired anti-Vietnam protest rally that April in Washington. Racial solidarity with Third World peoples and dismay that black youths were fighting and dying disproportionately in the Vietnamese rice paddies moved King and Moses. But they also feared that Vietnam was starving the Great Society. "Do we love the war on poverty or do we love Vietnam?" asked King during this first year of full-scale war.[3]

Nineteen sixty-six brought the antiwar movement to full, robust life. Thousands marched in the spring and fall rallies on both coasts under the banners of the Fifth Avenue Parade Committee and the International Days of Protest. Clergy, women's groups, and war veterans joined the circle of protesters, and that fall the first peace candidates' names appeared on local ballots. Anti-Vietnam doves came to see the president as an ogre. In February 1966 Johnson attended a dinner in New York's Waldorf Astoria Hotel to receive an award from Freedom House for his efforts for peace and justice. Outside four thousand protesters, led by radical pacifist A. J. Muste, denounced the war and the president. And each day more and more civil rights activists assailed the president's policies.

The defection of the nation's academics, students, and intellectuals from the administration would be especially wounding. Johnson's relations with the intellectuals had never been an easy one. He knew he could not do without them. He tried to keep open the channels of communication with the academics by sending Califano, McPherson, and other aides on visits to the campuses to pick the professors' brains. No administration appointed more Ph.D.'s to high office. But LBJ never felt comfortable with the thinkers. They had supported him against Goldwater in 1964 and generally had favored his social initiatives. The literati might have condemned the war but spared the Great Society, and some did. When poet Robert Lowell rudely rejected the invitation to attend the White House Festival of the Arts in June 1965, he acknowledged that he was "very enthusiastic" about most of the president's "domestic legislation and intentions."[4] Yet many of the academics and thinkers found it difficult to separate LBJ's good works at home from his bad works abroad. Johnson the hawk poisoned Johnson the liberal. Before long, for some, everything connected with LBJ came to seem false or problematic. After mid-1965 very little that the president said or did failed to provoke anger or arouse skepticism on the college campuses, in the editorial offices of the influential small magazines, and in the city neighborhoods and summer colonies where the intellectuals gathered. "How nice it is," declared the self-mocking *New Republic* in October, "to have a man who gives what liberals have asked for for generations plus the fun of kicking him around too."[5]

The students were another serious loss. Youthful idealism had brought volunteers to Head Start, VISTA, and the Teacher Corps. After 1966 much of that idealism would be deflected into the antiwar movement. In February 1966 Lady Bird wrote in her diary that she was counting the "months and the weeks" until she and Lyndon could leave the White House.[6]

But the war's damage went beyond political psychology. Vietnam also ate into the federal budget. The war cost a modest $5 billion in fiscal 1965–66, and during that first year the president was able to hide the expense in the general defense budget. But costs soon soared, reaching $26.5 billion in the fiscal year beginning July 1967. War outlays now competed with domestic outlays, and no matter how dazzling LBJ's financial wizardry he could not conceal it.

The competition put inexorable pressure on prices. The economy in 1966 was at full throttle. GNP would grow by 6.5 percent in 1966, even higher than the remarkable GNP surge of the previous year. Federal revenues would leap to $131 billion, $14 billion over 1965, the largest annual increase since the early 1950s. In the parlance of the day, the country might well have enjoyed both guns and butter without severe strain. But beginning in mid-1965 the consumer and producer price indexes, virtually flat since

1961, began to inch up. On December 1, in a telephone speech from the Ranch to the Business Council in Washington, the president acknowledged a rise of 2.3 percent in wholesale prices and 1.8 percent in consumer prices for the year.

In fact, the war by itself does not explain the rising rate of inflation. By 1966, surging investor outlays and consumer demand had hit the wall of virtual full employment, and the economy could not avoid price rises. Yet almost everyone considered the war to blame and assumed that if it continued, domestic federal spending would have to be restrained or even cut to hold down prices.

Johnson himself feared inflation. Though an old populist, he was a fiscal conservative who posed as protector of middle-class real incomes. And Americans as a whole were terrified of price increases. A Gallup poll in the fall of 1967, when the inflation rate was still only about 3 percent annually, disclosed that a full 60 percent of the American public considered "the high cost of living" their most "urgent problem."[7] Whatever he personally felt, the president realized that inflation gave his political enemies a powerful stick to beat him with.

The obvious way to fight price rises was to raise taxes: force the consuming public to surrender income to the government so it could continue the war against North Vietnam and the war against social inequality simultaneously. At the end of 1965 Gardner Ackley, Heller's successor as head of the Council of Economic Advisers, urged a tax increase. So did Heller, who was now back at the University of Minnesota, and Budget Bureau Director Charles Schultze. But raising taxes meant making both wars painful, and the president had no illusions about the public's willingness to sacrifice for either. As a result, Johnson used every trick he knew to fight price rises without asking for a tax increase. He sold off federal stockpiles of aluminum, copper, and other metals to increase government revenues. When shoe prices inched up he put export controls on hides to contain the cost of leather. To prevent lamb prices from surging he ordered the Defense Department to buy New Zealand lamb for the troops in Vietnam. Some of his cost-cutting maneuvers were comical. He turned off White House lights; he ordered the use of slower executive aircraft to save on fuel; he cut the number of White House staffers' phone lines.

None of these ploys worked, or worked for very long. The specter of inflation hovered over the entire second session.

Price pressures began to slow the Great Society even in 1966. During the congressional intersession Johnson was barraged with admonitions from conservatives that domestic programs be reined in or cut back to repress the evils of inflation. In October Arthur Krock, the conservative *New York Times* columnist, would blame both wage demands by organized labor and "welfare state programs" for the growing pressure on prices.[8] In December, the conservative weekly *U.S. News & World Report* would claim that guns and butter were simply too much. The president could avoid price controls, new taxes, and restraints on consumer credit only if he put "wraps on the Great Society."[9] The most telling warning would come, in early December, from George Mahon of Texas, chairman of the powerful House Appropriations Committee and a longtime LBJ political ally. "In light of the situation confronting us," it was urgent, Mahon told reporters, that both Congress and the administration slow outlays for enacted programs and postpone or eliminate others. All new programs should be made "to crawl before they can walk," he declared.[10]

And yet as the new legislative year opened, a broad center coalition remained in the president's corner and fought to save and even expand the Great Society, war and inflation notwithstanding. The general public still liked the administration's domestic programs. A Harris poll on January 9, 1966, noted that when Congress reconvened it would "be riding the crest of the highest public approval rating registered in modern times." More than 70 percent of the voters gave "a favorable rating to the job done by Congress in 1965." "The reason for the increase," the pollsters noted, was "the widespread almost uniform praise . . . for the legislative program adopted after President Johnson took [office]." The public backed Medicare by 82 percent, federal aid to education by 90 percent, and the tax cut by 92 percent.[11]

And the president still had most of the big bloc constituencies on his side. Union leaders went along with the president on the war itself. Like him, they felt that communism must be checked. But they did not feel it should come at the expense of the administration's social programs. Andrew Biemiller, former congressman and chief Washington lobbyist of the AFL-CIO, came by Califano's office just before Christmas 1965 to exhort him to spare the Great Society. George Meany had sent him, he told Califano, to express labor's concern "that the great Society programs not be gutted . . . because of the war in Vietnam." The AFL-CIO was "100 percent with" the president on Vietnam, but "they did not believe that Vietnam should result in a drastic reduction of the Great Society programs."[12] The civil rights movement was becoming more militant, moving beyond the administration's retraining and education programs to direct federal jobs creation and guaranteed income policies. But mainstream civil rights leaders still could be counted on to support any addition to the Great Society they could get for their constituency.

And by now, existing Great Society programs had created constituencies even among unlikely groups. When, during the recess, rumors of Great Society medical program budget cuts for fiscal 1966–67 began to circulate, the medical profession rushed to sound the alarm. James Shannon, director of the National Institutes of Health, said he was distressed and disappointed at the rumored budget figures for medical programs. On January 2, Dr. Howard Rusk, a prominent New York medical administrator, expressed fervent hope that they would prove untrue. Rusk asked that the programs to expand medical education, particularly, be spared the pruning knife. The nation needed eleven thousand new doctors a year to take care of its expanding medical needs. Now was not the time to stint on medical costs.[13]

Still, as they dipped their toes into the political waters in early 1966, the Washington cognoscenti foresaw little chance that the Great Society could do better than hold its own in the new session. Observers expected the war's immoderate cost to be raised against every proposal. "The money squeeze is awful," declared an unidentified White House aide; "there hasn't been anything like it for years."[14] Even the warmest friends of the Great Society seemed pessimistic. Just before Congress convened, Representative George Grider of Tennessee, a Southern liberal who had voted on the administration's side 93 percent of the time the previous session, warned that there was little chance that "the nation is going to be able to afford expansion of social programs in the next term and there may even be some cutting back."[15]

Johnson was torn himself about his domestic social programs. He wanted the Great Society to advance but he also sought fiscal restraint this session. Ironically, congressional committees, yielding to constituent pressure, would vote to raise his program budgets, forcing the president to scold and admonish them for their irresponsibility.

The general public first learned of the new round of Great Society proposals on January 12 in Johnson's "State of the Union" message, written by Richard Goodwin, the idealistic young aide who had authored the Ann Arbor Great Society address.

Johnson considered Goodwin's departure from the White House the previous September, ostensibly to further his career as a writer, an act of disloyalty. To LBJ, haunted by personal insecurity since childhood, there was no greater sin. When Califano suggested that Goodwin be asked to write the "State of the Union," he had responded with a curt no. But LBJ recognized Goodwin's special flair for framing grand themes, and relented. Goodwin accepted the assignment as his last service to an administration he had come to despise for its Vietnam policy.

The experience was punishing. Holed up at the Mayflower Hotel, Goodwin sweated over the speech for a week. In the final push he was at his typewriter thirty-six straight hours, until the keys blurred before his eyes. By the morning of January 12 the speech was still being polished, and Goodwin was totally exhausted. Rushed to the White House, the draft was picked over by Califano and Jack Valenti, another presidential assistant, and then reworked by LBJ himself. It was ready for delivery to the joint session of Congress at nine that evening.

Johnson had refused to see Goodwin during the drafting process, but he invited him along to the Capitol for the address. Bone tired and angry at the president's shabby treatment of him, he declined. He never saw LBJ again.

The January 12 address, despite Goodwin's talents, is not an eloquent document in print. It was interrupted by applause fifty-nine times, but that may have been because LBJ, leaving nothing to chance, had ordered aide Marvin Watson to start clapping at the end of specified lines. The applause may also have derived from the president's machine-gun delivery: LBJ fired off a hundred words a minute in a confident staccato style that electrified those who heard him.

Caught between the crossfires of left and right, of spenders and savers, Johnson chose the middle ground. "This nation is mighty enough, its society is healthy enough, its people are strong enough," he proclaimed, "to pursue our goals in the rest of the world while still building a Great Society here at home." The president asked for continuing support of his health and education programs and called on Congress to prosecute "with vigor and determination" the War on Poverty. He recommended a cabinet-level department of transportation, a federal highway safety act, and new laws to reduce air and water pollution. He announced his intention to protect the consumer against false labeling on packaging, against harmful drugs and cosmetics, and against deceptive interest and credit charges. His most ambitious proposal was a program "to rebuild completely, on a scale never before attempted, entire central and slum areas of several of our cities in America." He admitted that Vietnam imposed constraints, and recommended that excises on new cars and telephone calls, recently cut, be restored to raise additional money. But he insisted that surging federal revenues from economic growth would keep the deficit small even if all the programs he recommended were enacted. "I have not come here tonight to ask for pleasant luxuries or for idle pleasures. I have come here to recommend that . . . you bring the most urgent decencies of life to all your fellow Americans."[16]

That evening at the White House, the president and Califano watched the coverage of his speech in LBJ's bedroom on three TV sets simultaneously while they ate a late supper. Johnson was happy with the way the legislators had received the address and would be pleased with much of the press comment in the next few days. *Newsweek,* typically, called the speech "heady, bubbly, 100-proof Old Lyndon."[17] The magazine's columnist Kenneth Crawford judged his agenda "almost as sweeping as the one he presented to the same Congress a year ago. . . ." It would "take members a while to recover from the resulting shock."[18]

But in fact, as we saw, only a few items were new and only one, the Demonstration Cities program, was bold. The president's January 24 budget message only confirmed the loss of momentum for LBJ's domestic program. He was requesting $2 billion less for his Great Society programs than Congress had authorized in 1965. A few weeks into the session pundit Walter Lippmann cut to the truth. The president's claim of guns plus butter depended on a "thin end of the wedge" approach. His proposals focused primarily on pilot programs, with little immediate need for money, and postponed program growth to some vague future. Lippmann saw this approach as common to both the president's domestic and foreign policies. "This is the tactic by which the administration has managed to support the claim that it can construct the Great Society and can win the war," Lippmann noted.[19] Lippmann was right, but the months ahead would put to the test even these cautious hopes.

Among the administration's most urgent legislative concerns were two pieces of business left over from 1965: rent supplements and the Teacher Corps. Congress had approved the Teacher Corps as part of the Higher Education Act the previous session but had failed to give it any money. The rent supplement program had been pushed through the Senate during the first session, but then had been dropped in the House-Senate joint conference committee on the appropriations. In effect, both were dead.

This was not pure happenstance. Both measures touched sensitive nerves. The Teacher Corps raised visions of further federal intrusion into the American system of neighborhood schools, and alarmed all the foes of big government and defenders of local autonomy. But beyond this, it threatened the educational establishment. The not so "gentlelady" from Oregon, Congresswoman Edith Green of the powerful House Labor and Education Committee, considered the corps elitist. A former schoolteacher, Green disliked the government's promise of free graduate tuition and light teaching loads to Teacher Corps volunteers; regular teachers received no such benefits. She also feared that the inexperienced if enthusiastic Teacher Corps interns would dilute professional teaching standards. Green echoed the concerns of professional educators and deans of education, who insisted that they already were training teachers for service in ghetto and poor rural schools and objected to the competition. And there may have been a whiff of suspicion in Congress that the Teacher Corps would nurture squads of Mario Savios and Bettina Apthekers, leaders of the recent Berkeley Free Speech Movement, agitating and recruiting in public schools around the country.

The rent supplement program suggested other nightmares: black families moving into white neighborhoods followed by a surge in crime and the collapse of property values. The Watts upheaval, soaring crime rates, and a thousand other recent paroxysms of local social disorder had made many whites more uneasy than ever about black neighbors. During the very weeks that Congress debated the rent supplement, Martin Luther King and his supporters were being barraged with insults and stones as they marched through white Chicago neighborhoods demanding an end to lily-white housing restrictions. Chicago's white homeowners would prove to be racists on a scale with Birmingham rednecks, and the King demonstrations would reveal how thin the veneer of racial civility was when the issue of hearth and home was at stake.

Even before it stalled completely the rent supplement program was in trouble. During the first session the administration's original commitment of $30 million had been cut to $22 million and eligibility restricted to the poorest of the poor. But even this modest measure remained a hot potato. When Robert Weaver, the black head of the Housing and Home Finance Agency, predicted the creation of as many as 500,000 rental units under the law if funded, a nervous Congress deleted all money for the program from the appropriations bill. Johnson had intended to appoint Weaver as first head of the new Department of Housing and Urban Development, but he blamed Weaver's premature disclosure for frightening Congress. Displaying his periodic streak of cruelty, he let Weaver dangle. Not until the following January did he submit his name as the first black member of the cabinet.

Little of these lurking sensitivities broke the decorous surface when, in the new session, Congress considered the supplementary appropriations bills to fund both programs. But inflation did. In the Senate, Everett Dirksen, the Republican minority leader, demanded fiscal restraint. "Call it walking inflation, call it creeping inflation, I don't care what you call it," opined the Senate's sonorous "Wizard of Ooze." "Somewhere, somehow, there has to be a halt in programs of the Great Society." It's either cut spending or a tax increase, he noted, and he preferred the former.[20] And rising prices undoubtedly influenced votes on both these leftover bills, though the unspoken motives probably counted for more.

Teacher Corps and rent-supplement votes seesawed back and forth through most of the session. Even with the administration riding close herd on the Democrats, virtually all roll calls on these issues were close. In March the House approved a paltry $22 million rent-supplement bill by an eight-vote margin, only to have the Senate Appropriations Committee knock it out of the 1966–67 budget bill. After hard lobbying by the White House, the full Senate restored the sum by a vote of 46 to 45 and also approved the Teacher Corps, though at the miserly level of $9.5 million for the coming year. Back in the full House the rent supplement ran the gauntlet again as the lower chamber considered the $2.8 billion supplementary appropriations bill for fiscal 1967. It was a dramatic moment, and a hush fell over the normally noisy House chamber, as the rent-supplement provision finally squeaked through by a vote of 192 to 188 in early April. The measure at this point was at most a pale shadow of the original. Congress had provided only $1 million for a start-up budget. Not until September, as the session was winding down, did it appropriate a modest $22 million for the program. In the same late action the Teacher Corps received an additional $7.5 million.

Congressional approval of both programs was symbolically important; defeats would have humiliated the administration. Obviously the president still had some clout. Yet passage was not a famous victory. The rent-supplement bill applied only to families eligible for public housing—those with incomes of about $2,600 a year or less. The more generous, original proposal to include those with incomes slightly above public housing eligibility levels had not been restored. Participants would pay 25 percent of their income for the rental of rehabbed housing or new apartments to be constructed by nonprofit groups, co-ops, or limited dividend corporations. The difference between this payment and the actual rent of the apartments would be paid by the federal government. Aside from the modest scope of the program—$22 million did not many rent bills pay—the law as passed also knuckled under to white fears of black neighbors. To discourage integrated housing it gave local authorities the right to exclude from their bailiwicks any project they did not like. For all the controversy surrounding it, the bill was a feeble measure. Five years after passage it had produced only 46,000 units of new housing for the poor.

The Teacher Corps measure, as passed, did not warrant administration preening either. As a *New York Times* editorial noted, the final $7.5 million grant was little more than a "liquidation payment."[21] Modeled after the prestigious Peace Corps, as proposed in the expansive first session it was to have had a budget of $31 million to train and deploy six thousand teachers. With only the niggardly $9.5 million allotted to it in April 1966, the corps recruited 1,600 teachers and recent college graduates during the summer and began to train them on forty-two college campuses. During these start-up months the interns and experienced "master teachers" spent half a day in academic training and the other half in summer session classes at poverty-level area schools. By summer's end the initial grant had been exhausted, but the corps survived on a month-to-month basis under a special congressional funding resolution. When the regular school year opened it still lacked money, and actual teaching was unable to begin. Teachers and interns quit and the corps barely survived. Not until the end of September, when Congress came through with the additional $7.5 million, were the corpsmen finally able to begin their teaching assignments.

In fact this was not a "liquidation payment," as the *Times* had predicted. The corps would continue its perils-of-Pauline existence for some years by convincing the public and the education establishment that it was both safe and creative. But it would never be generously funded and never attract much public attention.

The Teacher Corps and rent supplements were only two of the bills the administration placed on the congressional agenda. In all, the White House introduced over a hundred significant bills during the second session, considerably more than in the first.

The president ultimately got much of what he wanted. Califano estimates that Congress passed ninety-seven of the 113 measures he proposed. But there was a big catch. Aside from the Demonstration Cities bill, none of these ninety-seven approached the breakthrough measures of 1964 and 1965 as installments of the Great Society. Clearly Johnson was trying to spare the public economic pain, and most of the proposals, as Lippmann had observed, were pilot programs that did not require much initial money. Johnson's strategy here was to plant the seed; the tree would ultimately follow.

Liberals had little patience with this approach. Four months into the session *The New Republic,* voice of the moderate left, gave the administration a *C* on its performance. In an April 1966 editorial, "The Late, Great Society," the magazine called the recently funded Teacher Corps and rent supplements "the only important Great Society legislation of the year." But they were "small potatoes." There had been no dramatic Great Society "cutbacks," it was true, but there *had* been "an almost random series of 'pull-backs,' " from the agenda of 1965. Echoing Lippmann, one of the magazine's founders before World War I, *The New Republic* called the administration's bills pilot programs that were grossly underfunded, when they were not intrinsically feeble. The editors had no doubt where the responsibility for this depressing reality lay. Quoting an unnamed Midwestern congressman, the magazine noted that "Vietnam hangs over everything we do." It was "not just politics, it's the psychological problems it causes."[22]

Yet even if the administration came up with few bold new proposals, it fought to keep the existing Great Society structure from being dismantled. The chief weight-bearing pillars—the War on Poverty, the education measures, health care—had to be protected from the ax wielders when Congress considered the appropriations bills for fiscal 1967. This required constant parliamentary vigilance and deployment of all Johnson's vaunted political skills. Most of these day-to-day maneuvers do not warrant spacious attention. They were further applications of the standard Johnson pharmacopoeia of the previous session: phone calls, stroking sessions, deal-making, appeals to patriotism, gentle threats, in-your-face intimidation.

One case, however, deserves scrutiny. The poverty programs of the Office of Economic Opportunity, like other federal programs, were subject to annual, fiscal-year review and renewal. In 1965 OEO's budget had been approved for fiscal 1966 with an increase to $1.78 billion without much difficulty. Since then, however, the bad press of the community action programs and the Job Corps had sowed doubt and confusion, and Congress began to balk. The administration tried to tighten up OEO management and cool down the OEO zeal to save the world. The president appointed a team under Bertrand Harding, an Internal Revenue Service bureaucrat, to improve OEO's management practices, and in June appointed Harding as Shriver's deputy to replace Bernard Boutin, a man considered by his freewheeling subordinates to be too straitlaced and rules-bound. But Johnson also continued to give serious consideration to breaking up the Office of Economic Opportunity and distributing its functions among existing cabinet departments—HEW, HUD, Agriculture, and Labor. Califano recommended that it be done and proposed that, to appease the liberals, Shriver be made secretary of Housing and Urban Development and assume some sort of overall direction of the curtailed War on Poverty. "My personal feeling," he told the president, is that "the whole package . . . would be a typically dramatic Johnsonian move that would be received with applause across the board."[23]

Johnson never had to accept the Califano plan. By the end of the year some of the OEO firebrands of the early months, including William Haddad, Theodore Berry, Sanford Kravitz, and Richard Boone, had departed, a number to try their hands at social engineering elsewhere. The effects were quickly felt. As Robert Levine, an OEO staffer in those years, has noted, during 1966 the community action division largely ceased its social experimentation role and zeroed in on getting community action agencies up and running as coordinators of services for the poor.

But the shift came too late. By now community action had lost support among members of Congress sensitive to the complaints of the mayors and other local elected officials in their districts. In its vulnerable state OEO was also susceptible to attack by other federal agencies, most notably the cannibalistic Labor Department, which wanted to claim its manpower training programs for itself. On the other hand it did not totally lack a constituency. The LBJ Library White House central files contain a thick folder of citizens' endorsements of the administration's 1966 poverty bill, some expressing serious concern, as the summer advanced, that the vote would be delayed until after the fall elections.[24] The liberal press too gave OEO, and even the community action programs, high marks. In early 1966 *The Washington Post* ran a long series of articles by Alfred Friendly, called "The Better War," praising the War on Poverty and portraying the community action programs as by-and-large moderate groups that had helped bring the poor into the mainstream.[25]

In fact, the administration was still toying with breaking up OEO and shuffling its programs to other agencies. When in September Congressman Sam Gibbons of Florida, second in command of the Education and Labor Committee, asked the president to respond to a newspaper story about reassigning War on

Poverty programs, Johnson attached a memo: "Call SG. Say no position on this. It's being studied."[26]

Whatever his doubts the president asked for $1.75 billion for OEO for fiscal 1966–67, and the House Committee on Education and Labor began consideration of the budget in early March. Eight days of one-sided, pro-OEO hearings incited leading Republican committee members Albert Quie of Minnesota and Charles Goodell of New York to charge they were a "whitewash."[27]

But the problem was Adam Clayton Powell, not the Republicans. Chairman Powell in many ways was as good a friend as the War on Poverty could have. His constituency, after all, was a major beneficiary of the antipoverty program. But he was also an instable, mercurial man who at the moment was in deep trouble with the law over failure to pay a $575,000 court judgment against him in a libel suit, and was on the outs with his colleagues over payroll padding and frequent trips to Miami and the Caribbean on committee business that he could not justify. In fact, even as the OEO budget bill wended its way through the legislative process, a special House subcommittee was investigating his expense account claims and the charges of payroll padding. Eventually, Powell would be expelled from Congress, a move that provoked outrage among blacks and civil rights partisans, who believed that the drastic action would not have been taken if Powell had been white. Distracted and self-involved, Powell failed to protect the administration's budget request from pruning.

Predictably, among the various Economic Opportunity Act titles, the cacophonous, irksome community action programs took the biggest hit, initially losing nearly half the $600 million requested for them, exclusive of Head Start. But the committee pumped up the budget for the Neighborhood Youth Corps, an EOA program established to keep high school dropouts in school, but administered by the Labor Department. The committee also limited the power of community action administrators to fund programs at their discretion by earmarking specific sums to Head Start, neighborhood health centers, and legal services.

Within the committee, the Republicans conducted a war against the War. GOP members on the House Education and Labor Committee assembled a hundred-page indictment of the administration's poverty programs that called for a complete new start. The Democratic War on Poverty, they asserted, merely raised expectations without providing the means to satisfy them. The programs, especially the Job Corps and community action, had been badly run and scandal-ridden, and even Head Start, though commendable in many ways, was sliding into "bureaucratic confusion." In place of the supposed Democratic boondoggles, the Republicans proposed their own "Opportunity Crusade," which would bring together local, state, and federal governments with private industry to educate, train, and motivate the poor. It would also remove the Job Corps and Neighborhood Youth Corps from OEO and hand them over to the Department of Labor. OEO would be reduced to VISTA and the community action programs. Every committee Republican except Ogden Reid, the blueblood liberal from New York, signed the document.[28]

Despite the attacks, the committee completed work on the OEO budget on June 1, but thanks to Powell, even this maimed measure barely made it out the House door. The congressman from Harlem was now battling with Sargent Shriver over the Jersey City community action program and over a new OEO policy, quietly adopted in March, to give the mayors veto power over poverty projects. Allowing the mayors to control the community action programs was "brutal," he declared, and he threatened to stop the War on Poverty in its tracks if the policy continued.[29]

Powell may also have been distracted by his mounting legal troubles. In fact he disappeared from Washington for weeks without telling his colleagues where he was. For two months past the fiscal year deadline, the bill was not officially reported to the House, forcing OEO to proceed blindly, not knowing how or if Congress would finally allocate the money. Administration stalwarts urged Speaker John McCormack to bypass Powell by invoking the twenty-one-day rule previously wielded against obstructive conservatives. He refused: The rule was a blunt, dangerous weapon to be used only sparingly, he insisted.

Powell's fellow committee Democrats were not as forbearing. On September 15 Congressman Sam Gibbons, a loyal administration Democrat, introduced a motion to strip Powell of his powers and assign them to the committee majority. In high dudgeon, Powell called a press conference and accused Gibbons of racism. His colleague was always quick to make that charge, Gibbons retorted, and countercharged that during the session the Harlem minister had missed 164 of 218 House roll calls. On September 22, by a vote of 27 to 1, the Labor and Education Committee adopted Gibbons's proposal. That finally got the Harlem congressman's attention, and on September 26 Powell sent the bill to the House for final action.

The House debated the measure for three days, with Gibbons serving as floor manager. Worried that their bickering had endangered the bill, the Democrats closed ranks. To applause and laughter, Powell declared: "On this side, we are in complete unanimity."[30] And united they were. The Democrats successfully beat back Republican efforts to transfer parts of the War on Poverty to the Office of Education and the Labor Department. The bill passed 210 to 156.

The Senate had approved a different, more generous measure. With a broader, more suburban constituency, senators heard only faintly the cries of pain from the mayors. Only one third, moreover, were up for reelection in November. Both political facts explain the Senate's expansive $2.5 billion budget. But the Senate version also backed off from community action, deflecting some of its money into a number of small-scale job creation programs.

In the end, within days of adjournment, the Senate, under strong pressure from the administration not to bust the overall federal budget, accepted the House total of $1.75 billion and passed the bill 49 to 20. The Office of Economic Opportunity had weathered the storm, but it would never enjoy the freewheeling, exuberant style of its first two years again. In late October *The Washington Post* summed up the decline. "The high spirits and sense of mission are rapidly leaking out of the Office of Economic Opportunity. . . . Its long, trying struggle this year to get even an inadequate budget has badly eroded its assurance." The liberal newspaper, located in a city with a black majority, gave OEO programs high marks for good intentions and for providing some modest benefits for the poor. According to the *Post* editors, the OEO deserved to survive, though perhaps parts of its mission should be assigned elsewhere. The important thing, however, was for Johnson to "take stock, publicly" of the past two years' performance, and provide some renewed leadership.[31]

In fact it was difficult for the president to lead on the home front. Faced with the imminent hazards of reelection, Congress was no longer as willing to accept direction from LBJ as the year before. Time and again during the session, even administration stalwarts refused to go along with the president, especially when it required inflicting pain on influential or deserving constituents. The most galling defiance came from the liberal end of the political spectrum. When LBJ demanded sharp cuts in the federal milk and food lunch programs for schoolchildren to save money, Northern liberals stoutly resisted. Bobby Kennedy fought every effort to reduce poverty funds and so outraged LBJ that Senate Minority Leader Everett Dirksen reported that the president "fulminated like Hurricane Inez about what we were doing to his budget."[32]

The list of actual congressional enhancements of presidential budget recommendations was a long one: rural electrification, higher education, vocational education, the National Institutes of Health, and a federal civil servant pay raise. The education bills had especially potent congressional lobbies, and Congress gave short shrift to LBJ's urge for economy. In late March HEW's liaison on the Hill, Ralph Huitt, told the White House that "there was scarcely a Democratic member" who was "interested in 'holding the line' " on education. A majority, in fact, were asking for new programs "with rather expensive price tags." The response in part was political window dressing. Many of the subcommittee majorities would not be too upset if, in the end, the appropriations committees did not allow the increases to get through.[33] After Congress returned from the July 4 break, defiance surged. Many members from urban districts discovered that the president feared inflation more than their city constituents and concluded they need not heed his warnings.

In the Senate the chief culprit in padding the Elementary and Secondary Education Act (ESEA) refunding bill was Wayne Morse of Oregon, head of the education subcommittee of the Labor and Public Welfare Committee and former dean of the University of Oregon Law School. One of only two senators to vote against the 1964 Gulf of Tonkin resolution, which gave Johnson legal sanction for the Vietnam War, Morse was the earliest of the brave band of congressional "doves" whose numbers would swell so fast during the months ahead. He undoubtedly wished to improve the nation's schools, but he also refused to accept the reasons for the administration's parsimony. Vietnam, he declared, should not starve the country's children of the help they needed to advance in life. The bill that Morse's subcommittee reported out on July 15 made costly changes in the federal aid formula and added expensive new programs. It more than doubled the administration's funding request and goaded Douglass Cater, chief White House education aide, into an outburst. Morse had "declared war on his President" and was "trying to use education legislation as his weapon."[34] In the end the administration was able to postpone several big-ticket additions to ESEA until fiscal year 1968 but could not deflect increases in other parts of the federal education budget.

Johnson also found Congress resistant to any attempt to discourage inflation through taxes. Early in the session it passed the administration's modest measure to restore auto and telephone excises and accelerate collection of corporate and personal income taxes. But then it balked. Raising taxes in an election year is a prescription for political oblivion, and few members were in a suicidal mood. The president himself was loath to inflict fiscal pain on the voters. Yet the pressure built inexorably. For months his closest economic advisers had been suggesting that some sort of significant revenue increase would be unavoidable if spending continued at the rate of fiscal 1966. A majority of economists, liberal as well as conservative, testifying before the Joint Economic Committee of Congress in February favored a tax hike of some sort to suppress the inflation surge. "The expansion of demand," noted liberal economist Richard Musgrave of Harvard, might well exceed the ability of the economy to keep up, and it looked as if "some further tax restraint, applicable early this year, would have been in order."[35] In May, Walter Heller, the prime author of the 1964 tax slash, proposed a temporary $5 billion tax increase.

In August the president met with congressional leaders in the White House to test the waters for a modest income tax increase. "You'd have trouble getting more than fifteen votes," exclaimed House Minority Leader Gerald Ford. "You won't even get that many," Carl Albert, his Democratic counterpart, added.[36] The one proposal to raise revenue they would go along with was the repeal of the investment tax credit given business in the Kennedy years. This would increase the federal tax take while at the same time helping to cool off inflation-enhancing business investment. LBJ signed the bill into law shortly after Labor Day.

The president was able to extract from Congress several consumer protection laws. The first Truth-in-Packaging Act of 1966 was a weak measure, however, that failed to achieve its sponsors' goal of mandating uniform standards of size and weight so consumers could compare prices of store items. Despite administration efforts to hold the line, fierce industry opposition converted the original bill into a toothless law that merely restricted the exaggerated size claims on packages and allowed voluntary limits on the confusing array of sizes the consumer was exposed to. Congress also passed a bill to ensure safe toys for children and outlaw "goof balls" and pep pills, two dangerous recreational drugs.

More significant was the administration's auto and highway safety measures. Consumer advocates had long pointed the finger at the automobile as an unrestrained killer. From 1956 on, congressional committees had held hearings on auto safety, and representatives and senators had introduced bills to set safety standards. But during these years Americans cherished their large, gussied-up gas-guzzlers and showed little interest in safety concerns. And the cocky Detroit automakers, convinced they made the best cars in the world, resented every critical word said against their products and every effort to impose safety standards.

The picture altered abruptly in 1966 with the advent of Ralph Nader, a brilliant, darkly handsome young Harvard Law School graduate. Nader was a hot-eyed zealot who saw the auto companies as unprincipled killers of the innocent and himself as the victims' anointed savior. In 1963–64 he joined the Labor Department as an aide to Daniel Moynihan to research auto safety for legislation moving slowly through the congressional mill. Drawing on this experience, in late 1965 Nader published *Unsafe at Any Speed,* a flaming exposé of Detroit's profit-over-safety policies. The book singled out General Motors for its refusal to alter the life-threatening defects in its best-selling Chevrolet Corvair.

LBJ had proposed a highway safety bill in the 1966 "State of the Union" and had created a task force to prepare such a measure. The proposal submitted to Congress in early March, however, was a tepid bill that delayed government action for two years while the industry considered voluntary standards. Nader, a witness before Senator Ribicoff's subcommittee, attacked it as a "no-law law."[37] Then, on March 10, *The New York Times* headlined the confession of GM president James Roche that the auto giant had hired detectives to tail Nader to determine if he was connected with plaintiffs in several pending Corvair liability suits and to dig out dirt on his private and professional life.

The sensational revelation made auto safety a hot issue. Instead of the gloomy and frightening statistics of death and dismemberment and the dull details of dashboards, seat belts, and door locks, the public now suddenly had a classic evil-versus-good, David-and-Goliath plot to chew on. *Unsafe at Any Speed,* a moderate, 25,000-copy seller until now, leaped into bestsellerdom. The public got another installment of the morality tale when, at televised hearings called by Ribicoff's subcommittee to look into GM's harassment of a government witness, Roche publicly apologized to Nader.

The swell of public indignation assured a stronger bill than the administration had submitted. In Congress pro-industry resistance virtually collapsed. As one senator noted, "Everybody was so outraged that a great corporation was out to clobber a guy because he wrote critically about them . . . [they] said the hell with them."[38] On June 23 Congress passed the National Traffic and Motor Vehicle Safety Act authorizing the secretary of transportation to set auto safety standards and impose civil sanctions on manufacturers who produced cars and car parts that failed to meet those standards. Manufacturers who detected defects in their product were required to inform customers of the fact. Signed by Johnson on September 9, the bill was an improvement over the original, but it lacked the criminal penalty provision the strongest consumer advocates wanted. Still, it was the first time the automobile industry had been subject to federal safety regulation, and it became the precedent for the flood of later auto regulation laws. In December the Commerce Department, under terms of this law, established a set of safety standards for automobile manufacturers, including head rests to guard against whiplash injuries, cushioned instrument panels, more outside reflectors for better night visibility, and six lap belts for six-passenger cars.

The administration also induced the balky Congress to pass a number of significant conservation measures. Pursuing LBJ's goal of locating parks and recreation areas close to the urban millions, Johnson signed bills establishing Point Reyes National Seashore near San Francisco, the Indiana Dunes National Lakeshore park on Lake Erie, close to Chicago, and designating Wolf Trap Farm, near Washington, as a performing arts center. He also approved creation of Bighorn Canyon National Park in Montana and Wyoming and Guadalupe Mountains National Park in western Texas.

The arts and humanities foundations survived a narrow defeat. The House Appropriations Committee voted to cut the $7 million sum recommended for the arts and drop the humanities appropriation entirely. Committee members felt the nation could not afford such frills with a war on. But the more conservative members also demanded a say in the content of sponsored works and performances. In the end the humanities foundation was saved, and both foundations together received slightly greater funding than they had the first year.

But the chief sign during the second session that the Great Society still had some momentum was the Model Cities program, called originally Demonstration Cities.

The paroxysms of the urban ghettos unambiguously provided the thrust for this Great Society bill. The administration's supporters, in Congress and out, made no bones about the relevance of the measure to the uprisings in the ghettos in the previous months. The riots shouted loudly that more had to be done or the nation would explode. And besides, many white Americans felt, it was probably better to make the ghettos more livable than to encourage blacks and other minorities to flee to the white suburbs.

Demonstration Cities seemed an imaginative, holistic experiment in urban planning, combining existing and new resources to deal with cities as "total" environments, social and cultural as well as physical. It was reminiscent of the Tennessee Valley Authority project, the New Deal's bold stab at regional social "planning," in its approach. It was one of the few items of the second-session legislative program that came close to meriting the "New Agenda" label that Johnson sought to give most of his post-1965 proposals. And even if the New Agenda tag for Model Cities is hyperbolic, it *was* clearly a "second generation" effort at urban reconstruction that built on the experience of the first. Absent Vietnam, inflation, backlash, and the rightward shift in the political climate, it might have heralded a new strategy to problems of class, race, and inequality in America.

Model Cities was the brainchild of United Automobile Workers president Walter Reuther. A resident of turbulent Detroit and leader of a union with thousands of black workers, Reuther could not help being sensitive to the problems of the cities. He was also an idealist whose roots in the socialist movement drew him to schemes of bold social planning. Reuther got the demonstration cities idea from Detroit mayor Jerome Cavanagh, a former member of the 1964 task force on cities. In a memo to the president in mid-May 1965, Reuther proposed creating "research laboratories for the war against poverty and ugliness in the urban environment." Invoking Johnson's Ann Arbor image of "the city of man" serving "the desire for beauty and the hunger for community," he urged the choice of six large cities—Washington, Detroit, Chicago, Philadelphia, Houston, and Los Angeles—in which the government would create "full and complete neighborhoods for 50,000 people to give meaning to our *ability* to create architecturally beautiful and socially meaningful communities of the twentieth century. . . ."[39]

In fact, of course, federal money had been pouring into the cities for years in the form of payments to individuals, and this process only accelerated under the Great Society. The cities themselves had also received money, but most of it had been devoted to improved housing. Under the New Deal the federal government had subsidized "slum clearance" and the construction of giant high-rise "projects" to house the poor on the cleared sites. From 1949 onward the focus shifted to "urban renewal," the replacement of decayed areas with new residential housing and new commercial construction to rescue city centers from the creeping blight of the automobile age and the middle-class flight to the suburbs. Under the renewal program the public authorities bought up real estate in the slums and sold it to private developers, absorbing the difference between the price paid for the sites and the price received for the cleared land. By the mid-sixties, new malls, new office skyscrapers, new courthouses, theaters, and hotels had revitalized some city centers and improved urban tax bases, but they had done little directly for the poor. By 1967 more than 400,000 housing units had been pulled down in renewal areas largely inhabited by blacks and Hispanics. Only 41,000 new units of private housing had been constructed on the cleared ground and only a quarter of this was housing to fit the slim pockets of the poor. In fact urban renewal, in the phrase of the day, had often become "Negro removal." As we saw, it was the failure of urban renewal to benefit the urban poor that had stirred to life the Ford Foundation's efforts to rescue the cities' "gray areas."

Reuther remained partially trapped in the old equation: Physical renewal equals social renewal. But he also talked about "new types of old age centers, recreational facilities, and social services" for a "socially sound" as well as "physically beautiful" America. Reuther's memo, arriving on his desk during the still yeasty months of mid-1965, prodded Johnson's imagination. And then, in August, came Watts with thirty-four dead, nine hundred injured, and 4,300 arrested. In mid-September Reuther visited the White House to convey his vision to the president face to face. After the meeting Johnson told Califano that he wanted to rebuild the nation's slums and turn its cities into gems. A month later he established a task force composed of liberal businessmen, federal and city officials, civil rights leaders, academics, and Reuther himself to consider an ambitious program targeted at the cities.

With a small support staff of urban experts, the new task force, headed by Robert Wood of MIT, began its deliberations on October 16 in space provided at the White House. All told, it met for five long weekends. The administration was generous in its help, providing transportation via air force jets to and from Washington and to proposed project sites, and giving the panel free access to the best minds in the administration. Following the usual Johnson plan, the deliberations were secret. Even HUD secretary Robert Weaver was ignorant of its work. Members fought over details but in the end agreed on a plan to reconstruct American cities that they hoped would avoid the mistakes both of community action and urban renewal. They issued their draft report on December 16.

The original Heller proposal for the War on Poverty had recommended a small-scale social experiment before jumping in with both feet. Politics, however, had decreed a big program and a broad constituency instead. Now, once again, political realities prevailed. In its proposal the task force expanded Reuther's small group of metropolises to sixty-six large-, small-, and middle-sized cities. These "demonstration cities" would be selected by a presidential commission from among those, presumably hundreds, that submitted renewal proposals. These proposals would be evaluated for rounded, integrated attention to all aspects of neighborhood rehabilitation, for anticipated zeal and competence in carrying out the plans, for willingness to accept racial integration of housing, and for willingness to encourage, wherever possible, community leadership and participation. The approved cities would be able to redirect existing federal grants to designated slum neighborhoods; in addition, they could tap $2.3 billion of new federal money to be matched by a 20 percent local contribution. The task force members also hoped that the programs would attract private and state money to the target neighborhoods. Those cities in the program would become experimental laboratories in which a wide array of plans could be tried out and tested. Eventually all cities would learn from the experiences of the experimental first round.

This basic proposal reached Congress on January 26, in a message delivered by LBJ clothed in the usual inspirational Great Society rhetoric. McPherson, the president's counsel, had written the speech and, he later admitted, it had been too "arty."[40] "This Congress . . . can set in motion forces of change in great urban areas that will make them the masterpieces of our civilization," Johnson intoned. The "rebirth of our cities" to be accomplished by the bill would mean "a more tolerable and hopeful life for millions of Americans." The program would keep middle-income people in the cities and even induce some to return. It would reduce welfare costs, preserve valuable human resources, and provide "a clean room and a patch of sky for every person, a chance to live near an open space, and to reach it on a safe street."[41] And how expensive would the measure be? According to the president, it would cost just $12 million in its initial planning and $2.3 billion for implementation, spread over six years.

The bill began its slow progress through Congress the following day, with Califano in the role of administration trail boss. It quickly bogged down in both houses. There were abundant reasons for difficulty and delay. Senator John Sparkman of Alabama, head of the Senate Banking and Currency Committee, refused to touch it because of its desegregation feature and handed it over to Paul Douglas of Illinois. A World War II marine and distinguished former University of Chicago economics professor, Douglas was a bone-deep liberal, but he was in the race of his life for reelection in a state campaign that promised to turn on growing white ethnic resentment of blacks and of federal policies perceived as pro-black. In the House, the amiable but weak-willed William Barrett of Pennsylvania, chair of the housing subcommittee of the Banking and Currency Committee, refused to push the administration bill aggressively. There were substantive impediments as well. Many important players disliked it. In the House hearings, the city mayors expressed fears that the new program would divert money from cherished established ones. Housing experts testified that the government had grossly underestimated the costs of the social services to be provided to slum dwellers. Liberals, in general, questioned the miserly funding of the program. And reinforcing the hostile voices was the mounting fatigue of men and women who had been yoked to the legislative treadmill for eighteen long and tumultuous months while economic fears and racial resentments seeped into the nation's pores. By early May, Barrett's committee had amended the original bill to weaken its innovative goals and strip from it all but the $12 million planning feature. Last-minute intervention by Vice President Humphrey got a three-week delay in reporting out this token measure, but all observers agreed that the Demonstration Cities bill was in deep trouble.

Faced with the imminent defeat of its most important proposal of the session, the White House rallied. On June 10 the special White House Demonstration Cities swat team met in Califano's office to consider the fate of the bill. HUD secretary Robert Weaver made an impassioned plea for it, as did Charles Haar, HUD's assistant secretary. But others were pessimistic, seeing no way to get the measure through. Then, Postmaster General O'Brien, the White House liaison for congressional relations, rallied the dispirited troops in words described as "Churchillian—with an Irish flavor." He had never before presided over the "premature burial of one of the President's bills," he announced, and he "wasn't about to begin." Pounding the table, he insisted that the administration must not surrender.[42]

That evening the White House team decided on a revised strategy. While the administration stepped up its lobbying efforts on the Hill, Weaver and other supporters would traverse the nation building the sort of grassroots enthusiasm that would impress an election-conscious Congress. O'Brien and his aides would also shift the focus from the House to the Senate. Passage in the Senate would induce the House to take action without fear that it had wasted its time, as it had in the previous weeks when the Senate vetoed a hard-fought House labor bill.

The Senate-first strategy required some agile maneuvering. With Sparkman and Douglas out of the picture, next in line to lead the charge on the Senate subcommittee was Edmund Muskie of Maine. But Maine was predominantly rural and, as Califano told his chief, the senator probably did not have a single city in his state that would be eligible for Demonstration City status. "Well, he has one now," LBJ responded. "What one?" Califano asked. "Whatever one he wants," the president replied.[43] During the next few days Califano, O'Brien, and Humphrey met several times with Muskie, who worried, with good reason, about the bill's involuted financing arrangements and the difficulties of coordinating so many federal bureaucracies.

Impatient with his staff's slow progress the president ordered O'Brien and Califano to see Muskie at his Kennebunkport home over the July 4 recess. The weather was foul as the small plane carrying the two officials approached its destination. The pilot radioed the White House that he might have to land in New York or Boston rather than Pease Air Force Base, as intended. Johnson vetoed the alternate landing sites. The plane would land at Pease, near-zero visibility or not! And so it did—surrounded by fire trucks and ambulances. Later at the Muskie home, the two men, over steaming bowls of Jane Muskie's legendary lobster stew, pounded out an acceptable bill with her husband.

Still one subcommittee vote short, Johnson called in Senator Thomas McIntyre of New Hampshire and promised to keep the scheduled closing of the Portsmouth Naval Base under wraps until after the fall election. To make the senator's frugal Granite State constituents happier still, McIntyre would be allowed to introduce an amendment to limit the Demonstration Cities budget commitment to the first two years.

Meanwhile, the administration's grassroots propaganda machine had gone into high gear. On June 14 Weaver and Humphrey addressed eight hundred delegates at the annual U.S. Conference of Mayors meeting in Dallas. Both announced that the administration intended to fight for the full $2.3 billion for the program. In what Charles Haar would later call a "bell-ringing" speech, Weaver assured the mayors that there would eventually be plenty of new money, that the program would not depend only on funds previously earmarked for the cities.[44] The next day, back in Washington, Weaver conferred with CIO-AFL lobbyist Andrew Biemiller on how to strong-arm Democratic holdouts on the House subcommittee. The administration also recruited for the cause the newly formed Urban Alliance, a loose coalition of civil rights activists, trade union leaders, homebuilders, and mortgage bankers, who were concerned with urban programs. At weekly strategy sessions at the Statler-Hilton in downtown Washington, Alliance representatives plotted how to rescue the bill. Nor was the famous Johnson treatment neglected. Phone calls from the White House, invitations to chat with the president in the Oval Office, promises of help with bills of local interest—all were deployed to get the undecided to take a pro-administration stand. Toward the end of the drawn-out enactment process HUD staffers personally visited undecided members of the House and promised each one that at least one city in their district would be eligible for federal money under the bill.

The big push began to show results by the end of June, when Barrett and his subcommittee colleagues finally reported the measure out largely intact. Still, final passage promised to prove difficult in the full Senate, and it was here that Muskie, functioning as a latter-day Henry Clay, skillfully reassured the timid and soothed the bothered. Muskie softened the bill's aggressive, proselytizing tone, broadened the prescription for city eligibility, and reduced the original strict desegregation requirement for all new housing to the weaker phrasing "maximum opportunities in the choice of housing."[45] Most important, perhaps, he agreed to cut back from a $2.3 billion, five-year commitment to a $900 million, two-year commitment, a change deemed acceptable by the administration because the original measure had promised only $900 million in the first two years in any case. The first year, fiscal 1967, moreover, would be a planning year with a minimal appropriation of $11 million. Senator McIntyre was allowed to introduce the reduction amendment as the president had promised.

But besides making the bill more palatable by revision, Muskie made it more acceptable by his personal sponsorship. For a rural State-of-Mainer to favor a bill with so exclusive an urban focus impressed other small-state senators. A bemused John Tower expressed his wonder at all the rural state support the bill was getting. He himself was born in Houston, the nation's sixth largest city, he told his Senate colleagues, and he was "not insisting on the needs of the cities." "I cannot understand why these rural gentlemen are advocating it."[46] Muskie's skillful maneuvering, plus the usual party imperatives, held the answer.

On July 23 the Muskie subcommittee reported the modified bill out by a vote of only 6 to 4. After further minor changes it squeaked through the full Senate Banking and Currency Committee by a vote of 8 to 6 on August 9. Full Senate passage came ten days later by the decisive and surprising 53 to 22, with Democrats split 39 to 9 and Republicans 14 to 13.

The House, however, still remained an uncertainty and a danger. But meanwhile the summer was proving cataclysmic for American cities as the full force of bottled-up black rage burst out. In late July Cleveland's Hough district erupted into a crescendo of firebombs, looting, and sniper fire. Crowds surged through the streets of the two-square-mile ghetto shouting new, disturbing slogans: "Black Power! Black Power!" and "Burn, Whitey, Burn!"[47] Chicago too spilled over that month in what was described as a "near Watts."[48] By summer's end thirty-eight cities had detonated in spasms of rage and lawlessness.

That summer marked the definitive surfacing of two social movements severely damaging to the Great Society: black power and white backlash, mirror images of each other. It was during the late spring of 1966, during the "walk against fear" from Memphis to Jackson staged by black civil rights leader James Meredith, that Willie Ricks and Stokely Carmichael of SNCC first proclaimed "black power" and drilled it into the consciousness of white Americans. "Backlash" had been identified three years earlier by an economist who detected strong racial resentments among white blue-collar workers competing with blacks on the job market. In 1964 Lyndon Johnson had used the term to explain the support by white wage earners of Alabama's segregationist governor George Wallace in the Democratic presidential primaries. By late summer of 1966 backlash and black power were both draining the moderate middle and there was a growing sense among Americans that race relations had taken a disastrous new turn. In August, *Newsweek* magazine devoted its entire weekly issue to the "Crisis of Color '66," summarizing the tumultuous state of race relations in the nation. One of its major conclusions was that a majority of white Americans believed blacks were "trying to move too fast." And of all the racial issues, moreover, housing was the "most perilous collision point."[49]

In this late dog-day stretch of summer Senator Abraham Ribicoff's subcommittee on executive reorganization began hearings on the state of the cities that revealed a deep fissure between the administration and the most liberal elements of the Democratic Party over how much to invest in America's urban communities. Both Ribicoff, John Kennedy's secretary of HEW, and Robert Kennedy, demanded an augmented and permanent commitment to solving city problems. "The city," Kennedy told his colleagues, was "a central problem of American life" and to assuage it would require "an outpouring of imagination, ingenuity, discipline, and hard work unmatched since the first adventurers set out to conquer the wilderness." The two liberal senators sailed into Robert Weaver for being too timid on urban policy, when he appeared as an administration witness. Kennedy, still not a full dove on Vietnam, insisted that the country could afford both the war and broad social programs.[50] The Kennedy-Ribicoff attack was so sharp, observers noted, that it seemed as if the two senators almost belonged to the opposition party. And in a sense they did. Wherever one places John Kennedy on the political map, by 1966 his younger brother, the senator from New York, had made himself the tribune of the people, the keeper of the liberal flame. In the months ahead he would lead the attack from the left against the Great Society as feeble and parsimonious. Vietnam undoubtedly drove the final wedge between Bobby and Lyndon, but by the time Robert Kennedy challenged LBJ's reelection in January 1968 he had already parted from the president's more pragmatic, centrist approach to domestic social problems.

But the administration was able to get in its licks too. Sargent Shriver, still loyal to the administration despite his Kennedy connection, told the committee that he strongly endorsed the proposal as an extension of the War on Poverty. Demonstration Cities would "pump in new resources." It would "coordinate physical and human planning in the cities." It would "increase the flow of local resources and focus them on the underlying causes of the urban crisis."[51] Attorney General Nicholas Katzenbach, the last witness before Ribicoff, called the Demonstration Cities bill the perfect response to the violence of the ghettos. "The genius of this program," he declared, lay "in its basic comprehension that the problems of the city are not ones of bricks alone, but also of men; that the only success worth having, or, indeed, possible—is for the problems of blight, unemployment, education, housing and all the rest to be considered in tandem."[52] And in the end, the hearings probably strengthened the bill's supporters. Yes, the government should do more, but this measure was better than nothing—as both Kennedy and Ribicoff were careful to say. For a certain moderate liberal, appalled by the swelling white backlash but not prepared to mortgage the nation's future to militants' demands, the bill was just right as an anodyne. As Senator Jacob Javits, the liberal Republican from New York, would say in the Senate debate: "If we let this slide, we are inviting what we will get —to wit, disorder in the cities, disorder and riots. If we do not pass it, we leave them no alternative but to loot and burn as a product of their despair."[53]

Referred back to the House in late August, the Senate bill was hit by the full blast of public reaction against the summer's racial disturbances. Right-wing voters bombarded wavering representatives with letters attacking the bill. Paul Fino of New York, the pugnacious Bronx conservative, warned his colleagues in early October that the bill could compel busing of school children to achieve racial balance. Soon after Fino sent Johnson a public letter urging him to abandon the bill.

In late August the liberal journalist Nicholas Von Hoffman provided powerful ammunition for the bill's enemies. In an article in *The Washington Post* Von Hoffman reported on the poverty program in Hunters Point, a black ghetto in San Francisco, where a month later police and National Guardsmen would put down a major race-based riot. An early associate of Saul Alinsky, Von Hoffman's own left-liberal political and social sympathies made the piece a particularly damaging indictment of community poverty programs across the board. The Youth Opportunity Center, the original Ford Foundation Gray Areas project in San Francisco, established in 1963 to train young people for jobs, had been a spectacular failure, Von Hoffman wrote. In the intervening three years the agency had placed about three hundred youths in full-time jobs. But these were not high-skilled, well-paid, open-future jobs. They were positions as office boys, groundskeepers, and clerk-typists. Given the agency's $500,000 outlay, each had cost between $5,000 and $10,000 to create.

Worse yet, Von Hoffman reported, was the effect of foundation, state, and OEO money on community morale and values. Oreitha Eggleston, a black social worker, described an OEO summer youth project as worthless. "The children didn't work. They did absolutely nothing." Gene Orro, a black psychologist with the Youth Opportunity Center, declared that "The people here don't want jobs, not real jobs. Jobs take away the one thing they want: leisure time, sitting in front of the liquor store over there and bulling." Like other poverty programs, that of Hunters Point benefited local residents primarily by creating administrative sinecures. A member of the California Department of Employment told Von Hoffman that the community "swarms with 'subprofessionals' and 'aides' whose duties are imprecisely described as attending meetings, providing contacts, passing out leaflets, 'interpreting needs,' and 'making resources available.' "

All this waste and self-aggrandizement went on without intervention. The poverty programs had spawned an infrastructure of black power militants who regularly snowed or intimidated visiting observers and evaluators from Washington. Orro described the system used to menace outsiders, which may have directly inspired Tom Wolfe's acerbic article on the poverty programs, called "Mau-Mauing the Flak Catchers" after the violent black anti-colonialists who, in the 1950s, used terror tactics to drive white European settlers and the British colonial government out of Kenya in East Africa. When visitors came, "People like me," Orro told Von Hoffman, "are trotted out of the way and the whole superstructure . . . takes over. Smile or be like a Mau Mau. You may James Baldwin it through. [Baldwin, the talented black novelist, had written *The Fire Next Time* in 1963 warning whites of racial Armageddon if black Americans were not given their due.] You know, kick him, stomp him in the guts, while the visitor says Yes, Yes, we're guilty. Even the ministry is saying kill the whites and the middle class."

None of this devastating indictment could have improved the reception in Congress of new federal legislation for the cities generally, but one segment gave special delight to opponents of Demonstration Cities. According to Von Hoffman, M. Justice Herman, head of the San Francisco Redevelopment Agency, had told him that the poverty program was fostering "open and overt revolution." Nevertheless the local black power leaders already had their eyes on the new Demonstration Cities program and were dickering with the poverty officials over who would control it if the bill passed.[54]

The prospect of another federal program falling under militant control told strongly against the bill. So powerful was the attack against Demonstration Cities that even the administration's most loyal supporters wobbled. Hale Boggs, the Democratic majority whip, for a time was heard expressing a preference for postponing the measure for the next Congress.

But in the end the White House was able to rally its supporters. As the House vote on the Senate bill approached the wire a score of religious, civic, and labor groups pounded the representatives with the urgency of passage. Most effective, perhaps, were "the big business progressives," as James Reston called them. Led by industrialist Edgar Kaiser, who had served on the task force that developed the bill, twenty-two manufacturers, bankers, and merchants, including some of the biggest names in American business, announced that "America needs the demonstration cities bill" to deal with "disease and despair, joblessness and hopelessness, excessive dependence on welfare and the . . . threats of crime, disorder, and delinquency." And not only was the bill necessary for the cities' health but it was fiscally responsible as well. "In our business judgement it deserves to be ranked as high on any list of national priorities as any program we know."[55]

The final House vote came on October 14 during a rare night session called so nervous and impatient members could get back to their districts in time to campaign for reelection. The bill passed 178 to 141, a close vote considering the lopsided House Democratic majority. Sixty Democrats, mostly Southerners, had joined eighty-one Republicans to oppose the bill. Only sixteen Republicans had favored it. The joint conference on October 17 and 18 had little to consider since the House had accepted the Senate bill virtually intact, and the measure reached the president's desk soon after. Johnson signed the bill on November 3 with the usual florid remarks and with generous thanks to Robert Wood and Secretary Weaver. Stung by claims that it pandered to angry demonstrators, he changed its name to the Model Cities

Bill. Its official title, however, remained the Demonstration Cities and Metropolitan Development Act of 1966.

Though only half a loaf, Model Cities was a victory for the Great Society at a time when one was sorely needed. But it was during the months when the bill was stumbling its way through Congress that one of the poverty warriors' pet programs suffered a blow.

Of all the EOA projects, Head Start had seemed the one solid success, and this perception had influenced its renewal and enlargement in the fall of 1965. An OEO in-house report in early 1966 announced the triumphs of the summer's improvised programs. The four- and five-year-olds did benefit. Head Start kids in Baltimore, declared child-psychology professor Leon Eisenberg of Johns Hopkins, gained ten IQ points on vocabulary tests. "There was a real difference, a real improvement."[56] At the Montessori school in Clovis, California, the predominantly Mexican-American children made gains in mental maturity of between four and twelve months. But even this upbeat document warned that the gains would be endangered if they were not followed up and reinforced by later schooling.

Then came the Coleman Report of July 1966. Produced by the Office of Education of HEW under mandate by the 1964 Civil Rights Act, this massive study of educational opportunity in the United States reached some startling conclusions. The report broadly questioned the conventional wisdom that the education gap between whites and minority groups derived from differences in quality of school facilities and dollar outlays per pupil. Even more devastating, it cast doubt on the view that school itself made a big difference in the educational achievement of students compared with student families' economic, social, and cultural backgrounds. In a long section evaluating summer Head Start of 1965, the report concluded that the measurable differences in test scores for Head Start participants and nonparticipants of comparable socioeconomic backgrounds were "small in many instances." Unwilling to rest with such a negative conclusion, however, it argued that "considering the short length of the program it may be unreasonable to assume that participation could immediately and universally affect the verbal and nonverbal reasoning abilities of pupils." And besides, the program may have improved motivation, and its effects would be felt down the road.[57] Such qualifiers clearly blunted the report's sharp edge, but they could not disguise how overstated Head Start's early acclaim had been.

By the end of the year further data on summer Head Start made its results seem still more problematical. An OEO study during the fall comparing several hundred summer of '65 Head Start graduates and nongraduates in New York City concluded that the program had been a "magnificent experience" for the young participants. But when they began regular kindergarten, most of their initial advantage disappeared. Six to eight weeks after Head Start, concluded Max Wolff, a senior research psychologist at Yeshiva University's respected Center for Urban Education, there was "no significant difference" between Head Start participants and the others.[58]

Fortunately for the reformers little of this doubt seeped into public consciousness at this point. Though the larger conclusions of the Coleman Report disputed a fundamental Great Society tenet—that by education we shall be saved—the journals of general opinion gave it virtually no attention at all. The skeptical early appraisals of Head Start made scarcely a deeper impression. As Johnson faced the midterm congressional elections, some of the Great Society programs still retained credibility with the voting public.

But not LBJ himself. By early summer of 1966 the pollsters reported that the president's public ratings had skidded badly. Only 46 percent of the public thought he was doing a good job, Gallup noted on June 10. By late September, as he finished his first "thousand days," a media benchmark based on the Kennedy administration's brief span, *Newsweek* reported that his "star is in eclipse." The public still flocked to his speeches, but "the polls he once brandished with such delight betray a strong erosion of support." A majority of the Republicans sampled, it noted, now believed the GOP could wrest the White House from the Democrats in 1968.[59]

The White House itself placed most of the blame for the administration's sagging approval ratings on Vietnam, with price rises next in line. But there were strong signals that a portion of the public had lost confidence in the administration's domestic social programs as well. In August, Califano and special presidential assistants Douglass Cater and Harry McPherson flew to several university towns to touch base with academe on the Great Society.

These "think-ins" had begun the year before when the professoriat still were enthusiastic about the Johnson administration. The 1966 round of "think-ins" was dismaying. Some of the country's best minds had lost faith in the administration's domestic social programs. There was a general feeling of "fumbling and bafflement" that derived, said one pundit, from a sense of futility. "I think what accounts for it," he remarked, "is the vast social legislation on every social problem that's been recognized, and yet people feel it isn't doing anything. It isn't changing anything."[60]

The deteriorating public mood undermined the president's campaign plans for the off-year congressional elections. Johnson had intended to canvass extensively for Democratic congressional candidates, stressing the administration's "historic" legislative record. As he told the state chairmen of "Dollars for Democrats" at the Shoreham Hotel in Washington, the Eighty-ninth Congress had "passed more legislation to do more good for more people than any other Congress since the Republic was founded."[61] And during late summer, before Congress adjourned, he whistle-stopped through New England, the Midwest, and the South singing the praises of the Great Society and the men and women who had enacted it into law. His audiences were large and friendly but, perplexingly, did not seem to be grateful to the administration for what it had accomplished. By mid-fall Democrats girding for re-election runs were politely declining the president's offers to campaign in their districts.

A week before the Eighty-ninth Congress adjourned on October 22, Johnson met with party congressional leaders and Democratic bigwigs in the East Room of the White House for a love feast of self-congratulation. Speaker McCormack called the achievements of the Eighty-ninth, including both sessions, "fabulous." Senate Majority Leader Mike Mansfield proclaimed its work "two years of towering achievement." Johnson ran through a checklist of accomplishments and exulted in its length. The Eighty-ninth was the Education Congress, the Health Congress, the Conservation Congress, the Cities Congress, the Consumers Congress.[62]

Soon after, the president and Lady Bird set off on a major tour of the Pacific region that included stops in Hawaii, Australia, the Philippines, Thailand, Malaysia, and Vietnam. The first family flew back to Washington on November 2. The president had made plans to begin almost immediately a grueling schedule of bill-signing ceremonies in locales around the country where the publicity could help local Democrats. He would assist Senator Paul Douglas of Illinois by signing the Indiana Dunes bill in Chicago. To boost the run for governor by Speaker McCormack's nephew in Massachusetts, he would sign the Model Cities bill in Boston. All together he made plans to race through eleven cities in four days, calling attention by his presidential presence to local Democratic campaigners.

However dubious of presidential coattails at this point, some of the selected beneficiaries rearranged their schedules and assigned personnel and resources to the visits. In Seattle a platform in a shopping center was already under construction for a presidential bill-signing ceremony. Suddenly LBJ had second thoughts. What if he risked his prestige and lost? Johnson had never officially announced his eleventh-hour campaign "blitz" to the media, though his plans were common knowledge. The day before he was supposed to set off he told reporters that, on recommendation of his doctors, he was retiring, instead, to the Ranch to begin "a reduced schedule of activity" to prepare for surgery to repair scars from his gallbladder operation and to remove a throat polyp.[63] When the journalists asked about the cancelled campaign trip, Johnson snapped back that he had never planned a campaign trip. The whole thing was in the imaginations of "people who phrase sentences and write columns."[64] The event, however trivial, typified LBJ's devious side and reinforced his image, even among his loyalists, of an untrustworthy man who was willing to sacrifice allies to save his own reputation. It further damaged his relations with the press. Once again, the reporters and columnists felt, the president had tried to deceive them.

The election was a Democratic disaster. The Republicans gained forty-seven seats in the House, three in the Senate. In 1967 there would also be eight more Republicans in the nation's state houses. Of the forty-four freshman congressional Democrats elected in the 1964 landslide, twenty-three had been defeated. The administration still retained big formal majorities in both houses of Congress—248 to 187 in the House and 64 to 36 in the Senate—but the voters had turned liberal working majorities into conservative working majorities. In the Eighty-ninth Congress the president could count on 191 Northern Democrats regularly. In the Ninetieth there would be only 156, a full sixty-two short of a majority.

Had the public repudiated the Great Society? At first look, it is hard to interpret these results as anything else. Obviously most voters did not consider the "historic" record of the Eighty-ninth Congress enough to offset the negatives of Vietnam, the ghetto upheavals, and rising prices at the store checkout counters. But wasn't the loss in Congress by the party in power the usual experience for a midterm election? That was the claim of the administration spin doctors. But they were wrong. Since the 1940s, the average midterm dropoff in the House for the party that controlled the White House had been only thirty-one seats. The defeat in 1966 was a full 50 percent worse.

And yet the election should be seen against the broader trajectory of American party history. The Democratic majorities in 1965–66 were not normal. In November 1964 the public had fled the GOP en masse out of nameless dread of Goldwater and handed the Democratic liberals the keys to the legislative kingdom. It was not intentional and it could not last. In November 1966, many voters were returning to their political home without much thought of the administration's legislative record. Admittedly, a more appealing or successful domestic program might have kept them voting Democrat longer, but that seems unlikely, on the whole. The swing voters were Republicans, after all.

But there is also a curious deviation in the repudiation, if repudiation it was. Throughout the fall campaign one wing of the Democratic Party defended the Great Society programs and even demanded their expansion. Ironically, it was the party wing that despised Lyndon Johnson the most; the one headed by Robert Kennedy, the junior senator from New York. Kennedy had campaigned for fellow Northern Democrats touting more spending on the ghettos, the poor, and the schools. The Great Society vision must not be abandoned, he proclaimed. He saw it as the continuation of his brother's programs and insisted that it had vastly improved the lot of Americans. In the process Bobby was, instinctively or consciously, positioning himself to be a major challenger to LBJ sometime in the future.

Whether the election results were a repudiation or not, they profoundly affected the course of the Great Society, draining away much of Johnson's own reformist enthusiasm. Even before the voting, LBJ was telling visitors to the Ranch that the outcome would not matter. "As for the Great Society," he mused, "it's just about all wrapped up. All I've got to do now is get the money to keep it going."[65] After the ax actually fell he sounded more positive. In the next Congress he did not intend to do nothing. "[W]e will have new recommendations. We will be briefing the members of Congress on them from time to time." But he also admitted it would be an uphill fight. "I think it will be more difficult for any new legislation we might propose."[66]

That Christmas there was little joy in the White House. In the absence of the president, gloom enveloped the staff at the president's official home. Meanwhile, back at the Ranch, visiting Democratic governors filled Johnson's ears with their complaints. It was not that the Great Society programs were bad in themselves, they said; they were just badly administered. That was why the voters had moved away from the Democrats. Johnson plied them with soothing words and good Christmas cheer but they were not so easily placated. The president could have little doubt that the road ahead presented an uncertain prospect.

SIX

"I Shall Not Seek"

LYNDON JOHNSON'S last two years as president began as a holding action for the Great Society. With each passing month anger, frustration, and despair tore at the fabric of national civility; governing the country became a near impossibility. These were the months when the dolorous words of Yeats were on every tongue: "Things fall apart; the center cannot hold; mere anarchy is loosed upon the world."

As the Ninetieth Congress convened in January 1967, the public mood was sour and disbelieving. In the White House living quarters Lady Bird wrote in her diary: "Now is indeed 'the Valley of the Black Pig.' A miasma of trouble hangs over everything."[1] Johnson himself had become an object of scorn and derision, accused of lying to the American people and pursuing mindless foreign policy goals that promised neither victory nor escape. Distracted and maligned, he lost much of his legislative power. But beyond this, the 1966 elections had restored the normal balance between executive and legislative branches in the American governing system; Johnson now faced the same congealed conservative coalition that had impeded his predecessor, and could no longer readily get his way on Capitol Hill. During its first session the Ninetieth Congress forced the administration on the defensive and it was all the president could do to fend off the sharp knives of the revived Southern Democrat-GOP alliance.

□　□　□　□

By the beginning of 1967 the president's public standing and reputation was woeful. Among the men who navigated the inner corridors of government, LBJ had been admired but seldom loved. During the 1964 presidential campaign the affection-starved incumbent had asked a White House gathering why the public did not like him better. Democratic elder statesman Dean Acheson, too old for discretion, bluntly answered: "Because, Mr. President, you are not a very likeable man."[2]

But skepticism this early in his administration required proximity to the Johnson modus operandi, and only a handful of people had it. The public at large knew little about LBJ until the days immediately following the assassination in Dallas, when he had emitted a quiet confidence and competence that had calmed their fears. The respect and admiration he earned in these earliest presidential weeks had lasted through the landslide of November 1964 and for a year beyond. At the beginning of 1966 he was still, according to the Gallup poll, the "most admired man in the world." By January 1967 the public had experienced high-intensity exposure to Johnson for two full years and many no longer liked what they saw.

LBJ did not seem trustworthy. The worst deceptions concerned Vietnam and had started with promises during the 1964 campaign not to "send American boys nine or ten thousand miles to do what Asian boys ought to be doing for themselves." Five months later Johnson had launched a sustained bombing campaign against North Vietnam, quickly followed by dispatch of the first U.S. combat troops. Thereafter he downplayed each increment of American commitment and exaggerated progress against the enemy.

And the public also came to distrust his domestic leadership. LBJ's overstatement, his braggadocio, was part of the American Western cultural tradition. Texans perhaps understood and discounted it. But the national media and the voters at large were not as generous in dismissing the hyperbole, especially when month after month the gap between promise and reality widened. The deception, domestic and foreign combined, produced the famous "credibility gap" that so damaged Lyndon Johnson's presidency. First used probably by Murray Marder of *The Washington Post* in December 1965, the expression stuck to the president like evil-smelling mud. A Louis Harris poll early in 1967 noted that the public at large considered LBJ devious, a "conner."[3] By the winter of 1966–67 Barbara Garson's play *MacBird,* a parody of *Macbeth* that depicted LBJ as a murderous hypocrite and schemer, had become a major hit. And the public's doubts penetrated even the inner sanctums of the White House itself. During a speech-writing session for the 1967 "State of the Union" address, Harry McPherson, the White House counsel, acknowledged: "The President is simply not believed."[4]

In the last two years of his administration Johnson ceased to be a legislative wizard. The loss of prowess stemmed in part from damaged personal morale. LBJ was a man of wide mood swings: Success brought towering emotional highs; failure abysmal lows. Few presidents could have felt his exhilaration in the early summer of 1965 when the fabulous Eighty-ninth Congress had virtually rubber-stamped the whole Great Society. Not only had he achieved his lifelong goal of equaling FDR's New Deal; he also felt truly loved. Bettering his mentor, he had assembled a consensus behind his programs and policies almost unique in American political history. A May 1965 Gallup poll showed that the president's performance was approved by 67 percent of all the American people. Even among Republicans a majority liked the way he was doing his job.

Then the roof fell in. By early 1967 the president felt besieged and depressed. Everywhere he looked, at home and abroad, clouds had gathered. And the public too had defected. By May 1967 Gallup would report his approval rating down to 48 percent. By August it would touch a woeful 39 percent.

An unhappy Johnson was a remote and distracted Johnson. At moments of challenge the president's old fire returned, but more often he shrugged off domestic defeats as inevitable. He also seemed prickly and quarrelsome. The Johnson that called on Americans to "reason together" was transformed into the Johnson who often squabbled with political friends and allies. He increasingly turned supporters into adversaries. In early 1968 the respected John Gardner would resign, over Vietnam, as secretary of HEW to become head of the liberal citizens' group the Urban Coalition, which at times would zing the administration for its deficiencies.

The president had also developed a neurotic preoccupation with Vietnam. As early as February 1966 Lady Bird noted in her diary that Vietnam represented "two thirds of what we [she and Lyndon] talk about these days."[5] Many nights, well past midnight, the president could be found in the Situation Room examining reconnaissance photos, peering at military maps, scrutinizing reports. When the bombing of North Vietnam began the president insisted on choosing himself many of the targets. No recent president maintained such direct daily contact with the joint chiefs of staff or the diplomats on the scene of important foreign policy events. Johnson later told his biographer Doris Kearns that he had never neglected domestic policy for the war and produced a chart to prove it. But as Kearns noted, many of the items included on the domestic side were purely ceremonial—presenting awards or delivering speeches in the Rose Garden. Subtract "these ritualized activities," she writes, and "the years 1966–1968 show a decided shift of time and attention . . . to the war in Vietnam."[6]

Vietnam could intrude into the legislative process at any point. William Friday, president of the University of North Carolina, recalled meeting with Johnson in late June 1967 to deliver the report of the second task force on education. (The first education task force was the one headed by John Gardner, which had hammered out the proposal for the Elementary and Second Education Act of 1965.) We talked, Friday later declared, "five minutes about education and forty-five about Vietnam."[7] Larry O'Brien noted that he would often visit the Hill in 1967 to "discuss, say, truth in lending," and find "the conversation diverted to 'What are you going to do about Vietnam?' "[8] Vietnam was not only distracting; it also undermined the administration's relations with the men and women in Congress it needed to pass its bills. Senators and representatives who had supported LBJ's domestic programs discovered that he had become a pariah to important groups in their home constituencies and that everything connected with him, including social legislation, had become tainted.

And the administration was also intellectually depleted. By 1966 the presidential task forces that had served as the Great Society's power cells were beginning to falter. Critics began to attack their power, their secretiveness, their elite nature. They should have more women; they should open their deliberations to public scrutiny, critics said. One White House lawyer even told Califano that the whole system was unlawful under statutes dating back almost sixty years. But in any case they were running out of fuel. According to Robert Wood, who chaired the Model Cities task force, by 1967 the "stockpile of ideas could not be replenished as quickly as it was being transformed into policy."[9] In 1967–68 Califano, Mc-Pherson, Douglass Cater, and other members of the administration once more toured the nation's high-powered campuses hoping for new stimulation and insight. The eager White House seekers discovered that the distinguished faculty were obsessed with Vietnam and were more interested in federal grants and per diem for themselves than in new ways to improve the nation.

Whatever the reasons, after three years the administration had lost some of the drive and enthusiasm needed to change minds and extract votes on Capitol Hill. In September 1967, *Newsweek* reported that neither the president nor O'Brien "invest the time and effort in legislation that they did during the great days of success in the 88th and 89th Congresses." Some recent administration efforts to pass bills seemed to be "the work of amateurs."[10] This was journalistic exaggeration for the sake of a better story, but it did not completely misread the facts.

The problems were not all internal, however. There were also the serious losses in Congress the previous fall. In late January, OEO general counsel Donald Baker outlined to Shriver the new congressional environment that the agency and the administration faced in the Ninetieth Congress. A "substantial number of Republicans fresh from the November elections" were "certain they have a mandate to slow down the Great Society," he wrote. On the other side of the aisle some Democrats were angry at the administration because they "need some one to blame for the November elections," or had concluded that the president was now a political liability. It would be best, Baker told his chief, to go slow on major legislation until the Democrats had rallied.[11]

Baker also faulted the Democratic congressional leadership. Party discipline, he noted, had become lax; the Democratic majority had simply been too large in the Eighty-ninth Congress and winning had been too easy. He was right about the leadership. Speaker John McCormack was approaching seventy-six and was beginning to show signs of mental decline. Second in command, Majority Leader Carl Albert of Oklahoma, was described politely as physically ill, but in reality was struggling against alcoholism. Larry O'Brien, always close-mouthed about party adversity, later admitted that the House Democratic leadership in 1967 was "getting a little tired.''[12] And the Senate Democrats were scarcely in better shape. The majority leader was the bland, introspective Mike Mansfield of Montana, who lacked the will and skill of his predecessor—that is, LBJ himself—in driving the stubborn and proud upper house. The Senate Democratic whip Russell Long of Louisiana was not an obstructionist Southern diehard, but he was also not an enthusiast of the Great Society and was easily attracted by quixotic issues, which called in question his emotional balance. In fact, these same men had ruled the previous Congress, but then the nation was riding the wave of hope and expectation that followed the 1964 liberal sweep. Getting anything through was a cinch. Now, when leadership was needed, their inadequacies clearly showed.

The first signs of Democratic infirmity in the Ninetieth Congress was McCormack's failure to stop House conservatives from repealing the twenty-one-day rule that, in the Eighty-ninth, had restricted the Ways and Means Committee's power to obstruct legislation. At the same time the speaker conceded a change in the party proportion of major House committees. Ways and Means, for example, with a 17 to 8 Democrat-Republican ratio in the Eighty-ninth Congress, went to 15 to 10. All-important Appropriations shifted from 34–16 to 30–21. "None of these failures," noted disgusted Missouri representative Richard Bolling of the liberal Democratic Study Group, "would have happened in Rayburn's Speakership."[13] McCormack had handed legislative control over to the usual coalition of conservatives. Meanwhile, in the upper house, conservatives shot down South Dakota senator George McGovern's resolution to weaken the tyranny of the Senate filibuster.

All told, as the new Congress assembled, things did not look good for the Great Society. The most skillful legislative tactician of the century was distracted and depleted at a time when his skills and attention were needed more than ever. His lieutenants seemed without commitment and force. And the reservoir of ideas stored up over a generation had been largely drained.

Johnson signaled his own limited expectations in the January 10 "State of the Union" address. The speech was scheduled at 9:30 P.M. to avoid blacking out the most popular Tuesday evening TV shows and offending the couch potatoes of the nation. Yet even the viewers whose weekly fix of *Petticoat Junction, Gomer Pyle,* and *Green Acres* was spared could not have been appeased. Emmett John Hughes, the *Newsweek* columnist, called the address the "dullest oration of his regime." The president's rhetoric had "soared to the leaden boast: 'We are moving and our direction is forward.' "[14] It had been guns and butter in 1966; now most of the butter was gone too. Johnson made only modest requests for augmented domestic programs: Social Security benefit increases, expansion of Medicare, Head Start for three-year-olds, federal funds for public radio and TV, and full funding for Model Cities. The speech reflected the new realities. It defended the country's Vietnam involvement. We would "stand firm" in Vietnam and show our adversary that we could hold out longer than he could. Responding to public panic over soaring violent crime and the "hideous narcotics problem," the president called for a tough federal crime control act. The domestic initiatives were not generous but the war was becoming costly and, to offset any possible revenue deficit, he asked for a 6 percent surcharge on personal and corporation income taxes for two years or for as long as the Vietnam operation lasted. There was some polite applause for social programs but the only real enthusiasm came when the president mentioned his "safe streets," anticrime proposal. Observers noted that the president used the phrase "Great Society" only once.[15]

Johnson was clearly drained and discouraged, but he did not intend to abandon what he had accomplished. It would be hard to add to the record, but if he wanted to save his programs he would have to maintain forward movement. Operating on the principle that attack was the best defense, the administration introduced sixty-six bills and transmitted twenty-four major messages to Congress between the opening of the Ninetieth Congress and early spring, a near record. The tactics fooled no one. The president's poverty message, almost three years to the day after he had declared war on want, requested a trivial increase of $400 million over the previous fiscal year, though 1967–68 was the year when appropriations for the poverty programs had been scheduled to take off. The president also submitted bills to renew and modestly increase funding for federal aid to education, for highway beautification, for Model Cities, the Teacher Corps, rent subsidies, and for other programs of the previous Congress. There were also a number of quality-of-life proposals, including a new national corporation for educational TV, a stricter air pollution measure, and an omnibus consumer protection law.

Republican opposition to virtually every proposal proved formidable. In the previous Congress GOP leaders, chastened by their spectacular drubbing in the Goldwater landslide, had tried to avoid an obstructionist image by formulating their own anti-poverty plan. They called their alternative—emphasizing tighter program administration, reduced federal presence, and private business involvement—the Opportunity Crusade. It got no further in Congress but was incorporated into the *Republican Papers,* a collection of "discussion papers" edited by influential Wisconsin congressman Melvin Laird that covered the full sweep of domestic policy.

One proposal in this volume was destined to have a significant future. For some years Laird had been pushing a scheme to return federal revenues to the states as "block grants," without strings, to use as they saw fit. Called revenue sharing, the approach sought to enlist the potent federal revenue-raising machine for public purposes while avoiding the federal red tape and centralized direction from Washington that marked the liberal Great Society approach. Stuck on hold for years, in late 1966 it had received the imprimatur of Walter Heller, the liberal economic adviser of both Kennedy and Johnson. During most of the Ninetieth Congress, almost as a reflex, GOP leaders would regularly propose strings-free block grants to the states to replace Great Society programs enacted in the two previous congresses.

But all things considered the GOP leaders made little attempt to disguise their role as the bulldog opposition. Even as Johnson delivered his lackluster "State of the Union," observers could see the tokens of change. As LBJ approached the middle of his speech he glanced down at GOP congressional leaders Gerry Ford and Everett Dirksen and wistfully asked that there "be light and reason" in the relations between the Republicans and the administration in the new Congress. The two men grinned back, but their smiles were mirthless, reporters thought.[16]

But it was ultimately the world outside the narrow purviews of 1600 Pennsylvania Avenue and Capitol Hill that dragged down the domestic initiatives of the administration.

Nineteen sixty-seven was the worst of the long, hot summers. It began on July 12, when New Jersey's largest city, Newark, detonated following rumors of brutal acts by the police against ghetto residents. The city of 400,000 was the bottom of the urban barrel. Once a prosperous manufacturing and commercial center that had sheltered and nurtured generations of newcomers, it had crashed since the later fifties. By 1967 it had the most substandard housing in the nation, the highest mortality figures for mothers giving birth, and the second highest infant mortality rate. It was also the first large city in the North with a black majority. On the evening of the twelfth Newark police arrested a black cab driver for a traffic violation, and rumors raced through the ghetto that the cops had beaten him to death. Out of the tenements and decayed frame houses erupted an angry, frustrated, and despairing mob led by male adolescents, who added to the explosive social mixture a giant dose of testosterone. Five days of arson, looting, sniping, and murder followed, leaving twenty-five people dead and inflicting damage accounted at $10 million.

After Newark, riots erupted in Detroit, the nation's fifth largest city. There too the police triggered ghetto rage when, on the early morning of July 23, they raided an after-hours club. Detroit had its large pockets of squalor and despair, but it was still the prosperous auto capital of the world and many of its black residents worked for top wages in Ford, Chrysler, and GM factories. Unlike Newark, moreover, the city had a liberal mayor and a raft of black officials. None of this made a difference. The violence lasted for a week, during which forty-three people died, many from National Guard fire. It cost the city's landlords and shopkeepers, black and white alike, $250 million in property losses.

Aftershocks from Newark and Detroit continued through July and August as neighborhoods in fifty American cities, large and small, went up in flames. There were riots and arson waves in Minneapolis, Cincinnati, Kansas City, Des Moines, Tampa, Jersey City, Milwaukee, and Philadelphia. None of these explosions equaled those of Newark or Detroit but they added to the public's sense of coast-to-coast race war.

Though Watts in 1965 and Cleveland's Hough the next year had shocked the middle class and shaken liberal confidence, Newark and Detroit were visions of hell that forced the public to confront the connection between the Great Society and ghetto violence as never before. Few Americans, white or black, con-doned the ghetto uprisings. But the public response was confused and inconsistent. Polls taken soon after the summer's riots showed opinion curiously divided on the issue of how to respond to the seething unrest in the ghettos. A majority of white Americans had been sufficiently frightened by the violence to endorse expanded ghetto programs. According to a Harris poll in mid-August, 66 percent of whites favored a major public works program to give jobs to all the unemployed; 63 percent supported federal programs to rebuild the ghettos; 55 percent favored establishing large summer camps for ghetto youths; and 59 percent supported federal programs to exterminate rats, a blight in ghetto neighborhoods. But at the same time fewer white Americans now believed that blacks were oppressed and many felt that there was no excuse for the ghetto violence. *Newsweek* noted in its three-page review of the poll that among whites even "moderate comments" were "tainted with bitterness." A fifty-four-year-old Oklahoma oil field worker charged that "the colored people" had "asked for a better chance, but when they got it, it went to their heads." An elderly Californian told the pollster: "They need food, work, and education, but . . . they use these as excuses to riot." White Americans had lost their reluctance to work beside Negroes or sit next to them on buses or in a movie theater, but 70 percent considered them less ambitious than white people.[17]

Ordinary white Americans, it seemed, could be frightened into accepting ghetto demands, but they resented it. Their commitment was not heartfelt or robust and could easily go into reverse. Many would drift into a confused rage that linked the Great Society, and especially the War on Poverty, with the growing violence and disorder in the inner cities. To a growing segment of the public the riots were proof that government social programs did not work; in fact, they did more harm than good by raising expectations beyond any realistic possibility of satisfaction. Nor were the riots the only sour fruits of liberalism. Liberal permissiveness was also responsible for the nation's unsafe city streets. After years of little change, suddenly in the mid-sixties the incidences of murder, rape, armed robbery, and assault had soared. This appalling mutation coincided with the very programs liberals had concocted to alleviate the problems of the poor. The timing, conservatives declared, said it all.

As the months passed more and more white Americans quietly

slipped their liberal moorings and drifted to the GOP or enlisted in the backlash under the leadership of George Wallace.

In Congress the riots and swelling white reaction strengthened the Great Society's enemies. When Shriver appeared before the House Appropriations Committee in early August for the annual congressional grilling on OEO's budget, he was pressed hard by the doubters. Mayor Jerome Cavanagh of Detroit, another witness for the War on Poverty appropriation bill, outraged chairman George Mahon, a conservative Democrat, when he asserted that Congress was encouraging rioting by a cheese-paring approach to antipoverty measures. Mahon shouted back: "The problem is not one of more dollars, but of discipline. The more we have appropriated for these programs, the more violence we have had."[18] Mahon sat down to a standing ovation in the committee room.

The hostile response was inflated by reports that antipoverty workers had actively encouraged rioters during the summer spasms. In Newark Willie Wright, an employee of the local OEO agency, supposedly urged a rally of blacks just after the city's riot to buy guns and keep them for use during the next eruption. Wright refused to appear before his superiors when summoned to explain his remarks, issuing an incendiary statement instead. It was his "firm conviction," he announced, "that complete chaos will have to prevail in the streets of America and blood will have to flow like water before the black man will become an accepted citizen of this society."[19] Wright was not speaking for a majority of black Americans, of course, but rage such as his frightened many whites and fanned the already hot embers of backlash.

Nothing expressed the new resistance to "rewarding rioters" so well as the notorious rat abatement incident. In a special message on urban and rural poverty, Johnson had proposed a $20 million federal program to improve garbage collection and reduce rat infestation in slum neighborhoods. The project drew on "Operation Rat," a 1965 OEO rodent extermination proposal that promised to improve health, preserve food supplies, and create jobs. Moved by blurry memories of the medieval Black Death and reports that thousands of ghetto children each year were bitten by rodents while they slept, Johnson signed on. In previous years the plight of slum children had never failed to touch a sympathetic nerve in the nation's legislators and a generous response seemed a sure thing. Not this time. The bill reached the floor of the House just three days before Detroit exploded.

The last thing Johnson wanted was to link administration policies to ghetto violence. He had been relieved when New Jersey governor Richard Hughes declined to ask for federal troops for Newark. But he did not reckon with his shoot-from-the-lip vice president. On July 15 Humphrey had called Hughes and offered to send federal antipoverty aid to help pacify the city. The president exploded. His Great Society programs must not be seen as rewards for rioters. Inform Humphrey, he screamed at Califano, that he had "no authority . . . N-O-N-E, to provide any federal aid to Newark or any other town or county in America."[20]

The aversion to paying off rioters was even stronger among Johnson's conservative congressional critics, and they saw the rat abatement bill as both laughable and vulnerable. Incensed at the rioters, House Republicans turned consideration of the measure into a circus. Joel Broyhill of Virginia remarked in a put-on Dixie accent: "Mr. Speaker, I think the 'rat smart thing' for us to do is to vote down the rat bill 'rat now.' " Other conservatives called it a "civil rats bill" designed to create a "rat bureaucracy" presided over by a "high commissioner of rats." There were references inevitably to throwing money down a "rat hole." One congressman proposed that the president just "buy a lot of cats and turn them loose."[21] In a fit of heartless levity the House voted down the bill 207 to 170.

The House tantrum even offended *The Wall Street Journal* and the president took advantage of it. The House's action had been a "cruel blow to the poor children of America," he announced in an angry statement. The nation was spending federal funds to protect livestock from rodents and the "least that we can do is give our children the same protection. . . ."[22] The House should immediately reconsider its ill-considered action. That evening he remarked to Califano that the bill would have passed the previous summer when the White House had first considered the issue of vermin control. It was the riots that had turned the country around. Congress later reconsidered and approved a rat control provision in the Partnership for Health Act, which Johnson signed in December.

Committed liberals drew a different moral from the ghetto eruptions: The nation must spend more money and enact better programs. On July 25, in the middle of the Detroit riot, Martin Luther King, Jr. telegraphed Johnson deploring the "blind revolt" in the ghettos against the conditions that LBJ had "set out to remedy" when he came to the White House. But King also demanded a federal jobs creation program for every poor person in the cities.[23] King by now had moved well beyond demands for civil rights and was contemplating an interracial "poor people's" march on Washington the following spring to goad Congress into vastly expanded antipoverty programs. He would later tell a journalist that the campaign would demand nothing less than a "redistribution of economic power" in America.[24]

King spoke for many on the left. Back in the previous October, A. Philip Randolph, the revered black union leader, had proposed a $185 billion "freedom budget" to rebuild slums, raise health standards, improve schools, create full employment, and provide a guaranteed annual income for all. In August 1967, after the summer riots, the Urban Coalition, a creation of prominent liberals dedicated to more "positive and progressive legislation" for the cities,[25] proposed that Congress create a million new jobs. In late September Americans for Democratic Action passed a resolution demanding massive outlays for social programs. Meanwhile, the AFL-CIO endorsed the concept of the federal government as the "employer of last resort." In Congress liberals and other civil rights leaders demanded a "Marshall Plan for the cities," a massive injection of money and effort into the slums modeled after the original Marshall Plan, which had revived a prostrate Europe after 1945. That August, liberal senator Joseph Clark of Pennsylvania introduced an amendment to the administration's antipoverty bill to allot $1.5 billion for low-skill-job creation for the urban poor. All nine Democratic members of Clark's labor committee, as well as liberal Republican Jacob Javits of New York, approved the proposal, and Clark was soon mobilizing support among the experts and influential public figures.

The direct federal jobs approach did not stand a chance. It reminded critics of the WPA and other expensive make-work programs of the Great Depression that had often amounted to useless "leaf-raking." That was acceptable in 1935, when there were 10.5 million unemployed. But unemployment was now at a historic low point and anyone, it seemed, could find work who wanted to. A new federal jobs program, moreover, would over-

whelmingly benefit unskilled, undisciplined black males, the core
element of the mobs rampaging through ghetto streets. Of all the
categories of "undeserving poor" in our history, these young
men seemed to many white Americans to have the least claim on
the nation's compassion.

The administration opposed the Clark initiative as excessive. It
was already asking Congress for a $2.3 billion package for its fiscal
1968 antipoverty programs and was under enormous pressure to
economize in a time of rising prices. The liberals' jobs initiative
seemed a danger to the president's remaining antipoverty program. But even Johnson was beginning to reassess the emphasis
on massive programs run from Washington. They no longer
seemed either possible or desirable. The administration had a
jobs plan waiting in the wings that promised to be both cheaper
and simpler. Derived from a June 1967 task force report on urban
unemployment, this scheme proposed to create paid work in the
private sector for the "hard-core unemployed" through a govern-
ment-business partnership. In mid-1967 the Commerce Department and several other agencies began pilot programs to test the
concept.

For many reasons, then, the administration objected to the
Clark bill. Califano recounts his own apoplectic response when he
discovered from an article in *The Washington Post* what Clark had
in mind. "That son of a bitch," he exclaimed to the president.
"He's got one helluva nerve. If his job proposal is hooked to the
poverty program on the floor, it'll kill the bill!"[26] Johnson wanted
desperately to steer a middle path. The country must not pay off
rioters, but runaway backlash must be prevented from unraveling
the Great Society. Working behind the scenes with friendly senators, the administration succeeded in killing the Clark initiative.
Clark retreated to a more modest scheme that would cost $875
million. But this too failed to get by the administration blockade.

During the Ninetieth Congress the fear of inflation, far more than
in 1966, dogged the administration's domestic programs. The
economy overall continued to perform well in 1967–68 measured
by expansion of the gross national product. By late 1967 the boom
that began in 1961 had entered its eightieth month, making it the
longest sustained economic expansion in U.S. history. During
that six-and-a-half-year period real GNP had climbed 34 percent.

But budget deficits had grown as well. In the fiscal year ending June 30, 1966, the government had taken in $3.8 billion less than it had disbursed. The deficit would climb to $8.7 billion in fiscal 1967 and leap to $25.2 billion the accounting year following. The inevitable ensued. By mid-1967, after five months of relative stability, prices began to surge again. They would continue to grow at an accelerating rate for the next three years.

Students of the Johnson era have condemned LBJ for failing to react soon enough and vigorously enough to the deficits and inflation. Some critics see it as *the* fatal misstep of his administration. Bill Moyers has said that Johnson's delays and indecision over a tax increase irreparably damaged his presidency. "It was the beginning of the end, a time when he lost control of the administration, lost control of events," he later asserted.[27]

But it is not clear what the critics of LBJ's fiscal behavior mean. If their point is that Vietnam, through its impact on prices, damaged the Great Society, they are right. The war in Southeast Asia not only distracted the administration and undermined its credibility with the public; it also forced a reallocation of revenues that squeezed domestic-program growth. To increase the guns, the butter had to be stinted. But how would asking for higher taxes sooner, say in late 1965, when some of the administration's economic advisers first urged it, have saved the Great Society programs? It can be as convincingly argued that if LBJ had gone to Congress with a tax hike request during the Eighty-ninth Congress, when inflation pressure first appeared, there would never have been a Great Society. The delay, given Vietnam, saved the Great Society programs. Johnson may have deceived the American public over the cost of the Vietnam adventure, but it was not, as David Halberstam and other antiwar partisans insist, merely to get a war. It was also, and perhaps foremost, to get a Great Society.

The epic struggle over the budget deficit in the Ninetieth Congress confirms this point. By early 1967 Johnson no longer denied that a major tax hike was needed and, as we saw, he included a recommendation for a 6 percent surcharge on each personal and corporate tax return in his "State of the Union" address. At this point, apparently, he considered a tax increase primarily as a way to rescue his domestic programs. He did not yet accept that to get it he would have to trim his sails.

The opposition to any tax hike was formidable. Conservatives in both parties, led by Chairman Mills, questioned the necessity of a tax increase when Johnson had first proposed it and demanded that any hike be accompanied, or preferably preceded, by a great whack at domestic spending. Among the president's most important constituencies, support for a tax increase was soft. Labor Secretary Willard Wirtz reported in July that the labor union czars were unhappy at the government taking a bigger bite from the pay envelopes of their membership. Johnson stalwarts, they were willing to go along with the president, especially if it meant saving the Great Society, but they felt "there would be a real protest and possible strong negative reaction on the part of union membership as a whole."[28] The business community also proved tepid. Prompted by the White House, a group of pro-administration businessmen endorsed a tax hike and higher interest rates to combat inflation, but only if accompanied by cuts in "nonessential spending."[29]

In January 1967 the Federal Reserve had tripped off a minor economic downturn by raising interest rates, and Johnson held off sending a tax bill to Congress for fear of further depressing business. Through the summer the president and Mills sparred over the size, the timing, and the circumstances of a tax surcharge. Mills continued to express doubt that a tax hike was needed. Ever the chameleon, the former small-town banker no longer had much use for the Great Society. Back in 1965, when the tide of opinion was running for the president, he not only supported Medicare but had tacked Medicaid onto the original bill as well. But now he had reverted to the stern economizer, a more congenial role. "If the American people are going to be asked to pay more taxes," he announced, "one condition that would have to be met in order for me to sponsor it would be some reduction in the rate of federal spending."[30]

Mills was jealous of his prerogatives and unfazed by the prestige and standing of the president, even if he was a fellow Democrat. With ambitions beyond the chairmanship of Ways and Means, he saw a chance, by defying the president's spendthrift ways, to win friends and grab headlines. Mills wanted to be consulted directly by the president on the dimensions of the new taxes and the administration's spending plans. Reluctant to dilute his own prerogatives, Johnson at first balked, but on July 26 he invited Mills to the White House to consider a tax bill. Mills helped with the bill's drafting but refused to give it his full support until the president agreed to further spending cuts. Despite the chairman's resistance, on August 3 LBJ finally sent his tax surcharge proposal, now raised to 10 percent, to the House accompanied by warnings about the size of the deficit if Congress did not comply. At a press conference in the Fish Room of the White House he promised to cut programs.

Months of tedious negotiating followed with Mills flexing his legislative muscles and glorying in the attention of the media. The chairman, as usual, hid behind the screen of realism. It was not he who was demanding the cuts in programs; Congress simply would not pass a tax surcharge bill without them. ''I was merely trying to tell him [i.e., Johnson] what it would do to pass a bill.''[31] In mid-September he announced that he had gotten a flood of mail on the tax surcharge, and ninety-nine letters out of a hundred opposed it. He would wait to see if inflation grew stronger before supporting the tax increase, but in any case, for him to approve it there would have to be substantial spending cuts. Three weeks later, unable to extract specific promises of reductions from the administration, Mills got Ways and Means to shelve the surcharge for the session. ''The climate in the country,'' he announced, ''was not yet ready for it.''[32] The move was accompanied by a signal. ''We are trying to get this message across: We want a pause in this headlong rush toward ever bigger government.''[33]

Johnson fought back. The tax hike must not become an excuse to destroy the Great Society. Inflation and war had made the public uneasy about generous domestic spending, but social programs had important constituencies, and if aroused they could light a backfire that would scorch Wilbur Mills and Congress alike. In October Johnson proposed drastic cuts in programs that channeled federal money to the states and cities. The governors, state legislators, and local officials, he hoped, would get the message. When this tack failed to work, he attacked his opponents personally. Mills and Gerry Ford, he announced at a November news conference, would ''live to rue the day'' they quashed the surcharge. It was a ''dangerous decision . . . an unwise decision.'' The nation could afford both to ''fight this war abroad . . . and the problems in our cities at home. . . .''[34] Several days later Mills fired back that he would not retreat from his demand for budget cuts even if it cost him ''a friendship of 29 years.''[35]

But it was Johnson who blinked. In late November the press reported the president ready to propose a list of specific spending cuts in exchange for the tax boost. They were not enough to move the representative from Arkansas's 2nd District, however. The president must check long-term as well as short-term spending, Mills declared. For another week or two the two sides continued to wrestle. In early December Johnson invited Mills to the White House and the two conferred for three hours. The meeting relaxed strained personal relations, but the session ended without Ways and Means reporting out a surcharge bill.

As guardian of the fiscal gates, Mills did get a cut in 1967 in one major social program: Aid to Families with Dependent Children (AFDC). Established in 1935 as part of the landmark New Deal Social Security Act, it was assumed in those innocent days that AFDC would apply primarily to families headed by widowed women and would replace the scores of private and local charities that had evolved over generations to help such unfortunates. As Daniel Moynihan has noted, the authors of the original Social Security Act expected that the typical AFDC beneficiary would be the wife of a West Virginia coal miner killed in an accident. It did not work out that way. After World War II more and more of the AFDC families were headed by abandoned wives or divorced women. Then came a wave of beneficiaries whose children were conceived "out of wedlock," to use the quaint old phrase. Few in number in the mid-1930s, they became a growing class of AFDC recipients with each passing year. In 1961, in a final burst of social generosity, Congress also accepted the right of long-term-unemployed fathers to receive welfare under the Social Security Act, though this program was kept small.

In the next six years the welfare rolls took off. Between 1962 and 1967 the number of AFDC families climbed from 3.8 million to 5.3 million. The surge reflected the decline of family cohesion during the sixties that conservatives would link to the more permissive atmosphere of the era. But it also followed the rise of the welfare rights movement, fostered by the ever-creative Richard Cloward and his associate Frances Piven. Having concluded from their own research that twice as many poor families were eligible for relief than were actually receiving it, the two social theorists in late 1965 proposed that social workers and "other activists" organize a movement "with the express purpose of getting thousands of families on the relief rolls." Booming rolls, they concluded, "would mean procedural turmoil in the cumbersome welfare bureaucracies, fiscal turmoil in the localities where existing sources of tax revenue were already overburdened, and political turmoil as an alerted electorate divided on the question of how to overcome this disruption in local government." Their goal was "to establish a federally financed minimum income."[36]

Cloward and Piven found a ready instrument in George Wiley, a black former professor of chemistry at Syracuse who had quit academe to become associate director of the Congress of Racial Equality (CORE), a militant civil rights organization that advocated civil disobedience tactics against discrimination. In May 1966 Wiley organized the Poverty Rights Action Center with national headquarters in Washington to encourage activist attacks on the existing paternalistic and tightfisted welfare structure as a step toward replacing welfare with a system more generous toward the indigent. In the spring of 1966 the action center began to demonstrate for improved benefits from state and local governments and that August assembled one hundred welfare groups to form the National Coordinating Committee of Welfare Rights Groups. A year later 178 delegates representing seventy-five local welfare rights organizations from around the country met in Washington to establish the National Welfare Rights Organization (NWRO).

NWRO operated on both local and national levels. In the cities, following the overload theory of Cloward and Piven, it challenged strict rules of welfare eligibility and found loopholes that allowed more of the poor to claim public money. In New York City NWRO activists forced local officials to pay for winter clothing for welfare recipients under a "minimum standard," mandated by law but seldom utilized. Modest success in this initial campaign spurred further drives for money for furniture and back-to-school clothing for welfare families.

The welfare rights advocates deployed a range of tactics in their New York campaign. They made sure the poor knew their rights and guided them through the bureaucratic maze to the goal of welfare eligibility. They advised them on protest tactics: picketing at City Hall for more money and improved services, and disruptive invasions of local welfare centers to force officials to comply with their demands. Some of the demonstrations made it impossible for welfare officials to function at all. Undoubtedly the New York welfare kamikazes achieved part of their goal: The city's welfare caseload soared from 84,700 in 1965 to 175,400 in 1968. Between 1965 and 1970 the number of New Yorkers on welfare leaped from 531,000 to 1,165,000, though the economy was booming.

The welfare rights movement provoked polar responses among middle-class Americans. Zealous liberals, however battered and discouraged, supported the drive as they had the War on Poverty. The NWRO received money from liberal foundations and from the National Organization of Social Workers. Most of its funding, however, came from the predominantly white liberal Protestant churches, the denominations that made up the National Council of Churches. The drive for welfare rights advocates seemed to many other Americans another outrage against the nation's cherished values of individual responsibility and the work ethic. As Henry Cohen, the New York City deputy human resources administrator, later insisted, the welfare rights movement had been counterproductive for the poor. It "attacked the American concern for the work ethic at its core" and was "bound to bring considerable counter-reaction over time."[37]

By 1967 the middle-class public, much as today, had come to perceive the nation as trapped in a "welfare mess" marked by fraud, abuse, extravagance, and incentives for the lazy to sponge off the hardworking taxpayers of the nation. During the Ninetieth Congress, playing to the general erosion of social benevolence, Mills and other conservatives sought to freeze the Aid to Families with Dependent Children program as a condition of accepting Johnson's request for a 15 percent across-the-board hike in Social Security benefits and other augmentations. Under the "freeze" there would be no additional federal matching funds to the states beyond those needed to maintain the existing proportion of each state's children receiving the program's benefits. Johnson called Mills to the White House to berate him on his harsh response to the nation's poorest people. The Arkansan argued back. The black woman who lived near his mother back home, he told the president, managed to have a baby every year. She now had eleven children and the cost was being borne by the state and federal governments. "My proposal," he said, "will stop this. Let the states pay for more than a small number of children if they want to." LBJ pressed Mills hard but the congressman would not be moved. When he left the White House, Johnson turned to Califano and remarked: "You hear that good, now. That's what we're dealing with. That's the way most members feel. They're just not willing to say it publicly unless they come from redneck districts."[38]

Mills got his freeze but Congress also tackled the larger issue, still festering today, of income divorced from work. To get benefits, recipients would have to work. There would be a carrot—family heads could earn $30 a month without having their monthly welfare check reduced dollar for dollar—and a stick—adult AFDC recipients would enter a training program to prepare to work. To receive federal money, states would have to cut off welfare payments to able-bodied adults who could work or benefit from training if they refused to register for work. To make the scheme practicable, Congress established a work incentive program (WIN) to fund jobs and training programs and to provide day care centers for the children of enrollees.

The work provisions were in reality weak. Employable AFDC recipients were not required to work; they need only register for it. Yet the bill released a torrent of protest. Zealots for the poor attempted to disrupt the Senate Finance Committee hearings on the bill. When that failed, they took turns denouncing the pending legislation. Red-hot New York welfare-rights activist Beulah Sanders told the lawmakers bluntly:

> I do not believe that we should be forced to work. I do not believe we should be forced to take training if it is not meaningful. . . . We, the welfare recipients, have tried to keep down the disturbances among our people, but the unrest is steadily growing. The welfare recipients are tired. They are tired of people dictating to them, telling them how they must live.[39]

In December, as the bill worked its way through the House-Senate Conference Committee, the president came under a liberal barrage to do something to stop the freeze and the work requirement. The Social Security bill, along with the pending federal crime bill, were "repressive measures aimed at the poor," wrote Leon Shull, director of Americans for Democratic Action. The freeze on AFDC was "cruel" and the work requirement was "callously wrong."[40] James Fogerty, executive director of the

Community Council of Greater New York, told Johnson that the words used to justify the measure, "to strengthen family life," were only a "cover to launch the most destructive attack on public welfare since its inception . . . in 1935."[41] In the camp of organized labor, Meany and Reuther both urged a veto, as did mayors John Lindsay of New York, James Tate of Philadelphia, Thomas D'Alesandro of Baltimore, and a flock of liberal governors. Within the administration itself, John Gardner, now HEW secretary, urged the president to try to get the conference bill modified. Mayor Lindsay and Bobby Kennedy, he noted, were ready to make political hay of punishing poor children. The freeze and compulsory work provisions, moreover, had "anti-Negro overtones" and would be used "as rallying points for civil disobedience and violence in the great urban centers." Gardner thought LBJ should sign the omnibus Social Security measure because of its other features, but suggested that he make his opposition to the freeze and work incentive known to Congress before it came to his desk.[42]

The White House actually worked hard to improve the bill. But late 1967 was not 1964. Much had happened since the War on Poverty declaration to arouse resentment of welfare recipients. It was about this time that bumper stickers and placards appeared on American streets with the slogan: END POVERTY; GET A JOB. And in the end the administration could not head off the two controversial proposals. The president signed the bill on January 2 with fulsome praise of its generous benefits to the aged. He said almost nothing of the conservative provisions.

Ironically, after all the fuss, WIN did nothing to slow the surging welfare rolls. In the year before its passage they had grown by 7 percent; in 1971, after enactment, they climbed by 28 percent. The training programs did not provide jobs that most welfare mothers could perform; the day-care system was spotty and many mothers could not find sitters for their children. In the end only one in ten welfare recipients ever enrolled and only a fifth of these ever finished a training course. Still, it put on the federal agenda, for the first time, the explicit issue of work versus handouts. Its appearance at this moment was a measure of how far class generosity had declined since 1964.

□   □   □   □

Taken as a whole, the first session of the Ninetieth Congress was a near disaster for the administration. In mid-Congress the Capitol Hill columnist for *The Wall Street Journal* pronounced it "dispirited" and quoted a liberal House Democrat as saying he had "never seen a Congress . . . so devoid of any sense of purpose."[43] By late October, as the session drew to a close, liberal fears seemed to have been realized. "Some of the Johnson Administration's major programs may well be dismantled by Congress," a Washington reporter noted. The president had "lost control of the increasingly bitter fight" and in fact his "disorganized and demoralized lieutenants no longer have even a battle plan."[44]

It was all the administration could do to save what had already been achieved. Once more rent subsidies and the Teacher Corps, programs with small and scattered constituencies, seemed especially vulnerable. Johnson may have lost faith in bold new programs, but these, like sickly children, touched his heart and he fought for both. The corps, he insisted, was a "symbol of new hope for America's poor children and their parents."[45] However lackluster administration efforts for other programs, the president's lieutenants lobbied Congress intensely for these. The White House proffered presidential têtes-à-têtes and escorted tours of Teacher Corps projects to key representatives, and handed around testimonials from pleased school officials in hopes of collecting votes for sustaining the corps and getting $12.5 million to support summer training programs for 1967. The push paid off. Congress proved stingy during the first session, but before the Ninetieth Congress adjourned it had granted the Teacher Corps almost $21 million for fiscal 1969, $7.4 million more than for the previous year, and extended its life through 1971.

The administration was also able to fund other existing Great Society programs for fiscal 1968. The War on Poverty survived despite ominous predictions, though once more its fate resembled the perils of Pauline.

As the first session opened things had looked chancy for Shriver's agency. On January 24 Larry O'Brien warned the president of a rough legislative ride ahead. A head count by Sam Gibbons of Ways and Means showed there were only 190 votes for the program as it existed. The Republicans would not try seriously to shut down all the poverty programs; the GOP "cannot afford to sink Poverty" for political reasons. But they would certainly try to cut the budget, and their main effort would be to dismantle OEO as an agency. The question was not whether the poverty program could be extended; it was whether "it can be retained as a meaningful entity in the 90th Congress."[46] Shriver too feared the worst. "Mouthing cynical noises about efficiency and sound organization," the Republicans, he declared after the GOP had shown its hand, were attempting "to scrap OEO, denying their efforts are a disservice to the poor and ignoring the national commitment to the elimination of poverty."[47]

In part OEO's unpopularity with the GOP was the fault of Shriver himself. A vigorous idea man but a lax administrator, "Sarge" offended both the political and fiscal conservatives. He also inevitably became the scapegoat for all the misadventures of the antipoverty programs, especially community action. By the end of 1966 he considered himself a liability to the War on Poverty and, worn down by three grueling years in the trenches, offered to resign. In December 1966 he told Johnson he was prepared to leave before the new OEO budget went to Congress to avoid clouding the issue of the agency's funding. "I believe it is in the president's interest and OEO's interest for the war on poverty to have a new face and a new image," he wrote. "I have exhausted my bargaining power in the congress. I am out of IOU's up there."[48] Johnson disagreed. At the Ranch over Christmas he pledged him to continue at OEO for at least one more year. Shriver would remain in the thick of the 1967 battle over preserving OEO.

The administration expended much of its depleted energies that first session to save OEO. In a mid-March speech, "America's Unfinished Business—Urban and Rural Poverty," Johnson called for a 25 percent increase in funding for programs that showed special promise, a major hike in Head Start follow-through programs, and a modest new Concentrated Employment Program for the hard-core jobless. During the remainder of the session the White House staff kept in constant touch with Shriver on the bill. Califano alone reported fifty personal meetings with the OEO director through mid-September, as well as scores of telephone calls on the subject of the poverty program. The president himself conferred frequently with Shriver during the preparation of the administration proposal. In March he met with the newly appointed National Council on Economic Opportunity, authorized by Congress in late 1966 to oversee the War on Poverty, and quickly put the notables to work on getting the OEO renewal bill through. At a mid-April meeting in the White House Indian Treaty Room, Shriver briefed the council members of the threat to OEO and urged everyone present to fight for the president's bill. The administration also rallied big labor and tried to capture the press. In mid-February OEO held a three-day seminar in Washington for print and TV reporters at which OEO officials delivered papers explaining the agency's programs and clarifying the new bill. Shriver came at the end to answer questions.

The really heavy politicking for OEO funding for 1967–68 began in June with hearings presided over by Carl Perkins, Powell's successor on the Education and Labor Committee. The administration bill requested an increase of $400 million over the previous accounting year. Meanwhile OEO had to operate on a "continuing resolution" that allowed temporary funding pending an actual appropriation until early November. The administration forces mustered a flock of witnesses who testified against breaking up OEO and urged the lawmakers to generously fund the antipoverty programs generally. Administration officials, recognizing the potential damage of divided counsels, carefully coordinated their testimony.

The debate in Congress over OEO was so protracted that all the agency's money under the "continuing resolution" ran out without renewal. By October Shriver had to drop proposed projects, including portions of the still popular Head Start, and stop paying the salaries of local staffers. *The Washington Post* reported soon after that forty community action agencies had closed down or were about to owing to congressional delays.

Johnson was helped by a powerful if undramatic procedural reality of the American legislative equation: "iron triangles." Tacit alliances between voter constituencies, congressional subcommittees, and administrators, these informal structures are instruments of a political second law of thermodynamics: Programs in motion tend to remain in motion. The "iron triangles" provide a powerful forward momentum once a program is in place and dispensing bounty. They continue to nurture programs incrementally long after they are enacted and fend off even the most determined foes. Now, suddenly, with jobs threatened, the relevant public discovered that the War on Poverty had its practical uses after all. In October and November there were more than four hundred newspaper editorials endorsing OEO and accusing Congress of irresponsible action. Congress began feeling the heat, and the immobile wheels abruptly jerked into motion.

In the end the OEO bill that Johnson signed in December was far better than he had anticipated in January. The House bill reduced the administration's requested $2.3 billion to $1.6 billion, transferred some minor OEO functions to other federal agencies, and required that all community action agencies be state or local entities, in effect put under elected officials. This last proviso was the work of Edith Green of Oregon, whose motive, besides orneriness, was to appease Southern members who blamed the community action groups for the guerrilla war against local establishments. All told, the House action was not a startling administration triumph. The Senate was the more liberal body, but that initially had a downside; the administration had to beat back Joe Clark's $1.5 billion Emergency Employment Act before it could get the antipoverty bill through. The final Senate bill, stripped of Clark's proposal, authorized almost $2 billion for each of two years, and allowed OEO to keep all its programs. In the conference committee it was essentially the Senate version that prevailed. Days before the session's end the president signed a measure assuring a two-year program at a little under $2 billion average per year, with a softened Green amendment allowing the OEO director to provide financial resources to private community action agencies under specified circumstances.

The outcome was a startling win considering the early prospects. Shriver himself called it an "unexpected success."[49] It was, said the *Washington Star*, "a major victory for the Administration and a stunning reversal of the political fortunes of Sargent Shriver's beleaguered Office of Economic Opportunity."[50] The administration's efforts had undoubtedly worked some magic. And the Republicans had been divided. Still more potent was the reluctance of many members to cut back benefits to constituents in an election year. But whatever the cause there was every reason for the administration to be pleased.

□   □   □   □

The administration's major education achievement—the 1965 Elementary and Secondary Education Act—also survived the legislative gauntlet. But even as it was moving through Congress, evidence was piling up that ESEA's key Title I was not producing the results that its champions had predicted in the Eighty-ninth Congress.

The bad news, ironically, was partly Johnson's own fault. The president's admiration for Defense Secretary Robert McNamara had induced him to mandate Pentagon-style cost-benefits evaluation, called Planning-Programing-Budgeting-System (PPBS), for all major federal departments. It soon gave rise to a flood of program evaluations that would challenge many of the Great Society's premises.

The first rigorous test of Great Society programs was the discouraging 1966 Coleman Report. Its conclusion that there was little linkage between the money spent on education and the test scores of pupils cast doubt, as we saw, on Title I of ESEA, the major program to raise student achievement in poor school districts. Fortunately for the Great Society planners, Congress and the general public seemed not to notice the Coleman Report conclusions, though the bureaucrats and the academic policy-crafters did.

But Coleman was only the first of a series of blows. In early 1967 the Civil Rights Commission published a study of the educational effects of racial segregation, *Racial Isolation in the Public Schools,* that further undermined the premises of Title I. The study dealt primarily with the impact of Jim Crow laws rather than poor funding on school achievement, but its conclusion—that racial mixing was the best predictor of improved black performance—raised doubts that more dollars for ghetto schools made a difference. Soon after, Alice Rivlin, HEW's assistant secretary for planning and evaluation, hired the TEMPO division of the General Electric Company to examine specific Title I projects to identify successful features. These HEW would emphasize and support; the others would be cut or eliminated.

The Tempo Report, in two volumes, was as disappointing as the other evaluations. It compared pupil achievement in the years 1965–66, before federal money had arrived, with 1966–67, after the billion dollars plus of the ESEA had been liberally scattered across the nation. Two devastating conclusions emerged from the study. One was that it was almost impossible to identify specific Title I programs or a specific Title I population. Local school officials had kept few records of how ESEA money had been spent, and it was almost impossible to determine whether federal funds had truly been devoted to programs aimed at poor children. Clearly, much of the money had been spread so thinly and erratically that any possible effect of the ESEA nationally had been lost. The second conclusion was equally dismaying. Five districts where the students were indeed poor and where a decent amount of Title I money had been expended were selected for detailed study. In these, the broad effects on pupil achievement of extra education money could be determined. Alas, it seemed to have had little positive impact. In fact, there appeared to have "been a very slight decline in average pupil achievement in the Title I schools studied."

The results were greeted at HEW with "something approaching disbelief," according to Bayla White, a senior analyst with HEW.[51] The TEMPO study, like two previous negative reports, was effectively buried by the bureaucrats at HEW and the Office of Education. Though these reports would be discovered by conservatives in the years ahead, they did not affect the debate on refunding the ESEA for fiscal 1968 and 1969.

During the first session of the Ninetieth Congress the ESEA stalled in the House as the Democrats fought off a Republican amendment to change the way education money was allocated. Conservatives remained unreconciled to the federal presence in the public schools and the bias against suburban districts. To restore local control and allow suburbanites to share in the federal boon, Representative Albert Quie introduced an amendment to the ESEA early in the session to allot much of the federal money as block grants to state education departments for distribution as they saw fit. Administration officials balked. State control, especially in education, meant stodgy, poorly administered programs, they felt. Southern state education officials, moreover, could evade more easily federal desegregation guidelines, and parochial school students, owing to state constitutional provisions for separation of church and state, might lose hard-won benefits. Finally, the block-grant approach was a Republican Trojan horse in the Great Society camp. It could be applied to almost every federal program with damaging political results.

The administration jumped on the Quie amendment with both feet. On April 26 HEW secretary Gardner called it "disastrous." It would "strike at the very heart" of the delicate ESEA consensus.[52] The next day, in a talk at the Crossland Vocational Center in Maryland, the president denounced the amendment as harmful to poor states and to the cities. In May, Johnson warned that the Republican proposal threatened to undo twenty years of effort to get a federal-aid-to-education bill through dangerous shoals. The so-called "friends of education" had stirred up "ancient and bitter feuds between church and public school leaders" and aroused the fears of big-city-school superintendents.[53] To defeat the Republicans, the White House rounded up congressional support from every threatened quarter: Northern liberals, Catholics, moderate Southerners.

In the end the administration was forced to accept a compromise midwived by Edith Green. The Green amendment preserved the direct federal aid and aid-to-the-child features of the ESEA. But Green, always solicitous of the state education establishments, managed to reallocate $500 million in Title III funds for locally initiated programs from the U.S. commissioner of education and give it to the state education departments. Though the administration fought the Green amendment, it passed with the support of the Southern Democrats. Liberals denounced Mrs. Green's "mini-Quie" as a betrayal, but the basic principles of the ESEA were conserved and federal aid to education received funding at levels close to previous years'.

The task of the first session of the Ninetieth Congress had been primarily to conserve past gains, but the administration could also take credit for enacting several innovative programs during 1967.

Intellectuals and sophisticates had long denounced commercial American radio and TV as a "vast wasteland," the phrase used by Kennedy's FCC chairman, Newton Minow. It was dominated by sitcoms, quiz shows, soap operas, sports events, and vulgar pop culture. Their voices had not been unheeded. By the mid-sixties there were more than one hundred educational TV and three hundred educational radio stations in existence, brought to life by the 1962 Educational Television Facilities Act of the New Frontier, which provided stations with federal funds for transmission equipment.

Unfortunately, these did not satisfy elite yearnings for higher cultural standards. The act made no provision for programming, and the stations were all low-wattage enterprises, both in a cultural and a technical sense. Within the administration Douglass Cater, Wilbur Cohen, Francis Keppel, John Gardner, and other top aides hoped to see this feeble system upgraded and sought to bring the president into the process. Johnson did not oppose additional federal funding for educational broadcasting but preferred to stay in the background.

A 1966 report by the Carnegie Commission on Educational Television recommended that a private, nonprofit broadcasting corporation, financed by a special excise tax on receivers, be created for television alone. The corporation would operate an actual network. HEW and the Bureau of the Budget preferred a bill that included radio as well, that avoided a politically divisive special excise tax, and that eschewed direct control of stations, changes that were included in the administration measure that went to Congress.

HEW Secretary John Gardner was White House point man on the Hill for the proposed Corporation for Public Broadcasting. The former head of the Carnegie Foundation refused to pander to the demotic urge in Congress when he testified before the House committee considering the bill. The measure was aimed at providing economic support to "those creative people" who were willing "to explore the potential" of the broadcast media, he said. The time had "come to match technological sophistication with program excellence." Did the nation want "excellence"? He, for one, believed it did. Gardner rattled off the usual high-culture statistics: soaring museum attendance, the number of new symphony orchestras, the leap in sales of classical records. This suggested, he said, that the American people were interested in the sorts of programs that were not being offered by commercial broadcasting. And if better programs were made available, they would "stimulate an even greater interest."[54]

The measure as passed extended for three years the equipment construction program already in force and added educational radio to the original TV focus. Title II created a federally chartered, nonprofit corporation to be financed by federal revenues. The corporation would not own or operate stations of its own but would make grants to local noncommercial stations and to educational networks to encourage existing TV stations to experiment with more imaginative programming and to establish new public broadcasting stations, including radio stations, to provide fare that the profit motive could not justify. It would eschew any effort to connect its TV affiliates, though not its radio affiliates, into another network that might compete with the three commercial ones and dilute local station initiative. The new stations, besides relying on federal funds, would seek financing from private individuals and organizations.[55]

Congress gave the corporation no money in 1967, but by the mid-1970s there would be more than four hundred public broadcasting stations receiving federal block grants to provide listeners and viewers with a diet of hard news, sophisticated discussions, classical music, and serious jazz.

The administration also sought a raft of environmental and consumer protection laws from Congress. Johnson opened his consumer-environment campaign in the Ninetieth Congress with a special message on February 16, 1967, proposing twelve new laws: a pipeline safety measure, mutual fund and pension regulations, a stricter meat and poultry inspection act, new rules to prevent power system blackouts, a bill to frustrate fraud in mail order land sales, safety legislation for power tools and kitchen appliances, and a law to regulate clinical laboratories. The most important measure, reviving legislation long blocked in Congress, would be a truth-in-lending bill to protect consumers from credit gougers and from the most painful consequences of consumer credit abuse. To dramatize his push, in April he announced the appointment of Betty Furness, famous as a TV huckster for Westinghouse refrigerators, to replace the abrasive Esther Peterson as special assistant for consumer affairs. *The Nation,* critical of the Great Society from its position on the left, would call the selection of Ms. Furness, a successful actress who seldom did her own shopping, "another case of image making."[56] But her thespian flair and visibility would make her an effective consumer advocate in the months ahead.

Johnson got only a thin slice of the consumer protection-environmental program he wanted in the first session. The Air Quality Act of 1967 gave HEW the responsibility for designating air quality control regions in polluted areas but left to the states the job of setting and enforcing air quality standards. The Senate passed a weak Truth-in-Lending bill in July, but the House would not budge and the bill was held over to the next session. Congress also approved a Wholesome Meat Act and passed a fire standards act for fabrics. But the rest of the president's wish list remained bottled up.

All told, it had not been a good session, certainly not compared with the year before. The White House tried to put a good face on it, calling the record "impressive." Califano announced that "the Great Society's programs are here to stay. They are clearly a part of the American way of life."[57] But almost no one else agreed. When Congress finally adjourned in mid-December after one of the longest sessions on record, few praised it. *Newsweek* called it the "Do-Little" Congress. There was no way, it said, to deny its "abysmal record of shortcomings."[58] *The Washington Post* noted that "in 1967 Congress sat longer and did less than any session in recent years. And Lyndon Johnson's reputation as a great parliamentary magician was tarnished in the process."[59]

As Americans slid into an uneasy 1967–68 Christmas–New Year's holiday season, they had little reason to feel that the nation's domestic affairs were in order or that the drift into confusion and turmoil had ceased.

Nineteen sixty-eight has been described as the worst year of the century. In late January the Vietcong launched a massive offensive on Tet, the Vietnamese lunar New Year, that shattered the administration's remaining credibility on Vietnam. The attackers seized public buildings in many of the provincial capitals, captured the old capital city of Hue, and even occupied the American embassy compound in Saigon. American and South Vietnamese troops soon retook the embassy, recaptured the overrun towns, and inflicted crushing losses on the Vietcong. But after January 30, LBJ's claims that victory was near seemed laughable.

Meanwhile, at home, things spun out of control. In April, a white racist assassinated Martin Luther King in Memphis, setting off the most destructive wave of ghetto riots of the decade. Arson, rock-throwing, and looting swept over 125 cities in twenty-eight states; forty-six died and thousands were injured. That spring the nation's campuses, led by Columbia, exploded in a round of building occupations, violent demonstrations, and police "busts" that marked the apogee of student violence and radical efforts to destabilize the liberal order. In June, Bobby Kennedy, running against Eugene McCarthy in the California presidential primary for the right to challenge LBJ at the Chicago Democratic Convention, was assassinated by a Palestinian immigrant who resented his pro-Israel stand. With each passing week, the antiwar movement grew more militant. What started in 1965–66 with peaceful rallies, marches, and teach-ins soon became an angry cacophony of draft card burnings, arson, and even fiery self-immolations.

It would not be an auspicious year for the Democrats, the party in uneasy power, but as it began Lyndon Johnson intended to run for reelection and win. Always the practical politician, LBJ tailored his January "State of the Union" address to suit the tumultuous political season now unfolding. Not once during the lackluster fifty-one-minute speech did he utter the phrase "Great Society." Clearly it had become a political liability. But if the public had lost faith in the program as a whole, it had not repudiated many of its components. Johnson promised to fight for what he had already accomplished in education, health care, consumer protection, conservation, and model cities. He also proposed a half-billion-dollar JOBS (Job Opportunities in the Business Sector) program to promote a joint government-industry effort to train 500,000 of the hard-core unemployed, a major housing bill to improve the shelter of the poor and the lower middle class, and a clutch of new environmental and consumer protection measures. None of these aroused his congressional audience; the president himself seemed detached when he described them. Ominously, the few bursts of enthusiasm from the nation's representatives came when the president deplored inflation, crime in the streets, and riots.

A panel of seventeen GOP congressional leaders replied to the president on TV, denouncing the administration for prolonging the Vietnam War, for runaway federal deficits, for the growing chaos in the ghettos and crime on the streets. Marking the recent retreat of public favor, Johnson's political adversaries began the process of demonizing the Great Society. Melvin Laird proposed to replace "the Great Planned Society" with "true federalism" in the form of revenue sharing with the states. Albert Quie, the ranking Republican on the House Education and Labor Committee, recommended, in place of the federal War on Poverty giveaways, a joint government-industry program to create jobs and an "industry youth corps" to "mobilize the communities to help the poor get off the welfare rolls."[60]

The Tet offensive, two weeks later, wounded the administration badly. The astonishing Vietcong attack made the president seem either a fool or a liar and emboldened the antiwar movement. And the failures in Southeast Asia undermined Johnson's social programs as well. By early 1968 large elements of the public no longer cared about the administration's domestic programs, or even understood them. Aide James Gaither, dispatched to California to scout the local political scene, reported back that the state's Democrats were hostile to the president and would not give him credit for anything. If they thought about Great Society programs at all, they considered them "a continuation of the welfare programs of the '30's and didn't understand that it was an entirely different concept, one of opportunity rather than a handout."[61]

By this time the administration felt besieged. Johnson could not appear in public without angry squads of protesters showing up with signs accusing him of murder in Vietnam. Wherever he went he could hear their chant: "Hey, hey, LBJ, how many kids did you kill today?" On the campuses students wore buttons inscribed: STERILIZE LBJ: NO MORE UGLY CHILDREN, HITLER IS ALIVE—IN THE WHITE HOUSE, and the particularly vicious LEE HARVEY OSWALD—WHERE ARE YOU NOW THAT WE NEED YOU? On March 12, Eugene McCarthy, the reflective senator from Minnesota, came within 230 votes of edging out the president in the New Hampshire Democratic primary. Four days later, Bobby Kennedy, LBJ's nemesis, announced that he too would challenge Johnson for the Democratic presidential nomination.

The president now faced a wrenching fight for the nomination with imminent defeat looming in the impending Wisconsin primary. A lifelong hypochondriac whose forebears had died young, he feared his health would not hold up to a vigorous campaign and a second full term. But he also concluded that he had become a jinx to his own domestic programs. If he withdrew from the fall race he would be in a better position to save his Great Society. On March 31 Johnson delivered a major televised speech to the American public on Vietnam. He spoke mostly of a bombing halt in Vietnam and new peace negotiations. But as he approached the end of the speech he shifted gears. He pleaded for national unity and for preserving "the American commitment for all of our people." What the nation had won during the months following the "moment of tragedy and trauma" that brought him to office in 1963 must not be lost. "Accordingly," he concluded, "I shall not seek, and I will not accept the nomination of my party for another term as your president."[62]

Johnson had guessed right. The public's response echoed Malcolm's to the Thane of Cawdor's death in *Macbeth:* "Nothing in his life became him like the leaving it." Just before the withdrawal speech, the president's approval rating was an abysmal 36 percent, the lowest level of his presidency. On April 17 Gallup reported that 49 percent of the people polled now approved his performance. When Johnson flew to Chicago on April 1 to address the National Association of Broadcasters, he encountered the usual rude placards. But he also saw one saying: LBJ IS A GREAT AMERICAN. A trip to New York for the installation of the Catholic archbishop yielded other signs of favor. As the president walked down the aisle of St. Patrick's Cathedral, the congregation rose and cheered.

Johnson's renunciation initially staggered the White House staffers. A lame duck president would have absolutely no political leverage, they were certain. Yet the renunciation gave a lift to the administration's legislative program. Writing in early May, Califano noted that since the March 31 speech the administration had been "moving with increased power and ability to get things done. . . ." The American people now believed that the president was acting "without any ax to grind and only because it is right."[63] Some members of Congress, moreover, especially conservative Democrats, apparently felt sorry for the president and regretted treating him and his programs so shabbily. During the second session of the Ninetieth Congress, programs bottled up since the previous session suddenly shook loose and began to roll down the legislative assembly line.

The most important legislative venture of the session was an ambitious housing bill unveiled in a special message, "The Crisis of the Cities," on February 22, 1968. Johnson hoped to reignite some of the visionary fire of the past while keeping his feet on the ground. He asked for a new housing and urban development act that would fund, over the next ten years, 26 million new homes and apartments. The program would start with 300,000 new housing units for the inner cities during fiscal 1969 at a cost of $4.6 billion. These would not be limited to rental apartments in public housing projects. A hundred thousand poor families would actually become home owners. Congress should also expand the rent supplement program and boost the funding for Model Cities: $500 million for fiscal 1969 and $1 billion for each of the next two fiscal years.

The proposal struck a new note of humility on the part of the administration. Johnson never accepted the Republican concept of revenue sharing. He always favored central federal administration over devolution of power. He also trusted government over private initiatives. That's the way the New Deal had worked and it was, he believed, more consistent and effective than state management. But by 1968, if only because the money was no longer there, he was willing to consider other approaches. The administration had begun to take seriously proposals from Bobby Kennedy and others to enlist private business in the rescue campaign for the inner cities, and "The Crisis of the Cities" made this one of its core principles. Construction of low-cost housing units would be undertaken by new national housing partnerships funded by banks, construction companies, and manufacturers, but with government directors on their boards. Constructing decent shelter for the poor had never been profitable, despite generations of reformers who sought magic formulas to do good and make money simultaneously. To protect investors, the new scheme allowed any losses incurred to be applied against personal income taxes. Investors in housing for the poor would make as much money, then, as investors in cars or cloth. It would, the president said, be "a new partnership between business and government."[64]

The new law would also allow eligible poor families to obtain mortgages to purchase private homes at 1 percent interest, with the government paying the difference between that figure and market rates. It also authorized the HUD secretary to provide technical assistance and interest-free loans to nonprofit sponsors of low-cost housing, and subsidized construction and rehabilitation of rental and co-op housing for poor families. It proposed extending the rent supplement program in both eligibility and amount, provided additional money for model cities projects, authorized a program to protect insurers against losses from riots or civil disorders, and offered federal subsidies for creating entire new towns and planned communities. This last proposal for "New Cities"—self-contained, detached communities—was actually a supplement announced a week later. Authored by Charles Haar, now Weaver's deputy at HUD, it reflected several generations of speculative thinking among social planners and architects as an approach to urban problems.

Taken together this was by far the most ambitious piece of new social legislation proposed in the Ninetieth Congress, and by all rights, given the nation's newfound fears and frugality, it should have had heavy going. The New Cities project came under fire as visionary and likely to accelerate "white flight" from the cities. The House Banking Committee cut it from the lower house's bill. But it was restored in the Senate and survived the conference. And the rest of the program, buoyed up by the president's surge in popularity, sailed through Congress with remarkable ease and few changes.

In fact, the bill appealed to a broad range of political appetites. For liberals it embodied a tradition of social betterment through slum improvement that had begun with the early twentieth century progressives and accelerated with the New Deal. It also was a pledge of concern for the unhappy and restless ghetto poor. One of its provisions, obviously crafted to fit the new mood, required, for example, that wherever feasible, construction projects should employ local people (read: "residents of the ghetto") and construction contracts should be awarded to companies owned by locals. For conservatives and Republicans, on the other hand, the measure seemed less a boon to the poor than a massive pork barrel for every section of the country. But in an election year, this feature was compelling, even to Republicans, fiscal scruples notwithstanding.

The majorities for the bill were decisive. The Senate approved the Housing and Urban Development Act of 1968 on May 28 by a vote of 67 to 4; the House passed its own version on June 25 by 295 to 114. Reconciled by conference, the bill went to the president in late July. On August 1, on the plaza in front of the sparkling new headquarters for the Department of Housing and Urban Development, Johnson signed it before an audience of government workers, media crews, and blue-suited dignitaries with his usual embellishments. The new law was "the most farsighted, most comprehensive, most massive housing act in all of American history," he announced. It could be "the Magna Carta to liberate our cities."[65] It was standard Johnson hyperbole, but who could begrudge him the verbal flourish of happier days?

LBJ remained attuned to environmental and consumer issues in 1968. The first session of the Eighty-ninth Congress had broken new ground with the anti-billboard, highway beautification law and with environmental measures to enhance the quality of the nation's air and water. Aided by the dramatic Nader-General Motors encounter, in the following session Congress had passed the National Traffic and Motor Vehicle Safety Act and the Highway Safety Act. During the Eighty-ninth Congress the administration treated environmental and consumer legislation as grace notes of the Great Society. In the Ninetieth, laws to protect the consumer and the environment would have special appeal.

For LBJ they served to sustain the sense of liberal momentum and were simultaneously cheap and appropriate for a time of budget constraints and diminished legislative expectations. They also suited Congress. Liberals in the House and Senate, like the president, could preserve their populist credentials; conservatives could claim that they too had the best interests of the endangered public at heart. And not just "the poor" this time, but all Americans—white as well as black, suburban as well as urban, affluent as well as impoverished. All were consumers, and so deserved protection. Only when environmentalism became a threat to jobs and the preserve of folk with an antibusiness social agenda would conservatives balk at further environmental regulation. But that came later, during the 1970s and 1980s.

During the first session of the Ninetieth Congress many of the administration's consumer and environmental initiatives had stalled. Early in the second session, Johnson came back with another consumer protection message praising the bills still stuck in committee and adding proposals to guard against appliance radiation hazards, to improve pleasure boat safety, and to study the causes and cures of high auto insurance rates. Soon after, the photogenic Betty Furness presided at a high-profile White House press conference where reporters questioned Transportation Secretary Alan Boyd, HEW Undersecretary Wilbur Cohen, and the head of the Security and Exchange Commission on the roles of their agencies in consumer protection. Furness told the reporters that Lyndon Johnson would go down in history as the "consumer conscious President," who began and nurtured the movement and "stayed with it until everybody else caught up."[66]

Once again the second session proved more accommodating than the first. In an election year, members feared returning to their constituents in the fall with little to show for two years of lawmaking. Even Republicans hoped to use their consumer protection records to bolster their candidacies in November. The end result was an avalanche of new laws that went far to justify Furness's flattery.

The major consumer law passed by the Ninetieth Congress was the Truth-in-Lending Act, which had failed to make it through Congress the previous session. Efforts to get a federal credit disclosure law dated back to a 1960 proposal by Illinois senator Paul Douglas. John Kennedy had supported a credit disclosure bill but had been unable to overrule the banks, retail businesses, and finance companies, which considered it another federal intrusion into their affairs and a threat to their profits. As introduced in the House during the first session, the Johnson bill required that banks, finance companies, and sellers on credit clearly state annual finance charges in writing.

This was a consumer protection bill, pure and simple. But it soon acquired unsettling additional baggage in the form of a garnishment restriction. At congressional hearings activists and civil rights spokesmen had linked the existing consumer credit regime to exploitation of the poor. A worker whose wages were legally garnished, for example, was often fired by his employer. The cause of garnishment relief was taken up by Representative Leonor Sullivan of Missouri, head of the House subcommittee on bankruptcy, who succeeded in making it a feature of the truth-in-lending debate. The garnishment issue touched sensitive nerves. Credit sellers saw it as a danger to their business; deadbeats would escape their obligations. Southern congressmen considered it another misguided civil rights proposal that would allow blacks to evade their debts.

Inclusion of "revolving credit" was another problem for the bill's supporters. The department stores and other big retailers like Sears, Roebuck, claiming it was impossible to convert revolving credit to an understandable, simple interest figure, feared telling customers that annual interest charges on unpaid balances ran as high as 18 percent.

The president recognized the limits of his power in this waning period of his administration and proved willing to compromise. His chief ally was organized labor, but no consumer constituency had as much to gain as the business groups had to lose and the fight promised to be hard. Johnson's critics from the left considered his pragmatism hypocrisy. According to Robert Sherrill of *The Nation* he wanted credit for a consumer protection measure but had no heart for a fight. He had asked the unions to back off a tough law that included garnishment reform, Sherrill claimed, and AFL-CIO lobbyist Andrew Biemiller had obliged in his testimony before the House Banking Committee. In fact Biemiller, a savvy legislative tactician himself, was probably responsible for choosing realism over purity.

During the summer of 1967 the Senate passed a weak bill that required some disclosure of credit costs but exempted department store revolving credit accounts and failed to limit garnishment. This was enough for the embattled president, but not for Leonor Sullivan. The dogged congresswoman, helped by Betty Furness, who "supplied glamor and a human appeal,"[67] induced the House in the second session to top it with a stronger bill. Yet the final measure, worked out by the joint conference and passed on May 15, 1968, was a compromise. Representative Sullivan had proposed an absolute prohibition of garnishment, but under the new law workers were allowed to exempt from garnishment only 75 percent of their take-home pay, or a maximum of $48 per week. They could not be fired by their bosses for a first garnishment, though they could if they became chronic offenders. Consumers had to be informed of the true cost of credit in writing, but small loans were exempt from most disclosure provisions and only limited disclosure was required on first mortgages.

On consumer protection issues the Ninetieth Congress gave the administration a batting average as high as the overall legislative record of its predecessor. Besides the consumer credit bill, Congress passed laws to establish state systems of poultry inspection, to regulate pipelines, to reduce air and water pollution, radiation hazards, and aircraft noise, to set auto insurance rates, and to supervise dangerous drugs. Exuberant and obsequious at once, Vice President Humphrey gave LBJ most of the credit for the successes. The present administration, he chortled in mid-May, had "done more for the consumer in the past four years" than any other "in the previous hundred."[68] In fact the legislation suited the public mood and Congress was happy to oblige the president. In roll calls for several of the bills the "yea" majorities were overwhelming, close to unanimous.

The president also won some victories in the war for culture. The 1965 law establishing the National Endowments in the Arts and in the Humanities had broken new ground by making scholarship and the arts federal concerns. But once staff and guidelines were in place and grants and fellowships began to flow to artists and academics, the abstract became concrete. The world of the politicians, and of average Americans, did not correspond to the worlds of scholars and artists, and the inevitable ridicule and outrage soon erupted.

The opening moves of the endowments were exemplary. The first grant of the humanities endowment in mid-1966 went to the Modern Language Association, the professional body of the professors of modern languages and the literatures thereof, to prepare definitive editions of the collected works of classic nineteenth-century American writers. Early the next year the NEH awarded grants for an edition of the papers of Founding Father John Jay and for the collected works of philosopher John Dewey. In August the director of the arts endowment announced $220,000 in individual grants to promising younger writers, especially those in the West and South who were not members in good standing of the "Eastern Seaboard Literary Grants and Gravy Society."[69] Endowment officials, both for expedient and principled reasons, sought to even out the regional inequalities of American cultural life by liberally watering local and regional orchestras, dance companies, and theater repertory groups.

All this evoked little but applause. But trouble was unavoidable. Run by sophisticates and cosmopolitans—men and women from the universities, museums, and arts, music, and theater worlds— the endowments inevitably offended the sensibilities of mid-Americans, distant in geography and taste from the culture capitals of the nation.

Among the sixty-nine grants announced by the NEH in February 1967 was $8,700 to David Kunzle of the University of California at Santa Barbara for a study of the political and social influence of cartoons and comic strips in the United States. The topic was not preposterous. Cartoons have always been potent political weapons, more powerful often than editorials and pamphlets in changing people's minds. But to Representative Durward Hall of Missouri's 7th District, the grant proved a godsend. A sympathizer with the far-right-wing John Birch Society, and no friend of the endowments from the beginning, Hall ridiculed the cartoon study grant and denounced Kunzle, an antiwar activist, for "biting the hand that feeds him."[70] At Senate hearings on a three-year extension of the program in the fall, defenders of traditional art denounced the arts endowment for grants to the abstract expressionists' "frauds and doodles, . . . drippings and droppings."[71]

During the second session the administration proposed to roughly triple the amount authorized for the previous year. The congressional defenders of truth and beauty considered this paltry and tried to double the administration's request to $135 million over two years. The economizers and skeptics fought back. Mississippi Democrat William Colmer said that while opposing the bill was like attacking motherhood, he could not justify spending the taxpayers' good money in a time of budget crunch. GOP Congressman Frank Bow of Ohio invoked Vietnam. "Certainly at this time there is not a soul on this floor who does not realize that we are at war [and] we cannot have guns and butter. And this Endowment is guns with strawberry shortcake covered with whipped cream and a cherry on top."[72] After the dust settled the arts endowment received a modest $8 million; the humanities endowment about the same. Congress also appropriated $5 million for the Public Broadcasting Corporation, established the previous session, and another $4.3 million for educational broadcasting facilities. Clearly, as yet, federal subsidies for culture and learning were still at the pilot-program stage.

The administration's record on conservation issues during the Ninetieth Congress was far more impressive. On March 8 Johnson submitted to Congress a roster of environmental and conservation proposals he called "To Renew a Nation." The president recommended giving the secretary of the interior authority to regulate strip-mining if the states failed to act. The HEW secretary would develop and enforce standards regarding chemical as well as biological contaminants of drinking water. Firms responsible for oil spills would pay the full cost of their clean-up. There would be additional federal money for municipal waste treatment plants. The president also asked for a system of scenic trails and for two new national parks. The message won the plaudits of all the major conservation and recreation organizations.

Johnson got much of what he asked for. Congress established the Redwood National Park in Northern California, passed the Scenic Trails and Rivers bill for a network of wilderness hiking trails, and created a system of national wild and scenic rivers, designating streams to be kept free of development and reserved for nature enthusiasts.

The most controversial item on the March 8 list was the ambitious Central Arizona project, eventually expected to cost $1.3 billion. This was the kind of old-fashioned resource development project popular in the early part of the century among "scientific management" conservationists and pushed hard by business-oriented community boosters and private developers. The bill authorized construction of major dams on the Colorado to provide hydroelectric power and drinking and irrigation water for the fast-growing central-Arizona region. The chief beneficiaries would be the exploding cities of Tucson and Phoenix, fruit and vegetable farmers, and private utility investors. Stalled in Congress for two decades by fierce struggles among the Southwestern states over division of the region's limited water resources, it had recently faced the wrath of the new ecologists. Led by the Sierra Club, they charged that the proposed two dams on the Colorado River would destroy the scenic Grand Canyon and forced the administration to abandon them. But the full thrust of the "no growth" ecological movement lay ahead, and the remainder of the bill, including a controversial dam on the Gila River in Utah, passed with administration blessing. Johnson signed it on September 30 with a self-congratulatory little speech in the East Room of the White House, describing the bill as a "proud companion to the 250 separate conservation measures" that he had signed since he had become president.[73]

But it was one step back for every two steps forward. During the Ninetieth Congress the highway beautification program got pounded by its adversaries, and the cause of riding the nation's roads without exposure to visual blight suffered serious setbacks.

The pathbreaking 1965 Highway Beautification bill had barely tamed the billboard lobby, and in 1967 it struck back. One provision of the beautification act allowed the Bureau of Public Roads to establish zoning standards for billboards and arrange compliance pacts with the states to avoid having federal highway funds withheld. The standards as proposed by Secretary of Transportation Alan Boyd were stricter than anticipated and provoked a heated response from the billboard lobby. Before a single agreement between Boyd and the states had been reached, Representative John Kluczynski, chair of the House Public Roads Committee, actively intervened on behalf of the billboard lobby. Early in the first session of the new Congress he wired the nation's governors that the proposed regulations were unworkable and "the basic law" would "have to be revised if we are to accomplish our goals."[74] In April the Chicago Democrat opened hearings on a new bill to limit Washington's power to impose standards. Many Republicans wanted no law at all and prepared to fight for its full repeal.

The administration brought out its big guns to save the beautification act. The women's clubs, conservation groups, and roadside councils rallied to the bill, and administration lobbyists made the trek to the Hill in force. But the hearings, managed by Kluczynski, were generally anti-administration, and its witnesses, with exceptions, denounced the administration's tough interpretation of the law. Congressmen themselves were "generally hostile," reported Secretary Boyd.[75] Jim Wright of Texas told Boyd that "Congress feels . . . that you fellows are trying to do things . . . that were not contemplated in the act." Republican William Cramer of Florida, reflecting the impatience of conservatives with domestic quality-of-life programs while Americans were dying in Southeast Asia, asked Boyd bluntly: "Why is this before us during the Vietnam crisis?"[76]

Despite the initial tough talk Boyd soon backed down and negotiated an agreement with Kluczynski. The federal government would leave the regulation of billboards to local zoning authorities, would relax the definition of an unzoned commercial area subject to regulation, and would not impose penalties during 1967–68 on those states that failed to reach agreement on enforcement with the federal authorities.

The House hearings ended in early May and were followed by parallel Senate hearings. Boyd appeared once again, armed with the concessions he had already made to the House committee.

With his promises in mind, the Senate ratified a bill that gave the beautification act funding for another year of nuisance removal, but only at about half the level the administration had requested.

The House postponed action until the next session. The delay only undermined the administration position further. By early 1968 the original law had come under fire from its erstwhile supporters, the conservationists, who had concluded that it was "a fraud on the public expectations."[77] In his March 8 "Renew A Nation" message the president had called for revitalizing the Highway Beautification Act. But without many friends, except Lady Bird and the White House, the Federal-Aid Highway Act of 1968 was a weak measure. The bill as passed authorized just $8.5 million for billboard removal, only 10 percent of what the administration had requested. It weakened federal power to set standards for billboards and reduced the protection afforded roadside parklands by the 1965 measure. Senator Clark called it "a significant victory for the uglifiers," and for a time the president considered vetoing it.[78] Fearing that his veto would be overridden and embarrass the administration, he finally signed the bill.

The lesson of the highway beautification measure was that if the country's sour mood and the loss of liberal momentum could not annul the Great Society core benefit programs, they could shrivel the "frills." Lady Bird's 1965 beautification bill represented the fragile late flowering of a rich and confident society's concern for the finer things. It could not survive in a time when anger, doubt, and fear had overtaken the American people. Representative Cramer's question about the relevance of highway beauty during an agonizing war undoubtedly expressed a wider public mood: Was this issue worth worrying about, all things considered?

The second session also saw passage of the Health Manpower Act, which reinforced earlier Kennedy and Johnson measures to encourage the training of health workers. Better medical care for Americans, of course, had been one goal of the bill. The country had a shortage of health professionals, the experts believed, making good medical attention hard to get in many areas. But as with the 1965 Health Professions Education Act, another purpose was cost containment. As the president's Advisory Commission on Health Manpower reported in late 1967, the nation's cost for medical care, some $37.3 billion in 1965, would reach $94 billion by 1975. The federal government was expected to be a major contributor to this inflation through Medicare and Medicaid reimbursement formulas that "do *nothing* to encourage efficiency."[79] The pressure, the panel believed, could be relieved by expanding the number of medical professionals and the health facilities they practiced in.

Responding to this prognosis, the measure aimed at increasing enrollments of medical and dental schools by 2.5 percent. Already dependent on the federal gravy train, the schools would get twice as much for each of these new students as for those already enrolled. The federal government, moreover, would pay up to 100 percent of the additional cost imposed by the augmented student body, including added construction outlays, extra expenses for curriculum development, and so forth. The bill encountered little opposition and became law in mid-August.

Johnson finally got his tax surcharge in mid-1968 but he paid a price for it. By the time Congress passed the tax hike bill and sent it to his desk for signature in late June, LBJ had already withdrawn from the presidential race and become a lame duck, but the tribute exacted by Mills and the fiscal conservatives vexed him sorely.

Johnson had invited Wilbur Mills to the Ranch over the Christmas recess in 1967 to join the discussions on the fiscal '69 budget. If the president expected to win over the powerful chairman he was disappointed. Mills returned to Washington in January convinced more than ever that the people back home did not want higher taxes. The way to cut the deficit was to cut the programs and he intended, he told reporters, to devote most of his energies during the second session to that pursuit. Though Mills's budget-cutting intentions were unmistakable, it was not clear how drastic a trimming would satisfy the congressman. In one version, he was said to favor slashing programs back to their fiscal 1967 level. But Mills was saying something different to the administration privately. In a meeting on January 24 with Treasury Secretary Fowler and his congressional liaison man, Joseph Bowman, Mills acknowledged that spending had probably been reduced as much as possible and that in fact Congress might not buy the cuts already made. He did not believe the tax surcharge on individual incomes, as opposed to a surcharge on corporate income and various excises, could be passed. The "recent Gallup poll on the tax bill had the members scared.'' Fowler told the chairman that Bowman would take a House head count. Mills agreed that it should be done soon.[80]

Whatever took place in private, the public sparring between the administration and the chairman continued for weeks. In March the treasury chimed in with a warning that failure to enact a tax increase bill would jeopardize the dollar, already under severe siege on international markets. There was ''no feasible substitute for tax action to curtail the inflationary excesses in domestic demand that are now spilling over into imports,'' reported a treasury advisory committee chaired by ex-Treasury Secretary Douglas Dillon.[81] On March 12 the president told the National Alliance of Businessmen, an advisory group for his JOBS program (see p. 293), that ''some desirable programs of lesser priority and urgency are going to have to be deferred.''[82] The next day the administration leaked reports that the president would accept cuts of $3 billion to $4 billion in spending for fiscal 1969. In his speech of March 31 announcing his withdrawal from the presidential race, LBJ once more asked for a tax increase and promised to cut domestic programs.

Though Johnson had accepted Mills's general demands for cuts, the fighting over their extent went down to the buzzer. The White House wanted no more than $4 billion, an amount Majority Leader Mike Mansfield said could be squeezed from defense, from research and development contracts, and from foreign aid, the space program, and expenditures for U.S. troops in Europe. If the sum was $6 billion, Mansfield noted, the cuts would inevitably reach into food stamps, aid to education, model cities, and the poverty programs. Secretary Fowler took a more conservative tack. The ''time of guns and butter [was] over,'' he believed. The country, he told George Meany, could ''no longer do both.''[83] But Fowler's position was unique in the administration. Writing shortly after Johnson's renunciation of a second full term, Califano, closer to the inner circle, urged his chief to hold fast. All the effort the president had expended ''should not be thrown away by dismantling large pieces of the Great Society.''[84]

Congress defied the president. On April 2 the Senate approved a 10 percent income tax surcharge to last until June 30, 1969, with a mandated budget ceiling for the new fiscal year of $180 billion, $6 billion below the president's January budget proposal.

But for tax legislation it was the House that counted and here Mills took a hard line. On April 30, Mills and other Democratic leaders met with the president and agreed on a pattern of cutbacks called the "10-8-4 formula." In 1968 Congress would be mandated to reduce future authorizations by $10 billion. It would also cut $8 billion from authorizations for spending already made. Finally, it would actually cut $4 billion from fiscal 1969. Though he agreed to the formula, Johnson was so resistant that he jeopardized its acceptance by Congress by publicly calling it "blackmail."[85] But then Mills was not able to deliver the 10-8-4 formula. In early May the House Republicans caucused and approved a full $6 billion cut for fiscal 1969. Claiming it the best he could get, Mills went along.

The prospect of drastic budget cuts brought out the liberals in force. At a meeting in the White House cabinet room, George Meany and the other labor czars told the president that the unions would fight with everything they had to stop a "meat ax," across-the-board budget slash. Meany said he would prefer a $23 billion deficit to lopping off big amounts for housing, health, education, and welfare, the large Great Society programs.[86] That same day Joe Barr, undersecretary of the treasury, and Arthur Okun, new chairman of the Council of Economic Advisers, met with the agitated Democratic Study Group, the liberal House Democrat caucus, to explain what was happening. Okun told the liberals that the $6 billion cut was more than warranted, but the "need for a tax increase was so overriding" that the administration would have to pay the price. Richard Bolling, the liberal majority whip, informed his colleagues that a $4 billion reduction would win only two or three Republican votes for the tax bill. A $6 billion cut would get from sixty to ninety. The only thing that comforted the liberals was that the proposed measure allowed the president to choose where to cut. They could trust him to spare the social programs.

The administration tried one last time to get Congress to restore the lower figure. "Little Wilbur," Wilbur Cohen, newly elevated to the top post at HEW, rushed to the Hill to inveigle members into a more reasonable course. Usually adept as a lobbyist, this time Cohen only offended the conservatives. One Republican senator said he deeply regretted he had not been present to vote against Cohen when he'd come before the upper house for confirmation as HEW secretary. The president bowed to the inevitable. On May 29 he sent a statement to Congress regretting the $6 billion cut but acknowledging that if the lawmakers gave him his tax increase he would accept it and sign the bill.

In the end the law did little harm to the Great Society programs already in place. It proved difficult in an election year to cut outlays. Congressional committees sweated over the butchering process but failed to get beyond half the authorized $6 billion cuts and left the rest to the administration. Johnson did as little as possible to help the economizers out during the few months that remained of his term. Budget Director Charles Zwick actually came up with $6 billion in cuts that targeted defense, various federal loan programs, highway construction, the space program, and foreign aid. Though it is difficult to calculate differences between funding of Great Society programs in fiscal 1969 and fiscal 1968, it was clearly not great. And the tax bill did the job—fiscal 1969 ended with a $3.2 billion budget surplus—sparing further fiscal pressure to cut domestic social programs. Joseph Califano's judgment about the impact of the surcharge bill is correct: "The Great Society programs survived."[87]

Squeezed from the right, the Great Society was also prodded by the left. In 1968 Johnson found himself simultaneously fending off campaigns for economy from conservatives, and aggressive, sometimes menacing demands from white liberals and black civil rights activists that the country do more for the poor.

In the wake of the 1967 ghetto riots he had appointed a commission headed by Governor Otto Kerner of Illinois to investigate the causes of "civil disorders" and to recommend solutions. But Kerner was a weak and indecisive man, and the dominant figure on the National Advisory Commission on Civil Disorders was Mayor John Lindsay of New York, a white liberal whose own privileged status seemed to reinforce his concern for the poor. While blue-collar and middle-class whites had begun to bridle at compensatory antipoverty policies by 1968, Lindsay and his Kerner Commission staff, headed by David Ginsburg, a Washington lawyer and a White House aide, did not. For elite liberals, beset by guilt and insulated from the painful costs of racial readjustment, funneling money into the ghettos still seemed a reasonable antidote to the horrors of inner-city life.

The eleven-member board met forty-four times, often at night and frequently in the former snack bar of the Senate office building. They visited eight ghetto communities to see and hear for themselves what conditions were like on the ground.

From the outset, though his own creation, the commission aroused Johnson's suspicions. The president did not want recommendations to spend more money and told Kerner and his colleagues to shun them. His advice fell on deaf ears. In late February, as a courtesy to the White House, Ginsburg gave Califano an advanced copy of the final report. It appalled the president.

As finally released to the public on March 2, the 1,400-page Kerner Report bluntly denied the optimists' view of race relations in America. Ignoring the gains that had been made since the mid-1950s, and especially under Johnson, it proclaimed that the nation was "moving toward two societies, one black, one white— separate and unequal." It also seemed to excuse the rioters for their violent actions. "White racism," virtually without qualification, according to the report, was the cause of the ghetto riots. White society was "deeply implicated in the ghetto. White institutions created it and white society condones it."[88]

Johnson deeply resented the report's omission of the Civil Rights and Voting Rights Acts and other landmark administration efforts to improve the lot of black Americans. He balked at the costs of the commission's recommended correctives. The appalling process of growing racial alienation could be checked, the Kerner commissioners declared, only by a massive social and economic rescue operation. Besides extensive efforts to improve community-police relations and to respond more effectively to community grievances, there must be nothing less than a new, better funded War on Poverty. Merely maintaining the current level of expenditures for the disadvantaged would be disastrous. The nation must make a commitment "to national action on an unprecedented scale" and tax itself "to the extent necessary to meet the vital needs of the Nation." More precisely, the United States must create 2 million jobs in the public and private sectors in the three years ahead, with federal subsidies for training to make the unskilled employable. It must expand Head Start to provide enriched year-round early education to every disadvantaged child. It must subsidize higher education opportunities for more young people. It must immediately establish a uniform national standard of welfare assistance that would bring every family up to the poverty line, and in the long run provide a "basic allowance" to all families as a step toward a guaranteed annual income. It must enlarge the rent supplement and bring 6 million dwelling units within reach of low- and middle-income people.[89] Johnson supported most of the Kerner Report housing guidelines, but the other proposals seemed utterly utopian to the president, wildly out of line with existing realities, and likely to make his dealings with the Ninetieth Congress even more difficult.

Angry and resentful, the president refused at first to respond to the commission's work. Not until March 22 did he formally comment on the report and then lukewarmly, acknowledging that he did not agree with all the recommendations.

The White House was even more dismayed by the Poor People's Campaign of the summer. In the last two years of his life Martin Luther King had been nudging the civil rights movement in a new direction. By 1966 Jim Crow was dead or dying and blacks in droves were registering to vote in Dixie. Phase one of the movement was largely complete. Now the problem was the swelling frustration and anger in the ghettos as quick advances in life's outcomes failed to materialize for most poor blacks. Phase two would be a concerted drive against housing and job discrimination in the North. In January 1966 King moved to a Chicago ghetto to launch a campaign against anti-black housing covenants and bias in hiring black workers. The open housing drive faltered, turned back by the desperate, tribal resistance of white householders to a black presence, which threatened to disrupt their ethnic enclaves and undermine the market value of their homes. The job bias campaign ended in a vague voluntary agreement by Chicago employers to do better, which few believed would provide many good jobs.

By late 1967 King and his lieutenants in the Southern Christian Leadership Conference had moved to phase three. The civil rights movement had now been jolted by the rise of black power. A new generation of black activists, contemptuous of King's biracialism and pacifist civil disobedience tactics, had wrested control of the Student Nonviolent Coordinating Committee and CORE from the moderates and expelled their white members. In 1966 two students at Oakland's Merritt Community College organized the Black Panthers, a paramilitary group that dressed in menacing black leather jackets and black berets and carried rifles on city streets to proclaim their hatred of police brutality. Meanwhile, although Malcolm X, the charismatic leader of the black separatist Organization of Afro-American Unity, was dead of assassins' bullets, the militant Nation of Islam continued to flourish. Increasingly, King found himself falling behind the new radicals and felt the urgent need to get out in front of the troops once more or risk becoming irrelevant.

In early December, at a SCLC meeting, King proposed an interracial Poor People's Campaign to demand a $12 billion "economic bill of rights" that would assure employment to all able to work and a guaranteed minimum annual income. At the campaign's heart would be a march on Washington of representatives of all the poor: white, black, Native American, Hispanic, Asian. The delegates of the dispossessed would camp out near the White House in plywood shacks and tents and agitate and demonstrate to force federal agencies and Congress to recognize the urgent needs of the poor. They would stay in Washington until the government yielded.

King never saw the campaign come to fruition. On April 4 a sniper shot him down in Memphis, where he had gone to support striking sanitation workers, setting off the worst racial explosion of the decade. His successor, the Reverend Ralph Abernathy, pushed ahead to fulfill King's last "dream," and the advanced party of the campaign, a delegation of a hundred, arrived in Washington on April 29. There they lectured Secretary of Agriculture Orville Freeman about the "national disgrace" of hunger and malnutrition and demanded that Labor Secretary Willard Wirtz "eliminate programs that try to fit poor people to a system that has systematically excluded them from sharing in America's plenty," an attack on Great Society hand-up programs. Testifying before the Senate subcommittee on manpower, employment and poverty, Abernathy demanded "an immediate income maintenance program" as well as "thousands of new units of low income housing," and up to two million new jobs in the next four years. He ridiculed the Great Society's "training programs." They imposed "meaningless tests" and often, at the end, led to "dead-end jobs" that undermined the poor's "manhood."[90] Before they left Washington the delegates met with secretaries Weaver and

Cohen and important congressional leaders to make their pitch for an upgraded War on Poverty.

On May 13 Abernathy drove a ceremonial nail into the first structure erected on a sixteen-acre encampment in West Potomac Park near the Lincoln Memorial. Eventually some 2,500 people of all races and ethnicities lived in Resurrection City, though a majority were black. Their stay was not a triumph for either civil rights or the cause of the poor. It rained constantly that spring, turning the grounds into a loathsome goo of mud, garbage, and debris, and creating excruciating problems with sanitation and health. Shared poverty proved to be a weak bond among the residents, and Hispanics, American Indians, and Appalachian whites soon accused black leaders of ignoring them and militant blacks of abusing them. Among the youth contingent there was a criminal element of Detroit and Chicago street gang members brought to Washington in the wrong-headed belief that they could serve as effective security guards. Not only did they prove useless as guards, they ripped off and intimidated respectable residents. To top it all, the campaign was bedeviled by severe financial problems. Since King's death and the eruption of black power, money from whites for the civil rights movement had dried up. Resurrection City hovered at the edge of insolvency as well as chaos for most of its two-month existence.

Amid all the turmoil and clamor the campaign leaders managed to tout their Economic Bill of Rights. At a news conference on June 3, Bayard Rustin, of the A. Philip Randolph Institute, issued a set of "immediate demands" that, he declared, were "attainable even from this miserable Congress." These included creation by the federal government of a million "socially useful" jobs, 6 million new dwellings, repeal of the "punitive" work requirements of the 1967 Social Security Bill, and restoration of budget cuts for major Great Society programs—Head Start, OEO, and elementary and secondary education. Finally, Rustin insisted, the president should declare a "national emergency" to meet the needs of the poor.[91]

But many of the activities in and around Resurrection City that spring belonged more to the realm of "expressive" than practical politics. On May 23 George Wiley of the National Welfare Rights Organization led 230 welfare mothers to Wilbur Mills's office at the Longworth Building. Half the demonstrators burst into the building and began to sing in the lobby. The police arrested eighteen. Soon after a rump group marched to Mills's home and missed the fleeing congressman by only a few minutes. On May 31, five hundred demonstrators invaded the auditorium of the HEW building and demanded to see Secretary Cohen. When told he was not available they refused to leave. At 6 P.M. Cohen arrived and endorsed a uniform welfare system, an innocuous statement that pacified the militants.

In June the Poor People's Campaign collapsed. When the District of Columbia authorities announced that the encampment site must be vacated on June 23, there was some window-smashing and looting in Washington by angry local ghetto youths. Abernathy threatened civil disobedience and some of the remaining inhabitants resisted when the police came on June 24 to evict them from the site. But in the end the holdouts allowed themselves to be peaceably arrested and led away. At 4 P.M. workers from the Interior Department began to dismantle Resurrection City and by the next day nothing remained. What had started as a commemoration of the martyred King and a hopeful rebirth of the War on Poverty had been swallowed up by the despair and anguish that marked the decade's end.

Black militancy undoubtedly hurt the Great Society. The administration, despite misgivings, sought to quietly buy off the militants. Harry McPherson, the president's counsel, later admitted that Abernathy probably did extract some additional benefits for the ghettos—about $45 to $50 million, he guessed. And using poverty program money to prevent or douse ghetto fires was not new. Bertrand Harding, appointed acting director of OEO in March 1968 after Shriver finally left to become ambassador to France, acknowledged that his agency's summer programs were intended to cool off the ghettos. Officially OEO did not run antiriot programs, but the summer projects that community action had installed in the cities had made "a measurable contribution towards at least relative peace in the cities. . . ."[92]

The administration, however it responded, feared the political effects of black militancy. According to McPherson, Johnson resented the Kerner Report not only because it tweaked his pride of accomplishment, but also because he believed it would damage the coalition of blue-collar labor, blacks, intellectuals, big-city bosses, and white urban poor that had made the Great Society possible. The ghetto riots, McPherson told an interviewer in 1969, had scared the "be-Jesus out of a lot of members of this coalition." And now the Kerner Report, commissioned by the president, seemed to say to the nonblack members of the coalition that they were responsible for the conditions that triggered the riots. At that point, McPherson continued, the "Polaks who work on the line at River Rouge" abandon Walter Reuther, say "Fuck you," and seek out George Wallace. Did McPherson believe the president himself saw it this way, the interviewer asked? "You bet I do. It's the way Bayard Rustin saw it, and it's the way Pat Moynihan saw it, and it's the way Lyndon Johnson saw it."[93]

The administration felt compelled to come up with a major new program to deal with the "hard core" unemployed. These were the young men who had not been benefited by the Job Corps and other Great Society training programs and whose idleness and despair fueled the inner-city violence. By itself OEO was clearly not doing the job.

JOBS (Job Opportunities in the Business Sector), derived from the 1967 task force report on hard-core unemployment, was a substitute for OEO's troubled Job Corps and implied a loss of confidence in the original antipoverty program. It was also intended to deflect pressure for more radical or expensive programs such as a guaranteed annual income and massive, and unrealistically expensive, government public works programs and other direct federal job creation schemes.

In early 1968 Johnson proposed a new "partnership" between government and private industry to identify, train, and channel into jobs the hard-core unemployed. Under JOBS the government would find those eligible and pay private employers to help them acquire the skills they needed. The business firms would then hire them. Promoting the program would be the National Alliance of Businessmen, composed of fifteen nationally prominent executives headed by Henry Ford II. Other business leaders would spark-plug local efforts in fifty different cities. The president proposed an initial federal outlay of $350 million for the first eighteen months to put 100,000 people to work by June 1969. There would be a similar level of funding through fiscal 1969 and by mid-1971, according to the plan, a half million of the intractably idle would be working productively. Johnson did not wait for

Congress to appropriate new money. In February he transferred substantial funds from OEO's budget to the new program.

The transfer jarred OEO. Agency officials announced that they would have to cut thirteen thousand children from Head Start, close sixteen Job Corps centers, and reduce funds for legal services. There was much loose talk of mass staff resignations, especially now that Shriver was talking of leaving. Congress threatened to look into unauthorized shifts. Yet the JOBS program got a fast start under Leo Beebe, a Ford executive. By late April Beebe had signed up five hundred volunteer executives, recruited AFL-CIO executives in almost all the city offices, and secured pledges of 111,000 jobs. By September, after nine months of work, the job pledge figure was up to 165,000, with greatest progress made in Houston, Dallas, Fort Worth, El Paso, and San Antonio. During these first few months it looked as if the program would be a great success.

By the fall the Great Society faced the gauntlet of the quadrennial presidential election. The campaign season began in late 1967 with the announcement of Eugene McCarthy that he would challenge the incumbent president for the Democratic nomination. Bobby Kennedy entered the race in early March followed by Vice President Humphrey in April after Johnson withdrew. Following Kennedy's assassination in Los Angeles in June, the vice president pulled ahead of McCarthy. On the Republican side Richard Nixon initially battled a clutch of state governors but quickly outdistanced the rest of the pack.

During the yearlong election campaign the public heard more about inflation, race, crime, and Vietnam than about education, consumer protection, the environment, or the War on Poverty. But the Great Society, especially the poverty issue, was not neglected entirely. During the hectic primary months the three Democrats each presented his position on Great Society domestic programs. RFK, like the others, praised the party's legislative achievements and denounced attempts to cut outlays for health, education, housing, urban development, and jobs programs. During his last political journey he touched the hearts of the nation's outsiders and dissenters in a way that no other candidate could. The New York senator would talk about a new coalition of the poor—whites, blacks, browns—and be dubbed the "tribune of the underclass." But surprisingly, the man who had attacked LBJ's programs for not going far enough had few new domestic programs of his own to offer, certainly nothing that would rattle the social order. Bobby opposed "a great new outpouring of guidance counselors to give the poor more advice," but his tepid answer to "the welfare crisis" was to assure "jobs at decent pay for all who are able to work" and "adequate assistance provided in a dignified way for those unable to work."[94] He opposed a guaranteed annual income, a policy that Americans for Democratic Action, representing the most liberal wing of the party, formally endorsed in mid-May.

McCarthy was personally ill at ease with blacks and poor people; his core constituency was college-educated suburbanites. But he was marginally bolder in his social ideas than Kennedy. At a mass rally in Madison Square Garden he demanded the creation of a million new public jobs in the next three years, a giant push for more affordable housing, more money for education, and new programs to "provide an income for all Americans." The last of these hinted at a guaranteed annual income if it did not actually advocate it. During the primary campaign Humphrey did not have to endorse the administration's Great Society; he had been a part of it from the outset and he proudly claimed that the "whole liberal program" he "stood for" had been successfully enacted. McCarthy denounced the vice president's complacency. Despite the "liberal program" American cities were getting worse, not better. The administration's urban housing programs relied too much on incentives to private builders. And its welfare system, unchanged in the previous four years, "demeans dignity and destroys incentive."[95]

The Republicans, at their Miami convention in August, nominated Nixon on the first ballot. Their platform emphasized federal-state cooperation on programs for the poor and for education, and government-private cooperation wherever possible for housing, environmental protection, and jobs. Welfare would be reformed to encourage "work motivation" and federal money provided to operate day-care centers for working mothers. The Democratic health care schemes had inflated health-care costs, the platform stated, and to slow these increases the GOP would encourage broader private health insurance coverage and expand still faster the number of medical providers—doctors, nurses, and supporting staff. In his acceptance speech Nixon sounded a less liberal note. Government programs of the previous five years had produced "an ugly harvest of frustrations, violence, and failure." The direction had to be changed. "Instead of government jobs and government housing and government welfare, let government use its tax and credit policies to enlist in this battle the greatest engine of progress ever developed in the history of man —American private enterprise."[96]

Humphrey won the Democratic nomination in Chicago on August 28 after a bruising convention rocked by wild street demonstrations, police beatings, and untamed, inflammatory rhetoric. While the area around the convention hotels came to resemble a war zone, the Democratic delegates wrote a moderate party platform. It expressed "pride in the achievements of these Democratic years," but admitted that the cost of "trying the untried, of plowing new ground" had been an "occasional error." The War on Poverty had not been won. But it had been primarily a campaign "to test a series of pilot projects" and many of these—Head Start, the Job Corps, Neighborhood Youth Corps, Upward Bound —had worked, at least in updated, new versions. The platform also praised Great Society education and health programs. There had been a fourfold increase in investment in "the human resources represented by the youth of America." A similar expansion had occurred in federal outlays for health, and through Medicare 7 million older citizens had been receiving "modern medical care in dignity—no longer forced to depend on charity, no longer a burden on relatives, no longer in physical pain because they cannot afford to pay for the healing power of modern medicine." All of these programs needed improvement and they could be enhanced through close cooperation of government and "leaders of the free enterprise system."[97]

Domestic social programs and policies were generally at the periphery of the campaign itself as it unfolded during the fall. But at times they counted. Many had constituencies that made them valuable as vote-getters in November. Humphrey extolled the Great Society's education programs and demanded that they be expanded. A Humphrey-appointed party panel recommended large increases in federal aid to education, year-round classes, and school decentralization. The last proviso met the demands of black activists in New York City and elsewhere who were denouncing centralized school bureaucracies as racist and insisting that black-oriented school programs for the ghetto be developed. On October 7 at Erie, Pennsylvania, Humphrey attacked Republican education and social policy by positing a hypothetical Nixon administration during the preceding five years. "No Nixon Administration would have done a thing for your local schools and colleges," he announced. Nixon had fought federal aid to education "all his public life." "No Nixon Administration would have voted funds for low-rent housing. No Nixon Administration would have backed the urban renewal program."[98] Nixon for his part paid relatively little attention to the Great Society programs. He disliked the existing welfare system and toward the end mentioned reducing the rolls and equalizing state benefits. He also explicitly rejected a guaranteed income. Like most Republicans he preferred downsizing the federal government. The states, he said, should be the sources of planning for federally supported public schools. Some needy college students should get federal aid, but those who could afford it should pay. On the other hand he carefully avoided offending older voters. He supported Social Security and Medicare, and even favored enlarging benefits under them. But he did not make his predecessors' domestic programs a major target, and on domestic policy generally he always seemed vague and uninterested.

At times during the campaign, remarks about the Great Society were stand-ins for views of crime and racial turmoil. Humphrey and Nixon clashed over the best way to deal with the upsurge in crime that had afflicted the nation as the decade wound down. A conventional liberal, the vice president claimed that crime could best be handled through provision of better housing and education. Nixon called him "naive." "The war on poverty" was "not a war on crime and it [was] no substitute for a war on crime."[99] Humphrey bridled at "naive," and asked for an apology. But at the same time he promised a tough federal response to the tidal wave of violence sweeping the nation. Nixon too retreated a little. On November 3, on *Meet the Press,* he agreed to consider the grievances of the young and blacks as president but said he would avoid "overpromising" to placate the insurgents.

Spiro Agnew, the GOP vice presidential candidate, provided a more blatantly conservative gloss on the issues than the man at the head of the ticket. Agnew's assigned campaign role was to outflank George Wallace, the former governor of Alabama, avatar of all the backlash of racial, class, and age resentments that had surfaced over the previous eight years. Unable to win the Democratic nomination, Wallace had created the New American Party, with himself as its candidate and Curtis LeMay, the "bomb-them-back-to-the-stone-age" air force general, as his running mate. The Wallace agenda included regular denunciations of big government and attacks on the "briefcase-toting bureaucrats in the Department of Health, Education, and Welfare." But during the campaign he paid little attention to Great Society programs that did not have a primary racial focus. The New American Party denounced "minority appeasement" but avoided stands on consumer protection, pollution control, and Medicare, programs that the middle-class esteemed.[100]

Though Agnew took the low road, he carefully skirted racism. He called repeatedly for "law and order," the Aesopian metaphor for refusing to buy off ghetto rioters and student nihilists. But he also pledged intolerance of "the vicious conditions of poverty and prejudice that create violent men."[101] The Republican administration would listen to the raucous dissenters, he said, but "we will make the diagnosis and we, the Establishment, for which I make no apologies for being part of, will implement the cure." In the next few days Agnew further outraged liberals by his response to a question about his reluctance to visit the ghettos: "If you've seen one city slum you've seen them all." At St. Joseph, Missouri, on November 1, the former Maryland governor described the guaranteed annual wage as "the socialistic dreaming of a few people in high places in this country."[102] Yet he balanced this by calling for "a national strategy" to create jobs, housing, and better schools and provide decently for those who could not support themselves while giving the others incentives to become self-supporting.[103]

The campaign messages, then, were both mixed and qualified, but anyone who voted for a candidate in November based on his Great Society rating would certainly have chosen Humphrey. Committed liberals surely flipped the lever for the man whose views and record virtually defined sixties liberalism. It is unlikely that anyone in the voting booth exclaimed: "I'm voting for Hubert because he supported the Great Society." But their sense of

Hubert Humphrey was composed in part of his record as Johnson's loyal lieutenant during the critical Great Society years.

And to a degree the Humphrey forces consciously invoked the Great Society to rally the liberal troops. During the home stretch, with Humphrey lagging badly, organized labor appealed to union members to repudiate Wallace as a social reactionary. The AFL-CIO Committee on Political Education (COPE), attacked Wallace's anti-labor record and his favoritism toward the rich as governor of Alabama. If not a direct defense of the Great Society, it was an implied one. The appeal apparently did some good. As Election Day approached, the Wallace tide receded and Humphrey gained on his Republican opponent. But it was not enough. On November 5 Nixon won one of the closest presidential contests in this century. Only 300,000 popular votes out of 70 million separated him from Humphrey. The GOP made gains in both houses; there would be five more Republican senators and five more Republican representatives in the Ninety-first than in the Ninetieth Congress. It was not a decisive change, however, and both houses remained formally under Democratic control. It was the first time since 1844 that a victorious presidential candidate had not brought his party a congressional majority in at least one chamber.

In the closing days of the campaign Nixon had asked the voters for "a mandate to govern."[104] They did not give him one. But he would be president at least through 1972, and what that meant for the vast Great Society structure built the previous five years remained unsure.

SEVEN

Nixon's Good Deeds

RICHARD NIXON was one of the most puzzling practitioners of high-level politics in American history. Few of us are thoroughly consistent: We all have better and worse natures; we all change our minds. But seldom have even democratic political leaders, who must seek compromise and consensus, been as riven by contradictions as Nixon. It was this mutability that made believable the claim, at many points during his long political career, that there was a "new Nixon," a reformed Nixon, whom voters, previously repelled, could now admire and support.

Nixon's inconsistencies were not scattered randomly across the behavioral terrain. They fell into a pattern of duality as sharp as the ones and zeros of computer code. The man seemed to be at once liberal and conservative, generous and begrudging, cynical and idealistic, choleric and calm, resentful and forgiving. Some scholars have pinned these alternatives to the psychological legacy from his parents: his mother, a gentle Quaker whom he considered a saint; his father, an unsuccessful, punitive, and angry man.

And yet one is tempted to see one side of Nixon, the hard side, as the real one. This is the part that appears in private, that we encounter in the notorious Watergate tapes and in the private diary kept by Bob Haldeman, his White House chief of staff. In talking to Haldeman or one of his other staffers—men who had no importance beyond their connection to him—he allowed his bigotry, his mean-spiritedness, his resentments and vindictiveness free play. And, whether out of our natural cynicism or our memory of Watergate, most of us take this to be the real man.

Nowhere do Nixon's contradictions show in sharper relief than in his response to his predecessors' social programs. As we saw, during the 1968 presidential campaign, the Republican candidate had relatively little to say about domestic issues. Mostly he denounced the Democrats for inflation and crime and this focus, along with the conservative truculence of his running mate, Spiro Agnew, was enough to convince the pundits that he would seek to undo most Great Society programs if elected.

In fact Nixon had no well-formed domestic agenda. Republicans seldom did; theirs was the party of subtraction, not addition. Nixon, moreover, was always far more interested in the grand stage of international relations; his domestic concerns were distinctly secondary to extricating the country from Vietnam, achieving détente with the Soviet Union, and reestablishing relations with mainland China. On these glamorous foreign stages his fellow players would be Chou En-lai, Charles De Gaulle, and Leonid Brezhnev, not Wilbur Mills, Gerald Ford, and Abe Ribicoff.

And yet, if he did not have well-defined domestic policy ideas, he had a constellation of prejudices with policy implications. Johnson, despite his Southern origins, was relatively free of racial and ethnic bias. Nixon, despite his Quaker ancestry, was a bigot who disliked Jews, Negroes, Italians, and Hispanics and blamed them either for radicalism or for violence and crime. He considered the Great Society primarily a payoff to blacks and Hispanics and deplored the supposed kowtowing to black militants and white left-liberals of his predecessor. Nixon's social values, if not his bigotry, were informed by the culture of Whittier, the small Southern California town where he grew up. This culture emphasized self-reliance, hard work, sacrifice, ambition. Poverty was not a shame; it was a misfortune that could be overcome by people who applied themselves. He himself had been a poor boy who had succeeded without family advantages or outside help. So could others. Nixon's intolerance toward the poor had the special stamp of the self-made man. This assortment of small-town attitudes might have defined a man of rectitude, though of a narrow kind. It obviously did not. It was accompanied in Nixon by an opportunistic, anything-goes streak that enraged his opponents and led him down the catastrophic path to Watergate.

Yet in all things domestic the new president was only marginally engaged. Out of indifference he deferred to others with greater knowledge, stronger concerns, and more urgent goals. The president, for all his tough talk, had little taste for wheedling and bargaining with Congress. He could not bring himself to ask favors; he could not twist arms. He relied on official advisers for direction, although their conclusions might at first trigger his prejudices.

He despised the Washington bureaucrats but could not, especially during his first four years, extricate his administration from their toils. As often as during the Kennedy-Johnson era, high-level officials and staffers made fundamental domestic policy. And many of them were holdovers from his Democratic predecessors. As a study showed, in 1970, 47 percent of high-level career civil servants in Washington were Democrats, only 17 percent Republicans. Moreover, most of these functionaries (54 percent)—whatever their party—favored either "some" or "much more" federal social services. The study concluded that the "social service bureaucracy," as it existed in Nixon's first term, was "dominated by administrators ideologically hostile to many of the directions pursued by the Nixon administration in the realm of social policy."[1]

At the end of the day, it was this mixture of presidential indifference and psychic bipolarity, as well as bureaucratic immobility, that best explains the strange and mixed fate of the Great Society in Richard Nixon's hands.

If there was a general principle that informed Nixonite domestic policy it was the need to decentralize power and decision-making. As we saw, at least at the beginning, some Democrats placed their faith in local control through community action. War on Poverty liberals had endorsed community action in the spirit of social experimentalism and people empowerment. This was not the same as the Republicans' New Federalism. The Nixon administration, under this formula, proposed shifting power to a different set of officials. Johnson and the Great Society promoters had distrusted state agencies. They considered state departments of education, for example, inefficient, incompetent, and obstructionist. Local control to Johnsonian liberals meant the die-hard resistance of Southern state administrations to federal efforts to dismantle the region's racial caste system. The prevailing philosophy in the GOP was the reverse: It was the federal bureaucracy that was dangerous and inept. Power should be lodged with governors, state legislatures, mayors, and city councils.

The Republicans had first switched states'-rights clothes with the Democrats (Southerners excepted) during the New Deal and thereafter had opposed "big government" at every turn. But it was not until the Nixon era that they made devolution of power from Washington to the state capitals and city halls a White House theme. During the 1968 campaign Nixon had talked vaguely of sharing federal powers with the states, but the New Federalism emerged full-blown only in late 1969, when William Safire, a White House speechwriter, composed a lengthy memo, the "New Federalist Paper #1," and sent it to his chief. The paper did not recommend dismantling all the Great Society programs. Let them continue where useful. But they should be turned over to the states to be administered. And the federal government should pay the bill, though it should share its revenues with the states. Revenue sharing and block grants to the states, policies that LBJ had emphatically rejected, would become regular parts of the American federal system under this plan. Federal tax-raising powers would be harnessed to social purposes, Safire noted, but federal money would not further empower the intrusive Big Brother in Washington.

At times the revenue sharers like Safire sounded almost like the community action activists. By sending money for programs back to the localities, more citizens would feel empowered and become involved in local government. But Nixon never intended to surrender his own power. As he saw it, spinning off domestic programs would reduce the authority of Congress and the despised federal bureaucracy without diminishing his own. The anti–big government bias of the New Federalism (in 1971 he changed the term to the "New American Revolution"; it never caught on) informed many aspects of Nixon's legislative initiatives. Welfare reform was one.

No domestic issue received as much administration attention as the "welfare mess." "Mess" was a buzz word for many things simultaneously, depending on the critic's politics, perceptions, and predilections. First it meant that welfare rolls—the number of families receiving money under the federal Aid to Families with Dependent Children program—were climbing year by year. In

1960 there were 3 million recipients of AFDC; in 1965 there were 4.3 million; and in 1970 there would be an astounding 8.4 million. Second, there were the gross state-by-state inequalities. The federal government paid for only a portion of each state's AFDC bill, while the individual state itself paid the rest, leading to wide disparities in support. New York in 1965 gave the average AFDC family $197 a month; Mississippi paid $33, less than a fifth as much. Third, the program suffered from bureaucratic overload. Salaries for overpaid and inefficient social workers and functionaries piled up many millions in administrative costs. Fourth, its critics charged, the system encouraged sloth, illegitimacy, and family abandonment. Recipients who worked lost benefits; a father's presence usually disqualified a mother and children from eligibility; the more children the higher the benefits. Fifth, as almost everyone agreed, AFDC degraded its recipients. Receiving welfare was a stigma. Beneficiaries, moreover, were forced to submit to nosy social workers and bureaucrats trying to ferret out their income, assets, and the presence or absence of a father. Sixth, it created resentments, especially among the working poor, people in low-income jobs with intact two-parent families who felt indignant that only idlers received benefits. Finally, welfare was rife with fraud. Cheating was endemic in the system, despite the red tape; every community, many Americans believed, spawned a class of "welfare queens" who bilked the taxpayers with false claims.

The 1967 Social Security amendments, as we saw, had addressed several of these objections by placing a cap on overall federal spending for welfare, by allowing AFDC recipients to keep $30 per month of job earnings plus one third of the rest, and by compelling AFDC recipients, under the WIN provision, either to work or enter a training program. The law had unforeseen consequences. Because an earlier, 1962 measure had required the states to consider only *net* income from earnings, and because many states accepted a broad range of items as legitimate work expenses deductible from *gross* income—including such items as payments on car loans, union dues, and Social Security taxes—the law spawned a class of legal welfare receivers with gross incomes as high as $10,000 a year, three times the poverty level. At the same time WIN failed to compel welfare mothers to take jobs. Under its terms welfare mothers need not work or train unless the states provided day-care facilities. Few states could afford such facilities, and so few took jobs. These outcomes were not what Wilbur Mills and the other Ninetieth Congress champions of work incentives had intended.

As we have seen, a way to cut the welfare Gordian knot had been in the wings for some years in the form of a guaranteed minimum income, or annual wage, for the poor. In whatever model—and there were several versions—this promised to eliminate some of the anomalies and abuses of the existing AFDC program. Giving the poor a no-strings monthly dollop of cash would abolish the intrusive social worker bureaucracy, reduce the stigma of welfare, cut fraud, and equalize state benefits. On the other hand, its costs would be high: It would continue to reward the idle and discourage work. It would also not end resentment of the welfare system by the working poor.

The scheme appealed across ideological lines, creating strange alliances. On the left, the destigmatizing of welfare strongly recommended it. Still, not all liberals were in favor. Organized labor worried that a guaranteed income would undermine the drive for a higher federal minimum wage and deter employers from granting wage increases. "Decent wages are the obligation of the employer, not the taxpayer," pronounced CIO-AFL president George Meany.[2] Many conservatives found the idea utterly repulsive. It seemed the ultimate redistributionist scheme: robbing the competent to reward the lazy and unfit. Some of the income of the industrious middle class would be siphoned off by taxes and delivered to the poor.

It was the conservative economist Milton Friedman who, unexpectedly, placed a guaranteed income on the policy agenda in 1962 with his proposal for a "negative income tax." Under this plan those who earned too little money to pay federal income taxes would instead *receive* payments proportionate to their shortfall below the minimum tax line. The system preserved the work incentive by reducing the amount received by less than the amount a family could earn, but at the same time established a "floor below which no man's net income could fall."[3] That such a plan should come from the arch free-market conservative seemed improbable. But Friedman was a radical Libertarian who worried more about the dangers of big government than about discouraging work. Anything was acceptable if it meant scaling back on government intrusion into people's affairs. With cash in their pockets, poor people could control their own lives and not be beholden to distant welfare bureaucrats.

During the Johnson years a guaranteed income had been a shibboleth of the left, Friedman notwithstanding. Cloward and Piven, the activist social work professors, had favored it; that had been the ultimate goal of their swamp-the-welfare-system campaign. Robert Theobald, the left-wing English economist prominent in the "Triple Revolution" group, was also a strong defender of an "incomes" over a "services delivery" approach to aiding the poor. In June 1968, more than a thousand liberal economists, headed by Paul Samuelson, James Tobin, and John K. Galbraith, signed a petition urging adoption of a guaranteed annual income plan "both feasible and compatible with our economic system."[4]

Advanced liberals subsumed an assured minimum income under the concept of vested economic rights for all, which had begun to emerge from the progressive law schools as an element of the sixties ideological insurgency. A guaranteed income, this said, was a fundamental human right, not charity. In late 1964 the National Association of Social Workers endorsed "an adequate standard of living . . . as a matter of right for all Americans." The association—whose members were obviously capable of transcending their fears of unemployment—urged federal legislation to ensure "income . . . in amounts sufficient to maintain all persons throughout the nation at a uniformly adequate level of living."[5] Theobald demanded that the guaranteed income be incorporated into the Constitution.

> We will need to adopt the concept of an absolute constitutional right to an income. This would guarantee to every citizen of the United States . . . the right to an income from the federal government sufficient to enable him to live with dignity. No government agency, judicial body, or other organization whatsoever should have the right to suspend or limit any payment assured by these guarantees.[6]

Obviously not all the guaranteed-income partisans perceived it in the same way, but for the most radical, it promised, as conservatives feared, a long overdue reshuffling of income from richer to poorer Americans.

The Johnson administration had had a peculiarly ambivalent response to a guaranteed income. The War on Poverty, as we saw, had been called a "hand up," not a "hand out." As Sanford Kravitz, a founding father of the War on Poverty, later said of the early OEO, "We were talking about a new ownership of services, but it was still services. We were not talking about redistribution . . . of the goods of society. . . ."[7] William Capron, another early antipoverty warrior, noted that back in the summer of 1963, when the Kennedy task force was first brainstorming the poverty issue, he, Robert Lampman, and James Tobin discussed a negative income tax, but rejected it as a probable budget-buster and a political nonstarter.

And clearly, the public in the early and mid-sixties was unprepared for an abrupt change in welfare policy that promised to raise costs and legitimize what seemed to be handouts—notwithstanding disdain for the existing system. According to Gallup, in 1965 67 percent of those polled opposed a guaranteed income. Opinion shifted in the next few years so that the negative response declined to 58 percent by 1968 and to 50 percent by 1972. This change suggests a growing social generosity by the turn of the decade. But that conclusion defies one's sense of the times; other opinion surveys show that the resentments against the poor remained very much alive. In 1969, 58 percent of Americans believed that poverty was due to "a lack of thrift and proper money management by poor people," while a high 71 percent endorsed the statement that "many people getting welfare are not honest about their need," and a startling 84 percent agreed that there were "too many people receiving welfare who ought to be working."[8]

What seems to explain declining resistance to a guaranteed income, I believe, is not class generosity so much as class fears. In effect, a segment of the public had come to believe that, "deserving" or not, the poor must be bought off to avoid further violence and disruption. In fact, such coerced benevolence could only have pernicious effects in the long run.

Lyndon Johnson himself always remained skeptical of a guaranteed income policy. Democrats must not be associated with any scheme to enlarge the welfare rolls. Wilbur Cohen, his designated chief expert on welfare policy, for his part was certain that organized labor would desert the administration if it endorsed the scheme. A more important argument to Cohen, however, was that any social program that did not include the middle class, that taxed them to support the poor, would fail. It would only create resentment and, even if such legislation could be enacted, it would be perpetually besieged. Programs *only* for the poor, with "nothing in it for the middle and upper class," he later noted, were "lousy, no good, *poor* programs."[9]

But the Johnson administration detected difficulties beyond political expediency. The chief concern of those who addressed the practical side of the issue was that it would cost far more than anyone anticipated to bring every family up to the poverty line. In 1964 the Council of Economic Advisers had slipped into the president's annual economic report as an aside that as little as $11 billion a year, a mere 2 percent of the GNP, would be enough to end poverty as officially defined if just handed out to the poor. It would be better to provide the means through training and education for every American to *earn* enough, it acknowledged. But the option of an outright subsidy should not be dismissed out of hand. In fact, the hardheaded experts said, the CEA's figure was preposterous. Promise each family the difference between its current income and the official poverty line, and tens of thousands, possibly millions earning only a little more would quit their jobs and go on the dole. Eleven billion dollars would not begin to pay for the cost when low-income earners flocked to join the new leisure class. Robert Lampman, the Wisconsin economist who had helped design the War on Poverty, later told the American Economic Association that it was "a major disservice to rational discourse to suggest . . . that the United States could eliminate poverty if we were only willing to transfer an additional $10 billion to the poor." (For some reason the original $11 billion had by now declined to $10 billion.) To get that sum into the hands of those currently below the poverty line would require far more, owing to the work disincentive effect.[10]

But if the president and Cohen demurred, other administration officials were drawn to the idea of a guaranteed income, and the president allowed them to dabble while refusing to commit himself. Not surprisingly Shriver and other OEO enthusiasts found income maintenance worth looking into. As we saw, in the fall of 1965, inspired by a report by Joseph Kershaw, head of OEO's new Research, Plans, Programs, and Evaluations division (RPPE), Shriver sent LBJ a plan to "end poverty in the United

States, as we know it today, within a generation" that included a negative income tax.[11]

The president quickly shot down this particular scheme, but for the next three years administration officials continued to flirt with a guaranteed income. In 1966 the Advisory Council on Public Welfare, appointed much earlier by HEW Secretary Anthony Celebrezze, issued a report called "Having the Power, We Have the Duty," recommending a guaranteed annual income. This plan fell into a black hole and never surfaced again, but the liberal bureaucrats at OEO refused to give up. In 1967–68 RPPE launched an experiment with agency funds to see what the effect of a negative income tax would be on work effort among several hundred low-income New Jersey families. The experiment was later extended to several other communities and continued through 1978. The New Jersey trial suggested that few husbands worked less when families received a handout, but working wives quit their jobs in droves. On the whole an assured income seemed to reduce work effort and, for some reason, encourage family breakup. Still, the results of the extended trials overall were sufficiently mixed so that analysts could read them through their personal ideological lenses.[12] But in any case, the experimental results were not available until the late 1970s.

Meanwhile, however doubtful, Johnson shifted ground under growing pressure to meet the welfare crisis. In his 1967 economic report he announced that he would establish a commission to look into income maintenance, but then he delayed until Congress acted by itself to create the Commission on Income Maintenance. Johnson appointed one of his favorite businessmen, Ben Heineman of the Chicago and Northwestern Railroad, to chair the commission, which began hearings in 1968. By the time it completed its work LBJ was permanently back at the Ranch and the country had a new man in the White House. Unable to embarrass the president who had appointed them, the commission members recommended a negative income tax as the key to ending poverty.

The Heineman Commission Report in November 1969 overlapped Richard Nixon's own official guaranteed income bill, the Family Assistance Plan (FAP), which the president proposed in a nationwide televised speech on the welfare problem in early August, eight months into his first term.

Nixon himself was not the source of FAP. However much he despised the existing welfare regime, he did not, as we saw, give social programs high priority. But the new president surrounded himself with advisers who had stronger domestic agendas than himself. Some of these were old-line conservatives who had served Eisenhower and endorsed policies based on the traditional principles of the free market, a balanced budget, small-government, and rugged individualism. They hoped the new administration would chop out most of the do-gooder legislative and bureaucratic thicket that had grown atop the modest social welfare state that Ike had inherited from FDR and Truman and had reluctantly accepted. But there were also pragmatists in the new administration who recognized that many of the Great Society programs had developed strong constituencies and could not be slashed without major political cost. And there were even a few bona fide liberals, especially among the mid- and upper-level bureaucratic holdovers from the Great Society, who believed that a Republican president was the very person to solve the problems that the Great Society had addressed, though ineffectively. Nixon might be induced to accept the role of Tory democrat and, like nineteenth-century British Prime Minister Benjamin Disraeli, confound conventional wisdom by siding with the nation's dispossessed.

During the fall campaign Nixon had selected Paul McCracken, a centrist University of Michigan economist, to head a flock of policy-making task forces for the incoming Republican administration. Their proposals became the raw material for a team headed by conservative, budget-balancing Columbia economist Arthur Burns that included his young sidekick Martin Anderson, as well as Alan Greenspan and McCracken himself. After the election this group prepared a draft of the administration's legislative program. Just days before the inauguration Burns presented the president-elect with a final report containing more than a hundred domestic and foreign policy proposals, including suggestions for revenue sharing, welfare reform, federal aid to inner-city schools, and for new job creation programs. Nixon was so delighted with the report that he induced a reluctant Burns to join the administration as counselor, with responsibility for program development.

Even at this point there were divided counsels among Nixon's inner circle. On what came to be the administration's boldest domestic innovation, welfare reform, Burns and the chairman of the public welfare task force, Richard Nathan, a liberal Republican from the Brookings Institution, disagreed. The Nathan committee, addressing the nagging issue of state inequalities, had proposed a minimum welfare payment under the AFDC provision of the basic Social Security law. The federal government, which had previously paid half of what each state provided, would now pay all of a minimum nationwide welfare standard, plus half of any additional state supplement. Burns, in his final report on the McCracken task forces, objected. Nathan, he claimed—mistakenly in fact—had "basically accepted the Johnson administration's approach to welfare problems." The costs of the plan would be exorbitant. "Another study . . . [was] urgently needed."[13]

But disagreement over domestic policy, especially social programs, was built into the new administration's composite human material. Surprisingly, most of the new administration's domestic-policy cabinet posts were filled by moderate, or even liberal, Republicans: Robert Finch of California at HEW; George Romney of Michigan at Housing and Urban Development; and George Shultz, a University of Chicago economist, at Labor.

The most interesting voice in the White House advisers' circle was that of former Kennedy-Johnson subcabinet member, forty-two-year-old Daniel Patrick Moynihan, now of the Harvard-MIT Joint Center for Urban Studies. Moynihan was an interesting combination of hard-drinking Irish "pol" and academic intellectual. No one in late-twentieth-century American political life had a more speculative mind or a better feel for new political and ideological winds. A man who never allowed the precise facts to interfere with a witty aphorism or a novel opinion, he impressed everyone with his brilliance. Nixon found him particularly intriguing. Here was a bold, amusing, and clever man, so different from the run-of-the-mill hacks who populated his own Republican Party. Though a Democrat who had helped formulate the War on Poverty, Moynihan was rethinking social policy in 1969 and was on a path that would take him into the camp of the 1970s neoconservatives. In 1965, while a member of the Johnson administration, he had written a memo that pointed to disintegration of ghetto families as the root of black poverty and urged policies to keep black males from abandoning their wives and children. The response to the "Moynihan Report" had jolted its author. Black militants denounced him for "blaming the victim." They also charged that he had no business prying into the sexual behavior of black people.

Yet Moynihan would be a prime mover in Nixon's "good deed." Just three days after the inauguration the president established an urban affairs council as his domestic counterpart to the National Security Council. The new body would consist of the president himself, the vice president, and the seven cabinet officers concerned with urban issues and their staffs. Nixon chose Moynihan as its executive secretary. With Burns as White House counselor, he would have men on both ends of the policy band.

The council soon had its marching orders. Just five days before he took the oath of office Nixon sent Finch and Moynihan a memo calling for an analysis of welfare. The American people, he noted, were "outraged" by the existing system. "The whole system smells to high heaven and we should get charging on it immediately."[14]

Eager to get a welfare reform proposal before the president, Moynihan and Secretary Finch presented a condensed version of the Nathan AFDC state equalization scheme to the Urban Affairs Council welfare subcommittee just two weeks after Nixon's inauguration. At the subcommittee meeting, Nathan defended his plan and came under hot fire from Shultz, Agriculture Secretary Clifford Hardin, Commerce Secretary Maurice Stans, and Attorney General John Mitchell. Unable to get their scheme by the subcommittee, the welfare reformers decided to refer it back for further study to a lower-level task force where HEW and Budget Bureau experts could collaborate on revising it.

This committee, headed by John Veneman, a liberal Republican businessman from California, in turn farmed it out to a working group composed of several holdover Democrats, including Worth Bateman, Alice Rivlin's former deputy at HEW, and James Lyday, a young economist at OEO's Office of Research, Plans, Progress, and Evaluation who had been a spark plug of OEO's guaranteed income efforts under Johnson. The official group in turn consulted a number of guaranteed-wage zealots outside their own circle, whom they treated almost as equals. The efforts of this working group bear an uncanny resemblance to the 1964 Johnson poverty task force that produced the Economic Opportunity Act, and they underscore again the significant role of the technocrats as animators of the modern social welfare state.

The Bateman-Lyday working group scuttled the Nathan minimum welfare payment plan as too limited and decided instead to go for "structural reform," as Bateman later said.[15] But they sought to keep the cost the same as the Nathan scheme: no more than $1.4 billion. Their solution was a negative income tax for all poor families with children, whether they included a wage earner or not. A family of four would get at least $1,500 a year and the amount would increase with family size. A family with earned income would lose only fifty cents for each dollar in wages and so would have an incentive to work, but beneficiaries would not be required to work to receive benefits. In addition there would be a federal across-the-board payment for every needy adult and AFDC could continue as a state program. This plan went to Secretary Finch for his approval in early March with the whimsical surefire cover title: "Christian Working Man's Anti-Communist National Defense Rivers and Harbors Act of 1969."[16]

The meeting in Finch's office on March 3 was bumpy. Finch himself raised the issue of scope. "How are you going to explain why we have to add six million to the welfare rolls?" But Finch trusted Veneman enough to give him the green light to bring it before the full Urban Affairs Council welfare subcommittee. Renamed the Family Security System, it was presented for consideration on March 24 with a fallback plan that closely resembled the original Nathan scheme.

Moynihan had not himself been part of the Bateman-Lyday working group, but he thoroughly approved of their proposal. Now, at the subcommittee meeting, he rushed to defend it against an anticipated attack by the conservatives. "I want to say this is a great historic plan," he announced at the outset. "I think we should go to the president with it immediately. If we worked on it for five years I don't think we could come up with a better plan."[17] Martin Anderson, Burns's assistant, objected. No, it wasn't a good plan and it should not go to the president. It was an out-an-out negative income tax that resembled the evil Speenhamland scheme of late-eighteenth-century Britain, when parish officials had given handouts from local taxes to family heads earning less than subsistence. Speenhamland had helped to create a permanently pauperized segment of the English working class. Besides, it would cost too much and would hurt the administration politically. When Anderson announced that he believed in "calling a spade a spade," Moynihan retorted: "I agree with Oscar Wilde: Anyone who insists on calling a spade a spade should be forced to use one." This riposte made Secretary of Commerce Stans laugh but it did not change his mind. He could not approve a federal minimum income guarantee to all families, he said. Nor could hard-nosed conservative Attorney General John Mitchell. Finch noted that the president, besieged by the press to move faster on domestic policy, wanted a welfare plan by April 15. Couldn't the Family Security System be brought to a full cabinet meeting before then? No, said Mitchell, it would need more work.[18]

It was during Easter weekend at Nixon's winter hideaway at Key Biscayne that the president finally got down to cases on his domestic agenda in discussions with Burns, Finch, Moynihan, administration congressional liaison Bryce Harlow, and White House aide John D. Ehrlichman, now beginning to move into a key position as domestic affairs adviser. Moynihan and Finch presented FSS as the administration's number-one domestic program. It was not a negative income tax, they insisted, because it covered only families with children and did not eliminate other income support arrangements like AFDC. It also did not mandate income unrelated to need or work. When Burns protested that the scheme would, in effect, swell the welfare rolls by 7 million people, Nixon pointedly asked him if he had a better way of reforming the system. The president's relatively positive response was surprising. Burns would later declare that "it ran counter to every thing I knew about Dick Nixon."[19] This was not the man who had exploded in mid-January when he heard about the fraud and waste uncovered in the New York City welfare system. But one exchange between the president and Moynihan reveals the consistent conservative, anti-welfare thread. At one point Nixon asked Moynihan: "Will FSS get rid of social workers?" He was pleased when the Urban Affairs Council executive secretary snapped back, it "would wipe them out."[20] To Nixon the most appealing part of the plan, then, was that it would evict the evil bureaucrats from people's lives.

The president did not actually give the green light to FSS at this meeting, but he also did not say no. Clearly, a guaranteed income plan of some sort would be a serious contender in the debate over a welfare reform package to be presented to Congress. And indeed, during the next four months, FSS was the proposal to beat as the welfare discussion within the administration ranged back and forth along the ideological spectrum.

FSS's opponents offered two major alternatives. Burns on April 21 sent the president a plan that, unlike FSS, refused payment to families with low-earning working fathers and required that welfare recipients work. But it sought to address a very real problem that almost all contemporary observers acknowledged: the inequality in national levels of welfare benefits. Under the 1935 Social Security Act, AFDC levels were determined by the states, with their contributions matched by the federal government. In the South they were appallingly low. At the same time taxpayers in the more generous Northern states were heavily burdened. The Burns plan would set a federal welfare standard. Any state that met or exceeded that standard would receive money from the federal government. Those that fell short would not. Besides the problem of unequal standards, the scheme could be expected to appeal to Nixon's desire to reduce federal influence through revenue sharing. The federal government would pay the states directly for the program; Washington would not administer it.

The swirl of memos, discussions, and presentations pushing either the Burns plan or FSS confused the president, and in mid-May he asked Labor Secretary George Shultz to analyze the feasibility of FSS. Generally speaking, Shultz favored the guaranteed income approach but believed the figures of the original FSS proposal suspect. To penalize a welfare parent for working to the extent of fifty cents on the dollar would, in effect, given work expenses, provide little incentive to take a job. Why not exclude from consideration the first $20 a week in earnings? This "disregard" would cost the treasury about $1 billion, but it would effectively encourage work and so be well worth it.

In late June Nixon finally took the welfare reform process in hand personally. The president had now come to favor some sort of bold guaranteed income policy that would show up the Democrats and put his own stamp on American social history. He rejected the Burns counterproposal as an entity. But he liked the idea of compelling welfare recipients to work and so embraced both the Burns compulsory work feature and the Shultz work incentive. He handed the job of reconciling the differing features to Ehrlichman, who turned over the task to Edward Morgan, a lawyer on his staff, who in turn handed it off for actual line-by-line drafting to a group of high-level staffers at HEW. Ehrlichman provided the drafters with a set of guidelines that included work and job training packages, an end to social worker snoops, day care for working mothers, and a federal income floor.

Finch presented the working group plan to an audience of some thirty key players in the administration's domestic policy area at Camp David on August 6. Seated around the president at the long table in Laurel Cottage were the secretaries of eleven cabinet departments plus Vice President Agnew, Burns, Ehrlichman, Moynihan, Anderson, the HEW drafters, and a clutch of other interested parties. The plan itself was close to the Shultz scheme, though the figures for a family-of-four minimum and the earned income "disregard" were different. Burns, allied with budget director Robert Mayo, denounced FSS. But the president defended it. "We're doing it because we can't go on with the present system," he said.[21] With the president its champion, it was clear that the plan would go forward. But preferably under another name. Family Security System seemed too New Dealish, said Defense Secretary Melvin Laird, not appropriate for a Republican administration. One issue raised was the scheme's complexity. Even its defenders agreed that it was difficult to understand or, more significantly, easy to misunderstand. That opacity would help in the end to doom the plan.

By the time Nixon took to the airwaves on August 8 to introduce his welfare reform program to the American people, FSS had become the Family Assistance Plan, FAP. But in fact the thirty-five-minute address covered the whole range of Nixon's domestic agenda, not just welfare reform.

Nixon opened with an attack on his liberal predecessors' domestic policies. Despite "a third of a century of centralizing power and responsibility in Washington," the nation faced an "urban crisis, a social crisis." Government itself had evolved into "a bureaucratic monstrosity, cumbersome, unresponsive, ineffective." The nation was now left with a "legacy of entrenched programs that have outlived their time or outgrown their purposes."

He then swung into the welfare issue, being careful not to sound callous or cruel. Nowhere was the inadequacy of government so evident than in its failure "to help the poor and especially in its system of public welfare." Whether measured by the pain of the poor or the pain of the taxpayers, the existing welfare system had to be considered "a colossal failure." States and cities were sinking under the financial burden, dependency was growing, and the poor themselves were not receiving "the elementary human, social, and financial" benefits they needed. The existing system, moreover, encouraged paternal desertion: In most states the presence of a father disqualified a family for aid. It discouraged work: Families on welfare often earned more than self-supporting ones. Then there were the inequalities among the states that lured poor families into the Northern urban ghettos but left them "as unprepared for city life as they are for city jobs." If the present regime were to continue, "the financial cost" would "be crushing" and "the human cost . . . suffocating."

His family assistance system would replace the current scheme, continuing federal aid to the aged, blind, and disabled but setting a federal minimum standard of payments, with Washington sharing the cost of benefits above that minimum. The big change would come with AFDC. The existing system would be abolished. In its place would be one based on three principles: equal benefits for all nationally, a work requirement, and a work incentive. Benefits would go to both the working poor and those unable to work; they would go to both father-headed and mother-headed families.

For a family of four currently on welfare there would be a basic federal payment of $1,600. States could add to that amount if they wished. In addition, a welfare family would be encouraged to earn money by allowing its members who worked to keep the first $60 a month of earnings without penalty. Any amount above that would reduce benefits only by fifty cents per dollar. For a poor working family not currently on AFDC, there would be a "family assistance supplement" that would, for example, raise the income of a family of five that earned only $2,000 a year to $3,260.

The benefits would not be cost free, however. Everyone receiving them would have to get a job or enter a training program, not merely, as under WIN, *register* to work or to train. The only exceptions would be the handicapped and the mothers of preschool children. But even they would have the chance to work if they chose; there would be a major expansion of day-care centers. All states would benefit through federal money. The citizens of those states with low current welfare payments would come closer to receiving a living income. More generous states would have a part of their financial burden lifted.

Nixon went out of his way to deny that he was proposing a guaranteed income. He opposed that scheme and had said so during the presidential campaign, he noted. A guaranteed income, he explained, handed out money without demanding responsibility. It undermined the work incentive. It taxed one person "so that another can choose to live idly." His proposal increased "the incentive to work."

Nixon estimated costs the first year to be about $4 billion, but the system would not go into effect until fiscal 1971. Besides, the existing system was also costly and promised to become still more expensive in the future.

The speech encompassed more than just welfare reform. It proposed alternatives to many of the Great Society's poverty programs. The president, who especially despised the Job Corps, talked of revised manpower training programs to replace the existing "terrible tangle of confusion and waste." He said that the Office of Economic Opportunity needed "reshaping, reforming, and innovating." Surprisingly, at this point Nixon did not favor abolishing OEO. The antipoverty agency had "a vital place in our efforts to develop new programs and apply new knowledge." But in the past it had sought to do everything at once. OEO should be cut back to a "laboratory agency" to test new antipoverty programs. Those that worked should then be "spun off" to existing departments for actual application.

Nixon concluded with a pitch for revenue sharing. Appealing to the ingrained mid-American prejudice against centralized government, he proposed that a portion of federal revenues be handed over to the states with few strings attached, except that a portion be allotted to local government. This revenue sharing would be a first step in the "New Federalism" that would end "nearly 40 years of moving power from the states to Washington" and usher in "a decade of decentralization, a shifting of power away from the center. . . ."[22]

□   □   □   □

The welfare plan that Nixon announced that August evening was indeed a daring initiative, given America's fundamentally conservative political culture. However loudly Nixon denied that it was a guaranteed income scheme, it essentially was, and represented a quantum leap in public obligation to the poor as well as a commitment to at least a modest redistribution of income. It is hard to see it any other way. Moynihan later estimated that "under FAP thirteen million people were to begin receiving income payments who had not previously been receiving any."[23] Martin Anderson calls it "the most ambitious attempt to redistribute income ever undertaken in the United States."[24]

In its improbability FAP resembles Nixon's startling resumption of diplomatic contacts with China in 1971 after two decades of total rejection. In his policy toward the People's Republic, the arch red-baiter and intransigent Cold Warrior had abruptly reversed field, and his impeccable anti-communist credentials legitimized the move in the eyes of most Americans. For a time the same process seemed to apply to the Family Assistance Plan. The initial public response to the speech was remarkably enthusiastic. Even conservative newspapers like the *Chicago Tribune* praised it, though they especially liked the work incentive feature. In *The New York Times,* liberal commentator James Reston wrote: "Mr. Nixon has taken a great step forward. He has cloaked a remarkably progressive welfare policy in conservative language. . . . He has insisted that poverty in a prosperous country must be eliminated."[25] A White House team estimated that 95 percent of the press editorials were favorable. Ordinary citizens also applauded. Between August 9 and September 10 the White House received almost three thousand letters and telegrams on FAP. Eighty-one percent approved of it; only 9 percent out-and-out opposed it. But there was one ominous note. Just a day before Nixon's August speech, George Wiley and Johnnie Tillmon of the militant National Welfare Rights Organization blasted his proposal. In a public letter to the president they complained that poor people had not been consulted in the composing of FAP. And the bill showed it. The proposed $1,600 for a family of four was ludicrous. The government's own research indicated that the correct minimum support figure should be $5,500. Taken together the plan was "anti-poor, and anti-black" and "a flagrant example of institutional racism."[26] An influential component of public opinion had just pinned the racist tail on the donkey. NWRO did not speak directly for more than twenty or thirty thousand people, but its voice in this overheated, apocalyptic year 1969 would touch a sensitive chord in the liberal community.

Nixon probably had less leverage with the Ninety-first Congress than Johnson with its predecessor. Though not the ideological preponderance of 1965–66, LBJ had Ninetieth Congress party majorities in both houses, guaranteeing the Democrats the valuable formal control of the congressional machinery. Nixon, on the other hand, had failed to carry enough Republicans into office to gain either house for his party.

The situation appeared different, however, when one took into account the ideological factors. A. James Reichley of the Brookings Institution has estimated that conservatives, drawn from both parties, represented about two fifths of the Ninety-first Congress. If this core could attract half the Republican "moderates" and Democratic "centrists," they could forge a majority. In addition, as under Johnson, Democratic "traditionalists," mostly conservative Southerners, continued to dominate the key committees of both houses.

But FAP, like much other Nixon legislation, could not be easily classified as conservative or liberal. Bryce Harlow, Nixon's counterpart to Larry O'Brien as head of White House congressional liaison, recognized this dilemma and employed a "floating coalition strategy" to deal with it. William Timmons, Harlow's assistant for House relations, explained Republican legislative strategy this way: "We would begin by solidifying the Republicans. Then we would reach out for whatever Democrats we needed." On many issues the Democrats Harlow courted would be Southern conservatives. But on some, including FAP, "the liberals were the ones to whom we had to appeal."[27] In fact, on FAP, the most liberal representatives, the members of the Democratic Study Group, were the resource to tap. According to an aide of Timmons's, Phillip Burton of California, the DSG chair, was "very effective in delivering votes for welfare reform."[28] The floating coalition worked better in the House than the Senate, however. In the upper chamber the Republican minority was less cohesive than in the lower. Compared with earlier years, there were now few strong Senate chieftains to whip individualistic senators into line, and the Republican rank-and-file readily defected from administration leads. It was in the undisciplined Senate that FAP would encounter its greatest difficulties.

House hearings on FAP opened on October 15 before Wilbur Mills's Ways and Means Committee and the sides were quickly defined. Secretary Finch was the first to testify, followed by HEW undersecretary Veneman, Secretary Shultz, and other administration stalwarts. Finch spoke to the inadequacies of the current AFDC system and the heavy burdens welfare imposed on the states. His deputy, Veneman, emphasized FAP's work incentives and sought to demonstrate that they were better designed than those of WIN, the failed work program of the 1967 Social Security revisions. Shultz denied that FAP was a guaranteed income law and emphasized the work and training requirements. Members of the committee were on the whole polite, but there was an obvious political undertone to the statements and questions of the committee members. Virtually all the Republicans, regardless of their place on the ideological spectrum, supported the administration. Not so all the Democrats. Representative Al Ullman of Oregon, a middle-of-the-road Democrat, said he was "shocked . . . almost to the point of being speechless" by FAP. "It looks to me," he declared, "like you are opening up the Treasury of the United States in a way it has never been opened up before."[29] Liberal Democratic Congresswoman Martha Griffiths of Michigan also proved skeptical, though she was less negative than Ullman. On the other hand Shirley Chisholm, representing the all-black Bedford-Stuyvesant district of Brooklyn, called the benefit levels "patently inadequate" and denounced the compulsory work requirement as "involuntary servitude." Foreshadowing the militant position that ultimately destroyed FAP, she announced that it would "not be a great disaster" if the administration allowed the proposals "to die."[30]

During the hearings the traditional pressure group blocs divided without apparent consistency. The U.S. Chamber of Commerce took out a full-page newspaper advertisement to assert that FAP "would triple our welfare rolls. Double our welfare costs."[31] Yet the National Association of Manufacturers, usually a close ally of the Chamber of Commerce, sent a letter to every member of the House calling FAP "an opportunity to end the cycle of dependency."[32]

House hearings concluded on November 13, and for the next

few months the bill remained stuck in committee while Chairman Mills brooded. In December he announced that "the public isn't ready for [FAP]—and won't be for years."[33] But then, under pressure from his committee colleagues, Democrat Hale Boggs of Louisiana and Republican John Byrnes of Wisconsin, he relented. Ways and Means approved the bill on March 5, 1970, by a bipartisan majority of 21 to 3.

On April 16 the full House passed FAP by a vote of 243 to 155. As Reichley shows, almost none of the most conservative Democrats voted for it, while virtually all of the liberal Democrats did. Three fourths of the most conservative Republicans deserted the president, but the GOP middle, whatever they believed in their heart of hearts, held. It was a coalition of administration loyalists and the liberal element of both parties in the House that passed the bill.

In the Senate FAP crashed in flames. Senate Finance Committee hearings began on April 29. They were devastating.

The administration's chief antagonists were Chairman Russell Long, the erratic traditionalist Democrat from Louisiana, and conservative Republican John Williams of Delaware. Long believed the bill, whatever its other virtues, would fail to end the fraud and general abuse—the overpayments, the benefits to ineligibles, the hiding of earned income—permitted by the existing welfare system. In Moynihan's view Long had taken too seriously Nixon's claim that FAP was a "reform" of AFDC, not an entirely new approach. Williams focused on detailed charts Finch and his staff had prepared at his demand that seemed to show that FAP had strange anomalies. A working mother on welfare could get a pay raise and, because she would lose food stamps or other "in-kind" benefits, be worse off than on AFDC. An intact family with a working father could suffer if he worked full time rather than part time. Williams bludgeoned Finch, Veneman, and Robert Patricelli, deputy assistant secretary of HEW, into admitting inadequacies in the measure. FAP might have been saved at this point if the liberals had rushed to its support. But they did not. As Moynihan later complained: "No senator spoke a word in support of the president's bill."[34] Indeed, one of the most liberal, populist Fred Harris of Oklahoma—friend of Native Americans, of black Americans, of hard-scrabble mid-American farmers—complained that the work provisions of the bill failed to take into account that there simply were no jobs out there for the poor.

After three days of damaging Senate hearings the administration agreed to revise the existing proposal to take into account the various in-kind benefits that were essential parts of any welfare reform. On May 18, as Finch was about to speak to a group of HEW employees, he physically collapsed, a victim he later claimed of burnout. In early June Nixon replaced him with the Boston Brahmin Elliot Richardson, a moderate Republican sympathetic to FAP.

On June 21 Richardson brought a revised FAP to the Finance Committee. The new version sought to prevent the anomaly of wages reducing income in certain circumstances, primarily by lowering some welfare benefits. But this version too came under attack. Hearings on the new bill dragged on, with Williams resuming his offensive from the right and Harris objecting that the revision was at the expense of the poor, from the left.

Friends of FAP tried to get the bill back on track. In a widely reported speech Moynihan warned that if some version of FAP were not enacted by the Ninety-first Congress it would take a decade to get an equivalent. His prediction was echoed by Tom Wicker, the liberal *New York Times* columnist, and by the old Robert La Follette journal, *The Progressive,* of Madison, Wisconsin. Alice Rivlin and Worth Bateman, two of the Democratic welfare technocrats who had fought for a guaranteed income long before Nixon had taken it up, condemned the motives of many of their Democratic colleagues. Too many liberal Democrats were "reluctant to embrace FAP because they apparently do not want to see the President winning points for welfare reform."[35]

Meanwhile George Wiley and the National Welfare Rights Organization launched a barrage against the revised version of FAP. Though NWRO leaders had reservations about the original FAP bill, they had not opposed House passage in April. But by the summer, after the Richardson revisions, they had changed their minds. They now saw FAP as a threat to their chief constituency, AFDC welfare mothers. The bill, they said, would coerce welfare mothers to take jobs. It would make it harder for AFDC recipients in the future to increase benefits. It would take money from welfare recipients and give it to the working poor. On July 25, at its annual conference, the NWRO denounced every aspect of the new FAP and concluded with a resolution calling the bill "on the whole, an act of political repression."[36]

A still better forum for NWRO was provided by two days of testimony on November 18 and 19 arranged by Senator Eugene McCarthy at Wiley's urging. McCarthy had advocated a guaranteed income even before Nixon considered it. Then, in 1969, at the bidding of NWRO, he proposed a substitute for the administration plan that promised a minimum of $6,500 to each welfare family. This was a totally unrealistic figure that would have caused fiscal collapse and plunged the private labor market into chaos. Now, on the verge of leaving the Senate, he made another quixotic gesture by agreeing to provide a platform for Wiley and his colleagues.

The "people's hearings" in room 1202 of the Senate Office Building were conducted by Wiley, wearing an African dashiki; listening and watching from the dais were senators collected by McCarthy. The proceedings were an exercise in what writer Tom Wolfe would later call "radical chic." White liberals, filled with middle-class guilt, looked on approvingly as black people vented their anger against the status quo and made unreasonable demands for instant transformation.

Most of the witnesses were unapologetic, even defiant, displaying an "in your face" attitude. Ethel Camp from Arlington County, Virginia, a mother of five separated from her husband and receiving $5,400 in cash and food stamps, announced: "We only want the kind of jobs that pay $10,000 or $20,000. . . . [W]e aren't going to do anybody's laundry or babysitting except for ourselves." The fiery Beulah Sanders, WRO's New York City vice chairman, shouted, "You can't force me to work! You'd better give me something better than I'm getting on welfare. I ain't taking it." Each rebellious sally was accompanied by cheers, clapping, and cries of "That's telling 'em!" and "Hear that!" from the spectators.[37]

The "people's hearings" exasperated a large sector of the moderate public. Members of Congress, it was reported, were deluged with letters from working women asking what right did welfare mothers have to sit at home while others labored. But the performance apparently played well to several of the senators on the dais. The next day the *Times* reported that Harris was going to vote against the proposal and that other liberals might join him.

And they did. On the twentieth, after an appeal from the president, Long permitted the committee to vote on sending a one-year trial FAP bill to the Senate floor. It was defeated 10 to 6, with liberals McCarthy and Harris, and two Democratic centrists, Albert Gore of Tennessee and Clinton Anderson of New Mexico, voting against it. The left and the center had defeated it. Interviewed by the Washington *Evening Star,* Wiley declared himself "very pleased. . . . It's a big win."[38]

That finished FAP for 1970. That fall the midterm elections produced a slightly more conservative Congress. Yet the roadblock still seemed to be the liberals, not their opponents.

FAP reappeared in the Ninety-second Congress as Title IV of H.R. 1, a comprehensive bill to upgrade Social Security. The new version of FAP as introduced in the House raised the guaranteed income for a family of four from $1,600 to $2,400 to make it more palatable to liberals though it made welfare recipients ineligible for food stamps. In late June the House defeated a motion of Congressman Ullman to delete the FAP provision from the bill by 234 to 187, confirming FAP by a narrower margin than in 1970. Most of the lost votes were of liberal Democrats; eleven of the twelve black Democrats had opposed.

The Senate promised to be the roadblock once again. Abe Ribicoff of Connecticut tried to get around the barrier by attaching his own version of FAP to another bill. To win over the liberals Ribicoff's proposal was more generous than the administration's. It raised the minimum payment to the standard family of four to $3,000, provided for graduated increases yearly, and allowed recipients to keep the first $720 of earned income plus 40 percent of the rest. Ribicoff estimated that the measure would make 30 million Americans eligible for benefits in year one and would add $13 billion to the national welfare bill. HEW's own estimates were that it would hike the eligibles to 40 million, one fifth of the entire country; by 1976 it would soar to 72 million, a full third.

Ribicoff's maneuver failed. In late March 1972, while both the Ribicoff proposal and the administration's FAP plan as part of the Social Security revision languished in the Senate Finance Committee, the NWRO conducted a "Children's March for Survival" to the Washington Monument to denounce FAP even in its more generous version. The children carried posters proclaiming Ribicoff, Nixon, Long, and Mills as "the D.C. Four Against the Poor." These villains had "conspired to starve children, destroy families, force women into slavery."[39]

Soon after, the Finance Committee rejected the FAP provision of the Social Security bill and substituted one of its own that abolished AFDC for families with children of school age and promised jobs to parents instead. It also proposed wage subsidies for low-wage workers privately employed and set a floor of $2,400 for remaining AFDC families of four.

The ball was now in the administration's court. It could seek a workable, passable compromise, or stand pat. In June the Budget Office had joined with HEW and the Labor Department to analyze the three options presented by the administration's original bill, the Long proposal, and the Ribicoff amendment. It concluded that hammering out a compromise with Ribicoff presented "the only possible strategy which will get us a bill. . . ."[40] On June 16 Richardson advised Nixon to compromise with Ribicoff to the extent of $2,600 for a four-person family, plus cost-of-living increases.

Nixon refused. His role in the long legislative drive for FAP had been, to put it bluntly, two-faced. In public he took every opportunity to bolster his welfare reform proposals, but in private he was more than skeptical. The president's waning enthusiasm is traceable in part to the declining influence of Moynihan. In November 1969 Nixon had kicked him upstairs to become his counselor, a rather vague position as an idea man, while Ehrlichman was put in charge of domestic policy generally.

The unsmiling, laconic Ehrlichman was linked by the media with Bob Haldeman as one of the hard-nosed White House "Prussians." A Seattle lawyer who had been Nixon's effective "tour manager" during the 1968 campaign, Ehrlichman had never held elective office and understood far less than Moynihan about the give and take of American democratic politics. Once he grasped the domestic policy reins he worked to push Moynihan further out of the loop to consolidate his own power. Moynihan's own gaffes hurt him with the president. In December 1969 militants turned his Conference on Food and Nutrition into a collective diatribe against the administration's policies. Then, in January, Moynihan sent his boss a memo on "the American Negro" that touched on the growing "social alienation" between the races.

The time had come, he noted, "when the issue of race could benefit from a period of 'benign neglect.' " Leaked to the press a few months later, the comment suggested that the administration was callously indifferent to the plight of black America and produced a firestorm. Moynihan offered his resignation, and although the president refused to accept it, the New Yorker had little leverage thereafter in the White House. He resigned in December to return to Harvard.

But Moynihan's fall and Ehrlichman's rise was not the whole story. Nixon in truth had never been fully comfortable with the FAP program. It appealed to the "good" Nixon, the generous, more liberal man. But the resentful, bigoted Nixon, while concealed from public view, was never far from the surface. In explaining the necessity for welfare reform Nixon talked sympathetically about the plight of the poor. But he despised most of those on welfare. In late April 1969, in a private discussion with Haldeman and Ehrlichman, the president remarked that the whole welfare problem was "really the blacks." The key was to devise a system that recognized "this while not appearing to." The nation would have to "get rid of this veil of hypocrisy and guilt and face reality."[41]

All through the FAP legislative process Nixon's private responses belied his public ones. In late February 1970 he called Wilbur Mills to thank him for getting FAP through Ways and Means, though he told Haldeman in the Oval Office that the Democrats were really trying to trap him into an unworkable scheme. That July, Haldeman recorded in his diary: "About Family Assistance Plan, [the president] wants to be sure it's killed by Democrats, that we make big play for it, but don't let it pass, can't afford it."[42] In early November, shortly before the fatal vote in the Senate, seeing the bill as a certain loser, the president sent the White House staff a curt private note: "sink FAP."[43]

Early the next year, as the Ninety-second Congress was about to convene, Nixon told a team of CBS television interviewers that his greatest disappointment thus far had been "the failure to get welfare reform."[44] But by now, stung by what he felt was lack of credit from the left, he was drawing away generally from all the purveyors of liberal domestic programs. "We're going to quit meeting with the people who are against us," he told Haldeman on a plane ride to New York in early May, "and playing to the issues such as consumers, environment, youth, press, business elite, intellectuals, volunteers, . . ." The administration should avoid such groups "except when it's solely a question of delaying action."[45]

By 1972 a new element had entered the FAP equation: the presidential election. For months the Democrats had been painfully torn over the party nomination. The moderates and old-fashioned liberals had rallied to Humphrey or to Maine senator Edmund Muskie. To their left was a coalition of antiwar activists, civil rights advocates, and a circle of crusaders for new social causes—women's liberation, gay rights, Indian rights, ecological and environmental rigor—engendered by the sixties. Some of these were regular Democrats radicalized by the past years' events; many were young firebrands, newcomers to party politics, who now saw the Democratic Party they had denounced at the 1968 Chicago convention as a useful vehicle for change.

The activists' candidate was George McGovern, the amiable but bland senator from South Dakota. A historian with a Ph.D. in American history from Northwestern, McGovern was "Mr. Entitlement" writ large. By now, a new liberalism was emerging to challenge the traditional equality of opportunity with an equality of results. One thread derived from the new militants of the National Welfare Rights Organization sort, who had much to gain from a definition of "rights" that did not balk at income redistribution policies. Whether they learned their rhetoric from Cloward and Piven, or whether homegrown, NWRO leaders made no bones about claiming a decent income as a matter of right. Another thread arose from an intellectual process that carried the sixties idea of rights to new, and seemingly logical, conclusions.

We have seen the beginnings of this impetus in the work of Charles Reich, who interpreted government benefits as a species of property deserving the same protection as rights to land, earnings, or profits. By 1971 John Rawls's *A Theory of Justice*, a work that denied that equal opportunity was sufficient for a truly just society, was becoming the bible of the new liberals. In Rawls's view, inherent differences in merit and natural ability would still lead to inequality. Justice therefore required what amounted to affirmative action and that beyond this society must provide "a social minimum either by family allowances and special payments for sickness and employment, or more systematically by such devices as a graded income supplement."[46]

Though no long-haired, besandaled youth, McGovern had absorbed the new sensibility and recently given it political embodiment. In January 1972, early in the campaign, he had almost absentmindedly endorsed a position paper calling for a lump-sum federal grant (a "demogrant") of $1,000 to every man, woman, and child in the nation regardless of need, paid for by progressive income taxes. The plan provoked a storm of disapproval. Critics, including Humphrey, pointed out that it would siphon off income from everyone who earned only a little more than the national median of about $10,000 a year and would cost billions. After admitting he had submitted the proposal as a courtesy to the NWRO, McGovern retreated in awkward haste. The incident confirmed Nixon's conclusion that anything seen as a guaranteed income was a political liability.

In late June 1972, faced with the option of negotiating with Ribicoff and his liberal Senate colleagues, the president announced that he would stay with the FAP proposal in the Social Security bill. That decision doomed FAP. On October 15 the Senate-House conference committee to reconcile the differing versions of the Social Security act removed FAP from the final bill. The measure that passed, and the president signed, made no mention of the FAP proposal that Nixon had introduced with such fanfare three years before. It was a straight Social Security measure, though an exceptionally generous one, that increased benefits to retirees by a whopping 20 percent and tied future old-age payments to the cost of living, a scheme that built inflation into the Social Security system.

It also included a section establishing SSI, Supplemental Security Income, a provision that retained a trace of a guaranteed income. SSI closed a large hole in the Social Security safety net by establishing a minimum income for the needy blind, the elderly, and the disabled even though they had never paid a nickel into the Social Security fund. Under the existing Social Security legislation the federal government already contributed to state programs to aid such presumably unemployable people. But, as with AFDC, benefits and eligibility requirements were uneven, and some states did not participate in the program at all. The new law federalized the programs and made them uniform. It was, in effect, a guaranteed minimum income for certain preferred classes of Americans.

Passage of SSI, after the defeat of FAP, seemed a bitter irony to liberals: The nation could create an income floor for millions of adults, but not for young families with children! Critics have charged that race explains why the two programs met different fates: AFDC families were too often black, in effect. But this is unfair. Many SSI beneficiaries, especially those who qualified by age, were also black. Thousands of black seniors, notwithstanding their spotty employment histories or work as domestics or casual laborers—jobs where employers notoriously neglected paying into the Social Security fund—would receive incomes when they reached sixty-five. SSI beneficiaries, regardless of race, were another segment of the "deserving poor," a group that did not include welfare mothers. If prejudice played a part in defeating FAP, it was prejudice against illegitimacy, and welfare recipients' assumed contempt for work, rather than race.

The differing fate of SSI and the Family Assistance Program undoubtedly owed much to the special power of the "seniors" lobby—and of the lobbies for the blind and disabled, as well as to pressures from richer states that paid their own versions of SSI and would now be relieved. But FAP's defeat was also the work of lobbyists: the welfare rights militants who opposed it in the only form passage was possible. A wiser opposition would have taken the modest program offered and then worked to expand it. In the years since 1972 there would be other drives to establish a federally guaranteed minimum income for poor Americans. None has succeeded. The chance lost in the early seventies was never regained.

The story of the Family Assistance Plan lends some support to recent depictions of Nixon as a closet liberal. From Joan Hoff's *Nixon Reconsidered,* one might almost conclude that Hubert Humphrey, or even Robert Kennedy, had won the 1968 presidential election, not the avowed enemy of the "bleeding heart" liberals. Are Professor Hoff and her allies right? Was Nixon actually a covert progressive?

I think not. A good test of Nixon's place on the political spectrum is his response to the Great Society legislation he inherited from his predecessor.

Nixon did not like the Office of Economic Opportunity and, as we saw, recommended in August 1969 that it be stripped of several programs and remodeled as an experimental agency. Under his own executive authority he closed fifty-nine Job Corps centers and managed to get the funding for the controversial program sharply cut. He also disliked OEO's legal services programs. Though a low-budget enterprise that devoted most of its energies to "service case work"—day-to-day disputes between tenants and landlords, husbands and wives, "perpetrators" and police—it also brought class action suits that challenged property rights and establishment institutions. Under the rubric of "law reform," it attempted to redefine "rights" through court challenge in the absence of legislative mandate. In 1967, legal services director Earl Johnson had described law reform as "bringing about changes in the structures of the world in which poor people live in order to provide . . . a legal system in which the poor enjoy the same legal opportunities as the rich."[47] Conservatives especially bridled at the role legal services lawyers played in disputes between the poor and their adversaries. In late 1970 Donald Rumsfeld, the Republican head of OEO, dismissed the director of the legal services program and his assistant for resisting efforts to subordinate legal services personnel to local officials. Director Terry Lenzner did not leave quietly. Rumsfeld, he charged, was "caving in to the political interests" represented by governors Reagan in California and Claude Kirk in Florida, who were "determined to keep us from suing special interests close to them on behalf of the poor."[48] He was quickly seconded by leading Democrats, by Americans for Democratic Action, and by Poverty Lawyers for Effective Advocacy. In the end Rumsfeld retreated, but the incident revealed the true state of the administration's feelings about the program's judicial zealots for the poor. Legal services managed to survive, but under the separate Legal Services Corporation and with its law reform propensities sharply curtailed.

Nixon also looked askance at OEO's Head Start. Like many Americans he had initially accepted the program's value and benevolence. The 1966 Coleman Report and other critical early evaluations had analyzed only the 1965 summer Head Start. It was not necessarily relevant for a year-round program. But in early 1969, there appeared a new study of children who had taken a full year of Head Start and then entered regular school programs. This study, administered by the Westinghouse Learning Corporation, rocked Head Start's friends by showing that even full-year programs made little difference in cognition test scores of children who had participated in Head Start, compared with other pupils, after a relatively brief exposure to regular schooling. Head Start's defenders at OEO, as well as Secretary Finch, considered the test design sloppy, but it changed the administration's preconceptions. What had started as an endorsement in the president's 1969 education message was revised to a note of caution. In 1971–72 Head Start was transferred to HEW. Though its friends in Congress were able to increase its funding, its growth slowed to a very modest rate. Then, in 1971, Nixon vetoed the Comprehensive Child Development Act sponsored by liberal Democrats Walter Mondale and John Brademas on the grounds that it favored "communal approaches" to early childhood education and development over family nurture.[49]

OEO survived for a time but it was effectively gutted, losing the Job Corps to the Labor Department and other manpower training programs to local governments under the Comprehensive Employment and Training Act (CETA) of 1973. By fiscal 1974 its budget, some $1.9 billion in 1969, had dropped to $328 million. It went out of business as a separate agency soon after.

Nixon obviously did not bleed for the cities either. That's not where his supporters lived. In fact, many Republican voters defined their politics in opposition to people who lived in the cities and all they represented. Yet as president, Nixon could not reverse the currents created during the previous decade and appears, improbably, as a preserver of urban benefits programs, though without the special sympathy for the poor of his predecessor.

Nixon sought change in national housing programs. In 1970 he proposed a measure to consolidate the roster of housing programs and to allow people in "the projects" to buy their apartments. It never passed Congress. In 1973, after denouncing federal housing programs since the New Deal as a waste of "$90 billion of the taxpayers' money," and declaring a moratorium on new housing projects, he plumped for a government voucher for the poor to pay their private rent. He did not feel he could goad the ghettos into insurgency.

Nixon despised Model Cities as an example of liberal utopianism run amok. In fact, the scheme had not worked especially well even under Johnson, its originator. The Ninetieth Congress, though more conservative than its predecessor, in mid-1967 had actually voted the half billion dollars for Model Cities authorized for fiscal 1968. But money was not the issue. The core problem was that the program was too unwieldy. White House aide James Gaither later called it "a very interesting dream, that you could get everybody to work together, and you could get all the segments in the political system . . . to work together." In reality, even "the federal government . . . couldn't deliver their [sic] programs." "We knew long before Model Cities got into trouble," he noted, "that it wasn't going to work."[50]

In the first round sixty-three cities, including all the largest ones except Los Angeles, where Mayor Sam Yorty had offended LBJ, were awarded planning grants. In March 1967 twelve additional cities were added to this group. Choices were made for both merit and politics. Detailed, thoughtful applications helped. But so did voting the right way. In November 1968, as Johnson was preparing to leave the White House, legislative counsel Barefoot Sanders told the president that HUD intended to reject the application of Amsterdam, New York, for a Model Cities grant. The application had been only mediocre by HUD's criteria. Moreover, Congressman Sam Stratton had urged its acceptance, and Stratton had opposed the administration on implementing the highway beautification bill. "I have not gone out of my way to help him on this," Sanders remarked dryly.[51]

There would be further additions to the eligible list in the months that followed, each occasion milked for maximum Democratic political gain. But under the rules of the bill, four steps were to follow the planning grant, which was only "Stage I."[52] By the time Nixon took office in January 1969, only nine cities had actually received "execution" money.

Nixon considered the Model Cities program another example of misguided social engineering that pandered to rioters and looters and would have preferred to bury the program. Early on he called Moynihan into the Oval Office and told him: "fold up Model Cities." The program was "going to be a failure and a waste of money. . . ."[53]

Nixon had not reckoned with political realities. Within Housing and Urban Development, the program had the support of many holdover officials. They, in turn, had "brainwashed" their impressionable chief, George Romney.[54] Moving with the times, the department leaders now claimed that the Model Cities program was consistent with the president's desire to devolve administration of federal programs to the localities. It was a form of revenue sharing and, stripped of its social experimentalism and its concern for community autonomy, should be retained as an administrative mechanism.

In early 1969 a HUD report signed by Romney called for improved administration of the program but concluded that its "goals are sound."[55] Instead of cutbacks, Romney proposed increased funding. Nixon balked, but rather than insisting on his way ordered another study, this one by his Urban Affairs Council. Its report proposed a shift of control from Washington to the states and cities in line with the New Federalism, and the enlistment "of private efforts and voluntary organizations" in line with Republican preference for the private sector.[56]

The Urban Affairs Council report was followed by at least six more before the president was convinced. One report was conducted by a task force headed by Edward Banfield, a conservative urbanist whose book, *The Unheavenly City,* became a defining work of the emerging neoconservative movement. Surprisingly, the Banfield task force report praised the program for having made "some city halls more aware of the special problems of their poor neighborhoods" and had led to the "improvement of management methods" for delivering services to the cities.[57] In fact, Banfield himself had little faith in this or other government urban programs; the task force's bureaucrats had merely overruled him. Meanwhile, from within the administration, Budget Director Robert Mayo and HUD Assistant Secretary Floyd Hyde were reassuring the president that Model Cities fit both his revenue-sharing and decentralization goals.

Nixon approved funding for Model Cities in 1970, but despite the urgings of Mayo, Romney, and Moynihan, remained unhappy with the program. But he could not, or would not, take on its supporters. Like so many other money-dispensing federal programs, Model Cities had begat an iron triangle, a mesh of constituencies and congressional committees, that would not let it die. In the spring of 1970 Model Cities' defenders barely beat off a proposal to deflect most of its appropriation into a Southern school desegregation effort. Civil rights groups, liberal reformers, and social workers wrote and called their congressmen. The National League of Cities and the U.S. Conference of Mayors rallied to the endangered program. At least fifty mayors contacted the White House. Few congressmen were brave enough to defy the tide. Even Barry Goldwater expressed concern for the Model Cities money for Tucson, his state's second largest city. Moynihan told the president: "Now you worry about our treaties in southeast Asia and I'll worry about our treaties with the cities."[58] In the end Nixon cried "uncle." On May 14 he met with Romney and said the scheme would be dropped.

But Nixon remained skeptical to the end. In 1971 he tried to allot Model Cities funds to a new revenue-sharing program for urban development. When Congress rejected this plan he ordered the Budget office to impound a half billion dollars of the program's funds. Yet in the end Nixon retreated and approved $2.3 billion to fund Model Cities for 1969 to 1973, a rate consistent with LBJ's recommendations.

The final demise of the program in 1973 was part of a larger Nixon victory in the state-federal battle. Backed by governors and mayors desperate for any new source of revenue, he finally had his way on revenue sharing. In 1972 Congress passed the State and Local Fiscal Assistance Act, a measure that promised to channel $30 billion of federal revenues over five years to state and local governments. Almost without strings, this money could be used for any purpose the local communities wanted, including local tax reduction. General revenue sharing, to use the political scientists' term, ended up making little difference. Local governments used the money to supplement existing federal programs; almost none was used for innovation. It did not, as its supporters predicted, democratically involve more voters in civic processes. On the other hand, it did help hold down local taxes in a minor way. The program was terminated in 1986 without anyone the better for it, only to reappear more recently as a panacea for big government and bureaucratic inefficiency.

Nixon had less faith than LBJ in education as a magic cure for social failure and economic inequality and liked the ESEA Title I programs—those providing federal money for poor school districts—scarcely better than Head Start. Ignoring the educationists' caveats, he had little doubt that the recent studies of Title I's effects proved that it had not worked as predicted and was quick to say so. "We must recognize that our present knowledge about how to overcome poor background," he declared in March 1970, "is so limited that major expansion of such programs could not confidently be based on their results."[59] The president fought efforts to increase spending on the ESEA, but Congress was uninterested in whether the programs had achieved their stated goals or not. By now taxpayers, teachers, and school administrators in their home districts were used to having federal funds and fought to keep their annual fix. In fiscal 1970 Congress padded the ESEA appropriation in the HEW funding bill by $300 million more than Nixon requested. Nixon vetoed it. Later in 1970, when Congress tried once more to hike the ESEA's appropriation beyond Nixon's request, he again vetoed the bill. Congress overrode the president; in the Senate only three Republicans spoke out in favor of the president's position. But the same confrontation over appropriations took place in 1972 and this time Nixon won.

Yet all told Nixon failed to stop the expansion of Great Society education programs. The ESEA survived and grew. The appropriation for its core component, Title I, funded at $1.1 billion in 1969, rose to $1.8 billion in 1973. Outlays on higher education programs meanwhile expanded from $424 million to $927 million during the same period. Once again, despite what the president wanted, political realities—the built-in iron triangles of all benefit programs—plus Nixon's own relative indifference to what went on domestically and his disinclination to confront Congress helped ensure continuation of the Great Society programs.

In the same way Nixon was not an enthusiast for the environment. If he was insensitive to cities, he was also indifferent to nature. LBJ had roots in the soil; one imagined him astride a horse, riding the range. Nixon's native habitat was the speaker's rostrum and the conference table. Whenever he appeared outdoors he always looked uncomfortable. Photographers loved to catch him walking on the beach outside his Pacific White House in California dressed in a suit and wearing dress shoes.

Before becoming president he had thought little about environmental issues. His advisers were more aware of them. Ehrlichman had been involved in land-use issues as a lawyer in Seattle.

John Whitaker, undersecretary of the Interior Department, and his assistant, Christopher Demuth, were also sensitive to environmental issues. But these men were less committed environmentalists than political pragmatists. As the seventies began, Americans were worried about pollution and environmental degradation; they had become hot, popular issues. The administration had to respond or Congress would, and take the lead ahead of the White House. One member of the Nixon administration was a true enthusiast, however: Nixon's Interior Secretary Walter Hickel, the former governor of Alaska. At the time of his appointment Hickel was considered a friend of the oil companies and other industries that exploited natural resources. At a preinauguration press conference Hickel declared that he had little use for "conservation for conservation's sake."[60] But then the Alaska politician did an about-face, embracing environmentalism and surprising all his critics. Most improbable of all, he resisted the enormous pressure to push a pipeline through eight hundred miles of virgin Alaska terrain to tap the newly discovered oil pool off the state's North Slope.

It was during Nixon's presidency that environmentalism first developed a large constituency. In many ways it was an outgrowth of the antiwar movement, the civil rights movement, and the New Left all at once. As the American presence in Vietnam declined under Nixon's Vietnamization policy, the antiwar rallies, marches, and sit-ins petered out. In 1969 Students for a Democratic Society split into warring factions. One, the Weathermen, disappeared into "the belly of the beast," determined to destroy "Amerika" from within. The other, dominated by rigid Leninists, soon disbanded. By this time white militants had been effectively evicted from the civil rights movement as black power advocates seized control of SNCC, CORE, and other groups. Deprived of these outlets for idealistic dissent, many of the young political activists lugged their placards, backpacks, and mimeograph machines to the new environmental-ecological sites, where they could deploy their polemical and organizational skills to denounce capitalism, bourgeois materialism, and American industry for their crimes against the nation's forests, streams, and air.

Obviously, this was not Nixon's natural constituency. Indeed, he despised these "deep" environmentalists as much as the campus radicals and the antiwar demonstrators. The depth of his contempt can be heard on the Watergate tapes, for example, as Nixon discusses emission controls with Henry Ford II and Lee Iacocca, then still a Ford executive. Nixon denounces consumer advocates as "enemies of the system" who weren't "one really damn bit interested in safety or clean air. . . ." They were, rather, interested in "destroying the system. . . ."[61] In a diary entry of February 9, 1971, Haldeman quotes Nixon as saying: "The environment is not an issue that's worth a damn to us." It was an issue of the political leftists, he noted, and the administration should not play into their hands.[62]

Yet Nixon was under extraordinary pressure to comply with environmentalist demands. The process of public arousal and awakening that began during the Johnson years had now turned into a mass movement. Adversarial dissent had merged with public health fears to create a hybrid crusade epitomized by Earth Day, 1970, inspired by liberal Democratic senator Gaylord Nelson of Wisconsin. That April 22, millions across the country participated in demonstrations to protect the environment, denounce polluters, and pledge themselves to ecological purity. In New York thousands marched for the environment down an auto-free Fifth Avenue. In Hoboken a crowd dumped into the Hudson a coffin containing the names of America's polluted rivers. At Boston's Logan Airport environmentalists demonstrated against federal funding of the ozone-depleting Supersonic Transport. At the University of New Mexico students presented an "enemy of the earth" award to twenty-eight state legislators accused of gutting a recent law to protect the environment. A few civically conscious industrial firms joined the celebration, but business was also the demonstrators' chief target. In Minneapolis students from the university, carrying a coffin crammed with small General Electric appliances, broke into a GE stockholders' meeting to attack the corporation. In Philadelphia Ralph Nader called manufacturers the worst polluters and urged consumers to develop a "radical militant ethic" to curb their excesses.[63]

Nixon could not resist the message. By the fall of 1969, according to John C. Whitaker, who became undersecretary of the interior about this time, the "Washington mood" on the environment could be described only by the word *"hysteria."* The "words *pollution* and *environment* were on every politician's lips," and Nixon was in danger of being left behind.[64] The president went along, but he was never a convert. At one point he told a speech-writer: "In a flat choice between smoke and jobs, we're for jobs."[65]

The president moved cautiously. In May 1969 he created a task force on the environment and in late August turned it over to Whitaker. This group composed a sixty-five-page outline of proposals that Nixon incorporated into his environmental message to Congress in February 1970.

The message did little to please the environmental puritans, who demanded villains and doubted the goodwill of the private sector. Nixon refused to identify villains. The damage done to the environment "has not been the work of evil men." Nor could environmental repair be exclusively the work of the government. It would have to be a collaboration among government, business, and individuals. Nixon outlined a comprehensive, thirty-seven-point program that included twenty-three legislative proposals and fourteen executive orders in the areas of water and air pollution, solid waste management, and parks and recreation. He also proposed reorganizing and consolidating the existing agencies devoted to environmental issues. All told, his proposals added up to a respectable environmental platform, though they clearly sought a balance between the environmentalist enthusiasts and the defenders of jobs, profits, and "progress."[66]

Congress considered Nixon's program tepid. It approved his plan to create an independent Environmental Protection Agency as a central federal agency to monitor, coordinate, and enforce antipollution laws, to set antipollution standards, and to conduct research into environmental problems. But it exceeded the administration's wishes when, over the strong resistance of the oil and auto industries, it passed the Clean Air Act, a tough air pollution bill that mandated car exhaust standards to be phased in over the next few years, and established national air quality standards, also to be gradually applied. Nixon signed the bill but without enthusiasm. Following the 1969 Pacific oil spills off Santa Barbara he signed the Water Quality Improvement Act, authorizing federal clean-ups of oil spills and establishing liability for willful negligence or misconduct connected with oil spills. Nixon also accepted or initiated other environmental measures. In 1969 he approved the National Environmental Policy Act requiring all federal agencies to accompany executive department actions and legislative proposals with an environmental impact statement. That same year the Department of Agriculture ordered an early end to the use of DDT in residential areas and a quick phase-out of its use generally. In late 1970 the president signed the Occupational Safety and Health Act, mandating employers to provide a safe and healthy work environment for workers and establishing federal standards for workplace environments and federal enforcement of those standards.

But all told the president's record on the environment was mixed. In late 1970 he fired Walter Hickel, the watchdog of the Alaskan wilderness, from the Department of the Interior. Though the grounds were disloyalty, it was taken by many to be a setback to environmental protection. In 1972 he vetoed a clean water act on the grounds that it was too expensive. Congress overrode his veto, but the president then sought to "impound" portions of congressional clean water appropriations that he did not consider warranted. Nixon also supported the Supersonic Transport, considered by environmentalists a danger to the ozone barrier to lethal ultraviolet radiation. Meanwhile, the Office of Management and Budget, a new executive agency, began intruding into the tough regulatory decisions of the EPA to ease the burden on accused polluters. All told, Nixon was a less committed environmentalist than his predecessor. He chose not to resist the current but he tried to tame and deflect it.

Nixon did, however, prove to be surprisingly generous on that other Great Society quality-of-life program, federal funding of the arts and humanities. The president had little use for "modern," nonrepresentational painting and atonal music—but then, few Americans did. But he enjoyed and respected the classics and was willing to support them. Even more enthusiastic was Leonard Garment, a former Nixon law associate at Mudge, Rose, who came with him to Washington to serve as a White House domestic policy aide. A cultivated liberal, a one-time clarinetist with The Woody Herman Band, Garment took a special interest in the arts and scholarship and Nixon allowed him to serve as his cultural adviser. Howard Phillips, an arch-conservative Nixon aide, said that Garment had "a whole cultural and social portfolio at the White House."[67]

Nixon's choice as chair of the national arts endowment was

Nancy Hanks, an associate of New York governor Nelson Rockefeller. A soft-voiced Southerner, Hanks proved to be a remarkably adept politician who knew how to handle both Congress and the president. On one occasion she asked Nixon to describe his highest priority for the arts endowment. It should reach more people, the president said. "What you are talking about, sir," she responded, "is totally impossible to accomplish without money."[68]

Meanwhile Garment was playing to Nixon's political instincts. Responding to Hanks's request for funding the NEA eightfold over the Johnson figure, Garment wrote the president: "Support for the arts is, increasingly, good politics. . . ." Arts boards were made up "very largely, of business, corporate, and community interests." Not all of these people were his friends. "[Y]ou will gain support from groups which have hitherto not been favorable to this administration."[69] But there was more than mere expediency in Nixon's positive response. As Garment later noted, Nixon "liked to surprise people" and in the end his support for expanded funding was "one-third politics, one-third substance, and one-third irony."[70]

In late 1969 Nixon asked Congress to increase federal expenditures for the arts and humanities in fiscal 1971 to $40 million and extend for three years the national foundations. In his message he admitted that the increase might seem extravagant in a time of budget constraints, but he believed "that the need for a new impetus to the understanding and expression of the American idea has a compelling claim on our resources."[71]

Under Nixon and Ford the arts endowment outlay would leap an extraordinary 1,400 percent despite denunciations by conservatives and traditionalists, even in the 1970s, that its money all too often subsidized obscenity or phony trendiness. In fiscal 1970 it was $8,250,000. In 1978 it reached over $123 million.

The humanities endowment was less successful under Nixon. In 1970 Barnaby Keeney left the endowment and Nixon nominated Stephen Hess, a middle-of-the-road journalist and White House speechwriter, to succeed him. Though a literate man, Hess had no advanced degree and immediately became a lightning rod for all those anti-Nixon feelings that academics had worked up over Vietnam and other issues. Letters poured in denouncing the appointment, and the American Council of Learned Societies came out against Hess. An embarrassed Nixon soon withdrew the nomination.

For two years the NEH languished without a director, falling behind its sister endowment. For a time Hanks, believing her agency the more popular and better able to tap the federal treasury if a solo act, sought to sever her agency's connection to the weaker sister. Matters improved for the humanities in 1971, when Nixon nominated Ronald Berman, a prominent Shakespeare scholar with conservative leanings, as chairman of NEH. Berman weathered the confirmation process in a still-liberal Senate by promising Senator Javits that he would not exclude radicals from benefits and assuring Claiborne Pell that he did not oppose "little grants to little people."[72]

But Berman represented a more elitist and traditional perspective than he admitted. He believed in an intellectual dialectic. The seventies, he felt, would inevitably be the antithesis of the activist, hedonistic sixties, a time when the humanities "had lost part of their professionalism" and given in to "what felt good and seemed relevant."[73] During his tenure at the NEH the agency sponsored major projects examining and publicizing "the American experience in its broadest sense."[74] As 1976 approached it devoted much of its energies to the bicentennial of American independence. But it continued to fund generously traditional academic research in history, classics, literature, and languages. Berman managed to restore much of the agency's prestige and extract a substantial sum from Congress. During his tenure the agency's funding went from about $11 million to a whopping $72 million. In 1975, however, he collided with Pell over what the Rhode Island senator considered excessive focus on scholarly enterprise and not enough concern for "diversified, popularly supported constructive programs at a grass roots level."[75] When Berman's reappointment came up in 1976, Pell succeeded in shooting it down.

Nixon and his advisers were less friendly to public broadcasting. The Corporation for Public Broadcasting, established in 1967, received its first funding, $5 million, in 1969. Over the next three years federal money increased to $31 million, while other sources of funds—viewer contributions, corporate contributions, local and state appropriations—raised the CPB's total budget to $158 million. In 1972 there were 233 TV stations affiliated with the Public Broadcasting Service, the private agency linking the stations supported by the CPB. During these early years public television enriched the airwaves with a breakthrough educational program for young children, *Sesame Street,* and with such adult programs as the irreverent view of public affairs *The Great American Dream Machine.* In 1969 the CPB, along with the Ford Foundation, made a study of the public radio system that led, the next year, to the creation of National Public Radio to distribute programs to public radio stations. By the late 1970s more than two hundred stations were part of the NPR group, each receiving about forty hours a week of packaged news and public affairs programming from the CPB.

The Democratic Congress admired the burgeoning public broadcasting system and in mid-1972 gave the CPB $155 million over two years. Nixon vetoed the bill. The administration did not like the liberal bias of the CPB's public affairs programs and believed that the agency intended to establish de facto a fourth national network, abandoning the principle of localism. Long-term funding would be unwise until the agency changed its policies, the president's veto message declared. The veto staggered the agency, and in its wake CPB president John Macy and many of his top aides resigned.

During the ensuing months the CPB, with new leadership, changed its practices to suit the White House objections. Appeased, in 1973 Nixon signed a bill authorizing a two-year CPB appropriation of $110 million. The joke was on Nixon. Alone among the media, public broadcasting offered gavel-to-gavel coverage of the Senate and House Watergate hearings in 1973–74 that destroyed Nixon's presidency.

One way to evaluate Nixon's impact on the Great Society is by looking at the figures. Did the total cost of domestic social programs fall or rise after 1968?

Joan Hoff, the Nixon partisan, notes that in the Nixon budget for fiscal 1971 annual spending on human resource programs for the first time since World War II exceeded spending on defense. By 1975, as she points out, after five Nixon budgets, defense expenditures were 25 percent of all federal outlays while social welfare outlays had reached 43 percent. In part the change in proportions was due to the Vietnam "peace dividend" as Vietnamization progressively reduced the American commitment to Saigon before total withdrawal in 1973. But at the same time federal social programs expanded in absolute dollar terms, from $37 billion in 1965 to $104 billion by 1972.

But the changes can be viewed another way—in relation to the economy's total size. The proportion of the federal budget devoted to expenditures on human resources and transfers— broadly defined as direct expenditures and grants-in-aid for education and training, health, cash assistance, and in-kind benefits (food stamps, e.g.)—increased from 6.3 percent of full-employment GNP in 1961 to 8.7 percent in 1969, and then to 13.4 percent in 1976. A substantial proportion of these outlays, however, went to the middle class—in the form of old-age pensions, for example. If we limit the figures just to the proportion spent on the poor, the growth was from 0.8 percent of GNP in 1961 to 1.4 percent in 1967. This fraction continued to grow during the Nixon period until 1973 (to 1.8 percent) and then declined by 1976 to only 1.5 percent, about where it had been in 1971.

Overall, then, Nixon-era social outlays represent an upward tilt from the Johnson period. If we confine our view solely to federal spending for "human resource" development programs (including the Job Corps, Model Cities, Appalachian development, and several other programs) the Nixon surge is less clear, however. In 1968 these programs reached 6.5 percent of total federal outlays. In 1972 they were down to 6.2 percent. But in absolute terms they were up: from $11.6 billion to $14.1 billion. All told, if there was not a great leap, there was also not a great drop.

Whatever his urges and intentions, in straight quantitative terms Nixon did not roll back the Great Society. In fact, as Hoff and others observe, the programs grew well into his administration.

Do these figures, then, confirm Professor Hoff's claim that Nixon was a reformer, a closet liberal? I do not believe so. Great Society programs survived, and some became bigger and costlier. But often they expanded simply because the nation's population grew and with it the number of people eligible, or because a Democratic Congress, under the iron triangle principle, overruled Nixon's wishes, or because the president, in a fit of absent-mindedness, allowed some of his more liberal aides to act as policy makers. Richard Nixon often had little to do with it. Obviously Nixon did not prove to be the antiliberal ogre that many on the left had feared, but at the same time his administration marked a transition to the truly conservative era of his Republican successors during the 1980s.

Richard Nixon was reelected in 1972 over George McGovern by one of the electoral tidal waves of this century. The South Dakota senator, as we saw, owed his nomination to the most liberal wing of his party. New affirmative action rules for state delegations that mandated racial-, gender-, class-, and youth-defined quotas for delegates had revolutionized the delegate distribution. Watching the convention proceedings from the convention hall balconies or on their flickering TV screens were the traditional Democratic power brokers: the mayors, labor leaders, and party benefactors. On the floor, voting on rules, platform, and nominees were an array of antiwar activists, progressives, counterculture experimenters, and youthful enthusiasts. Of the 388 California delegates and alternates, all McGovernites, eighty-nine were on welfare.

Inevitably the Democratic campaign was suffused with the most liberal shibboleths of the day. The party platform called for a major federal program of public service jobs; an "income security system" to replace "the present welfare system"; a more "progressive" tax system; a higher minimum wage; stricter environmental and occupational health and safety laws; legislation to protect farm workers' organizing rights; "a more equal distribution of power, income, and wealth"; the "right to be different" in "lifestyles and private habits" as well as in cultural, racial, and gender identities; the "right to legal services"; full funding for ESEA and measures to equalize spending among school districts; and further increases in outlays on the arts and humanities.[76] McGovern himself dropped the universal thousand-dollar-a-year "demogrant" and came out instead for a national income insurance plan of public service jobs for the employable on welfare and a minimum $4,000 in cash and food stamps per a welfare family of four, the whole to be paid for by higher taxes on the rich.[77] The candidate inevitably identified himself with the Great Society by selecting Sargent Shriver as his running mate, after his first choice, Senator Thomas Eagleton of Missouri, bowed out following revelations that he had been hospitalized for mental illness in the past. The Republicans said little of the New Federalism or FAP or Model Cities on the hustings during the fall, but no one doubted that the two candidates and the two parties represented different social philosophies. The administration sought to demonize McGovern and his followers as radicals. His opponent, Nixon told Ehrlichman, should be depicted by GOP campaigners as "a fanatical, dedicated, leftist extremist."[78]

In the end the American voters gave Nixon 60.7 percent of the popular vote, the third highest proportion in history. Had they disowned the Great Society itself? In reality much of what voters disliked in McGovern and his campaign was at most the marginalia of the Great Society. Lyndon Johnson did not favor peace marches, ghetto riots, permissive child raising, LSD, welfare handouts, or college takeovers by students any more than his successor. But however unfair, the middle-class public perceived McGovern and his entourage as the heirs of Lyndon Johnson and, forgetting how much they themselves had benefited from Great Society programs, they held it against the Democratic candidate in November 1972. And yet the Nixon sweep was not a mandate to dismantle the Great Society. The voters did not repudiate the congressional Democrats. The Republicans gained only twelve seats in the House and actually lost two in the Senate. They remained the minority party in both houses.

There is little more of our story to tell. During the election campaign the administration had been able to contain the Watergate scandal, calling the breakin at Democratic National Committee headquarters "a third-rate burglary" and denying any connection between the five men apprehended and the White House or the Committee to Reelect the President. Nixon interpreted the election as a personal, if not a party mandate, and planned to butt heads with the liberal Congress and liberal bureaucracy in his second term. He intended, Richard Nathan has written, to ignore both antagonistic power centers and create an "administrative presidency."[79] Success with this plan might at last have rolled back much of the Great Society. But in the months ahead the White House coverup of Watergate unraveled and the president and his staff were swept up in evermore frantic efforts to evade the investigators. By mid-1973 Nixon's domestic initiatives faltered as he fought to save himself and his administration.

Nixon never did tame the Great Society system. But then, neither did Ford or Reagan, his conservative successors. At this writing it remains to be seen if the vaunted Republican congressional victory of 1994 will come any closer to disassembling the baroque, if well-meant, structure of benefits, interests, entitlements, and commitments erected during the 1960s and early 1970s.

Epilogue

ON JANUARY 13, 1969, a week before leaving office, Lyndon Johnson attended a testimonial dinner in his honor at New York's Plaza Hotel. It was a resplendent black-tie affair with dancing in the grand ballroom and entertainment by Cab Calloway. The four hundred guests included high administration officials, prominent New York state and city leaders, cultural luminaries, and an array of liberal businessmen and Democratic benefactors. Johnson gave a brief speech reviewing his accomplishments in office. He did not touch all the Great Society bases but he hit the ones he considered the most significant. Black citizens were "finding their voice in the voting booth in every part of the nation," he declared. "The old in their illness . . . know the dignity of independence." Young minds had been "enriched and young horizons expanded." "Families who were poor—and men who were idle—[had] begun to know the dignity of decent incomes and jobs." "A larger share of American earth—of its shores and forests—[had been] set aside for all the American people." Reversing the usual cliché, he noted that what really mattered was "not the ultimate judgment" that historians would pass on his administration, but "whether there is a change for the better in the way our people live."[1] A week later he handed over the keys of the White House to his successor and retired to the banks of the Pedernales.

Did the Great Society make life better for Americans? Did it augment or diminish the nation's collective happiness and prosperity? Did it make the United States a more admirable country? On a civic balance sheet do we write its bottom line in red ink or black?

The questions are especially relevant in the mid-1990s. For a time after November 1992 it seemed as if the Great Society was to have a new lease on life. The first Democratic president in twelve years, Bill Clinton proposed expanding Head Start and manpower training programs, supported a new version of VISTA, and virtually bet his administration on a vast extension of federal health insurance. He won some minor legislative victories but failed totally at the sweeping plan to expand Medicare-Medicaid into universal health care coverage for all citizens. In 1994 he and his party suffered a devastating defeat in the midterm elections. As these words are being written the newspaper headlines trumpet the plans of Republican leaders in the 104th Congress to demolish the remaining Great Society programs as wasteful, ineffective, and noxious. The polls show that the public is inclined to go along with much of what the dismantlers propose.

The destructive urge derives in large measure from the collective national memory of the Great Society. Even more than in 1972 the general public today remembers the sixties as a time of turmoil and despair and conflates the Great Society with ghetto riots, welfare fraud, and campus turmoil. That vision has become part of the street wisdom of our day.

More sophisticated Americans may be wary of such simple images but many accept another negative version of the Great Society, one framed by right-wing social thinkers of the 1980s. These conservative policy experts claim that most Great Society programs failed. Lawrence Mead, a political scientist at New York University, says the record of the Great Society's education and training programs "was disappointing." They "often provided worthwhile services, but they had very limited impact on the skills of their recipients."[2] Charles Murray's 1984 conservative tract, *Losing Ground,* notes that "from the first evaluation reports in the mid-sixties and continuing to the present day, the results of these [Great Society antipoverty] programs have been disappointing to their advocates and evidence of failure to their critics."[3] Nor, in his view, did all that federal money for both lower and higher education accomplish much. Education for blacks improved during the decade preceding 1965 and then, after the ESEA and the Higher Education Act, the advance stopped. "[T]he federal investment . . . in elementary and secondary education for the disadvantaged," he insists, "bought nothing discernable."[4]

The indictment goes beyond the failure of specific programs. The Great Society, the detractors claim, also undermined personal self-reliance and corrupted civic life. Federal programs, Mead says, failed to "set standards for their clients."[5] They "emphasized giving recipients services, income, and other benefits directly,"[6] and did not effectively extract a price for benefits. By encouraging permissiveness, they spread the germs of social decay. Murray accuses the Great Society of refusing "to acknowledge moral inequality" in its response to the poor and thereby changing the moral climate so much for the worse as to undermine valid social norms.[7] In effect, the Great Society denied the distinction between worthy and unworthy poor, thereby withdrawing respect for work and personal effort. Conservative social scientist George Gilder is another major debunker of the Great Society. "What actually happened since 1964," he declaims in his 1981 polemic, *Wealth and Poverty,* "was a vast expansion of the welfare rolls that halted in its tracks an ongoing improvement in the lives of the poor, particularly blacks, and left behind . . . a wreckage of broken lives and families worse than the aftermath of slavery."[8]

In important ways the conservative critics, whether the streetwise or the educated, misread the Great Society. Most Kennedy-Johnson programs sought to encourage self-reliance. Instead of free gifts, the War on Poverty offered education and training to promote self-help. Johnson and his colleagues never did like "welfare." LBJ also rejected a guaranteed annual income policy. It is true that the president resisted WIN, the work requirement in the 1967 Social Security revision act, but from the outset of the War on Poverty the administration assumed that ignorance or disability, not laziness, explained poverty. Even community action, however it played out, sought to inspire responsibility and community competence. If these programs failed it was not because the targets were wrong, but because they missed those targets. Their ends were exemplary; their means and execution were flawed.

Many of the critics are wrong in another way, as well. Murray, Mead, and Gilder boil down the Great Society largely to programs to aid the poor. It was far more than that, of course. Any fair balance sheet must include the debits and credits of many other policies and programs. But for the moment let us ignore the reductionism and consider whether the War on Poverty by itself worked.

The answer cannot be crisply stated. Even the experts disagree. Their conclusions are blurred by qualifiers, semantical hair-splitting, statistical disagreements, and tendentious posturing. And in a sense there can be no objective answer. Poverty is in part a subjective phenomenon, a feeling of deprivation stirred in part by invidious comparison. Some people will feel poor as long as anyone else has more than they do. For such poverty the only cure is perfect equality, as hard to come by as perfect love.

But let us forego philosophy and assume that we can measure poverty objectively. A good place to start is with the officially defined poverty line, which, as we saw, was the minimum cash income presumably needed for subsistence of an average-sized family. This was determined by the cost of an adequate food basket multiplied by three to take into account other necessities. By 1972 inflation had raised the original $3,000 for an urban family of four to $4,200. It is important to note that the income figures used to place people above or below the poverty line were supplied by the poor themselves and included only money income, not "transfers" to them of noncash benefits with real value. Using this imperfect measure, did the collective efforts by government after 1964 actually reduce the proportion of Americans below the poverty line?

The answer is yes. The *officially designated* poor declined between 1965 and 1969 from 17.3 percent of the total population to 12.1 percent. It remained close to that 12 percent level through 1973. This means that if we use all forms of legal *money* income as the measure, there were fewer poor people after the War on Poverty was declared than before, roughly one third fewer.

But what actually accomplished this decrease in poverty? Was it federal antipoverty programs or other mechanisms? Could the advance have resulted from the sheer growth of the economy?

The reduction of unemployment and hence poverty had, of course, been the goal of Walter Heller and his colleagues when they proposed the tax cut in the Kennedy years. And they succeeded. When economic growth reached more than 5 percent per year in the mid-sixties, it pushed unemployment rates to below 4 percent. A tight job market in turn raised wages. Together these two effects reduced the number of families and individuals below the poverty line. By how much? In fact, despite the steady decline in officially defined unemployment, the proportion of all Americans below the poverty line dropped only a modest three percentage points, from 21.3 percent in 1965 to 18.2 percent in 1968, as a result of rising employment—*if we subtract the transfers of income from government programs.* By 1972, after the economy hit some bumps, another percentage point of the population had joined the "pretransfer poor." All told, our best estimate is that between 1965 and 1972 the country's vigorous economic growth by itself reduced the percentage at or below the poverty level by only about a tenth of the total.

A rising tide really did not lift all boats, then; many of the vessels, clearly, had leaky bottoms. Or to abandon the metaphor, too many poor people were detached from the economy and the labor market either because they were too unskilled, too old, too burdened by child care responsibilities, or too work averse, and so did not benefit from the economic boom. The seniors, the mothers, the invincibly lazy could not easily be reached. But what about all those hand-up programs—the Job Corps, manpower retraining, and educational enrichment—designed to make the unskilled and ignorant jobless more employable? These were the Great Society's professed means of dealing with the perceived structural unemployment that bedeviled the nation. Didn't they lift many above the poverty line by putting them in the running for jobs?

Money for all these human resources programs leaped in this period, as we saw. Outlays for "manpower training" climbed from $450 million in fiscal 1964 to $2.6 billion by fiscal 1970. They jumped to new highs during Nixon's first term—$4.9 billion in fiscal 1973. During this decade several million men and women received training under these measures, some 2.2 million under the Manpower Development and Training Act (MDTA) alone between 1964 and 1973. But the evidence suggests that relatively few who enrolled and completed manpower training programs achieved gains great enough to carry them over the poverty line. Trainees did improve their income compared with those who received no training, but generally the gain was not enough to raise them from the ranks of the official poor. In social scientist Henry Levin's summary, the MDTA training programs "had a slight impact, but not a profound one," on poverty.[9]

And even if training programs helped given individuals to rise out of poverty, they may well have had only a marginal net effect on total poverty. More than one expert in the field has called attention to the musical chairs effect: Each man or woman who got a job through Job Corps, MDTA, and the other training programs may have merely displaced someone else who did not have the training. One person rose out of poverty; another one dropped into it as a result.

As we saw, Lyndon Johnson was a pushover for education. He embraced it as the universal passport to success and achievement. Nor was he entirely mistaken. There is, at the very least, a well established correlation between income and years of schooling.[10]

How much did the Great Society general education programs—as opposed to "training"—affect the income of beneficiaries? Not very much. Upward Bound was a program designed to extend years of schooling among the poor to include college, but as we have seen it was largely a subsidy to students on their way to college in any event. Its augmenting effect accordingly was limited. Neighborhood Youth Corps, intended in part to encourage youths to finish high school by giving them income, had little power, it seems, to keep poor kids from dropping out. Studies of Youth Corps programs in New York, Cincinnati, and Detroit found, in fact, that they also did not raise educational horizons or improve school performance.

The most massive education enhancement program of the sixties was Title I of the ESEA of 1965, the section designed to pump federal money into school districts with a high percentage of the poor. Did it reduce poverty?

In order to reduce poverty it would obviously be necessary for Title I to raise achievement and/or years of total schooling for its beneficiaries. It does not seem to have done either. We have already noted that the Coleman Report and the Westinghouse study failed to find any detectable effect on student achievement from federal money. Defenders of the ESEA fault the small scale of the program relative to total local outlays for elementary and secondary education. They point to the inefficiency and incompetence of local boards of education. They blame the misdirection of funds from programs for the poor into general budget use by these local boards. They note the weakness of the specific local compensatory programs themselves. All these are valid criticisms of Title I but they do not gainsay that it failed to raise achievement scores by an appreciable amount. Coleman himself summed it up early in the devastating process of evaluating ESEA: "In effect, what educators have found to their dismay, is that school is not as effective as a means of increasing opportunity as it has been expected to be."[11] Nor has opinion changed drastically since the mid-sixties. At the very end of 1992 the Commission on Chapter 1 (that is, Title I) submitted a report on the operations of the program, which is now funded at more than $6 billion a year. It praised the program for narrowing the skills gap between rich and poor but said it was "hobbled by obsolete methods and low standards," and recommended major changes.[12]

The most esteemed of all the Great Society education programs for the poor was Head Start. Though it dealt with young children years away from entering the job market, its rationale was that getting four- and five-year-olds started on the right track would eventually help them become self-supporting adults. After reviewing all the data on whether it achieved its aim, the verdict must be "not proven."

During the sixties and early seventies most of the evidence that Head Start permanently raised IQ or achievement levels generally was negative. It was this data that persuaded Nixon to seek cutbacks in the program. It is also the data used by conservative critics of the Great Society in the 1980s and 1990s to attack the program. Most recently Richard Herrnstein and Charles Murray, in their provocative book, *The Bell Curve,* have repeated the figures showing initial gains followed by subsequent "fade-out" and conclude, after examining the literature, that "cognitive benefits . . . are usually gone by third grade. By sixth grade, they have vanished entirely in aggregate statistics."[13]

But there is evidence on the other side as well. One of the more rigorous sixties studies of preschool enrichment compared black ghetto three- and four-year-olds in the same Ypsilanti, Michigan, school who received especially intensive preschool enrichment with a control group that did not. The results of the special Perry Preschool Program resembled the others: The test group's average IQ initially benefited, but then, after they were mainstreamed, their scores slipped back to the previous level. To this extent the initial Perry Preschool study merely confirmed the others. But unlike other Head Start test subjects, the Ypsilanti group was followed through to age nineteen, and then some significant *behavioral* gains became apparent. The former Perry Preschoolers were absent from school fewer days and more often graduated from high school. More to the point, they were less likely to be on welfare or to have committed a crime or, in the case of the young women, to have had large numbers of children. It was not through higher IQ's, then, or reading and math achievement, that they enhanced their life chances, but through developing the work ethic and the other social values that contribute to success in our American free market economy.[14] Admittedly the Ypsilanti program was more intensive than the regular Head Start program, but its effects are suggestive for preschool enrichment generally. There is still room to believe that if we really wanted to commit massive resources to early education that we might turn around a generation currently programmed to fail.

Yet when all is said, neither economic growth nor the "hand-up" policy accounts for most of the decline in the proportion of Americans considered poor. What did reduce poverty during the late 1960s and early 1970s was *transfers*—handouts. These were both cash payments—Social Security, "welfare," federal pensions, and unemployment insurance, for example—and "in-kind" transfers —food stamps, housing subsidies, legal services, subsidized health care, and so forth. Cash transfers to the poor grew from $22.4 billion in 1965 to $34.3 billion by 1972, an increase of almost $12 billion. In the former year these cash transfers already lifted one third of the pretransfer poor over the poverty line; by 1972 the larger amount pulled 44 percent of that group over the line. What additional effect did the *in-kind* transfers have? Although official poverty estimates consider only cash income, it is obvious that the in-kind transfers are also important in any consideration of real poverty trends. Food purchased with stamps is as nourishing as food bought with cash, and those who get stamps can devote their folding money to other purposes. In-kind transfers, amounting to $1.2 billion in 1965, $10.8 billion in 1969, and $26.6 billion in 1974,[15] had the effect of further reducing poverty levels. If the value of in-kind benefits is treated as transfer income and added to the cash transfers, then in 1972, 72 percent of the pretransfer poor were lifted over the official poverty line. Historian James Patterson has summarized the results as of 1974 as follows: "Without any public programs, 20.2 million American families, more than one-quarter of the total population, would have been poor. With social insurance and public aid added to their incomes, 9.1 million remained poor. Adding Medicaid, food stamps, and the other in-kind benefits, the number fell to 5.4 million, or 6.9 percent of all families."[16]

Some poverty experts would also like to factor in to the estimates extra-legal income. The poverty line is determined by *reported* income, but as we know much income is not reported. At every job level people fail to acknowledge income received. At lower levels many people work "off the books," as every employer of casual labor or household help knows. Professional services too are sometimes paid for in cash and never reported to the IRS. And some people—far too many—receive money from illegal activities. We cannot know precisely how much money sloshes around the underground economy, but it stands to reason that more than a few participants in it are raised above the official poverty line by ill-gotten gains.[17]

So, did the Great Society antipoverty programs work or fail? As Johnson envisioned it—as *opportunity* programs—they largely failed. It is this failure that fuels the collective public resentment of the Great Society. Working Americans want people to be self-supporting; they want everyone to earn their bread by the sweat of their brows. But they except the handicapped and the aged and, in fact, a very large part of the poverty reduction of the era was among the aged. The aged, once poorer than most Americans, by 1982 had a poverty rate below the national average, primarily through the generational cash transfer program known as old-age pensions, plus the in-kind transfer program called Medicare. These outlays soared during the late sixties and early seventies. Medicare leaped from zero in 1966 to $11.3 billion in 1974; old-age pensions rose from $16.6 billion in 1965 to $54 billion in 1974. The increase in pension outlays represents the flood of new retirees as the population aged as well as generous new benefits under Kennedy and Johnson. The culmination was the "indexing" of old-age pensions—tying them to the cost of living—under

Nixon in 1972. In recent years generational jealousies, budget stringencies, and actuarial doomsaying have created pressure for reducing the benefits to the retired, but few besides right-wing ideologues consider "social security" a pernicious program, and codgers are not yet treated as quasi-criminals.

The sharpest indictment of the War on Poverty today targets the welfare issue, left unsettled after the failure of Nixon's Family Assistance Program. Murray, Mead, and others believe that AFDC created a permanently crippled class of dependents by rewarding antisocial behavior. In effect, the Great Society denied the distinction between worthy and unworthy poor and so withdrew respect for work, personal effort, and individual responsibility. Not only did welfare go to the undeserving; it created an ever-larger cohort of the undeserving, now often called the "underclass," men and women stuck unalterably in a nightmare version of the culture of poverty—destitution, mental illness, drugs, violent crime, illegitimacy, prostitution—and doomed to pass it on to their children and grandchildren.

It would take us far afield to deal with these claims. They subsume a decade of social legislation and policy making beyond Kennedy, Johnson, and Nixon, and they target recent social experiences as well as those of the sixties and early seventies. They require us to consider more than the Great Society as defined here.

But leaving this objection aside for the moment, should we attribute the present plight of the ghettos and the present "welfare mess" to bad laws? Crime, illegitimacy, drug abuse, and divorce are undoubtedly more common among welfare families and the kind of people targeted by the War on Poverty than among middle-class suburbanites. But rates for all four social pathologies rose among white middle-class Americans who never got a cent from AFDC and never sent a son to the Job Corps, as well as among those who did. The social deterioration that we deplore, moreover, began in the mid-sixties, before any of the Great Society programs could have had much impact. Clearly some common toxin was at work besides the social legislation of the decade. It might be more valid to say "blame it on the sixties" than "blame it on the Great Society." The decade was a cultural watershed as well as a liberal interlude, and its moral and intellectual qualities eroded the guilt and the shame that hitherto had constrained behavior. In the end, Timothy Leary's "Turn on, tune in, drop out" might explain snowballing social pathologies better than Lyndon Johnson's Great Society.

We must keep other matters in mind as well. Any evaluation of the Great Society poverty programs must consider whether it was the quality of the programs or the extent of their funding that explains their limited results. Michael Harrington, a founding father, in 1968 attacked the War on Poverty as little more than a "skirmish." The country knew "how to abolish poverty" but did not want to invest the resources or accept the structural readjustments needed to accomplish it.[18] Tom Hayden of Students for a Democratic Society noted in 1966 that "the antipoverty program should evoke little optimism. The amount of money allotted is a pittance. . . ."[19] The Harrington-Hayden indictment is in fact part of a larger critique from the left that considers poverty a structural defect of capitalism which cannot be repaired except by massive income and wealth redistribution under some form of socialism.[20] No level of funding for categorical programs, they say, can solve the problems.[21]

Leaving aside the call for socialism—as likely now as universal peace—were the left critics right about the insufficiency of the Great Society? Certainly during the sixties itself, most of the programs were too modest to overcome the failings of existing social institutions. At no time during its life, for example, did OEO, the War on Poverty command-central, receive as much as $2 billion a year. As James Patterson notes, this was less than 1.5 percent of the federal budget, or one third of 1 percent of the gross national product. If every dollar had gone directly to the poor, they would have been between $50 and $70 richer individually per year.[22] The education programs suffered from the same miserly restraint. Title I of the ESEA, for example, received on average during the early 1970s about $1.5 billion a year, only 2.5 percent of the total national outlays on elementary and secondary public education.

Clearly the financial means to make the programs effective had not been forthcoming. But what if they had been? What if Head Start had not been at most a one-year program? What if the federal funds for the ESEA Title I had been five times the actual amount? What if the Job Corps had received $1 billion on average per year rather than $200 million? Conservatives would say that it would have been more money wasted. But of course there is no way of knowing. What we do know, however, is that to expect substantially more was not realistic. The War on Poverty, as it was, represented as much as the American public, in a time of unusual social generosity and middle-class optimism, would venture. The response was off the historical trend line of national behavior, reflecting an extraordinary convergence of short-lived political and economic circumstances, not to be repeated in the next thirty years.

The Great Society programs directed at the poor, then, were not spectacular successes in narrow terms. They did not eliminate poverty. But community well-being may be measured by feelings and mood as well as statistics. According to Sar Levitan, the veteran liberal social-policy expert, we must also factor in morale. "By offering hope for productive life and an escape from poverty, even relatively small investments in health care, education, employment, and training can make an important contribution to the nation's well-being."[23] Writing in 1972, Robert Levine, a former OEO official, suggested that the community action programs, at their best, served as substitutes for self-help agencies—unions, ethnic associations, cultural clubs—established early in the century by European immigrants. Like these, CAP's provided the experience and self-confidence needed to cope and prosper in the complex industrial society of the 1960s.

In effect, Levine is saying that community action, as its inventors and sponsors hoped and promised, did indeed nurture community competence. That in turn produced direct gains for specific individuals—advances that do not show up clearly in the aggregate statistics and the large-scale costs-benefits studies. Some of the poor used the programs, not as mechanisms for retraining and education, but to become administrators, community leaders, facilitators. Great Society programs provided the boost they needed to achieve middle-class status. Writing from the perspective of the mid-1990s, Paul Ylvisaker, another War on Poverty founder, described how community action had "built bridges between ghettos and the establishment over which an extraordinary percentage of contemporary [black] leaders have passed."[24] And it did. As early as 1966 a survey of community action agencies in nine large cities showed that they had hired more than five thousand nonprofessionals, 79 percent black, to work for the poverty programs. In fact, so pervasive was this policy that conservatives often denounced it as a boondoggle. What was a by-product in the case of community action was an explicit goal of Head Start: The programs would employ parents as aides in their children's programs.

And we should not ignore the benefits of summer job creation in the ghettos under the Neighborhood Youth Corps and other programs. Badly administered and even corrupt at times, they nevertheless kept thousands of young men occupied at something besides crime and mischief during the nervous summers of the mid-sixties.

But other conclusions, negative conclusions, are possible when considering diffuse, overall effects. One suggests that by providing jobs for the able and ambitious among the poor, the Great Society made the circumstances of the rest worse. The first effect of steady work at good wages was often, as Art Buchwald's imaginary community action board member remarked, to encourage beneficiaries to move out of the ghetto. Left behind without role models to encourage the work ethic and civic restraint were thousands who felt more helpless than ever.

And then there is the argument of dashed expectations. According to this proposition, the Great Society, by promising more than it could deliver, promoted disillusionment, rage, and violence among the poor. By this formula, the long, hot summers from 1965 on—and the white backlash and racial resentment that followed—derived from inevitably thwarted expectations. The Great Society, then, was at least indirectly a powerful corrosive reagent dissolving the connective tissue of America during the sixties.

The frustrated-expectations analysis serves a political purpose: It is a weapon of the political right aimed at the social welfare state. And yet it cannot be dismissed out of hand. The Johnson administration did in fact grossly oversell the Great Society programs. We only have to recall LBJ's dramatic bill-signing ceremonies proclaiming salvation at hand in some vital area of American life to clinch the point. All politicians exaggerate, but Lyndon Johnson carried overstatement to a new level—and at a time when millions yearned for change long delayed. It was not only a small circle of the politically literate who were exposed to these overheated enthusiasms. They were transmitted to the field by agents from 19th and M Street and disseminated through the nation's grassroots communities. They ignited hope among the poor and inevitably let them down. They were culpable in some measure for the bitterness and bile that stained the transactions of Americans as the sixties wound down.

But there was more to the Great Society than the War on Poverty. What about the health programs? How much did they improve the quality of American life?

National health care is terrain so craggy and forbidding that only the foolhardy venture to cross it. In the 1990s we live with an acute sense of crisis in the health field. Never before has medicine as science promised so much, and never before has medicine as a social institution seemed so problematical.

By now, after the great failed national debate of the mid-1990s, the tale is a familiar one. Medical costs are soaring in absolute real terms and as a proportion of the GNP. The United States has the most expensive health care system in the world, even in relation to its great wealth, and its outlays for medical services are rising faster than in many other places in the affluent world. At the same time few other national health systems are so capricious. Millions of Americans have no health insurance and rely on emergency rooms and other forms of medical handouts when they get sick or are injured. And even those with health insurance easily lose it through job loss or job change, while many who contract a serious illness or require some costly medical procedure do not qualify under their existing coverage and face bankruptcy or even death. And in the end we do not get very much for our money; Americans are not the longest-lived or healthiest people in the world. The problems of modern American health care overwhelm us by their intractability and, as we have in fact recently done, we want to throw up our hands in despair.

How much of our present plight derives from the Great Society? Clearly the medical programs of the 1960s did not contribute to the problem of inadequate coverage. Great Society health programs made medical services far more widely available than ever before. The proportion of the poor who failed to see a doctor in the course of the year fell from 28 percent in the mid-sixties, before Medicaid, to 17 percent in 1973. In fact, by 1970, the percentage of the poor who saw a doctor once a year or more approached that of high-income Americans. Annual hospital visits for the same group rose from fourteen per hundred in 1964 to twenty-four per hundred in 1974. In 1963, 58 percent of poor women saw doctors for prenatal care; 71 percent did so in 1970. The trend was similar for retirees. After Medicare, hospital utilization among those over sixty-five rose from 2,029 hospital days per thousand seniors in 1965–66 to almost three thousand days per thousand by 1968. Oldsters also went to the doctor more often after the adoption of Medicare than before. Undoubtedly some of this new medical involvement represents waste: subsidized hypochondria and other, more corrupt abuses. But much of it registers a reasonable search for health care previously unaffordable. And the positive results appear in the mortality statistics. One crucial index of the success of greater access to prenatal care is the rapid narrowing after 1965 of the infant mortality gap between white and black Americans. Similarly, life expectancy for all Americans rose more quickly in the fifteen years after 1965 than in the decade and a half preceding.

Liberals, then, may complain that Great Society health care and health delivery programs did not go far enough in meeting the needs of the American people, but no one can deny that they greatly expanded access to medical services and helped improve the health of Americans. It is in the matter of costs, primarily, that the Great Society medical programs have been faulted. Did Johnson and his colleagues, knowingly or carelessly, create a health care Dracula that is now draining the lifeblood of the nation?

In part. Medical cost increases are global and propelled by factors unrelated to the Great Society in the United States. Costs rise because of new medical technology, new clinical procedures, and new drugs. They rise because the population is aging. They rise because doctors are better trained. They rise because people want to live longer and feel better, but at the same time continue to smoke, drink, and loaf. None of this has very much to do with Great Society programs. In fact the surge in American medical costs began well before 1965. In 1950, for example, a day's stay in a hospital cost a patient $16. By 1960, before Medicare and Medicaid, it was up to $32, double the amount. By the early sixties, before the Great Society's impact, the rate of increase in hospital spending was already rising at the rate of almost 9 percent a year.

But some part of today's higher costs do come from Lyndon Johnson's programs. Joseph Califano, Johnson's right-hand man after mid-1965, admits it. Writing in the mid-eighties about the medical cost explosion, Califano embraces a central theme of this book: "We all contributed mightily" to the costs, he writes, "and most of the time we acted with the best of intentions."[25]

To enact Medicare Johnson allowed the hospitals leeway on reimbursement and permitted doctors to bill at rates that were "reasonable," "customary," and consistent with those "prevailing" in the local community. He allowed retirees to be insulated from the full cost of medical services. Medicare did have a "deductible" feature for physicians' fees but it was relatively small, and patients had only modest incentives to argue about the size of the bills the receptionist gave them as they left the doctor's office. Simultaneously, HEW officials, in interpreting the intent of the law, permitted hospitals to include as legitimate costs interest on debt and depreciation on buildings and equipment. Lacking serious cost containment features, Medicare and Medicaid allowed medical costs to balloon out of control.

The Johnson administration placed its faith in market forces to counteract medical cost inflation. To provide more doctors and health care workers, federal money during the 1960s, under the Health Professions and the Health Manpower acts, built a flock of new medical schools, induced established ones to increase their enrollments, and funded grants and loans to medical students. The number of doctors leaped. The nation's medical schools graduated eight thousand new MD's in 1965. They churned out double that number fourteen years later. In 1963 there were 143 doctors for every 100,000 Americans; by the mid-1980s there were 218. But the supply-side policies backfired. Many of the new doctors were specialists who, under the "reasonable" and "customary" formula, were entitled to charge more than their GP predecessors. As a whole physicians' fees rose between 1965–1974 by an average of 5.7 percent a year, quickly driving up the total cost of medical care.

The net outcome was frightening. Medicare in 1967, its first full fiscal year, covered 19 million people and cost a little more than $3 billion. Thereafter costs climbed at an average rate of 17 percent a year. By 1984 the nation was shelling out $63 billion annually, about twenty times as much as seventeen years before, though the amount covered only 30 million, less than 50 percent more people. Medicaid, subject to the same loose controls, also became a monster. A joint state-federal program for the poor and disabled that cost $3.6 billion in 1968, it grew to a $36 billion program by 1983, despite dedicated efforts from the mid-seventies on to clamp down on costs. This represents a rise in payments at an average rate between 1972 and 1981 of the same 17 percent per year as Medicare; far more, of course, than the growth of the overall consumer price index.

Adding it all up, it is not wrong to say that the Great Society helped make a healthier America. But it also—measured in non-medical ways—made a poorer America. On the other hand, it can be argued that the country is not made poorer by increasing its spending on health care, even if it is "disproportionate." After all, health is an economic "good" like automobiles or sirloin steaks, and if Americans want to spend their money on health, so be it. It can be said, however, that they are spending more per unit of health than they really need to; that they could get the amount of good health care they want at a lower price.

Better education to lift levels of understanding and awareness, not just to provide work skills and relieve poverty, was also a goal of the Great Society. Overall federal spending for all education expanded nearly seven times during the 1960s. During the years 1960–70 education's share of the GNP increased from 5.1 percent to 7.5 percent, an increase of almost half. All this money, it was assumed, would make Americans more knowledgeable and better informed.

It clearly did not. As everyone who reads the newspapers knows, Americans fall at the low end of almost every test of international science knowledge and mathematical competence. This abysmal performance apparently improved somewhat during the period of expanded federal education outlays, but substantial international differences remain and the results are not reassuring. Even less encouraging are the tests of absolute student performance over time. These strongly suggest deterioration during the very period that federal funding was climbing. During the mid-sixties SAT college-entrance scores began a long decline that lasted until about 1980. The argument that expanded opportunity for the poor and minorities to attend college explains the fall is probably not valid. The number taking the SAT's had already ballooned in the 1950s and scores remained as high as ever. Average test scores of high school pupils also show a flattening during the mid-1960s, though not as drastic as the SAT declines. And there is reason to believe that the deterioration took place disproportionately among the most able. Between the mid-1960s and the early 1980s, the proportion of the highest SAT scorers (at 700 plus) in the math portion declined from about 1.2 percent to well under 0.7 percent. A parallel trend occurred in the verbal part of the exam. Take all these together, and the reality is reasonably clear. As the chairman of the 1983 National Commission on Excellence in Education study noted, "For the first time in the history of our country, the educational skills of one generation will not surpass, will not equal, will not even approach, those of their parents."[26]

The Great Society, as we saw, also had a "new agenda," the policies aimed at enriching the quality of life in ways that appealed particularly to educated middle-class Americans. Can we factor it into our balance sheet?

It is easy to dismiss as insignificant or even frivolous Great Society programs like public broadcasting, the National Endowments in the Arts and Humanities, consumer and environmental protection, scenic beauty and billboard removal, and expanded national parks. Recent scholarly work on the endowments tends to dismiss their impact on culture. Alice Goldfarb Marquis, for example, while acknowledging the enormous surge after 1965 in the number of dance companies, theater troupes, symphony orchestras, opera groups, and museums, and a corresponding explosion of their public patronage, also claims that compared with arts and humanities funding by the states, by cities, and by private corporations, the federal government contributed rather modestly. As for overcoming "artistic deficit"—that is, encouraging excellence—the arts endowment accomplished very little, she says. America's most creative years of the post–World War Two period were the fifties and the early sixties, before the NEA was up and running.[27]

But that was just one sector. It is harder to fault public broadcasting, I believe. It did make accessible to millions information, knowledge, and experience that many would otherwise have found beyond easy reach. It made the "provinces" less provincial and nurtured the inner lives of thousands who could not afford frequent visits to New York, Boston, Chicago, or San Francisco.

As for Great Society environmental programs, however abused, inflated, bureaucratized, and distorted, they have cleaned the waters and the air, protected wildlife, preserved the landscape, and generally made America more beautiful and healthful. And by and large for most Americans the costs have been bearable, though some individuals and groups have no doubt paid a disproportionate price. Only if "wealth" is equated totally with personal ownership can one dismiss highway beautification, smoke abatement, cleaner water, new national recreation areas, and the rest as major additions to the American people's collective riches.

Praise for the quality-of-life programs may also appear indifferent to social equity. When millions are in want, when the ghettos are crumbling, when urban schools are grossly deficient, why should tax monies, even modest amounts, be diverted to the financially comfortable? In 1989 Robert Samuelson of *Newsweek* called public arts subsidies "a highbrow pork barrel."[28] I would argue that the middle class in this middle-class society also deserves regard. In any event, these were often the programs that worked best.

But times have changed and all aspects of the Great Society are under siege. We live in an era when globalization is creating a deep chasm between the best educated and skilled and everyone else. A relatively thin layer of highly literate and brainy Americans have left the rest behind and no longer have either contact with, or much sympathy for, them. Nor do they care very much about public goods. They can buy those they want—better schools, better access to art and culture, better vacation spots. They do not need the government to provide them.

But there was a time, a generation ago, when a significant portion of the upper middle class and the policy professionals felt more closely attached to their fellow Americans and believed they could make a great society for all. However imperfect the results, theirs were the best of intentions.

Notes

Prologue

1. Arthur Schlesinger, Jr., "The Challenge of Abundance," *The Reporter*, May 3, 1956, pp. 8–11.

2. Stephen Bailey, "A White House-Academic Dialogue," in Bertram Gross (ed.), *A Great Society?* (New York: Basic Books, 1968), p. xi.

3. Eric Goldman, *The Tragedy of Lyndon Johnson* (New York: Alfred A. Knopf, 1969), pp. 139 ff.

4. "SDS: Port Huron Statement," in Massimo Teodori (ed.), *The New Left: A Documentary History* (Indianapolis: The Bobbs-Merrill Company, 1969), p. 167. Goodwin, a kind of New Left fellow traveler, acknowledged his debt to the Port Huron Statement. See Goodwin, *Remembering America: A Voice From the Sixties* (Boston: Little, Brown and Company, 1988), p. 276.

5. *Public Papers of the Presidents of the United States, Lyndon B. Johnson, 1963–64* (Washington, D.C.: Government Printing Office, 1965), pp. 704–707.

6. Merle Miller, *Lyndon: An Oral Biography* (New York: G. P. Putnam's Sons, 1980), pp. 376–377.

Chapter One

1. Lawrence O'Brien Oral History, LBJ Library, Interview 1, p. 64.

2. Arthur M. Schlesinger, Jr., *A Thousand Days: John F. Kennedy in the White House* (Boston: Houghton Mifflin Company, 1965), pp. 99–100.

3. Lawrence O'Brien Oral History, LBJ Library, Interview 2, p. 310.

4. Lawrence O'Brien Oral History, LBJ Library, Interview 1, p. 102.

5. Robert Dallek, *Lone Star Rising: Lyndon Johnson and His Times, 1908–1960* (New York: Oxford University Press, 1991), p. 165.

6. Lawrence O'Brien Oral History, LBJ Library, Interview 1, p. 91.

7. Lawrence O'Brien, *No Final Victories: A Life in Politics, From John F. Kennedy to Watergate* (Garden City, N.Y.: Doubleday and Company, 1974), pp. 128–129.

8. *Newsweek,* April 16, 1962.

9. Harry McPherson Oral History, LBJ Library, Interview 1, p. 32.

10. Ewan Clague and Leon Greenberg, "Employment," in John T. Dunlop (ed.), *Automation and Technological Change* (Englewood Cliffs, N.J.: Prentice-Hall, 1962), p. 130.

11. John T. Dunlop, "Introduction: Problems and Potentials," in John T. Dunlop (ed.), *Automation and Technological Change* (Englewood Cliffs, N.J.: Prentice-Hall, 1962), p. 1.

12. Joseph Helfgot, *Professional Reforming: Mobilization for Youth and the Failure of Social Science* (Lexington, Mass.: Lexington Books, 1981), p. 47. In fact, Lewis was a liberal who blamed the dysfunctionality of the poor on their "marginal position in a class stratified . . . capitalist society." See Oscar Lewis, "The Culture of Poverty," in Daniel Moynihan (ed.), *On Understanding Poverty: Perspectives From the Social Sciences* (New York: Basic Books, 1968), p. 187. The term "blaming the victim" was actually used by William Ryan as the title of his book. See Ryan, *Blaming the Victim* (New York: Pantheon Books, 1971).

13. *Facts on File, 1962,* p. 93.

14. Leon Keyserling, for example. See Gardner Ackley, memo to the president, December 17, 1964. Papers of Lyndon Johnson, Welfare, Box 23, LBJ Library.

15. *Newsweek,* January 2, 1961.

16. *Facts on File, 1962,* p. 156.

17. Allen J. Matusow, *The Unravelling of America: A History of Liberalism in the 1960s* (New York: Harper and Row, 1984), p. 46.

18. Wilbur Cohen Oral History, LBJ Library, Tape 1, p. 9.

19. Quoted in Theodore Marmor, *The Politics of Medicare* (Chicago: Aldine Publishing Company, 1973), p. 36.

20. James L. Sundquist, *Politics and Policy: The Eisenhower, Kennedy, and Johnson Years* (Washington, D.C.: The Brookings Institution, 1968), p. 308.

21. Marmor, *The Politics of Medicare,* p. 40.

22. *Newsweek,* June 4, 1962.

23. Richard Harris, *A Sacred Trust* (New York: The New American Library, 1966), p. 124.

24. *Newsweek,* June 4, 1962.

25. Harris, *A Sacred Trust,* p. 142.

26. *Newsweek,* June 4, 1962.

27. Hugh Davis Graham, *The Uncertain Triumph: Federal Education Policy in the Kennedy and Johnson Years* (Chapel Hill: The University of North Carolina Press, 1984), p. 12.

28. *Ibid.,* p. 13.

29. *Ibid.,* p. 37.

30. Brandeis Conference, *Poverty and Urban Policy: Conference Transcript of 1973. Discussion of the Kennedy Administration Urban Poverty Programs and Policies* (JFK Library: Boston, Mass.), p. 162. Hereafter referred to as "Brandeis Transcript."

31. Brandeis Transcript, p. 182.

32. Daniel Moynihan, "The Professors and the Poor," in Moynihan (ed.), *On Understanding Poverty: Perspectives from the Social Sciences* (New York: Basic Books, 1969), p. 6.

33. Lawrence Friedman, "The Social and Political Context of the War on Poverty: An Overview," in Robert Haveman (ed.), *A Decade of Federal Antipoverty Programs* (New York: Academic Press, 1977), p. 51.

34. Theda Skocpol, *Protecting Soldiers and Mothers: The Political Origins of Social Policy in the United States* (Cambridge, Mass.: Harvard University Press, 1992), p. 41.

35. The term is that of Theodore White, the chronicler of presidential elections. See Robert Wood, *Whatever Possessed the President? Academic Experts and Presidential Policy, 1960–1988* (Amherst, Mass.: The University of Massachusetts Press, 1993), p. 33.

36. Brandeis Transcript, p. 159.

37. U.S. Senate, 88 Cong., 2 sess., *The War on Poverty: The Economic Opportunity Act of 1964* (Washington, D.C.: Government Printing Office, 1964), p. 2.

38. Quoted in Daniel Knapp and Kenneth Polk, *Scouting the War on Poverty: Social Reform Politics in the Kennedy Administration* (Lexington, Mass.: Heath Lexington Books, 1971), p. 27

39. Quoted in Daniel Moynihan, *Maximum Feasible Misunderstanding: Community Action in the War on Poverty* (New York: The Free Press, 1969), p. 54.

40. Richard Cloward and Lloyd E. Ohlin, *Delinquency and Opportunity: A Theory of Delinquent Gangs* (Glencoe, Ill.: The Free Press, 1960), p. 78.

41. *Ibid.*, p. 211.

42. Quote in Sar Levitan, *The Great Society's Poor Law: A New Approach to Poverty* (Baltimore: The Johns Hopkins Press, 1969), p. 19.

43. Quoted in Peter Marris and Martin Rein, *Dilemmas of Social Reform: Poverty and Community Action in the United States* (New York: Atherton Press, 1969), p. 14.

44. Moynihan, *Maximum Feasible Misunderstanding*, p. 44.

45. Mobilization for Youth, "A Proposal for the Prevention and Control of Delinquency by Expanding Opportunities" (second edition 1962), p. 21.

46. Moynihan, *Maximum Feasible Misunderstanding*, p. 58.

47. Marris and Rein, *Dilemmas of Social Reform*, p. 22.

48. Frances Fox Piven, "Low Income People and the Political Process," in Richard Cloward and Frances Fox Piven, *The Politics of Turmoil: Essay on Poverty, Race, and the Urban Crisis* (New York: Pantheon Books, 1972), pp. 85–86.

49. Jack Newfield, "The Story of Mobilization for Youth: An Old Theory Put to the Test," *New York Post*, August 30, 1964.

50. Harold H. Weissman, "Overview of the Community Development Program," in Harold H. Weissman (ed.), *Community Development in the Mobilization for Youth Experience* (New York: Association Press, 1969), p. 26.

51. See Newfield, "The Story of Mobilization for Youth."

52. Brandeis Transcript, p. 52.

53. Jack Conway Oral History, LBJ Library, Interview 1, p. 5.

54. Knapp and Polk, *Scouting the War on Poverty*, p. 109.

55. Quoted in James L. Sundquist, "Origins of the War on Poverty," in Sund-

quist (ed.), *On Fighting Poverty: Perspectives From Experience* (New York: Basic Books, 1969), p. 7.

56. Gardner Ackley Oral History, LBJ Library, Tape 1, p. 9.

57. Sundquist, "Origins of the War on Poverty," p. 20.

58. Quoted in Levitan, *The Great Society's Poor Law,* p. 15.

59. Matusow, *The Unravelling of America,* p. 120.

60. Sundquist, "Origins of the War on Poverty," p. 20.

61. Levitan, *The Great Society's Poor Law,* p. 17.

Chapter Two

1. Quoted in John C. Donovan, *The Politics of Poverty* (New York: Pegasus, 1967), p. 18.

2. Lawrence O'Brien Oral History, LBJ Library, Interview 8, p. 1,261.

3. Harry McPherson Oral History, LBJ Library, Interview 4, p. 3.

4. Quoted in Robert S. McNamara, *In Retrospect: The Tragedy and Lessons of Vietnam* (New York: Times Books, 1995), p. 198.

5. *Newsweek,* December 9, 1963.

6. Lawrence O'Brien Oral History, LBJ Library, Interview 6, p. 881.

7. Joseph A. Califano, Jr., *America's Health Care Revolution: Who Lives? Who Dies? Who Pays?* (New York: Random House, 1986), p. 50.

8. Cliff Carter, memo to Jack Valenti, March 7, 1964. White House Central Files, Box 76, LBJ Library.

9. Allen Matusow, *The Unravelling of America: A History of Liberalism in the 1960s* (New York: Harper and Row, 1984), p. 57.

10. Walter Heller, "President Johnson and the Economy," in James M. Burns (ed.), *To Heal and to Build: The Programs of President Lyndon B. Johnson* (New York: McGraw-Hill Book Company, 1968), p. 153.

11. Lyndon Baines Johnson, *The Vantage Point: Perspectives of the Presidency, 1963–1969* (New York: Holt, Rinehart and Winston, 1971), p. 71.

12. Matusow, *The Unravelling of America,* p. 121.

13. Walter Heller, memo to Theodore Sorensen, December 20, 1963. Papers of LBJ, Box 25, LBJ Library.

14. Johnson, *The Vantage Point,* p. 74.

15. Kermit Gordon Oral History, LBJ Library, Interview 4, p. 7.

16. Kermit Gordon Oral History, LBJ Library, Interview 4, p. 7.

17. *Public Papers of the Presidents of the United States, Lyndon B. Johnson, 1963–64,* vol. 1 (Washington, D.C.: U.S. Government Printing Office, 1965), pp. 112–118.

18. James L. Sundquist, *Politics and Policy: The Eisenhower, Kennedy, and Johnson Years* (Washington, D.C.: The Brookings Institution, 1968), p. 140.

19. Quoted in Harold Silver and Pamela Silver, *An Educational War on Poverty: American and British Policy-Making, 1960–1980* (Cambridge, England: Cambridge University Press, 1991), p. 81.

20. Brandeis Transcript, p. 92.

21. Charles Haar, *Between the Idea and the Reality: A Study in the Origin, Fate, and Legacy of the Model Cities Program* (Boston: Little, Brown and Company, 1975), p. 37.

22. Adam Yarmolinsky, "The Beginnings of OEO," in James L. Sundquist (ed.), *On Fighting Poverty: Perspectives From Experience* (New York: Basic Books, 1969), p. 51, footnote 2.

23. Yarmolinsky, Brandeis Conference, p. 287.

24. Yarmolinsky, "The Beginnings of OEO," in James Sundquist (ed.), *On Fighting Poverty*, p. 39.

25. U.S. Senate, 88 Cong., 2 sess., *The War on Poverty: The Economic Opportunity Act of 1964* (Washington, D.C.: Government Printing Office, 1964), p. 1.

26. *Ibid.*, pp. 1–6.

27. U.S. House of Representatives, 88 Cong., 2 sess., Committee on Education and Labor, Subcommittee on the War on Poverty, *Hearing on the War on Poverty*, pp. 21–22.

28. *Ibid.*, pp. 26–30.

29. *Ibid.*, p. 302.

30. *Ibid.*, p. 422.

31. Dr. R. H. Edwin Espy to Lyndon Johnson, New York, January 9, 1964. Papers of Lyndon Johnson, Welfare, Box 25, LBJ Library.

32. *New York Times,* July 1, 1964.

33. "Statement by the AFL-CIO Executive Council," February 21, 1964. Papers of Lyndon Johnson, Box 25, LBJ Library.

34. *New York Times,* "News of the Week in Review," March 29, 1964.

35. *New York Times,* April 1, 1964.

36. AUR Washington Newsletter by Congressman O. C. Fisher, August 13, 1964. Papers of Lyndon Johnson, Welfare, Box 25, LBJ Library.

37. U.S. House of Representatives, 88 Cong., 2 sess., War on Poverty Hearings, p. 332.

38. Lawrence O'Brien Oral History, LBJ Library, Interview 8, p. 1,266.

39. *New York Times,* April 10, 1964.

40. *New York Times,* March 23, 1964.

41. U.S. Senate, 88 Cong., 2 sess., Select Committee on Poverty Hearings, p. 207.

42. U.S. Senate, 88 Cong., 2 sess., Select Committee Hearings on the Economic Opportunity Act, pp. 72–73, 84, 107–108.

43. U.S. Senate, 88 Cong., 2 sess., War on Poverty Hearings, pp. 185–197.

44. *New York Times,* July 22, 1964.

45. Christopher Weeks, *Job Corps: Dollars and Dropouts* (Boston: Little, Brown, 1967), pp. 119–120.

46. *New York Times,* August 6, 1964.

47. Rowland Evans and Robert Novak, *Lyndon B. Johnson: The Exercise of Power* (New York: The New American Library, 1966), p. 432.

48. *New York Times,* August 21, 1964.

49. Nelson Polsby, "Strategic Considerations," in Milton C. Cummings, Jr., *The National Election of 1964* (Washington, D.C.: The Brookings Institution, 1966), pp. 87–88; *Facts on File Yearbook, 1964,* p. 314.

50. *Facts on File, 1964,* p. 314.

51. Eric Goldman, *The Tragedy of Lyndon Johnson* (New York: Alfred A. Knopf, 1969), pp. 232–233.

52. Vaughn Davis Bornet, *The Presidency of Lyndon B. Johnson* (Lawrence, Kans.: University Press of Kansas, 1983), p. 103.

Chapter Three

1. *Newsweek,* February 1, 1965.
2. Lawrence O'Brien Oral History, LBJ Library, Interview 11, p. 1485.
3. Eric Goldman, *The Tragedy of Lyndon Johnson* (New York: Alfred A. Knopf, 1969), p. 284.
4. Lawrence O'Brien, *No Final Victories: A Life in Politics from John F. Kennedy to Watergate* (Garden City, N.Y.: Doubleday and Company, 1974), p. 178.
5. Goldman, *The Tragedy of Lyndon Johnson,* p. 260.
6. O'Brien, *No Final Victories,* p. 182.
7. Lawrence O'Brien Oral History, LBJ Library, Interview 1, p. 64.
8. Lawrence O'Brien Oral History, LBJ Library, Interview 11, p. 1,487.
9. Joseph A. Califano, Jr., *The Triumph and Tragedy of Lyndon Johnson: The White House Years* (New York: Simon and Schuster, 1991), pp. 25–26.
10. Merle Miller, *Lyndon: An Oral Biography* (New York: G. P. Putnam's Sons, 1980), p. 390.
11. Lawrence O'Brien Oral History, LBJ Library, Interview 6, p. 840.
12. Peter A. Corning, *The Evolution of Medicare: From Idea to Law* (Washington, D.C.: Government Printing Office, 1969), p. 110.
13. Theodore R. Marmor, *The Politics of Medicare* (Chicago: The Aldine Publishing Company, 1973), p. 60.
14. Wilbur Mills Oral History, LBJ Library, Interview 1, p. 14.
15. Quoted in David Blumenthal, "Medicare: The Beginnings," in David Blumenthal, Mark Schlesinger, and Pamela Brown Drumheller (eds.), *Renewing the Promise: Medicare and Its Reform* (New York: Oxford University Press, 1988), p. 13.
16. Richard Harris, *A Sacred Trust* (New York: The New American Library, 1966), p. 187.
17. Miller, *Lyndon,* p. 410.
18. *New York Times,* March 24, 1965.
19. Harris, *A Sacred Trust,* pp. 190–191.
20. Lawrence O'Brien letter to Clinton Anderson, August 27, 1965. White House Central Files, Box 75, LBJ Library.
21. Eugene Feingold, *Medicare: Policy and Politics: A Case Study and Political Analysis* (San Francisco: Chandler Publishing Company, 1966), p. 144.
22. Marmor, *The Politics of Medicare,* p. 71.
23. Wilbur Cohen, memo to the president, June 17, 1965. White House Central Files, Box 75, LBJ Library.
24. Mike Manatos letter to Lawrence O'Brien, May 20, 1965. White House Central Files, Box 75, LBJ Library.
25. *New York Times,* June 9, 1965.
26. Feingold, *Medicare: Policy and Politics,* p. 147.
27. John Gardner Oral History, LBJ Library, Tape 1, pp. 14–15.
28. Harris, *A Sacred Trust,* p. 213.
29. Wilbur Cohen, "From Medicare to National Health Insurance," in David

C. Warner (ed.), *Toward New Human Rights: The Social Policies of the Kennedy and Johnson Administrations* (Austin: University of Texas Press, 1977), pp. 146–147.

30. Lawrence O'Brien Oral History, LBJ Library, Interview 11, p. 1,543.

31. Elizabeth Wickenden to Lyndon Johnson, New York City, August 5, 1965. White House Central Files, Box 75, LBJ Library.

32. Horace Busby, n.d., memo to Jack Valenti, Douglass Cater, Bill Moyers, and Marvin Watson. White House Central Files, Box 75, LBJ Library.

33. Goldman, *The Tragedy of Lyndon Johnson*, pp. 295–296.

34. Miller, *Lyndon*, p. 407.

35. Philip Meranto, *The Politics of Federal Aid to Education in 1965: A Study in Political Innovation* (Syracuse: Syracuse University Press, 1967), p. 109.

36. John Gardner Oral History, LBJ Library, Interview 1, p. 9.

37. Meranto, *The Politics of Federal Aid to Education in 1965*, p. 70.

38. Hugh Davis Graham, *The Uncertain Triumph: Federal Education Policy in the Kennedy and Johnson Years* (Chapel Hill: The University of North Carolina Press, 1984), p. 63.

39. Allen Matusow, *The Unraveling of America: A History of Liberalism in the 1960s* (New York: Harper and Row, 1984), p. 222.

40. Meranto, *The Politics of Federal Aid to Education in 1965*, p. 69.

41. Eugene Eidenberg and Roy D. Morey, *An Act of Congress: The Legislative Process and the Making of Education Policy* (New York: W. W. Norton and Company, 1969), p. 100.

42. Julie Roy Jeffrey, *Education for Children of the Poor: A Study of the Origins and Implementation of the Elementary and Secondary Education Act of 1965* (Columbus: Ohio State University Press, 1978), p. 83.

43. Eidenberg and Morey, *An Act of Congress*, p. 95.

44. *Ibid.*, p. 123.

45. *Ibid.*, p. 129.

46. U.S. Senate, 89 Cong., 1 sess., Hearings Before the Senate Subcommittee on Education of the Committee on Labor and Public Welfare, pp. 511, 513.

47. Jeffrey, *Education for Children of the Poor*, p. 97.

48. *New York Times,* July 16, 1965.

49. Lawrence O'Brien Oral History, LBJ Library, Interview 13, p. 1,724.

50. Quoted in Martin V. Melosi, "Lyndon Johnson and Environmental Policy," in Robert A. Divine (ed.), *The Johnson Years, Volume II: Vietnam, the Environment, and Science* (Lawrence, Kans.: University of Kansas Press, 1987), p. 121.

51. Lewis L. Gould, *Lady Bird Johnson and the Environment* (Lawrence, Kans.: University of Kansas Press, 1988), p. 39.

52. Charles Haar Oral History, LBJ Library, Tape 1, pp. 4, 17.

53. *Ibid.*, p. 23.

54. *Ibid.*, p. 32.

55. Gould, *Lady Bird Johnson and the Environment*, p. 54; *New York Times,* January 5, 1965.

56. Gould, *Lady Bird Johnson*, p. 55.

57. *Public Papers of the Presidents of the United States. Lyndon B. Johnson, 1965* (Washington, D.C.: Government Printing Office, 1966), Book 1, pp. 155–165.

58. *Ibid.*, p. 1,034.

59. Miller, *Lyndon,* p. 403.

60. Gould, *Lady Bird Johnson and the Environment,* p. 243.

61. *Ibid.,* p. 74.

62. *New York Times,* May 27, 1965.

63. Henry Wilson, memo to the president, September 12, 1965. Aides Files/ Wilson, Box 8, LBJ Library.

64. Gould, *Lady Bird Johnson and the Environment,* p. 146.

65. Larry O'Brien, memo to the president, September 18, 1965. Aides Files/ Wilson, Box 8, LBJ Library.

66. "Remarks of the President at the Signing Ceremony of the Highway Beautification Act." Highway Beautification Box 2, LBJ Library.

67. Gary O. Larson, *The Reluctant Patron: The United States Government and the Arts, 1943–1965* (Philadelphia: University of Pennsylvania Press, 1983), p. 181.

68. Larson, *The Reluctant Patron,* p. 162.

69. Quoted in Laura Louann Atkins Temple, "Pathfinders for the Imagination: The Evolution of Presidential Support for the Arts, 1961–1965," M.A. Thesis, University of Texas, Austin, 1990, p. 60.

70. Harry McPherson Oral History, LBJ Library, Interview 1, Tape 2, p. 28.

71. Gould, *Lady Bird Johnson and the Environment,* p. 23.

72. *Public Papers of the Presidents, Lyndon Johnson, 1965,* vol. 1, p. 8.

73. U.S. Senate Special Subcommittee on Arts and Humanities of the Committee on Labor and Public Welfare, *National Arts and Humanities Foundations, Hearings,* p. 219.

74. *Ibid.,* p. 416.

75. Legislative Background of the Arts and Humanities Foundation, 1965. Box 1, LBJ Library.

76. Larson, *The Reluctant Patron,* p. 216.

77. *The National Council on the Arts and the National Endowment for the Arts During the Administration of President Lyndon B. Johnson,* vol. 1, p. 21. Administrative History of the National Endowment of the Arts, Box 1, LBJ Library.

78. Joseph Wesley Zeigler, *Arts in Crisis: The National Endowment for the Arts Versus America* (Chicago: A Capella Books, 1994), p. 16.

79. *Washington Post,* September 30, 1965.

80. *New York Times,* August 10, 1965.

81. Vaughan Davis Bornet, *The Presidency of Lyndon B. Johnson* (Lawrence, Kans.: University Press of Kansas, 1983), p. 134.

82. James L. Sundquist, *Politics and Policy, The Eisenhower, Kennedy and Johnson Years* (Washington, D.C.: The Brookings Institution, 1968), p. 3.

83. Goldman, *The Tragedy of Lyndon Johnson,* p. 334.

84. Charles Haar Oral History, LBJ Library, Tape 1, pp. 35 ff.

Chapter Four

1. Lyndon B. Johnson, *The Vantage Point: Perspectives of the Presidency, 1963–1969* (New York: Holt, Rinehart and Winston, 1971), p. 323.

2. *Newsweek,* March 29, 1965, p. 23.

3. William Haddad, "Mr. Shriver and the Savage Politics of Poverty," *Harper's Magazine,* December 27, 1965, p. 45.

4. Edward Zigler and Jeanette Valentine (eds.), *Project Head Start: A Legacy of the War on Poverty* (New York: The Free Press, 1979), p. 56.

5. Remark at the Brandeis Conference. See Brandeis Transcript, p. 147.

6. Paul E. Peterson and J. David Greenstone, "The Mobilization of Low-Income Communities through Community Action," in Robert H. Haveman (ed.), *A Decade of Federal Antipoverty Programs* (New York: Academic Press, 1977), p. 246.

7. Bernard Gifford, "War on Poverty: Assumptions, History, and Results, a Flawed but Important Effort," in Marshall Kaplan and Peggy Cuciti (eds.), *The Great Society and Its Legacy: Twenty Years of U.S. Social Policy* (Durham, N.C.: Duke University Press, 1986), p. 68.

8. Robert Levine, *The Poor Ye Need Not Have With You: Lessons From the War on Poverty* (Cambridge, Mass.: The M.I.T. Press, 1970), p. 55.

9. The term was first publicized by Charles Silberman in his influential 1964 book, *Crisis in Black and White* (New York: Random House, 1964), pp. 308 ff.

10. R. H. Upton to Sargent Shriver, York, Alabama, August 8, 1965. Papers of LBJ, Box 127, LBJ Library.

11. *Sunday News,* August 16, 1964.

12. Joseph Helfgot, *Professional Reforming: Mobilization for Youth and the Failure of Social Science* (Lexington, Mass.: Lexington Books, 1981), p. 70 ff.

13. Herbert Krosney, *Beyond Welfare: Poverty in the Supercity* (New York: Holt, Rinehart, and Winston, 1966), p. 29.

14. The words are those of Harold H. Weissman in *Community Development in the Mobilization for Youth Experience* (New York: Association Press, 1969), p. 27.

15. *New York Times,* October 13, 1965.

16. U.S. House of Representatives, 88 Cong., 2 sess., Committee on Education and Labor, Subcommittee on the War on Poverty, p. 797.

17. Quoted in John C. Donovan, *The Politics of Poverty* (New York: Pegasus, 1967), p. 124.

18. Erwin Knoll and Jules Witcover, "Fighting Poverty—and City Hall," *The Reporter,* June 3, 1965, p. 21.

19. *New York Times,* December 3, 1965.

20. Allen Matusow, *The Unravelling of America: A History of Liberalism in the 1960s* (New York: Harper and Row, 1984), p. 248.

21. *Ibid.,* p. 248.

22. Tom Hayden and Carl Wittman, "Summer Report: Newark Community Union," pamphlet in the Tamiment Library, New York University.

23. *New York Times,* April 18, 1965.

24. *Washington Post,* April 14, 1965.

25. Harold Silver and Pamela Silver, *An Educational War on Poverty: American and British Policy-Making, 1960–1980* (Cambridge, England: Cambridge University Press, 1991), p. 121.

26. Quoted in Irving Lazar, "Which Citizens to Participate in What?" in Edgar S. Cahn and Barry A. Passett (eds.), *Citizen Participation: Effecting Community Change* (New York: Praeger Publishers, 1971), p. 104.

27. Tom Wolfe, *Radical Chic & Mau-Mauing the Flak-Catchers* (New York: Bantam Books, 1971), p. 144.

28. Louis A. Zurcher, Jr., *Poverty Warriors: The Human Experience of Planned Social Intervention* (Austin: University of Texas Press, 1970), pp. 243–245, 274–275.

29. Krosney, *Beyond Welfare*, pp. 35 ff.

30. *New York Times*, October 13, 1965.

31. *New York Times*, October 16, 1965.

32. *New York Times*, October 15, 1965.

33. *Ibid.*, October 15, 1965.

34. *New York Times*, October 16, 1965.

35. Gregory Farrell, "The View from the City: Community Action in Trenton," in James L. Sundquist (ed.), *On Fighting Poverty: Perspectives From Experience* (New York: Basic Books, 1969), p. 147.

36. *New York Times*, October 20, 1965.

37. Zurcher, *Poverty Warriors*, p. 16.

38. *Ibid.*, p. 26.

39. *Ibid.*, p. 39.

40. Mrs. I. Steinberg to President Johnson, Fairlawn, New Jersey, December 2, 1965. White House Central Files, Box 10, LBJ Library.

41. J. D. Magid to President Johnson, Bellrose, New York, December 4, 1965. White House Central Files, Box 10, LBJ Library.

42. Mrs. William Clark to President Johnson, Caseyville, Illinois, December 1, 1965. White House Central Files, Box 10, LBJ Library.

43. Jean Gettle to President Johnson, Tillamook, Oregon, December 7, 1965. White House Central Files, Box 10, LBJ Library.

44. Walter Hormell to President Johnson, Beverly Hills, California, December 1, 1965. White House Central Files, Box 10, LBJ Library.

45. Richard C. Schalich to President Johnson, Marietta, Georgia, November 19, 1965. White House Central Files, Box 10, LBJ Library.

46. Bill Crook, memo to Hayes Redmon, September 1, 1965. Papers of LBJ, Box 127, LBJ Library.

47. *New York Times*, June 1, 1965.

48. *New York Times*, June 2, 1965.

49. William C. Selover, "The View From Capitol Hill: Harassment and Survival," in Sundquist, *On Fighting Poverty*, p. 169.

50. *New York Times*, April 28, 1965.

51. Joseph A. Califano, Jr., *The Triumph and Tragedy of Lyndon Johnson: The White House Years* (New York: Simon and Schuster, 1991), p. 78.

52. Wilbur Cohen Oral History, LBJ Library, Tape 3, p. 10.

53. James Gaither Oral History, LBJ Library, Tape 1, p. 10.

54. Walter Reuther to Lyndon Johnson, Detroit, June 26, 1964. Papers of Lyndon Johnson, Welfare, Box 25, LBJ Library.

55. *New York Times*, April 15, 1966; Shirley Scheibla, *Poverty Is Where the Money Is* (New Rochelle, N.Y.: Arlington House, 1968), pp. 234–237.

56. *Washington Post*, July 6, 1965.

57. *Newsweek*, April 26, 1965, p. 29.

58. William Selover, "The View From Capitol Hill," p. 166.

59. *New York Times,* June 30, 1965.

60. John G. Woodford, "The Politics of Local Representation: The Administration of the Community Action Program, 1964–1966," in Sundquist, *On Fighting Poverty,* p. 83.

61. See enclosure in Sargent Shriver, memo to Bill Moyers and Jack Valenti, July 13, 1965. Papers of Lyndon Johnson, Box 26, LBJ Library.

62. *Washington Post,* August 1, 1965.

63. Mark Hatfield to the president, Salem, Oregon, July 2, 1965. Papers of Lyndon Johnson, Box 128, LBJ Library.

64. *New York Times,* June 8, 1965.

65. George Saunders to Lyndon Johnson, Austin, Texas, July 26, 1965. Papers of Lyndon Johnson, Box 129, LBJ Library.

66. *Newsweek,* September 13, 1965, p. 26.

67. *Washington Post,* August 4 and 21, 1965.

68. *New York Times,* February 6, 1966.

69. *U.S. News & World Report,* December 27, 1965, p. 55.

70. The best brief summaries of these results can be found in Sar A. Levitan, *The Great Society's Poor Law: A New Approach to Poverty* (Baltimore: The Johns Hopkins Press, 1969), pp. 291–306; and Levine, *The Poor Ye Need Not Have With You,* pp. 121–128.

71. Sargent Shriver to the editor of the *Washington Post,* March 15, 1965. Papers of Lyndon Johnson, Welfare, Box 23, LBJ Library.

72. Scheibla, *Poverty Is Where the Money Is,* p. 102.

73. Levitan, *The Great Society's Poor Law,* p. 166.

74. Edgar S. Cahn and Jean C. Cahn, "The War on Poverty: A Civilian Perspective," *The Yale Law Journal,* July 1964, pp. 1317–1352.

75. Reich, a Yale Law School professor, created a sensation in 1970 with the publication of *The Greening of America,* a book that predicted the demise of "Consciousness II," the repressive, "square" state of mind based on "the state, laws, technology, manufactured goods" that characterized America from the previous century through the early sixties. This old *Zeitgeist* was fast giving way to the freer, less inhibited culture Reich called Consciousness III.

76. Charles Reich, "The New Property," *The Yale Law Journal,* April 1964, pp. 733–787.

77. *New York Times,* February 20, 1966.

78. Levitan, *The Great Society's Poor Law,* p. 180.

79. Sargent Shriver, memo to Bill Moyers, April 14, 1965. Papers of Lyndon Johnson, Box 26, LBJ Library.

80. Edward Zigler and Karen Anderson, "An Idea Whose Time Had Come: The Intellectual and Political Climate For Head Start," in Zigler and Valentine (eds.), *Project Head Start,* p. 52.

81. Joseph A. Califano, Jr., "Head Start: A Retrospective View: The Founders," in Zigler and Valentine (eds.), *Project Head Start,* p. 77.

82. Edward Zigler and Susan Muenchow, *Head Start: The Inside Story of America's Most Successful Educational Experiment* (New York: Basic Books, 1992), p. 26.

83. Zigler and Anderson, "An Idea Whose Time Had Come," p. 16.

84. Zigler and Valentine (eds.), *Project Head Start,* p. 61.

85. Quoted in Zigler and Muenchow, *Head Start,* p. 43.

86. Polly Greenberg, *The Devil Has Slippery Shoes: A Biased Biography of the Child Development Group of Mississippi* (London: The Macmillan Company, 1969), p. 23.

87. *Ibid.,* p. 44.

88. *Ibid.,* p. 44.

89. *Ibid.,* p. 268.

90. See interview of Shriver in Zigler and Valentine (eds.), *Project Head Start,* pp. 61 ff.

91. Lady Bird Johnson writing in Califano, "Head Start, A Retrospective View," in Zigler and Valentine (eds.), *Project Head Start,* p. 45.

92. *New York Times,* September 1, 1965.

93. Sargent Shriver, memo to the president, October 20, 1965. Papers of Lyndon Johnson, Box 26, LBJ Library.

94. Charles Schultze, memo to the president, September 18, 1965. Papers of Lyndon Johnson, Box 26, LBJ Library.

95. Califano, *The Triumph and Tragedy of Lyndon Johnson,* pp. 79–80.

Chapter Five

1. Califano's own description. See Joseph A. Califano, Jr., *The Triumph and Tragedy of Lyndon Johnson: The White House Years* (New York: Simon and Schuster, 1991), p. 18.

2. Lyndon Baines Johnson, *The Vantage Point: Perspectives of the Presidency, 1963–1969* (New York: Holt, Rinehart and Winston, 1971), p. 324.

3. Nancy Zaroulis and Gerald Sullivan, *Who Spoke Up? American Protest Against the War in Vietnam, 1963–1975* (Garden City, N.Y.: Doubleday and Company, 1984), p. 108.

4. Quoted in Eric Goldman, *The Tragedy of Lyndon Johnson* (New York: Alfred A. Knopf, 1969), p. 427.

5. *The New Republic,* October 16, 1965, p. 4.

6. Lady Bird Johnson, *A White House Diary* (New York: Holt, Rinehart and Winston, 1970), entry for February 22, 1966, p. 362.

7. Quoted in Allen Matusow, *The Unravelling of America: A History of Liberalism in the 1960s* (New York: Harper and Row, 1984), p. 175.

8. *New York Times,* October 19, 1965.

9. *U.S. News & World Report,* December 13, 1965, p. 29.

10. *New York Times,* December 5, 1965.

11. Merle Miller, *Lyndon: An Oral Biography* (New York: G. P. Putnam's Sons, 1980), p. 453.

12. Joseph Califano, memo to the president, December 23, 1965. Papers of Lyndon B. Johnson, Box 26, LBJ Library.

13. *New York Times,* January 2, 1966.

14. *New York Times,* January 3, 1966.

15. *Ibid.*

16. *Public Papers of the Presidents of the United States, Lyndon B. Johnson, 1966,* Book 1, p. 4.

17. *Newsweek,* January 24, 1966, p. 21.

18. *Ibid.,* p. 35.

19. *Newsweek,* February 14, 1966, p. 15.

20. *New York Times,* April 26, 1966.

21. *New York Times,* September 29, 1966.

22. "The Late, Great Society," *The New Republic,* April 9, 1966, pp. 5–6.

23. Califano, memo to the president, December 18, 1965. Papers of Lyndon Johnson, Box 26, LBJ Library.

24. White House Central Files, Box 166, LBJ Library.

25. *Washington Post,* February 2–13, 1966.

26. Sam Gibbons to Lyndon Johnson, September 13, 1966. Papers of Lyndon, Box 125, LBJ Library.

27. *New York Times,* March 26, 1966.

28. *New York Times,* May 29, 1966; *Washington Post,* May 29, 1966.

29. *Washington Post,* March 28, 1966.

30. *New York Times,* September 27, 1966.

31. *Washington Post,* October 24, 1966.

32. Quoted in Arthur Schlesinger, Jr., *Robert Kennedy and His Times* (New York: Ballantine Books, 1973), p. 842.

33. Hugh Davis Graham, *The Uncertain Triumph: Federal Education Policy in the Kennedy and Johnson Years* (Chapel Hill: The University of North Carolina Press, 1984), p. 126.

34. *Ibid.,* p. 128.

35. *New York Times,* February 11, 1966.

36. Califano, *The Triumph and Tragedy of Lyndon Johnson,* p. 147.

37. Mark V. Nadel, *The Politics of Consumer Protection* (Indianapolis: The Bobbs-Merrill Company, 1971), p. 140.

38. *Ibid.,* p. 141.

39. Charles M. Haar, *Between the Idea and the Reality: A Study in the Origin, Fate and Legacy of the Model Cities Program* (Boston: Little, Brown and Company, 1975), p. 289–290.

40. Harry McPherson Oral History, LBJ Library, Interview 4, p. 15.

41. Haar, *Between the Idea and the Reality,* p. 59.

42. *New York Times,* November 4, 1966. This is from a long article written after Model Cities passage.

43. Califano, *The Triumph and the Tragedy of Lyndon Johnson,* p. 132.

44. Haar, *Between the Idea and the Reality,* p. 70.

45. *Ibid.,* p. 82.

46. *Ibid.,* pp. 73–74.

47. *Newsweek,* August 1, 1966.

48. *Newsweek,* July 25, 1966.

49. *Newsweek,* August 22, 1966, pp. 20–58.

50. U.S. Senate, 88 Cong., 2 sess., Hearing Before the Subcommittee on Executive Reorganization of the Committee on Government Operations of the U.S. Senate, Part I, pp. 25–26, 187–190.

51. Attachment to Califano memo to the president, August 19, 1966. Papers of Lyndon Johnson, Box 124, LBJ Library.

52. Haar, *Between the Idea and the Reality*, p. 80.

53. Quoted in Haar, *Between the Idea and the Reality*, p. 82.

54. *Washington Post*, August 28, 1966, p. E1.

55. *New York Times*, October 11, 1966.

56. *Newsweek*, February 21, 1966, p. 87.

57. James S. Coleman et al., *Equality of Educational Opportunity* (Washington, D.C.: U.S. Government Printing Office, 1966), p. 516.

58. *Newsweek*, November 7, 1966, p. 100.

59. *Newsweek*, September 26, 1966, p. 25.

60. *Newsweek*, September 19, 1966, pp. 30–31.

61. "Remarks of the President at a Luncheon for State Chairman of Dollars for Democrats Drive," August 24, 1966. Aides Files, Califano, Box 47, LBJ Library.

62. "Remarks of the President, Senate Majority Leader . . . and the Speaker of the House . . . on the Accomplishments of the 89th Congress . . ." Aides Files, Califano, Box 47, LBJ Library.

63. *New York Times*, November 4, 1966.

64. *New York Times*, "News of the Week in Review," November 6, 1966.

65. *Newsweek*, November 21, 1966, p. 34.

66. *Ibid.*, p. 28.

Chapter Six

1. Lady Bird Johnson, *A White House Diary* (New York: Holt, Rinehart and Winston, 1970), entry for January 5, 1967, p. 469.

2. Eric Goldman, *The Tragedy of Lyndon Johnson* (New York: Alfred A. Knopf, 1969), p. 521.

3. *Newsweek*, January 9, 1967.

4. Joseph Califano, Jr., *The Triumph and Tragedy of Lyndon Johnson* (New York: Simon and Schuster, 1991), p. 172.

5. Lady Bird Johnson, *A White House Diary*, entry for February 20, 1966, p. 362.

6. Doris Kearns, *Lyndon Johnson and the American Dream* (New York: Harper and Row, 1976), p. 295.

7. Robert Wood, *Whatever Possessed the President? Academic Experts and Presidential Policy, 1960–1988* (Amherst, Mass.: University of Massachusetts Press, 1993), p. 83.

8. Lawrence O'Brien Oral History, LBJ Library, Interview 19, p. 2,262.

9. Robert Wood, *Whatever Possessed the President?*, p. 82.

10. *Newsweek*, September 4, 1967.

11. Donald M. Baker, memo to the director (Shriver), January 20, 1967. Califano Files, Box 7, LBJ Library.

12. Lawrence O'Brien Oral History, LBJ Library, Interview 19, p. 2,262.

13. Richard Bolling, *Power in the House: A History of the Leadership of the House of Representatives* (New York: E. P. Dutton and Co., 1968), pp. 241–242, 251.

14. *Newsweek*, January 23, 1967.

15. *Wall Street Journal*, January 12, 1967.

16. *Newsweek*, January 23, 1967.

17. *Newsweek,* August 21, 1967.

18. *Newsweek,* August 14, 1967.

19. *Ibid.*

20. Joseph Califano, Jr., *The Triumph and Tragedy of Lyndon Johnson,* p. 210.

21. Lyndon Johnson, *The Vantage Point: Perspectives of the Presidency, 1963–1969* (New York: Holt, Rinehart and Winston, 1971), p. 84; Califano, *The Triumph and Tragedy of Lyndon Johnson,* p. 212.

22. Califano, *The Triumph and Tragedy of Lyndon Johnson,* p. 212.

23. *Ibid.,* p. 218.

24. Irwin Unger and Debi Unger, *Turning Point: 1968* (New York: Charles Scribner's Sons, 1988), p. 182.

25. *Facts On File, 1967,* p. 328.

26. Califano, *The Triumph and Tragedy of Lyndon Johnson,* p. 234.

27. Quoted in Donald Kettl, "The Economic Education of Lyndon Johnson: Guns, Butter, and Taxes," in Robert Divine (ed.), *The Johnson Years, Volume Two: Vietnam, the Environment, and Science* (Lawrence, Kans.: University of Kansas Press, 1987), p. 54.

28. Willard Wirtz to the president, July 21, 1967. Califano Files, Economy, Box 12, LBJ Library.

29. "Muriel," memo to Califano, April 11, 1967. Califano Files, Economy, Box 12, LBJ Library.

30. *Wall Street Journal,* June 21, 1967.

31. Wilbur Mills Oral History, LBJ Library, Interview 1, p. 14.

32. Quoted in Kettl, "The Economic Education of Lyndon Johnson," in Divine, *The Johnson Years,* p. 68.

33. *Wall Street Journal,* October 9, 1967.

34. Califano, *The Triumph and Tragedy of Lyndon Johnson,* p. 245.

35. *Wall Street Journal,* January 22, 1968.

36. Larry R. Jackson and William A. Johnson, *Protest by the Poor: The Welfare Rights Movement in New York City* (Lexington, Mass.: Lexington Books, 1974), p. 32.

37. The remark was made at the 1973 Brandeis Conference. See Brandeis Transcript, John F. Kennedy Library, pp. 345–346.

38. Califano, *The Triumph and Tragedy of Lyndon Johnson,* p. 246.

39. Jackson and Johnson, *Protest by the Poor,* p. 13.

40. Leon Shull to the president, Washington, D.C., December 21, 1967. White House Central Files, Box 164, LBJ Library.

41. James Fogerty to the president, New York, December 15, 1967. White House Central Files, Box 164, LBJ Library.

42. John Gardner, memo to the president, December 11, 1967. White House Central Files, Box 164, LBJ Library.

43. *Wall Street Journal,* July 19, 1967.

44. *Wall Street Journal,* October 20, 1967.

45. *Wall Street Journal,* May 4, 1967.

46. Lawrence O'Brien, memo to the president, January 24, 1967. LBJ Official Files, Califano, Box 7, LBJ Library.

47. Sargent Shriver, memo to Joseph Califano, April 25, 1967. Califano Files, Box 7, LBJ Library.

48. Bill Moyers, memo to the president (received LBJ Ranch, December 19, 1966). Papers of LBJ, Box 125, LBJ Library.

49. Sargent Shriver to the president, December 22, 1967. Papers of LBJ, Box 126.

50. Quoted in Herbert Kramer to Lloyd Hackler, December 1967. Papers of LBJ, Box 126, LBJ Library.

51. Quoted in Milbrey Wallin McLaughlin, *Evaluation and Reform: The Elementary Education Act of 1965, Title I* (Cambridge, Mass.: Ballinger Publishing Company, 1975), p. 37.

52. Hugh Davis Graham, *The Uncertain Triumph: Federal Education Policy in the Kennedy and Johnson Years* (Chapel Hill: The University of North Carolina Press, 1984), p. 151.

53. "Statement of the President on the ESEA and Proposed Quie Amendment," LBJ Papers, Califano, Box 12.

54. "Statement of . . . John Gardner . . . Before the Interstate and Foreign Commerce Committee of the . . . House . . . ," Legislative Background, Public Broadcasting, Box 1, LBJ Library.

55. Carnegie Commission on the Future of Public Broadcasting, *A Public Trust* (New York: Bantam Books, 1979), pp. 36–38.

56. *The Nation,* April 3, 1967, p. 421.

57. *Washington Post,* December 17, 1967.

58. *Newsweek,* December 25, 1967.

59. *Washington Post,* December 17, 1967.

60. *Facts On File, 1968,* p. 35.

61. James Gaither Oral History, LBJ Library, Tape 5, p. 27.

62. *Facts On File, 1968,* p. 123.

63. Califano, memo to the president, May 2, 1968. Califano Office Files, Box 17, LBJ Library.

64. *Wall Street Journal,* February 23, 1968.

65. Joseph P. Fried, *Housing Crisis U.S.A.* (New York: Praeger Publishers, 1971), p. 58.

66. *Business Week,* February 10, 1968, p. 24.

67. Joseph Barr, memo to the president, February 7, 1968. Legislative Background Truth-in-Lending, Box 3, LBJ Library.

68. *Business Week,* May 18, 1968.

69. *Saturday Review,* August 12, 1967.

70. *New Republic,* April 22, 1967.

71. *Wall Street Journal,* October 2, 1967.

72. Zeigler, *Arts in Crisis,* p. 20.

73. *New York Times,* October 1, 1968.

74. Alan Boyd, memo to the president, February 7, 1967. Aides Files, Douglass Cater, Box 96, LBJ Library.

75. Lewis Gould, *Lady Bird Johnson and the Environment* (Lawrence, Kans.: University of Kansas Press, 1988), p. 180.

76. *Ibid.,* p. 180.

77. This was the conclusion of the Washington State Roadside Council. See Gould, *Lady Bird Johnson and the Environment,* p. 186.

78. Gould, *Lady Bird Johnson and the Environment,* p. 193.

79. Califano, memo to the president, November 15, 1967. Califano Office Files, Box 16, LBJ Library.

80. Henry Fowler, memo to the president, January 27, 1968. Califano Office Files, Box 9, LBJ Library.

81. *Facts On File, 1968,* p. 111.

82. *Facts On File, 1968,* pp. 111–112.

83. Califano, memo to the president, March 28, 1968. Califano Office Files, Box 16, LBJ Library.

84. Califano, memo to the president, April 3, 1968. Califano Office Files, Box 17, LBJ Library.

85. *Facts On File, 1968,* p. 173.

86. Quoted in memo, Califano to the president, May 17, 1968. Califano Files, Box 17, LBJ Library.

87. Califano, *The Triumph and Tragedy of Lyndon Johnson,* p. 288.

88. *Report of the National Advisory Commission on Civil Disorders* (Washington, D.C., Government Printing Office, 1968), p. 1.

89. *Facts On File, 1968,* pp. 79–86.

90. *Ibid.,* pp. 210–211.

91. *Ibid.,* pp. 233–234.

92. Bertrand Harding Oral History, LBJ Library, Tape 2, p. 9.

93. Harry McPherson Oral History, LBJ Library, Interview 4, Tape 2, p. 19.

94. *Facts On File, 1968,* p. 198.

95. *Ibid.,* p. 277.

96. *Ibid.,* pp. 327–331.

97. *New York Times,* August 27, 1968.

98. *Facts On File, 1968,* p. 437.

99. *Ibid.,* p. 393.

100. Stephan Lesher, *George Wallace, American Populist* (Reading, Mass.: Addison-Wesley Publishing Company, 1994), p. 400.

101. *Facts On File Yearbook, 1968,* p. 414.

102. *Ibid.,* p. 455.

103. *Ibid.,* p. 414.

104. *Ibid.,* p. 453.

Chapter Seven

1. A. James Reichley, *Conservatives in an Age of Change: The Nixon and Ford Administrations* (Washington, D.C.: The Brookings Institution, 1981), pp. 235–236.

2. Vincent J. Burke and Vee Burke, *Nixon's Good Deed: Welfare Reform* (New York: Columbia University Press, 1974), p. 93.

3. James Patterson, *America's Struggle Against Poverty, 1900–1980* (Cambridge, Mass.: Harvard University Press, 1981), p. 187.

4. *Newsweek,* July 1, 1968, p. 29.

5. Edward E. Schwartz, "An End to the Means Test," in Robert Theobald (ed.), *The Guaranteed Income: Next Step in Economic Evolution?* (Garden City, N.Y.: Doubleday and Company, 1966), p. 132.

6. Quoted in Martin Anderson, *Welfare: The Political Economy of Welfare Reform in the United States* (Stanford, Calif.: The Hoover Institution, 1978), pp. 72–73.

7. Brandeis Transcript, pp. 56–57.

8. Patterson, *America's Struggle Against Poverty*, p. 172.

9. Burke and Burke, *Nixon's Good Deed*, p. 38.

10. *Ibid.*, p. 13.

11. Joseph A. Califano, Jr., *The Triumph and Tragedy of Lyndon Johnson: The White House Years* (New York: Simon and Schuster, 1991), p. 79.

12. See Robert H. Havemen, *Poverty Policy and Poverty Research: The Great Society and the Social Sciences* (Madison, Wis.: University of Wisconsin Press, 197), pp. 178 ff. For an especially harsh conclusion see Charles Murray, *Losing Ground: American Social Policy, 1950–1980* (New York: Basic Books, 1984), pp. 148–153.

13. Reichley, *Conservatives in an Age of Change*, p. 76.

14. Burke and Burke, *Nixon's Good Deed*, p. 45.

15. *Ibid.*, p. 56.

16. *Ibid.*, p. 59.

17. *Ibid.*, p. 63.

18. *Ibid.*, pp. 63–65.

19. *Ibid.*, p. 68.

20. *Ibid.*, p. 67.

21. *Ibid.*, p. 106.

22. Congressional Quarterly, *Nixon: The First Year of His Presidency* (Washington, D.C.: Congressional Quarterly, 1970), pp. 81A–84A.

23. Daniel Moynihan, *The Politics of a Guaranteed Income* (New York: Random House, 1973), p. 355.

24. Anderson, *Welfare*, p. 16.

25. Burke and Burke, *Nixon's Good Deed*, p. 127.

26. Moynihan, *The Politics of a Guaranteed Income*, pp. 226, 236.

27. Reichley, *Conservatives in an Age of Change*, p. 86.

28. *Ibid.*, p. 90.

29. Moynihan, *The Politics of a Guaranteed Income*, p. 403.

30. *Ibid.*, p. 412.

31. Burke and Burke, *Nixon's Good Deed*, p. 131.

32. *Ibid.*, p. 131.

33. Reichley, *Conservatives in an Age of Change*, p. 145.

34. Moynihan, *The Politics of a Guaranteed Income*, p. 473.

35. *Ibid.*, p. 513.

36. *Ibid.*, p. 514.

37. Burke and Burke, *Nixon's Good Deed*, pp. 161–163.

38. Moynihan, *The Politics of a Guaranteed Income*, p. 533.

39. Burke and Burke, *Nixon's Good Deed*, p. 183.

40. *Ibid.*, p. 184.

41. H. R. Haldeman, *The Haldeman Diaries: Inside the Nixon White House* (New York: G. P. Putnam's Sons, 1994), entry for April 28, 1969, p. 53.

42. *Ibid.*, entry for July 13, 1970, p. 181.

43. The order comes from Ehrlichman's notes dated November 7, 1970, in the White House Central Files, at the Nixon Library. Quoted in John Richard Greene, *The Limits of Power: The Nixon and Ford Administrations* (Bloomington, Ind.: Indiana University Press, 1992), p. 51.

44. Stephen E. Ambrose, *Nixon, Volume II: The Triumph of a Politician, 1962–1972* (New York: Simon and Schuster, 1989), p. 403.

45. Haldeman, *The Haldeman Diaries,* entry of May 10, 1971, p. 285.

46. Quoted in Michael B. Katz, *The Undeserving Poor: From the War on Poverty to the War on Welfare* (New York: Pantheon Books, 1989), pp. 111–112.

47. Ellen Jane Hollingsworth, "Ten Years of Legal Services for the Poor," in Robert Haveman (ed.), *A Decade of Federal Antipoverty Programs: Achievements, Failures, and Lessons* (New York: Academic Press, 1977), p. 296, n. 28.

48. *Facts on File, 1970,* p. 852.

49. Francis Palmer and Lucille Woolis Andersen, "Long-term Gains from Early Intervention: Findings from Longitudinal Studies," in Edward Zigler and Jeanette Valentine (eds.), *Project Head Start* (New York: The Free Press, 1979), p. 434.

50. James Gaither Oral History, LBJ Library, Tape 1, p. 7.

51. Barefoot Sanders, memo to the president, November 12, 1968. Sanders Personal Papers, Box 26, LBJ Library.

52. Robert Wood, memo to Joseph Califano, November 2, 1968. Office Files James Gaither, Box 22, LBJ Library.

53. William Safire, *Before the Fall: An Inside View of the Pre-Watergate White House* (Garden City, N.Y.: Doubleday and Company, 1975), p. 248.

54. *Ibid.,* p. 248.

55. Charles M. Haar, *Between the Idea and the Reality: A Study in the Origin, Fate, and Legacy of the Model Cities Program* (Boston: Little, Brown and Company, 1975), p. 152.

56. Bernard J. Frieden and Marshall Kaplan, *The Politics of Neglect: Urban Aid from Model Cities to Revenue Sharing* (Cambridge, Mass.: MIT Press, 1975), p. 201.

57. *Ibid.,* p. 205.

58. This remark is reported by Joan Hoff from an interview with Raymond Price in 1983. See Joan Hoff, *Nixon Reconsidered* (New York: Basic Books, 1994), p. 57.

59. Julie Roy Jeffrey, *Education for Children of the Poor: A Study of the Origins and Implementation of the Elementary and Secondary Education Act of 1965* (Columbus, Ohio: Ohio State University Press, 1978), p. 204.

60. John Osborne, *The Second Year of the Nixon Watch* (New York: Liveright Publishing Corporation, 1971), p. 184.

61. Quoted in Joan Hoff, *Nixon Reconsidered,* p. 24.

62. Haldeman, *The Haldeman Diaries,* February 9, 1971, p. 246.

63. John C. Whitaker, *Striking a Balance: Environment and Natural Resources Policy in the Nixon-Ford Years* (Washington, D.C.: American Enterprise Institute, 1976), pp. 2–4.

64. *Ibid.,* p. 27.

65. Quoted in Tom Wicker, *One of Us: Richard Nixon and the American Dream* (New York: Random House, 1991), p. 515.

66. Congressional Quarterly, *Nixon: The Second Year of His Presidency* (Washington, D.C.: Congressional Quarterly, 1971), pp. 22A–26A.

67. Gerald S. Strober and Deborah H. Strober, *Nixon: An Oral History of His Presidency* (New York: HarperCollins Publishers, 1994), p. 111.

68. Joseph Wesely Zeigler, *Arts in Crisis: The National Endowment for the Arts Versus America* (Chicago: A Capella Press, 1994), p. 26.

69. Alice Goldfarb Marquis, *Art Lessons: Learning From the Rise and Fall of Public Arts Funding* (New York: Basic Books, 1995), p. 93.

70. *Ibid.*, p. 93.

71. Congressional Quarterly, *Nixon: The First Year of His Presidency,* p. 14.

72. Ronald Berman, *Culture Politics* (Lanham, Md.: University Press of America, 1984), pp. 12–13.

73. *Ibid.*, pp. 18–19.

74. Stephen Miller, *Excellence and Equity: The National Endowment for the Humanities* (Lexington, Ky.: The University Press of Kentucky, 1984), pp. 32–33.

75. *Ibid.*, p. 41.

76. *Facts On File, 1972,* pp. 536 ff.

77. *Ibid.*, p. 678.

78. Ambrose, *Nixon, Volume II: The Triumph of a Politician,* p. 556.

79. Richard P. Nathan, *The Plot that Failed: Nixon and the Administrative Presidency* (New York: John Wiley and Sons, 1975), p. 8.

Epilogue

1. *New York Times,* January 14, 1969.

2. Lawrence M. Mead, *Beyond Entitlement: The Social Obligations of Citizenship* (New York: The Free Press, 1986), p. 27.

3. Charles Murray, *Losing Ground: American Social Policy, 1950–1980* (New York: Basic Books, 1984), p. 36.

4. *Ibid.*, p. 101.

5. Mead, *Beyond Entitlement: The Social Obligations of Citizenship,* p. x.

6. *Ibid.*, p. 26.

7. Murray, *Losing Ground,* p. 183.

8. George Gilder, *Wealth and Poverty* (New York: Basic Books, 1981), p. 12.

9. Henry M. Levin, "A Decade of Policy Developments in Improving Education and Training for Low-Income Populations," in Robert H. Haveman (ed.), *A Decade of Federal Antipoverty Programs* (New York: Academic Press, 1977), p. 178.

10. Though in their recent book, *The Bell Curve,* Richard Herrnstein and Charles Murray note that years of schooling correlates with income primarily because it reflects IQ levels, it is not, they say, an important *independent* factor. See Richard J. Herrnstein and Charles Murray, *The Bell Curve: Intelligence and Class Structure in American Life* (New York: The Free Press, 1994), pp. 94–101.

11. Julie Roy Jeffrey, *Education for Children of the Poor: A Study of the Origins and Implementation of the Elementary and Secondary Education Act of 1965* (Columbus, Ohio: Ohio State University Press, 1978), p. 172.

12. *New York Times,* December 11, 1992.

13. Herrnstein and Murray, *The Bell Curve,* p. 403.

14. Peter Passell, " 'Bell Curve' Critics Say Early I.Q. Isn't Destiny," *New York Times,* November 9, 1994.

15. Medicaid grew from zero in 1965 to $9 billion in 1974; housing subsidies rose from $236 million to $1.2 billion in the same period; food stamp outlays rose from $36 million in 1965 to $4.3 billion in 1975. See James Patterson, *America's Struggle* . . . , pp. 164–165.

16. James Patterson, *America's Struggle Against Poverty, 1900–1980* (Cambridge, Mass.: Harvard University Press, 1981), pp. 165–166.

17. Martin Anderson, *Welfare: The Political Economy of Welfare Reform in the United States* (Stanford, Calif.: The Hoover Institution, 1978), pp. 15–42.

18. Bernard Gifford, "War on Poverty: Assumptions, History, and Results, a Flawed but Important Effort," in Marshall Kaplan and Peggy Cuciti (eds.), *The Great Society and Its Legacy: Twenty Years of U.S. Social Policy* (Durham, N.C.: Duke University Press, 1986), p. 69.

19. Tom Hayden, "Welfare Liberalism and Social Change," in Marvin E. Gettleman and David Mermelstein (eds.), *The Great Society Reader: The Failure of American Liberalism* (New York: Random House, 1967), p. 479.

20. Sar Levitan and Clifford M. Johnson, "Did the Great Society and Subsequent Initiatives Work?," in Kaplan and Cuciti (eds.), *The Great Society and Its Legacy,* p. 87; and Robert Wood, "The Great Society in 1984," *Ibid.,* p. 21.

21. Brandeis Transcript, p. 370.

22. Patterson, *America's Struggle Against Poverty,* p. 151.

23. Levitan and Johnson, "Did the Great Society and Subsequent Initiatives Work?" in Kaplan and Cuciti (eds.), *The Great Society and Its Legacy,* p. 74.

24. Paul N. Ylvisaker, "Poverty in the United States," in *Ibid.,* p. 51.

25. Joseph A. Califano, *America's Health Care Revolution: Who Lives? Who Dies? Who Pays?* (New York: Random House, 1986), p. 36.

26. Quoted in Herrnstein and Murray, *The Bell Curve,* p. 420.

27. Alice Goldfarb Marquis, *Art Lessons: Learning From the Rise and Fall of Public Arts Funding* (New York: Basic Books, 1995), pp. 200–291.

28. *Ibid.,* p. 202.

Index

ABOUT THE AUTHOR

Irwin Unger, Ph.D., is a historian at New York University. The editor of several history textbooks, he is the author of *The Greenback Era* (which won the Pulitzer Prize in 1965); *The Movement: The American New Left*; *Postwar America: The United States Since 1945*; and several other works. He lives in New York City.